CISTERCIAN STUDIES SERIES: NUMBER ONE HUNDRED TWENTY-ONE

Roger De Ganck

BEATRICE OF NAZARETH IN HER CONTEXT

CISTERCIAN STUDIES SERIES: NUMBER ONE HUNDRED TWENTY-ONE

Beatrice of Nazareth in her Context

by

Roger De Ganck

Cistercian Publications
Kalamazoo, Michigan

© Copyright Cistercian Publications, 1991.

The work of Cistercian Publications is made possible in part
by support from Western Michigan University to the
Institute of Cistercian Studies.

Available in Britain and Europe from
Cassell plc
London

Available elsewhere from
Cistercian Publications (Distribution)
St Joseph's Abbey
Spencer, MA 01562

Volume Two of a series of three:

The Life of Beatrice of Nazareth
(Cistercian Fathers Series, Number 50)

Beatrice of Nazareth in Her Context
(Cistercian Studies Series, Number 121)

Towards Unification with God
Beatrice of Nazareth in Her Context, Volume Two, Part Three
(Cistercian Studies Series, Number 122)

Library of Congress Cataloguing-in-Publication Data
Ganck, Roger de, 1908-
    Beatrice of Nazareth in her context / by Roger De Ganck.
        p. cm. — (Cistercian studies series; no. 121)
    Includes bibliographical references.
    ISBN 0-87907-421-3. — ISBN 0-87907-721-2 (pbk.)
    1. Beatrijs, van Tienen, ca. 1200-1268. 2. Theology — Middle Ages,
600-1500. 3. Asceticism — History — Middle Ages, 600-1500.
I. Title. II. Series.
BV5095.B42G26 1990
271'.97—dc20
[B]   90-35817
                                                                  CIP

Printed in the United States of America

PREFACE

TO COME TO A GOOD UNDERSTANDING of the biography of Beatrice of Nazareth and her treatise on *Seven Manieren van Minne* (*Seven Experiences of Love*), we need to study her in her context; that is, in connection with five of her contemporaries: Ida of Nivelles, Ida Lewis, Alice of Schaarbeek, Ida of Leuven, and the gifted Hadewijch, a *mulier religiosa* of whom there is no biography, but whose writings are amazingly rich in content and extent.

The spirituality and mysticism of these women were an integral part of their christian belief and tradition. What they said and did will therefore be studied in connection with their 'mentors': Gregory of Nyssa to some extent, Augustine, occasionally Gregory the Great, Bernard of Clairvaux, William of Saint Thierry, Aelred of Rievaulx, and Hugh and Richard of Saint Victor—who will be spoken of in the following pages simply as Bernard, William, Aelred, Hugh, and Richard. Since these women lived before scholasticism, Thomas Aquinas, Bonaventure, and their contemporaries will not be considered here. To write as objectively as possible, I have not consulted manuals by Augustine Poulain, Auguste Saudreau, Pierre Pourrat, Réginald Garrigou-Lagrange, or even Cuthbert Butler's *Western Mysticism*.

The Life of Beatrice, translated into English, and two volumes of studies on her significance and place along religious women, the *mulieres religiosae*, of the thirteenth century, form a single continuous study. Volumes two and three of this work (the study proper) have therefore continuous pagination; the bibliography and indices for the first two chapters of Volume One (the *Life of Beatrice*) and for volumes two and three will appear at the end of volume three.

This work should be considered a stepping stone for more and improved studies in the future. Our spiritual heritage is too rich to be allowed to remain unknown or to be ignored. These medieval women did not know what we today call a catechism, but what

v

they have to say surpasses one. Though not always consonant with our current vocabulary, their mystical terminology is very instructive and helpful to any interested reader.

I wish to express grateful appreciation to the reverend John Baptist Hasbrouck of Guadalupe Abbey, Lafayette, Oregon; to the reverend Charles Cummings of Holy Trinity Abbey, Utah; and to Dr Karen Carlton, professor of English at the State University of California at Arcata, all of whom have helped me a great deal in presenting these two books on Beatrice's world in readable English. No less gratitude is expressed to all the persons who sent photocopies of papers and studies beyond the reach of the very beautiful but remote place where this work has been composed. I thank especially the reverend John Baptist Van Damme and the reverend Rik Meren of the Abbey of Westmalle, Belgium; Dr Paul Wackers of the University of Nijmegen, the Netherlands; and Miss Jana Cloward of Hacienda Heights, California, who provided more than a substantial share of source material.

A great support has been the observations and constructive criticism offered by Professor David N. Bell of the Memorial University of Newfoundland, Canada; Professor Peter Dinzelbacher, then of the Historisches Institut at the University of Stuttgart, Germany; the reverend Robert Javelet, professor at the University of Strassbourg, France; Dr Joris Reynaert of the Rijksuniversiteit at Ghent, Belgium; and Professor Herman Vekeman of the Institut für Niederländlische Philologie of the University of Cologne, Germany.

It would be unfair of me not to thank the community of Cistercian nuns of Redwoods Monastery, Whitethorn, California, who have let me have the time needed over several years to complete this work. Finally, I express my gratitude to Dr Rozanne Elder of Cistercian Publications for her devoted assistance in preparing this work and bringing it to completion and publication.

Roger De Ganck

Redwoods Monastery
Easter 1987

TABLE OF CONTENTS

vii

ABBREVIATIONS

Abbreviations of Journals and Series

AA SS	*Acta Sanctorum*
AB	*Acta Bollandiana.* Brussels.
AC	*Analecta Sacri Ordinis Cisterciensis* (1945–64); *Analecta Cisterciensia* (1966 –). Rome.
AFP	*Archivum Patrum Praedicatorum.* Rome.
AHDL	*Archives d'Histoire doctrinale et littéraire du moyen âge.* Paris.
AHEB	*Analectes pour servir à l'Histoire Ecclésiastique de la Belgique.* Leuven.
BGHB	*Bijdragen tot de geschiedenis van het aloude Hertogdom Brabant.* Leuven.
Bijdragen	*Bijdragen. Tijdschrift voor Filosofie en Theologie.* Maastricht.
CBQ	*Catholic Biblical Quarterly.* Washington, D.C.
CCCM	Corpus Christianorum. Continuatio Mediaevalis. Turnhout.
CCH	*Catalogus Codicum Hagiographorum Bibliothecae Regiae Bruxellensis.* Brussels.
CF	Cistercian Fathers Series. Spencer, Kalamazoo.
Cîteaux	Cîteaux *Cîteaux in de Nederlanden* (1950–1958); *Cîteaux* (1959–). Westmalle. Achel.
Coll	*Collectanea Ordinis Cisterciensium Reformatorum* (1934–64); *Collectanea Cisterciensia* (1966–). Scourmont.
CS	Cistercian Studies Series. Kalamazoo, Michigan.
CSt	*Cistercian Studies.* Gethsemani, Kentucky.
DHGE	*Dictionnaire d'Histoire et de Géographie ecclésiastique.* Paris.
DSp	*Dictionnaire de Spiritualité.* Paris.
DThC	*Dictionnaire de Théologie catholique.* Paris.
ETL	*Ephemerides Theologicae Lovanienses.* Leuven.

GL	*Geist und Leben. Zeitschrift für Aszese und Mystik.* Munich/Würzburg.
HJ	*Heythrop Journal.* London.
HL	*Handelingen. Koninklijke Zuidnederlandse Maatschappij voor Taal- en Letterkunde en Geschiedenis.* Brussels.
IPQ	*International Philosophical Quarterly.* Fordham, New York-Namur.
LThK	*Lexikon für Theologie und Kirche.* Freiburg im Breisgau.
LV	*Lumière et Vie.* Savoie/Paris.
MnS	*Monastic Studies.* Pine City, New York. Montreal.
MS	*Medieval Studies.* Toronto.
MSR	*Mélanges de science religieuse.* Lille.
NRT	*Nouvelle Revue Théologique.* Tournai.
NTS	*New Testament Studies.* Cambridge.
OGE	*Ons Geestelijk Erf.* Antwerp.
OXP	*Orientalia Christiana Periodica.* Rome.
PL	*Patrologiae cursus completus, Series Latina.* Paris.
RAM	*Revue d'ascétique et de mystique.* Toulouse.
RBén	*Revue Bénédictine.* Maredsous.
RBibl	*Revue Biblique.* Paris.
RechSR	*Recherches de science religieuse.* Paris/ Strasbourg.
RHE	*Revue d'Histoire Ecclésiastique.* Leuven.
RMAL	*Revue du moyen-âge latin.* Strasbourg.
RSR	*Revue des sciences religieuses.* Paris.
RSt	*Religious Studies.* Cambridge.
RTAM	*Recherches de Théologie anncienne et médiévale.* Leuven.
SCh	Sources chrétiennes. Paris.
StM	*Studia Monastica.* Barcelona.
SVS	*Supplément à la Vie Spirituelle.* Paris.
TDNT	*Theological Dictionary of the New Testament.* Grand Rapids, Michigan.

TDOT	*Theological Dictionary of the Old Testament.* Grand Rapids, Michigan.
TNTL	*Tijdschrift voor Nederlandse Taal- en Letterkunde.* Leiden.
TS	*Theological Studies.* Baltimore, Maryland.
TT	*Tijdschrift voor theologie.* Nijmegen/Leuven.
VMKVA	*Verslagen en Mededelingen van de Koninklijke Vlaamse Academie voor Taal- en Letterkunde.* Brussels.
VS	*La Vie Spirituelle.* Paris.
ZKT	*Zeitschrift für katholische Theologie.* Innsbruck.

Abbreviations for Books

AM	*Augustinus Magister. Congrès international augustinien, Paris 21–24 Septembre 1954.* Three volumes. F. Cayré, ed.. Paris. 1954.
ET	English translation (or) English text.
Quinque	*Quinque prudentes virgines.* Chrysostom Henriquez, ed. Antwerp, 1630. (199–298: *Vita Idae Nivellensis)*
R-VM	*Beatrijs van Nazareth. Seven Manieren van Minne.* L. Reypens and J. Van Mierlo, edd. Leuven, 1926.
SBOp	*Sancti Bernardi Opera.* Ten volumes. Jean Leclercq, C.H. Talbot, H.M. Rochais, edd. Rome. 1957–1977.
SM	*Sacramentum Mundi.* Six volumes. Karl Rahner, C. Ernst, K. Smyth, edd., New York. 1968–1970.
Statuta	*Statuta Capitulorum Generalium Ordinis Cisterciensis ab anno 1116 ad annum 1786.* Eight volumes. J.M. Canivez, ed. Leuven. 1933–1941.

VM	Van Mierlo, Joseph, editor of the works of Hadewijch: *Hadewijch: Visioenen.* Two volumes. Leuven. 1924–1925. *Hadewijch: Strophische Gedichten.* Two volumes. Antwerp. 1942. *Hadewijch: Brieven.* Two volumes. Antwerp. 1947. *Hadewijch: Mengeldichten.* Antwerp. 1952.

Abbreviations for the Works of Bernard of Clarivaux and William of Saint Thierry

The abbreviations used in this study are those recommended by the Board of Editors of Cistercian Publications.

Abbreviations for the Works of Bernard of Clairvaux

Adv	*Sermo in adventu Domini*
And	*Sermo in natali sancti Andreae*
Ann	*Sermo in annuntiatione dominica*
Asc	*Sermo in ascensione Domini*
Conv	*Sermo de conversione ad clericos*
Csi	*De consideratione libri v*
Ded	*Sermo in dedicatione ecclesiae*
Dil	*Liber de diligendo Deo*
Div	*Sermones de diversis*
Ep	*Epistola*
Gra	*Liber de gratia et libero arbitrio*
IV HM	*Sermo in feria iv hebdomadae sanctae*
Hum	*Liber de gradibus humilitatis et superbiae*
Miss	*Homelia super* missus est *in laudibus Virginis Mater*
Nat	*Sermon in nativitate domini*
I Nov	*Sermo in dominica I novembris*
O Pasc	*Sermo in octava Paschae*
OS	*Sermo in festivitate Omnium Sanctorum*
Par	*Parabolae*
Pasc	*Sermo in die Paschae*
Pent	*Sermo in die pentecostes*
Pre	*Liber de praecepto et dispensatione*

QH	*Sermo super psalmum* Qui habitat
SC	*Sermon super Cantica canticorum*
V Nat	*Sermo in vigilia nativitatis domini*

Abbreviations for the Works of William of Saint Thierry

Adv Abl	*Disputatio adversus Petrum Abaelardum*
Aenig	*Aenigma fidei*
Cant	*Expositio super Cantica canticorum*
Contemp	*De contemplando Deo*
Ep frat	*Epistola [aurea] ad fratres de Monte Dei*
Exp Rm	*Expositio in epistolam Pauli ad Romanos*
Med	*Meditativae orationes*
Nat am	*De natura et dignitate amoris*
Nat corp	*De natura corporis et animae*
Sacr altar	*De sacramento altaris liber*
Spec fid	*Speculum fidei*

A NOTE
ON THE REFERENCES USED

1. All patristic and medieval works are referred to according to the printed editions contained in Migne's *Patrologia Latina*, except when more recent and better editions are available.
2. The titles of all other books and articles are given in full in the bibliography contained in volume three.
3. All biblical references follow the enumeration of the Vulgate text.

PART ONE

GOD AND MAN MADE TO HIS IMAGE AND LIKENESS

CHAPTER ONE

THE HISTORICAL CONTEXT OF THE *MULIERES RELIGIOSAE*

B EATRICE WAS A WOMAN OF HER TIME, and her life should therefore be set in its historical and spiritual background. Before joining the Cistercian community of Florival or Bloemendaal she had lived with a group of beguines who in the first half of the thirteenth century formed the major part of the *mulieres religiosae* movement, particularly active in Belgium.[1] She spent fifty-eight years as a Cistercian nun in three different communities, all of them located in her home country, the duchy of Brabant,[2] which, like its neighboring principalities, had

---

1 In these pages 'Belgium' refers to the contemporary country of that name, and also to that part of Flanders annexed to France in 1685 by Louis XIV.

2 In feudal times Belgium was formed by several principalities whose boundary lines shifted frequently but not radically. The duchy of Brabant was one of them, and during Beatrice's lifetime it grew in political, social, and economic importance. In church matters a large part of the duchy was under the jurisdiction of the prince-bishop of Liège. His principality was part of the Holy Roman Empire, while his ecclesiastical jurisdiction covered a much greater territory than his principality. Both the diocese of Liège and the duchy of Brabant ran from north to south through the Flemish and French speaking sections of these countries. For a convenient map, see *DHGE* 7, between columns 528 and 529.

1

become a country of towns.[3] Beatrice cannot be presumed to have
been unaffected by the socio-economic and religious trends of her
time and country.

THE *MULIERES RELIGIOSAE*

What we call the *mulieres religiosae* movement flourished
from about 1180 till about 1270. It was characterized in 1882 as
the problem of too many unmarried women, '*die Frauenfrage*'.[4]
This thesis provided socio-economic reasons for an abundance of
marriageable women who could not or would not marry: the
disproportion between the longevity of men and women due to
the hardships of physical labor, wars and crusades, the canonical
celibacy of the quite numerous clergy, and guild regulations

---

3 Henri Pirenne, 'The Place of the Netherlands [here = Belgium] in the
Economic History of Medieval Europe', reprinted in his *Histoire économique de
l'Occident Médiéval* (Bruges, 1951) 433–57; 447: 'Thanks to the commercial
currents from the Meuse [=Liège] to the sea [=Flanders], Brabant, situated
between the two, revived and in its turn became covered with towns. About
1150 Antwerp, Malines, Brussels and particularly Leuven, began to compete
with their rivals in the East and West. At the same time secondary towns grew
up, in increasing proximity to each other, around all the centers where urban life
had first sprung up, along the roads and rivers which penetrated the country.
They were so numerous that in the thirteenth century, the urban population may
be said to have been as large and perhaps larger than the rural'. Before the
nineteenth-century industrial revolution a megalopolis was unknown. According
to scholarly studies the population density of major, entirely walled-in cities in
the twelfth and thirteenth centuries—London, Paris, Ghent or Bruges—was
around fifty thousand. See Henri Pirenne, *Ecomomic and Social History of
Medieval Europe*, 2nd ed., ET by E.G. Clegg (New York-London, 1937) 169–71
and note 10.
4 C. Bücher, 'Die Frauenfrage im Mittelalter', *Zeitschrift für die gesamte
Staatswissenschaften* 38 (1882) 344–97. Although it is a century old, this study
is in some ways more balanced than the treatment of this question found in a
contemporary work: Daniel Herlily, *The Social History of Italy and Western
Europe* 700–1500 (London, 1979), particularly Chapter 13: 'Life Expectancy
for Women in Medieval Society', and Chapter 14, 'The Medieval Marriage
Market'. On p.12 of Chapter 14, Herlihy writes for example: 'there is no doubt
that a principal thrust behind the beguine movement was the difficulty girls were
encountering in finding a husband'. He attempts to prove the veracity of this
'thrust' by citing an observation of Louis of Male, count of Flanders (in 1345!),
that religious houses should be provided for many noble women because
crusades and wars had limited the number of men.

related to admission to masterhood.[5] A later study pointed out
that the expanding towns and cities with their incipient industrial-
ization and commerce, particularly in the flourishing cloth industry, attracted women as well as men but not only or chiefly for
socio-economic factors. The 'unusual surplus of women over
men' and 'the celibate condition of large numbers of women was
not an unusual circumstance producing novel and somewhat
mysterious psychic and economic pressure, but a normal aspect
of medieval life'.[6]

Today it is more customary to speak about the *mulieres religiosae* movement than about a *Frauenfrage*. A number of excellent studies have treated this phenomenon.[7] Without denying the
socio-economic reasons, modern scholars have brought religious
motivations abundantly and convincingly to the fore, showing
why a great number of women decided to live a celibate life. The
term *mulieres religiosae* is,[8] in fact, an 'umbrella title' covering
several sub-groups of nuns, recluses, and virgins living at home
or in small groups. The last-named formed the mainstream of the
movement and were called beguines.

Originally, beguine was a nickname. Its origin remains unknown and in one of its earliest occurrences the name was

5 Pirenne, 'La hiérarchie des artisans', *Histoire économique, 326–27; Id.,
Economic and Social History of Medieval Europe*, 176–88.
6 A. Phillips, *Beguines in Medieval Strasburg* (Stanford, CA, 1941) 19–24.
7 J. Greven, *Die Anfänge der Beginen. Ein Beitrag zur Geschichte der Volks-
frommigkeit und des Ordenswesen im Hochmittelalter*, Vorreformations-
geschichtliche Forschungen 8, (Munich, 1912); L.J.M. Philippen, *De
Begijnhoven. Oosprong, Geschiedenis, Inrichting* (Antwerp, 1918; henceforth
cited as *Begijnhoven*); Herbert Grundmann, *Religiöse Bewegungen im Mittelalter*, Historische Studien 267 (Berlin, 1935; rpt Wiesbaden, 1961; (henceforth:
Religiöse Bewegungen); Alcantara Mens, *Oorsprong en betekenis van de Nederlandse Begijnen en Begardenbeweging* (Antwerp, 1947; henceforth: *Oorsprong*); Ernest McDonnell, *The Beguines and Begards in Medieval Culture,
with Special Emphasis on the Belgian Scene* (New Brunswick, NJ, 1954;
henceforth: *The beguines*); O. Nübel, *Mittelalterliche Beginen-und Sozialsiedlungen in den Niederlanden* (Tübingen, 1970). See also the article 'Beginen' in
Lexikon des Mittelalters, 1:1799–1803, with bibliography up to 1980.
8 For a short overview of the term, see J. Huyben, 'Le mouvement spirituel
dans les Pays-Bas au XIIIe siècle', *SVS* 39 (1947) 29–45;36–40, and Joseph Van
Mierlo, 'Béguines. Histoire du mot', *DSp* 1: 1341–43.

applied to Cistercian nuns in the duchy of Brabant at the turn of the twelfth century.[9] Soon the name acquired a respectable ring and was used for the large numbers of *mulieres religiosae* (devout women), poor or well-to-do *sanctae mulieres* (holy women),—or *virgines continentes*, virgins determined to remain in virginity.[10] They were intent on a life of prayer and charitable works at a time when there were no institutions or organizations such as hospitals, homes for elderly, or even a school system.[11] Their lifestyle was almost identical with that of certain heterodox women,[12] a similarity which caused trouble for the orthodox beguines.

---

9 Caesarius of Heisterbach in his *Dialogus miraculorum*, ed., Joseph Strange (Cologne, 1851) vol.1: 89, written in 1220, told the story of Charles who in 1185 joined the Cistercians of Himmerod (Rhineland) and was soon afterwards, at his request, allowed to visit the ecstatic Cistercian nuns in Brabant of whom he had heard. A woman asked for information inquired why he was so particularly interested in 'those beguines'. The ET of the *Dialogus* by H.von E. Scott and C.C. Swinton Eland (London, 1929) 90, has ungraciously translated beguines as 'fanatics'. Charles was sent to Heisterbach, a foundation made by Himmerod, where he acted as prior. In 1197 the community of Villers elected him to be its abbot. After he resigned in 1209, he went back to Himmerod. See Edouard de Moreau, *L'Histoire de l'Abbaye de Villers-en-Brabant aux XIIe et XIIIe siècles* [henceforth: L'Histoire de Villers], (Brussels, 1909) 43–48.

10 Philippen, *Begijnhoven*, 31–32.

11 Beguines lived at a mere subsistence level and had to make a living by working at home at their looms for a patron (Philippen, *Begijnhoven*, 201; Pirenne, *Histoire économique*, 451). This aspect is particularly stressed in Brenda Bolton's 'Some Thirteenth-century Women in the Low Countries. A Special Case?', *Nederlands Archief voor Kerkgeschiedenis* 61 (1981) 7–29. Beguines were also of service in homes when institutional health care was in its infancy. (Theo Luyckx, *Johanna van Vlaanderen en Henegouwen (1205–1244)* [Antwerp-Utrecht, 1946] 316–18; 417–18). To foster the solidity of her incipient hospitals, countess Johanna tried and succeeded in having laysisters from some Cistercian communities involved in hospitals (Roger De Ganck, 'Het kloosterslot der Bijloke in het gedrang', Citeaux 3 [1952] 90–111). For a specific look at the working conditions at the time, see John Gimpel, *The Medieval Machine. The Industrial Revolution of the Middle Ages* (New York, 1976). For an interesting account of the living standards, see Urban T. Holmes, *Daily Living in the Twelfth Century Based on the Observations of Alexander Neckam (1157–1217) in London and Paris*, (Madison-Milwaukee-London, 1966) or Robert Delort, *Life in the Middle Ages*, ET by R. Allen (New York, 1983).

12 This is not the place to elaborate on the antecedents of those heterodox women.They go back to the eleventh century, the Gregorian Reform, the inadequate response of ecclesiastical authorities to beliefs and practices of those women and their reactions against what is called today 'the institution'. One can

Ecclesiastical authorities felt uneasy with beguines partly because they did not belong to any established religious Order or follow an officially recognized canonical rule, and were therefore seen as 'extra-regulars', i.e. groups of laypeople not directly controlled by the hierarchy. It was only in 1216 that the bishop of Acre, James of Vitry (d.1240), an admirer of Mary of Oignies, was able to announce from Perugia that he had secured permission from Pope Honorius III for the *mulieres religiosae* to 'live piously in common', a permission valid not only for the diocese of Liège, but for France and Germany as well. In 1233 Gregory IX who had meanwhile made his friend James of Vitry a cardinal (1229) gave the beguines a more explicit written recognition.[13]

From 1242 on the beguines grouped their numerous small houses together in *curtes* or walled-off beguinages, a kind of city within a city. This arrangement was found chiefly, though not exclusively, in Belgium.[14] Estimates of the number of beguines have ranged from (a too modest) five thousand to (an exaggerated) two hundred thousand.[15] Their number was certainly high, and many of them, both individually and as groups, tried to become associated with or integrated into Orders of men; autonomous congregations of women were still a long way off.

As in every movement, there emerged outstanding persons whose lives exemplified its ideals. The so-called beguine Mary of Oignies (now Aiseau) in the Hainaut (d.1213) was the model, or at least one of the early models, as James of Vitry made evident in his biography.[16] The greatest of all the *mulieres religiosae* we know of was undoubtedly Hadewijch,[17] who seems to have

find solid information in the publications of Arno Borst, *Die Katharer* (Stuttgart, 1953), and in Christine Thouzellier, *Catharisme et Valdéisme en Languedoc à la fin du XIIe et au XIIIe siècle*, 2nd ed. (Leuven-Paris, 1969), or in J.L. Tobey, *The History of Ideas. A Bibliographical Introduction*, vol.2 (Santa Barbara, CA-London, 1977), and Carl. T. Berkhout and Jeffrey Burton Russell, *Medieval Heresies: A Bibliography, 1960–1979* (Toronto, 1981).

13 Grundmann, *Religiöse Bewegungen*, 170–74.
14 Philippen, *Begijnhoven*, 89–129; Nübel, *Mittelalterliche Beginen*, 57–94.
15 Mens, *Oorsprong*, 319, n.112.
16 *AA SS* June 5: 524–72.
17 Norbert De Paepe, *Hadewijch: Strofische Gedichten*. Een studie van de Minne in het kader der 12e en 13e eeuwse mystiek en profane minnelyriek

been the leader of a small group. The spiritual and mystical content of her various extant writings are of an exceptionally high quality.[18] As prose writer, poetess, and mystic Hadewijch was unquestionably the most prominent of all who wrote in medieval Dutch (or *Diets*) before John of Ruusbroec (d.1381). It would be unfair to the *mulieres religiosae* movement to concentrate on Mary of Oignies, Hadewijch, or Beatrice of Nazareth, and leave the movement untouched. An important source of the knowledge of the *mulieres religiosae* movement are the *Vitae* that have come down to us. Their number, relatively high in Belgium, is nevertheless infinitesimal when compared with the number of women who were seeking a more authentic christian life and a deeper spirituality than they found among most contemporary churchmen.[19] The following is a short, but by no means comprehensive, list of women whose *Vitae* have been published. More than half of them are Cistercian nuns, and nearly all the others were in close contact with Cistercians.

―――――――――

(Ghent, 1967) 159, n.101, stands by his impression that Hadewijch was not born before 1200 and opines that she wrote her visions between 1239 and 1246. Joris Reynaert accepts the possibility that she was still alive in the second half of the thirteenth century. See his 'Over Hadewijch naar aanleiding van drie recente publikaties, OGE 54 (1980) 280–92; 284, and J. Van Mierlo, *Visioenen*, 2: 121 [see next note] admits 1260 at the latest. That Hadewijch and her small group were beguines has not yet been proved beyond doubt.

18 The pioneer in the field of Hadewijch's writings is indisputably Joseph Van Mierlo, who published the results of his research in *Leuvense Studiën en Tekstuitgaven*. See Section A.2 of the Primary Sources given in the Bibliography of this series. An ET by Columba Hart appeared recently in The Classics of Western Spirituality series: *Hadewijch. The Complete Works* (New York-Ramsey-Toronto, 1980). References to Hadewijch's writings are given according to the publications of Van Mierlo (cited as VM), indicating the volume number, page, and lines. Since the (not always too accurate) English translation indicates VM's lines, the references are not hard to find in the ET.

19 Charles Duggan, 'Equity and Compassion in Papal Marriage Decretals to England', in *Love and Marriage in the Twelfth Century*, W. Van Hoecke and A. Welkenhuysen, eds. (Leuven, 1981) 59–87; 63, and Charles Lefevre, 'Formation du Droit classique', in *Histoire du Droit et des Institutions de l'Église en Occident*. I: *L'Age Classique 1140–1378* (Paris, 1965) 133–345; 147 and 163.

Name and dates	Biographer	Publication
Mary of Oignies, 1171–1213	James of Vitry	*AA SS* June 5: 542–72
Odilia, beguine, d.1220	A cleric of Liège	*AB* 13 (1894) 197–287
Christine of St.Trond, d.1224	Thomas Cantimpré	*AA SS* July 5: 650–60
Yvette of Huy, d.1228	Hugh of Floreffe	*AA SS* Jan.2: 145–69
Ida of Nivelles, 1199–1231	Goswin of Villers?	*Quinque*, 199–297
Margaret of Ypres, d.1237	Thomas Cantimpré	*AFP* 18 (1948) 106–30
Lutgard of Tongres, d.1246	Thomas Cantimpré	*AA SS* June 5: 187–209
Alice of Schaarbeek, d.1250	A Cistercian	*AA SS* June 2: 476–83
Juliana of Cornillon, d.1258	A cleric of Liège	*AA SS* April 1: 435–75
Beatrice of Nazareth, d.1268	A Cistercian	Reypens, Antwerp, 1964
Ida Lewis, d.ca.1273	A monk of Villers?	*AA SS* Oct.13: 100–24
Ida of Leuven, 1211?–1290?	A Cistercian	*AA SS* April 2: 156–89
Beatrice of Zwijveke, 13th C.	A Cistercian	*OGE* 23 (1949) 225–46
Elisabeth of Spaalbeek, d.1304	Philip of Clairvaux	*CCH* 1: 362–78

CISTERCIAN NUNS AND *MULIERES RELIGIOSAE*

Some thirteenth-century Cistercian nuns had formerly been beguines or had at least been closely associated with them before, and after, they joined the Cistercian Order. Of Chrysostomus Henriquez' *Quinque prudentes virgines,* four indicate the familiarity these nuns had with beguines. Ida of Nivelles lived for six or seven years with a group of beguines in Nivelles,[20] and Ida de Lewis before she, like Ida of Nivelles, went to Rameya, had close contacts with beguines.[21] Beatrice herself spent a year with a group of beguines in Zoutleeuw (20,10). Ida of Leuven was a *mulier religiosa* before she became a nun in Roosendaal near Malines which traces its origin back to four recluses.[22] Twelve

20 She joined a group of seven 'poor virgins' at Nivelles, sharing their simple life style (*Quinque*, 291). Once a nun, Ida kept in touch with beguines (*Quinque*, 243; 253).
21 *AA SS* Oct. 13: 110. The Latin name *de Lewis* applied to the small country town of Gorsleeuw, some five miles from Borgloon, where Ida's father was the local rural nobleman *de Lewis*. See A. Steenwegen, 'De gelukz. Ida de Lewis of Ida van Gorsleeuw', OGE 57 (1983) 111–12. Since the name Lewis is more familiar to the readers than Gorsleeuw, Ida will henceforth be called Ida Lewis.
22 Before she became a nun at Roosendaal in 1233 at the age of twenty-two (Simone Roisin, *L' Hagiographie Cistercienne dans le diocèse de Liège au XIIIe Siècle* [Leuven-Brussels, 1947] 68 [henceforth cited: *L' Hagiographie*), she

communities of Cistercian nuns had been groups of beguines before their incorporation.[23] Cistercian nuns also had frequent relations with recluses, i.e. single women who lived a secluded life next to a church or oratory.[24]

CISTERCIAN MONKS AND *MULIERES RELIGIOSAE*

Abbots and monks often visited *mulieres religiosae* or were visited by them. They talked about what was the common desire and striving of their hearts: their love for God and God's love for them, Christ, spiritual progress, and love of neighbor. These interests were eagerly shared by people of religious inclinations at that time.

Conspicuous in these monk-beguine relationships were the abbots of Villers, an abbey some ten miles from Nivelles. Conrad of Urach (1209–1214) retained his sympathy for nuns and beguines alive throughout his life. As cardinal (1219–1227) he visited the tomb of the beguine Mary of Oignies, and later, we are told, she appeared to him.[25] Of his successor, abbot Walter of Utrecht (1214–1221), it was said that he could spend nearly a whole day praying without distractions, and that he committed no

---

often visited beguines, *AA SS* April 2: 165–68; 172. For the origins of Roosendaal, see Adrian Goetstouwers, 'De oorsprong der Abdij Roosendaal', *Bulletin de la Commission Royale d'Histoire* 119 (1949) 257–98; 275.

23 See Roger De Ganck, 'De stichting van Cisterciënser-monialenabdijen in de Zuidelijke Nederlanden in de 12e en 13e eeuwen', *De monialen van de Orde van Citeaux* (Westmalle, 1961) pro manuscripto, 21–32; 23.

24 Ida of Nivelles (*Quinque*: 199, 202); Ida Lewis (AA SS Oct.13: 110,11); Ida of Leuven (*AA SS* April 2: 172,175). Nübel (*Mittelalterliche Beginen-und Sozialsiedlungen*, 10–13) questions Mens about the relations between recluses and the early beguines, but he seems not to have known E. van Winterhoven's 'Recluseries et Ermitages dans l'ancien diocèse de Liège', in *Bulletin de la Société Scientifique et Littéraire du Limbourg* 23 (1905) 114, cited by L. Reypens in *OGE* 26 (1952) 332, n.13. Ida of Nivelles' biographer (*Quinque*, 199) describes the recluses thus: 'By their total exclusion from the world, they enclosed themselves completely with God'.

25 Edmond Martene and Usmer Durand, *Thesaurus novus Anecdotorum* (Paris, 1717) vol.3: 1276. [Henceforth cited as *Thesaurus*].

sin in forty years.[26] The *mulieres religiosae* with whom he was in contact held the same ideals. Walter's successor, William of Brussels (1221–1237), promoted the interests of many groups of nuns, supported beguines in their spiritual and economic needs, and appeared after his death to a recluse with whom he had a spiritual friendship.[27] All these abbots had a Christ- and Trinity-centered spirituality, as did the Cistercian nuns and the beguines. Of the eight first abbots of Villers, seven resigned to be able to enjoy 'the embraces of Rachel'.[28] Monks and laybrothers of Villers had no less contact with beguines than did their abbots, and the biographies of some of them show how frequent these contacts were and the extent to which they shared spiritual interests and concerns.[29] What is true of Villers is, though to a lesser extent, true also of the abbey of Aulne near Charleroi.[30]

Cistercian abbots, monks and laybrothers of Villers and Aulne supported the beguines financially by giving them pensions and making other provisions for them. The abbots of Villers, St.Bernards near Antwerp, the abbesses of Herkenrode near Hasselt and from 1233 on the abbess of Bijloke in Ghent had, because of their former support, a voice in the appointment of the beguines' chaplain after those in their vicinity became organized in their Beguinages.[31]

At the end of the twelfth century Robert of Arbrissel founded the monastery, and later the congregation, of Fontevrault, where the abbess had jurisdiction over all members, men as well as

---

26 de Moreau, *L'Abbaye de Villers*, 54–56; Martene and Durand, *Thesaurus*, 1275–78.

27 de Moreau, 57–62; Martene and Durand, *Thesaurus*, 1278–85.

28 de Moreau, 92.

29 *Ibid.*, 96–104: 'Le mysticisme à l'abbaye de Villers'; Simone Roisin, 'L'Efflorescence cistercienne et le courant féminin de piété au XIIIe siècle', *RHE* 39 (1943) 432–78; 373–74. [This study is henceforth cited as L'Efflorescence.]

30 Roisin, *L'Hagiographie*, 46–49.

31 Philippen, *Begijnhoven*, 95–97; particularly McDonnell, *The beguines*, 170–86, who devoted a whole chapter to this topic: 'beguine parochial organization under Cistercian auspices'. See also G.Meersseman, 'Les Frères Prêcheurs et le mouvement dévot en Flandre au XIIIe siècle, *AFP* 18 (1948) 69–130; 81–83.

women, who lived in buildings close to one another, but separate. Save for a few exceptions, Fontevrault did not extend its foundations outside France.[32] The first to integrate into his Order the flood of *mulieres religiosae* on a larger scale was Norbert of Xanten, founder of the Praemonstratensians, whose canons regular established a number of so-called double-monasteries in Belgium at the beginning of the twelfth century. The term double-monasteries is not completely appropriate, for the women became a kind of laysisterhood who did menial tasks and lived in separate quarters. They could not sing in choir, had to be content with silent prayer, and were subjected to rigorous enclosure.[33] For practical reasons they were, about 1137, gradually discouraged from joining the double-monasteries. Finally, in 1198, Innocent III approved the Norbertine General Chapter's decision to suppress this sisterhood completely. Meanwhile a number of monasteries exclusively for Praemonstratensian canonesses had been built in places more distant from the canons.[34]

CISTERCIANS AND CISTERCIAN NUNS

Stephen Harding, the establisher of Cîteaux as a monastic Order, was certainly involved in the beginnings of the nunnery at Tart (1125), some ten kilometers from Cîteaux. The nuns followed the Cistercian way of life under the supervision of the abbot of Cîteaux,[35] but apparently without the intervention of the

---

32 For a short and competent overview, see J. Daoust, 'Fontevrault', DHGE, vol.7 (1971) 961–71; and, in English, Penny Shine Gold, 'Male/Female Cooperation: The Example of Fontevrault', in *Medieval Religious Women*, CS 71 (Kalamazoo, MI, 1984) 151–68. See also Jacques Dalarum, *L'Impossible Sainteté: La vie retrouvée de Robert d'Abrissel* (Paris, 1986).

33 See Mens, *Oorsprong*, 345, n.64.

34 Micheline de Fontette, *Les religieuses à l'àge classique du Droit canon* (Paris, 1967) 13–25.

35 Anselme Dimier, 'Chapitres généraux d'abbesses cisterciennes', *Cîteaux* 11 (1960) 268–275; and Ernst Krenig, 'Mittelalterliche Frauenklöster nach den Konstitutionen von Citeaux, unter besonderer Berücksichtigung fränkischer Nonnenkonventen', in *AC* 10 (1954) 16–17. See also J. B. Bouton, Benoit Chauvin and E. Grosjean, 'L'abbaye de Tart et ses filles au Moyen Age', *Mélanges...A. Dimier*, vol.3:19–61. Citeaux is not a centralized Order. One

Order as such.[36] At a slow pace and mostly in France, communities of Cistercian nuns arose, founded under the wings of a local Cistercian abbot.[37] This informal situation was to change in 1187. In that year, king Alphonse VIII of Castille and his wife Eleanor of England requested and obtained permission that their foundation at Las Huelgas near Burgos be recognized by the General Chapter of Cistercians as the motherhouse of all Cistercian communities of nuns in Castille and Léon.[38] This seems to have been the first time that the General Chapter as the authoritative collegial body of the Cistercian Order explicitly made a decision regarding nuns. The Chapter stated that the nuns of Castille and Léon who lived according to the *Instituta* of the Order could hold a chapter, once a year, in Las Huelgas, just as the Order did at the abbey of Cîteaux.[39] There is some ambiguity in the question related to the full incorporation of the Spanish nuns into the Cistercian Order, for the General Chapter wrote in 1197 to the king of Castille that it could not oblige the abbesses to attend this [regional] chapter at Las Huelgas.[40]

There is as yet no modern monograph on Las Huelgas, but it looks as if king Alphonse VIII made his first request at a time

---

joined an autonomous Cistercian community and through this became connected with the Cistercian Order. This explains why women could become 'Cistercian' nuns without being under the authority of the General Chapter. The General Chapter itself is the supreme authority of the Order; it is a legal, collegial body made up of all the abbots of the autonomous houses, who authoritatively care for matters of common concern.

36 For an up to date study on Cistercian nuns in the twelfth century, see Brigitte Degler-Sprengler, 'Die Zistercienserinnen im 12. Jahrhundert', *Helvetia Sacra*, Part 3, vol.3, *Die Zistercienser und Zistercienserinnen...in der Schweiz* (Bern, 1982) 510–19.

37 *Addit. ad libros de Vita S.Bernardi*, PL 185: 1413–14, n.16.

38 A.Rodriguez Lopez, *El Real Monasterio de Las Huelgas* (Burgos, 1907) 1: 57, cited by A. Dimier, 'Chapitres', *Citeaux* 11 (1960) 272.

39 Angelus Manrique, *Annales Cistercienses* (Lyon, 1649; rpt Westmead, England, 1970) vol.3: 218, n.16.

40 *Statuta*; here 1191,27: 'Domino regi Castellae scribatur quia non possumus cogere abbatissas ire ad Capitulum de quo scripsit, et si vellent ire, sicut eis consulimus, multum nobis placeret'. The king's request was most probably spurred by the recalcitrance of the abbess of Tulebras (from whose community the founding nuns of Las Huelgas were taken), and a few others (equally founded by Tulebras) to assist at the king's favorite, Las Huelgas. This makes it rather a Spanish than a Cistercian issue.

when, independently from this, a movement was already in motion that would indeed result in the full juridical integration of the nuns into the Order of Cîteaux. Guy of Paray-le-monial, abbot of Cîteaux (1187–1202), in a charter issued between 1193 and 1199, stated that Tart was a daughter-house of Cîteaux and followed the *Instituta Cisterciensis Ordinis*. It was the prerogative of the abbot of Cîteaux to preside at abbatial elections at Tart as he did in Cîteaux' other daughterhouses. In the same charter Guy of Paray went even a step further: the abbot of Cîteaux had full jurisdiction in Tart (*plenam potestatem corrigendi et ordinandi*), and the abbesses of the eighteen communities related to Tart were obliged to participate in the [regional] Chapter of Tart.[41] The Chapters of Tart and Las Huelgas seem to have existed for some time.[42]

Between 1221 and 1240 the codification of Cistercian legislation began, in a fifteenth subtitle, to weaken the jurisdiction of abbesses.[43] The *Institutiones Capituli generalis* (around 1240) state clearly that the canonical visitation of nuns fell to the abbot. The same text reduced an abbess's visitation to a daughter-house to a mere visit.[44] Moreover, abbesses and nuns were not allowed to attend Cîteaux's General Chapter.[45] By 1200, there were in addition to the 'congregations' of Tart and Las Huelgas, some one hundred monasteries of nuns, all under the supervision, not of the order's General Chapter, but of a local abbot.[46]

Recognized by Rome as an Order in 1119, the Cistercians were not until 1184[47] completely exempt from the jurisdiction of the local bishop.[48] As the abbots came face to face with the *mulieres*

41 PL 185:1413–14.

42 Philippe Guignard, *Les monuments primitifs de la Règle cistercienne* (Dijon, 1878) 255.

43 Bernard Lucet, *La codification de 1212 et son évolution ultérieure* [henceforth cited as *Codification*], (Rome, 1964) 10.

44. Julien Paris, *Nomasticon Cisterciense* (Paris, 1664) 365; Hugo Séjalon, *Monasticon Cisterciense* (Solesmes, 1892) 361.

45 *Statuta* 1237, 4.

46 Jean Baptiste Van Damme, 'Les pouvoirs de l'Abbé de Citeaux aux XIIe et XIIIe siècles', *AC* 24 (1968) 73.

47 Jean Berthold Mahn, *L'Ordre Cistercien et son Gouvernement des origines au milieu du XII siècle (1098–1165)*, (Paris, 1945) 119–55.

48 Georg Schreiber, 'Studien zur Exemptionsgeschichte der Zisterzienser, zugleich ein Beitrag zur Veroneser Synode vom Jahre 1184', *Zeitschrift der*

religiosae movement at the end of the twelfth century, the General Chapter used its exemption for two purposes: on the one hand their exemption left them relatively free to shape their own legislation; and on the other they could require the same exemption for Cistercian nuns, making it at the same time more difficult for nuns to become fully incorporated into the Order. By longstanding custom, local bishops held more authority over communities of nuns than over those of monks in matters of monastic living, canonical visitations, elections, or professions. Cistercians could not simply ignore these rights, and certainly not all at once. Incorporation of the nuns of necessity obliged the abbots to deal with the long-established authority of the local bishop. But since both canonical and theological terminology was at that time still in a fluid stage, there seems to have been for a while a variety of consents by local bishops regarding the incorporation of nuns into the Order.[49]

In Belgium, the earliest indication of abbots having difficulties with the integration of nuns comes from a man who had an excellent record in understanding and fostering the *mulieres religiosae* movement and in founding monasteries of Cistercian nuns. When Walter of Utrecht, abbot of Villers (1214–1221) 'had planted (*plantavit*) many houses of our [Cistercian] Order in the diocese of Liège and because he was concerned about his own

---

Savigny-Stiftung für Rechtsgeschichte, Kanonistische Abteilung, 4 (1914) 74–116.

49 Between 1229 and 1235, for instance, the German bishops of Minden and Ratzeburg asked Gregory IX to integrate into the Cistercian Order the many monasteries of nuns not yet incorporated. In England the nuns were in a unique situation. In reality there were two wholly separate and distinct communities of nuns associated with the Cistercian tradition. The abbeys of Marham (Norfolk) and Tarrant (Dorset) were fully incorporated into the Order, 'but twenty-seven priories had no formal affiliation whatsoever with the white monks. The nuns of the latter group, at least those of the seven priories in the diocese of Lincoln, may uniquely be called "English Cistercians", for in the period between 1268 and 1270, a full century and more after their foundation, they won formal recognition but only from the English king and bishops. At precisely the same time, however, the abbot of Citeaux denied absolutely and unequivocally that they were any part of his order'. See Coburn V. Graves, 'The Organisation of an English Cistercian Nunnery in Lincolnshire', *Citeaux* 33 (1982) 333.

community for fear that his younger monks would have to miss the presence and example of a number of older monks serving as chaplains in monasteries of nuns, he handed over the paternity of eight houses to the abbot of Cîteaux'.[50]

The General Chapter of Cîteaux, realizing that the rush of so many women into the Order could overwhelm its control, took measures to stem the flow, or at least to restrict it. In 1219 it ordered that, in accordance with existing (but not closely observed) church laws for nuns, the newly incorporated nuns had to be cloistered.[51] The next year it decreed that henceforth no more monasteries of nuns would be incorporated.[52] Only foundations by existing communities would be tolerated.[53] Even this permission was abrogated in 1228: if nuns wished to follow the *Instituta* of the Order they were from September 1228 on, free to do so, but the Order took no pastoral responsibility for them.[54] The most famous community of this kind was Helfta, founded in 1229. This radical decision by the General Chapter proved to be as unsuccessful as the statute of 1152 forbidding new foundations and incorporations of monks.[55] In 1232 Fontenelles and Wauthier-Braine, two monasteries of Cistercian nuns in Belgium, received an explicit order to stop building a new foundation,[56] — a clear indication that nuns were not much perturbed by the General Chapter's earlier decision. Moreover, this legislative body soon attenuated its decrees: in 1235 it allowed future incorporations of nuns.[57]

The codification of Cistercian legislation, completed in 1240 after labors that lasted thirty-eight years, contains intentional loopholes: at the request of popes or when otherwise unavoidable,

---

50 Martene and Durand, *Thesaurus*, vol.3: 1277.
51 *Statuta* 1219, 12.
52 *Statuta* 1220, 4.
53 *Statuta* 1225, 7.
54 *Statuta* 1228, 16: 'Nulla monasteria monialium de cetero sub nomine aut iurisdictione Ordinis nostri construantur, vel Ordini socientur. Si quod vero monasterium monialium voluerit aemulari, non prohibemus; sed curam animarum earum non recipiemus, nec visitationis officium eis impendemus'.
55 *Statuta* 1152, 1.
56 *Statuta* 1232, 34.
57 *Statuta* 1235, 3.

new incorporations could be accepted,[58] on the condition already stipulated in 1225, that the buildings be completed, self-support guaranteed,[59] and cloister respected. Those cloister-stipulations in Cistercian legislation were certainly not absolute.[60] How elastic 'strict' enclosure was in the thirteenth century can be seen in Henriquez' *Quinque prudentes virgines*, particularly in the biography of Ida of Nivelles.

Before and after 1229 (though not in that year itself) popes, bishops, princes, noblemen and rich merchants requested incorporations,[61] particularly in Belgium.[62] This undoubtedly indicates a desire on the part of many *mulieres religiosae* and nuns to join the Cistercian Order. To this could be added the fact that at times whole families became enamored with the Cistercian way of life. The case of Bartholomew of Tienen and five of his six children provides one example. The same year that Bartholomew and his progeny made their profession in Florival (1216),[63] another family 'went Cistercian'. Geoffrey Pachomius, a native of Leuven, left the Augustinian canons regular to enter Villers where his two brothers and his father joined him and made profession on 8 September 1216. His sister Alice became a Cistercian nun in Vrouwenpark.[64] Abundus of Huy became a monk in Villers in 1206, his two brothers entered Val St. Lambert, one sister entered Rameya, another Val Notre Dame, and the

---

58 Julien Paris, *Nomasticon Cisterciense*, 364.

59 Self-support meant having sufficient income to ensure that nuns would not have to go out for fund-raising purposes, called in Cistercian parlance *mendicare* or *rubor mendicandi*: begging (*Statuta* 1276,15). Practically, this meant that they would have to support themselves mostly by means at variance with the stand taken by the founders of Citeaux, such as collecting profits from leasing lands and benefits from tithes and mills.

60 Gérard Huyghe, *La clôture des moniales des origines à la fin du XIIIe siècle. Étude historique et juridique* (Roubaix, 1944) 65–67; 74–87, concludes, 87: 'On ne peut dire qu'elle [enclosure] soit absolue [at the end of the thirteenth century]. D'ailleurs une clôture absolue ne tiendrait pas compte de certaines nécessités impérieuses'.

61 Krenig, 'Mittelalterliche Frauenklöster', *AC* 10 (1954) 21–31.

62 De Ganck, see above n.23.

63 Reypens, *Vita*, 49*.

64 Edmund Mikkers, 'Deux lettres inédites de Thomas chantre de Villers', *Coll* 10 (1948) 161–73; 163.

oldest remained home as a virgin.[65] Yvette of Huy (d.1228) married at thirteen, became a widow five years later and then a *mulier religiosa* who for eleven years took care of lepers before spending her last six years as a recluse. She was immured by the abbot of Orval but kept in contact with several Cistercians. Her father entered Villers,[66] one of her three sons became a monk at Troisfontaines and another at Orval.[67] The case of the knight Rainier of Udekem is the most fantastic. Not having the means to marry his eight daughters off by his standards, he tried unsuccessfully to have them accepted as Cistercians. Finally, in 1219, he transformed his castle into a convent of Praemonstratensian canonesses.[68]

The flow of *mulieres religiosae* toward Cîteaux ended around 1251 when Innocent IV allowed the Cistercians to ignore papal letters recommending, at the request of others, the incorporation of nuns if these letters did not mention word for word the privilege *Paci et tranquillitati* given to them to this effect.[69] After 1260 the *statuta* of the General Chapter mention few incorporations. They had already been made more difficult after 1244 because the General Chapter had demanded the explicit and officially recorded consent of the bishop to let them be exempt,[70] and—to avoid quibbling objections—the consent of the cathedral chapter by a charter with seal.[71] Clairefontaine near Arlon whose incorporation (1251) had dragged on for years,[72] is sometimes said to have had the oldest clearly formulated text.[73] Binderen near Helmond, provides a slightly older case. Empress Mary, sister of the duke of Brabant, had requested the incorporation of

---

65 A.M. Frenken, 'De *Vita* van Abundus van Hoei', *Citeaux* 10 (1959) 13.
66 Mens, *Oorsprong*, 385–87.
67 A. Frenken, 'De *Vita* van Abundus', *Citeaux* 10 (1959) 15.
68 Mens, *Oorsprong*, 367–68.
69 Manuscript 90 of the Epinal Library.
70 *Statuta* 1244, 7: no more incorporations 'donec chartam diocesanam habeant qua ipsas concedit Ordini absolutas ab omni iure episcopali secundum Ordinis instituta'.
71 *Statuta* 1245, 6.
72 *Statuta* 1247, 39; 1250, 41; 1251, 31.
73 Mahn, *L'Ordre Cistercien et son Gouvernement*, 152.

this, her foundation, in 1237.[74] Only in 1246 was the request granted, this time supported by the pope, the bishop of Liège and the chapter of his cathedral, for it included complete exemption.[75] It is remarkable that in the countries most affected by the *mulieres religiosae*, the foundation and incorporation of monasteries of Cistercian nuns was relatively high in the first half of the thirteenth century: more than one hundred and fifty in Germany,[76] and sixty-six in tiny Belgium.[77] Requests from the counts and countesses of Flanders to the General Chapter accounted for twenty two, or one-third, of them all. For how many the dukes of Brabant were responsible is difficult to ascertain given the scarcity of substantiating evidence. Their interventions, however, were not as frequent as those of their neighbors in Flanders.

James of Vitry in his *Historia Occidentalis* indicates that some communities of the 'older' Orders did not appeal to the *mulieres religiosae*, especially in Belgium.[78] Some eight formerly Benedictine and six Augustinian communities transferred to the Cistercian Order, while several individual beguines and at least twelve groups of them joined the Cistercians.[79] The movement toward Cîteaux ebbed after 1245 when the pope enjoined the Mendicants in that year to integrate women into their Orders.

The mutual relationships between Cistercians and the beguinal communities which dotted Belgium were numerous enough to lead J.Greven to assert that the beguines were an offshoot (Loslösung) of the Cistercians, and constituted an 'Order of

---

74 *Statuta* 1237, 31.

75 *Statuta* 1246, 56: 'cum pleno concessu privilegiorum, statutorum et libertatum Ordinis'.

76 Grundmann, *Religiöse Bewegungen*, 182, n.27.

77 De Ganck, 'The Cistercian Nuns of Belgium in the thirteenth Century', CSt 5 (1970) 169. See also above, n.23.

78 James of Vitry, *Historia Occidentalis*, Lib.1, cap.15, reproduced in Reypens, *Vita*, 122–23: 'The virgins devoted to God and holy women ...passed over to the tranquil harbor of the Cistercian Order, taking the regular habit, for they did not dare commit themselves securely to the other congregations of nuns because of the excessively dissolute life'.

79 See above n.23, p.23.

Cistercian nuns', a thesis rightly dismissed by Gregor Müller.[80]
Simone Roisin, after studying these two points of view, concluded first of all, that there was no Order of Cistercian nuns, but
a feminine branch of and within the Cistercian Order, and secondly, that although the beguines as an institution did not derive
from Cîteaux, they seem to have been an extension of the Cistercian 'apostolate' in the Low Countries.[81]

THE *CURA ANIMARUM*

It has been stated repeatedly that the Cistercians were unwilling to accept women as members of their Order.[82] Looking at the
sober wording of the General Chapters' decisions, one could
easily get that impression, for the phraseology is indeed masculine. The stand taken by the Cistercians, however, had less to
do with misogyny than with the *cura animarum*, care of souls, or
pastoral responsibility within the Order.[83] Before the sixteenth-
century Reformation the roughly seven hundred communities

---

80 Gregor Müller, 'Das Beginenwesen, eine Abzweigung von den Cistercien-
serinnen?', *Cistercienser Chronik* 27 (1913) 33–41.

81 Roisin, *L'Efflorescence*, 342–45 and 378.

82 Two recent publications keep this dubious assertion alive: Sally
Thompson, 'The Problem of Cistercian Nuns in the Twelfth and Early Thirteenth Centuries', *Medieval Women*, Festschrift Rosalind M. Hill, *Studies in
Church History* 7, Derek Baker ed. (Oxford, 1978) 227–52, writes 'that early
Cistercians were remarkable for their hostility to the feminine sex'. This opening
statement is based on a text from R.W. Southern, *Western Society and the
Church in the Middle Ages* (Harmondsworth, 1970) 314: 'No religious body was
more thoroughly masculine than the Cistercians; none that shunned female
contact with greater determination or that raised more formidable barriers
against the intrusion of women'. The problem with this kind of publications,
scholarly as they may be, is that they are too easily based on unchecked
references and texts of earlier publications. Nor should the particular case of
Cistercian nunneries in insular England presumed to be exactly the same as it
was in continental Europe. See above, n. 49. Nor should it be forgotten that in
England, most 'Cistercian priories' called themselves 'Cistercian' in order to
benefit from the numerous privileges and immunities the supposedly unworldly
Cistercians had been able to accumulate over the years.

83 Bede Lackner, 'Early Citeaux and the Care of Souls' in *Noble Piety and
Reformed Monasticism*, Studies in Medieval Cistercian History 7, R. Elder ed.
(Kalamazoo, 1981) 52–67, is mostly about *cura animarum* in the sense of
priestly ministry and administration of sacraments to laypeople.

of Cistercian monks were far outnumbered by nine hundred communities of Cistercian nuns,[84] which needed chaplains provided by the men. The *cura animarum*, touching both monks and the jurisdiction of the local bishop, was indeed a sensitive issue, and not only for the Cistercians. Cîteaux could at most be called 'neutral' rather than misogynist during the first century of its existence as a monastic reform by monks for monks. This attitude seems to have been part of their 'return' to an undiluted observance of Benedict's rule. This collegial body of all Cistercian abbots did not turn away the nuns out of hand. They allowed them at least the guidance of individual abbots who had some jurisdiction over them and some responsibility for them.

New solutions easily give rise to new problems. Though the Cistercians learned something from the experience of the Praemonstratensians, the abbots, soon after they agreed in 1187 to the establishment of the Las Huelgas' 'general chapter', found that they had to forbid equestrian travel together by Spanish abbots and abbesses or nuns.[85] By responding favorably to the influx of the *mulieres religiosae*, the century-old, all-male monastic Order of Cîteaux proved after all not to have been antagonistic to women. Was abbot Walter of Villers, one of the earliest supporters of the *mulieres religiosae* antagonistic when he deplored the absence from his community of eight solid members who were acting as chaplains to nuns?.[86] His successor, William of Brussels

---

84 Louis Lekai and Ambrose Schneider, *Geschichte und Wirken des Weissen Mönche* (Cologne, 1958) 54. A total reduced to 647 for monks and, 'at their peak', the total number of convents [of nuns] was probably greater than that of the monasteries [of men]. See Louis J. Lekai, *The Cistercians. Ideals and Reality* (Kent State University Press, 1977) 43–44 and 352.

85 *Statuta* 1191, 91; 1192, 6; 1199, 47.

86 One might wonder why an abbot of a daughterhouse of Clairvaux resigned the responsibility of eight houses of Cistercian nuns into the hands of the abbot of Citeaux. The abbots of Citeaux and of Clairvaux were usually eager to extend their own jurisdiction.Thanks to Bernard, Clairvaux claimed about fifty percent of all Cistercian houses and had developed a close relationship with its filiation. See Roger De Ganck, 'Les pouvoirs de l'Abbé de Citeaux, de la Bulle *Parvus fons* (1265) à la Révolution française', AC 27(1971) 3–63; 16. In Belgium, Clairvaux had more daughterhouses of nuns than did Citeaux, and both delegated local abbots to take care of the nuns. See R. De Ganck, 'Het "placet" voor buitenlandse Cisterciënser-visitators in de 16e eeuw', *Citeaux* 7 (1956)

(1221–1237), was not at all bothered by his predecessor's second thoughts and was very much at ease within the framework of the *mulieres religiosae* movement both among Cistercian nuns and among the beguines. And just as the above mentioned decision of the General Chapter of 1152 forbidding the incorporation of new communities of monks could not stop expansion, so the General Chapter's stand in 1228 in relation to nuns was likewise ineffective. In both instances the General Chapter's strongly-worded policy was not aimed against monks or nuns, but reflected the Order's doubt of being able conveniently to integrate the steady influx of new members without affecting the values it professed. Moreover the *cura animarum* of nuns was not limited to their 'souls' only, but comprehended them as persons with mind, soul, and body in need of assistance. This made the father abbot's responsibility that much heavier. When one considers that in Belgium the ratio of communities of nuns to those of monks was 4.4 to 1, the problem of integrating the nuns becomes apparent, and the accusation of anti-feminist bias against the General Chapter was somewhat strained, at least in so far as Belgium and Germany are concerned.

The *cura animarum* of nuns caused no greater enthusiasm in the budding mendicant Orders established in 1215 and 1216. The Castillian Dominic Gusman founded the first community of Dominican nuns in Prouille (1206–1207) with the help of the Cistercian bishop Fulk of Toulouse, even before the Order of Preachers had been established.[87] When Dominic died in 1221, there were only three monasteries of Dominican nuns, all under the jurisdiction of the Dominicans.[88] The text of the oldest constitutions of the Dominicans mentions a decision of 1220, forbidding any Dominican, under the penalty of excommunication, to

---

103. How else could Citeaux and Clairvaux have fulfilled the *cura animarum* of these nuns, or would they have found all the needed chaplains able to speak the different vernacular languages of these communities?.

87 M.H. Vicaire, *Saint Dominic and his Time* (New York-Toronto-London, 1964) 115–36.

88 A.H. Thomas, *De oudste constituties van de Dominicanen* (Leuven, 1965) 89, referring to O. Decker, *Die Stellung der Predigerordens zu den Dominikarerinnen* (1206–1267), (Vechter-Leipzig, 1935).

be or to become engaged in or entrusted with the *cura animarum* of nuns or of any other women grouped together.[89] Dominic's successor, Jordan of Saxony, had to make it clear that this decision did not jeopardize the communities of nuns founded by Dominic himself.[90] A few years later, in 1239, the Dominicans asked Gregory IX to relieve them of responsibility for nuns, i.e. their *cura animarum*, because it hindered their apostolate.[91]

The case of the Franciscans is somewhat more complicated, in no small part because the then cardinal Ugolino, Francis' patron, who became Gregory IX (1127–1241), tried in vain to have at least some *mulieres religiosae* integrated into the Franciscan Order. Francis had had no plans about including women until Clare Sciffi embraced the same ideal of poverty as Francis himself and settled in San Damiano.[92] In 1219 Francis explicitly said to Ugolino that he was against laying the *cura animarum* of any community of women on his brethren and he expressed this in so many words in his *Regula non bullata* of 1221. The sentence disappeared in the *Regula bullata* of 1223, to be replaced by a decision to limit the care of nuns exclusively to those to whom the pope would give special permission.[93] In fact, from 1228 until 1245 there is no record of any foundation of monasteries of Franciscan nuns, not even by the nuns at San Damiano.[94] It was only in 1245 that the pope was able to open the door to the integration of women into the Orders of the Dominicans and the Franciscans.[95] This measure relieved much of the pressure on the Cistercians. From 1245 on, monasteries of the 'second Order' of both mendicant Orders grew rapidly. The Franciscans flourished

---

89 Thomas, *De oudste consituties van de Dominicanen*, 360, n.27: 'In virtute Spiritus sancti et sub pena excommunicationis districte prohibemus ne aliquis fratrum nostrorum de cetero laboret vel procuret, ut cura vel custodia monialium seu quarumlibet aliarum mulierum nostris fratribus commitatur. Et si quis contraire presumpserit, pene graviori culpe subire subiaceat'.

90 Grundmann, *Religiöse Bewegungen*, 218–19.

91 Thomas, *De oudste constituties*, 89.

92 John Moorman, *A History of the Franciscan Order from its Origin to the Year 1517* (Oxford, 1968) 32–39.

93 Grundmann, *Religiöse Bewegungen*, 264–65.

94 *Ibid.*, 268.

95 *Ibid.*, 274–84.

in Mediterranean countries, while the Dominicans spread rather in Teutonic lands,[96] where Meister Eckhart, Heinrich Suso and John Tauler became the spiritual leaders of the fourteenth century.[97]

---

96 *Ibid.*, 312–18.

97 Martin Grabmann, *Mittelalterliches Geistesleben* (Munich, 1926) vol.1: 'Die deutsche Frauenmystik des Mittelalters. Ein Überblick', 469–83; 478:' Die grössten dieser Gottesfreunde sind die mystisch Dreigestirn des Dominikanerordens, Meister Eckhart, dessen Grössen in der spekulativen Mystik besteht; Johannes Tauler, der lebens-und herzenskundige gewaltige Prediger, und Heinrich Seuse, der Minnesänger untern den Mystikern'.

CHAPTER TWO

PRELIMINARY STEPS TO MEETING GOD

B EGUINES AND NUNS OF THE *MULIERES RELIGIOSAE* movement in Belgium were intent on leading a worthwhile
life. The ascetical implications of this endeavor will
become clearer as the study of Beatrice's 'context' progresses.
For now, it might be pointed out that their lifestyle, with all its
frugality and asceticism, was not accidental, *viz.* the result of
social and economic forces. Anyone who looks unbiasedly at
Western Europe in the twelfth and thirteenth centuries will
acknowledge that this was a Christian society, expressing its
Christianity in its own way within a feudal political system. It
certainly may not be labeled a 'dark ages'—something which had
already passed before the twelfth century.

The *mulieres religiosae* movement does not have the characteristics of the twelfth-century heterodox *Wanderprediger* phenomenon. These were not men and women roaming around
preaching and protesting against the contemporary church and
society, but persons in a positive movement, seeking and searching for the meaning of life. In their christian world view they
found this meaning in God, by whom and for whom they were
made. They gave it concrete expression by choosing a celibate
life lived in frugality, trying through self-knowledge to arrive at a
better knowledge of God and their mutual relationship. For clar-

23

ity's sake the following pages will consider frugality, virginity and self-knowledge, leading to the more basic question of the relationship between God and man, as the *mulieres religiosae* saw it.

FRUGALITY

The way of life of these women was marked by a great simplicity, by a poverty and frugality in spirit and in fact.[1] They practised what Bernard had praised in his time: 'By their own decision they gave priority not to possessions but to poverty, and if they had no possessions, they at least despised them'.[2] Frugality, as the *mulieres religiosae* lived it, was more than merely a refusal to become corrupted by or attached to possessions. Hadewijch wrote in her twenty-second Letter:

> I shared little in the eating, drinking and sleeping of people. I have not dressed up in their clothes, nor with their make-up, nor with their attire. And of all that gladdens the human heart, in what it can obtain or receive, I never derived any joy, except for the brief moments of experiencing *Minne* (Love) that conquers all.[3]

They considered frugality an indispensable, liberating means of freeing themselves in order to love and serve God and their neighbor. Their poverty was a deliberately chosen path,[4] taken to follow and imitate Christ.[5] Beguines were not infrequently called

---

1 Poverty is a customarily accepted expression referring to the vow made by religious not to own private property. Frugality describes more accurately the way of life of the *mulieres religiosae*.

2 IV HM 12; SBOp 5: 65: 'Voluntate divitias paupertate commutaverunt, vel etiam non habitas tamquam habitas contempserunt'.

3 VM, *Brieven*, 1: 243, ll.28–33. That Hadewijch could write that way could also indicate that, while belonging to the *mulieres religiosae* movement, she did not consider herself to be a beguine in the proper sense, at least not when she wrote that letter. Beguines, and even more so Cistercian nuns could not reasonably have written Hadewijch's quoted remark.

4 Herbert Grundmann, *Religiöse Bewegungen*, 194–95.

5 Matthäus Bernards, 'Nudus nudum Christum sequi', in *Wissenschaft und Weisheit* 14 (1951) 148–51, gives a fairly good overview of this poverty ideal.

pauperes mulieres religiosae, poor devout women,[6] leading a very simple life of 'apostolic poverty' as it was called.[7] Many of these women came from the middle class, though some stemmed from nobility.[8] Yet for love of the kingdom of God they despised the riches of the world, the wealth of their parents notwithstanding. 'Clinging to their heavenly Bridegroom in poverty and humility, they were content with a low income procured by the manual labor of their charitable services',[9] or the frugality of their monastic life. Voluntary poverty and frugality helped them also to create an outward environment advantageous to their spiritual life. In this connection someone has remarked that by choosing frugality they reduced their sensitivity to external impressions which could contaminate their spiritual ascent and mystical experiences.[10] All the new orders—Praemonstratensians, Cistercians, Carthusians—strongly emphasized poverty and simplicity. Abbots and monks of Villers were conspicuous for their frugality and their liberality toward others.[11] The monk Gobert summed up the mentality prevailing at Villers by saying, 'Christ's patrimony

---

6 Philippen, *Begijnhoven*, 31–32.

7 McDonnell, *The beguines*, 141–53.

8 Grundmann, *Religiöse Bewegungen*, 192: 'Soweit wir überhaupt über die sozialen und wirtschaftlichen Verhältnisse jener Frauen Bescheid wissen, die in freiwilliger Armut als Beginen oder in den Frauenklöster der Zisterzienser und Bettelorden lebten, sind es nicht etwa arme Frauen niederer Schichten, sondern reiche, zum mindensten wohlhabende Frauen der höheren Stände, des Hochadels, des Dienstadels, des städtlichen Patriziats und der reich gewordenen Kaufmannskreise. Aus dem Ritter-und Kaufmannsstand kamen alle jenen Frauen, die in der religiösen Bewegung Belgiens am Anfang des Jahrhunderts eine Rolle spielten'. See also Nübel, *Mittelalterliche Beginen-und Sozialsiedlungen*, 34.

9. James of Vitry, Prologue to Mary of Oignies' *Vita, AA SS* June 5: 542.

10 H. Grundmann, 'Geschichtliche Grundlagen der deutschen Mystik', *Deutsche Vierteljahrschrift für Literaturwissenschaften und Geistesgeschichte* 12 (1934) 405–29; 418–19, reprinted with slight additions in *Altdeutsche und Altniederländische Mystik*, K.Ruh, ed. (Darmstadt, 1964) 72–99; 87: 'Unverkennbar hat sich in die innere Anschauung solcher Erlebnisse [as ecstasies and raptures] sehr vieles von den Erfahrungen, Wünschen und Vorstellungen aus dem Sinnenwelt geflüchtet, von denen das Leben in religiöser Armut sich loslösen wollte'.

11 Roisin, *L'Hagiographie*, 94.

belongs to the poor'.[12] Prior Werric of Aulne is said to have been a typical representative of Cistercian charity.[13] Sharing with the needy was a customary expression of their spirit of poverty.[14]

Cistercian nuns, before and after they became Cistercians, embraced this ideal of poverty with enthusiasm, 'content only with what bodily needs required'.[15] Some from a well-to-do background refused to consent to their families' accumulation of goods. They were suspicious of, and sometimes resisted accepting and using their parental patrimony because it might be profit from 'sinful financial or commercial dealings'.[16] Their biographers call them *pauperculae Christi*, the little poor ones of Christ.[17]

The mendicant orders put poverty at the core of their way of life. They supported themselves, not by possessions and the income from manual labor, but by preaching, teaching and begging. Until then, seeking alms was considered unbecoming to religious women, and as a result the mendicants' second orders had difficulty obtaining ecclesiastical approval for living their ideal of poverty by actually depending on alms, though these nuns had no pastoral ministry that could contribute to their support.

VIRGINITY

The second emphasis of the *mulieres religiosae* movement was virginity. What has been said of their fervor for frugality applies equally to their zeal for virginity, for both were spoken of in the same breath. Those women were intent on remaining virgins (*virgines continentes*), not merely for societal or psychological

---

12 Martene and Durand, *Thesaurus* 3, 1324: 'patrimonia Christi propria sunt pauperum'.

13 Roisin, *L'Hagiographie*, 128.

14 McDonnell, *The beguines*, 323–25.

15 Alice of Schaarbeek, *AA SS* June: 478, 4: 'pro sola corporis necessitate utens'.

16 Ida of Nivelles, *Quinque*, 210; Ida of Leuven, *AA SS* April 2: 159, 4.

17 Roisin, *L'Hagiographie*, 94–95; Mens, *Oorsprong*, 258–61. The application of this term to Beatrice (37, 32) refers to an aspect of her poor health, not at this point to her spirit of poverty, as has sometimes been claimed:; see R. De Ganck, 'The Cistercian Nuns of Belgium in the thirteenth century', *CSt* 5 (1970) 177; Mens, *Oorsprong*, 260, n.22.

reasons, or for security's sake.[18] At the time this stand raised suspicions in the minds of some ecclesiastical authorities because there were, in fact, heterodox women who held a doctrine called Nicolaism which regarded marriage as something sinful, a form of fornication.[19] Virginity may also have appeared to be an implicit reproach of the sexual life of some clergy.[20] In 1233 Gregory IX issued a bull *Gloriam virginalem* approving the *mulieres religiosae*. In 1236 Geoffrey of Fontaine, bishop of Cambrai (1220–1237), followed suit and confirmed their way of life in his diocese,[21] which also covered a great part of the duchy of Brabant.

Virginity entails the renunciation not only of physical motherhood, of course, but also of marriage, a state of life these women esteemed.[22] They espoused virginity on a double level: the physical (*corporis*) and the spiritual (*cordis*).[23] As Gilbert of Hoyland expressed it, 'chastity is not judged so much by bodily continence, as by purity of heart'. [24] Just as true love is more related to the heart than to the body, so the ideal of virginity implied a conscious interiorization of virginity stabilized in the center of the

---

18 Jean Verdon pointed out that in the West of France in the eleventh and twelfth centuries, widows and even married women made up from 30% to 50% of the communities of Benedictine nuns, mostly for reasons of personal security. See his 'Les moniales dans la France de l'Ouest aux XIe et XIIe siècles. Étude d'histoire sociale', *Cahiers de Civilisation médiévale*, 19 (1976) 247–63.

19 Grundmann, *Religiöse Bewegungen*, 179–81; C. Thouzellier, *Catharisme et Valdéisme en Languedoc*, 77; Borst, *Die Katharer*,181: 'Ehe ist Hurerei'.

20 Ch. Duggan, 'Equity and Compassion' (see above Chapter I, n.19) 63–66. Although the author discusses circumstances existing in England, the behavior of some of the clergy on the continent was no different.

21 'Modum et honestatem vivendi sanctarum virginum in Begginarum habitu', see McDonnell, *The beguines*, 157–59.

22 Jean Leclercq, 'L'amour et mariage vus par des clercs et des religieux, spécialement au XIIe siècle', *Love and Marriage in the Twelfth Century*, W. Van Hoecke and A. Welkenhuyzen eds, (Leuven, 1981) 107.

23 Matthäus Bernards, *Speculum Virginum. Geistigkeit und Seelenleben der Frau im Hochmittelalter* (Cologne-Graz, 1955) 86–87.

24 SC 18.1; PL 184: 92A:' Non enim sola continentia castitas censetur; cordis multo magis est aestimanda puritate'; ET by Lawrence Braceland, CF 20: 227. The same theme had already been stressed by Augustine, see R. Herbert, 'Saint Augustin et la virginité de la foi', *AM* 2: 645–55; 646–47.

heart. The same ideal applied to male virgins.[25] Virginity of the heart had to be carefully guarded, for it could be subtly degraded by self-complacency [26] and disfigured by pride. [27] To be strong, such virginity demanded a deep love for Christ—their beloved, faithful lover, as he is frequently called in the *Vitae*. Juliana of Cornillon vowed her love to Christ from the days of her maidenhood: 'She was a virgin who gave herself up to the virginal Christ, the son of the Virgin'. [28] According to her biographer, on a certain day a huge cloud of smoke rose up when she was in prayer, a clear indication, he says, of the great fire of love that burned in her virginal heart. [29]

This does not mean that the ideal was realized by all the *mulieres religiosae*. [30] Yet when virginity of heart is missing,

---

25 As illustrated for example by a reference to two abbots of Villers. The handsome Charles (1197–1209) declined an offer from an influential lady of nobility who revealed to him that she was deeply in love with him. He had difficulty convincing her that her advances would always meet with a categorical no, because he was a monk. (Caesarius of Heisterbach, *Dialogus miraculorum*, ed. Strange [Cologne, 1851] vol.1: 162–63). When the body of abbot William of Brussels, former abbot of Villers (1221–1237), then abbot of Clairvaux (1237–1240), was being prepared for burial, his genitals radiated a light seemingly stronger than the sun (Martene and Durand, *Thesaurus*, 3: 1282). The authenticity of this so-called miracle is in itself irrelevant. The story was intended to show that the highly respected abbot, a great supporter of nuns and beguines, shared their appreciation of total virginity.

26 M. Bernards, *Speculum Virginum*, 51, n.159. 'A widow who is penitent and humble is more pleasing to God than an insolent, proud virgin'. 'Penitent and humble' together are opposed to 'insolent and proud', and do not imply that the widow should be penitent because she had been married.

27 Bernard, *Miss*, SBOp 4: 20: 'A [sexual] sinner turned humble is better than a proud virgin. The former cleanses through humility the impurity committed, whereas the pride of the latter taints the chastity'. See also Thomas Renna, 'Virginity and Chastity in Early Cistercian Thought', *StM* 26 (1984) 43–54.

28 *AA SS* April 1: 453.

29 Ibid., This *topos* was not uncommon at that time. See J[oris] Reynaert, *Beeldspraak van Hadewijch. Studiën en tekstuitgaven van Ons Geestelijk Erf* 21 (Tielt-Bussum, 1981; henceforth cited as *Beeldspraak*), 122, n.113. J.E. Cirlot, *A Dictionary of Symbols*, ET by J.Sage (New York, 1962) 285: 'The column of smoke is a symbol...of the relations between earth and heaven, pointing out the path through fire to salvation'.

30 Though Gregory IX spoke in 1233 of beguines as *virgines continentes*, virgins who promised perpetual chastity (Grundmann, *Religiöse Bewegungen*, 186, n.34), they certainly did not make solemn vows, and Gregory's talk about

virginity of body finds itself on a slippery path. The *Vitae* and *Exempla* illustrate more than one inglorious fall.[31] Virginity took its value from relatedness to Christ and from the efforts of the virgin to keep her bodily virginity spiritually virginal. There is no *Vita* in which this trait is not explicitly mentioned several times. Beatrice is a case in point. Called back from school, she pleased her father by her 'virginal resolve'. The biographer took care to stress that this was a decision taken of her own 'strong free will'(23,6), although it could well have been inspired in part by the beguines she had lived with in Zoutleeuw. Several times Beatrice was confirmed in her resolution: when Ida of Nivelles initiated her into bridal mysticism (50,47; 51,76); when she received her *consecratio virginum* (76,4); by her spiritual and ascetical endeavors (106,25;114,60; 141,5; 161,4) and during her mystical experiences in which Christ showed himself as the eager lover of his beloved. The biographer was fond of references to her virginity: Beatrice is the *virguncula* of Christ (29,113), the chosen virgin of Christ (22,52), the virgin (228,6), the holy virgin (274,24), Christ's or the Lord's virgin,[32] or his very devout virgin (36,13; 47,68). These virgin-appellations running through

---

perpetual chastity forces the meaning of this expression, since temporary and perpetual vows were then not yet a canonical matter. Philippen (*Begijnhoven*, 220) says that they did not make a perpetual commitment to virginity. The oldest known (fourteenth century) regulations of beguinages accept the possibility of beguines leaving their former way of life to marry (J. Philippen, *Begijnhoven*, 309). F.W. Koorn confirmed this in his paper, 'Ongebonden Vrouwen. Overeenkomsten en verschillen tussen Begijnen en Zusters des Gemenen Levens', *OGE* 59 [1985] 392–401; 395.

31 There are cases where authorities were provoked to take measures because nuns were not being faithful to their virginity. A former abbot of Villers, Conrad of Urach (1209–1214), acted as cardinal (1219–1227) forcefully at the synod of Mainz (1225) against clerics who, '*laxatis voluntatis habenis*' enticed nuns away from their virginity. (Martene and Durand, *Thesaurus*, 3: 1275] and in 1233 and 1244 the '*lapsus frequens et evidens*' of some beguines was of no small concern at other synods in the same Mainz archdiocese. See Grundmann, *Religiöse Bewegungen*, 326, n.15.

32 Christ's virgin: *Vita*, 19, 58; 49, 8; 91, 6; 151, 4; 170, 5; 192, 8; 212, 68; 230, 32; 243, 43; the Lord's virgin (Lord meaning Christ): 47, 55; 76, 4; 77, 49; 99, 22; 111, 10; 115, 74; 119, 21; 125, 4; 141, 5; 149, 86; 153, 32; 212, 84; 217, 86; 265, 54; 270, 6.

the whole biography begin to be interspersed with such titles as spouse, loving spouse, and venerable spouse, as soon as Beatrice heard from Ida of Nivelles that she had been chosen by the Lord to be his own most faithful spouse (51,76).

It should not be necessary to point out that the ideal of frugality and virginity of the *mulieres religiosae* demanded the support of more than a minimal ascesis. Whenever and wherever an outstanding orthodoxy is translated into practice it needs to be expressed in an orthopraxis of some quality. The writings of the Church Fathers, the sayings of the desert Fathers, the *Exempla* collections and the *Vitae* of the *mulieres religiosae* testify that a deep, interior life needs a supportive praxis of physical asceticism. A few Christians had such a compulsive need of it and practised it so excessively that their psychological and emotional balance could be questioned. But to whatever degree ascetical practices were part of the lives of most of these lovers of Christ,[33] they sprang chiefly from love rather than from a compulsive urge to satisfy a psychological complex. Frugality and virginity were undoubtedly important practices of the *mulieres religiosae*. But basically they were, like everything else in their lives, part of the answer to the how and the why of their existence. Peoples of all times and places have been asking basic questions about humankind's origin, purpose, and meaning. The *mulieres religiosae* were no less intrigued by them, though evidently within the frame of their belief and culture.

SELF-KNOWLEDGE

The self-knowledge we are speaking of is not that of philosophy, limiting its reflections to ordinary consciousness, [34] or 'one's own self'.[35] It is rather a self-knowledge which opens on to

---

33 For some practices in the Cistercian and Beguinal milieu, see Roisin, *L'Hagiographie*, 91–104.

34 Robert Ehman, 'Two Basic Concepts of the Self', *IPQ* 6 (1965) 594–611.

35 Sydney Shoemaker, *Self-knowledge and Self-identity* (Ithaca-London: Cornell, 1963) 165: 'Philosophical theories about the nature of "the self" generally have little to say about the nature of the knowledge one has of other selves than one's *own* self'.

knowledge of the transcendent God,[36] and it is not uniquely Christian. The three monotheistic religions, Judaism, Christianity and Islam have always viewed self-knowledge in relation to God.[37] Gershom Scholem has paid particular attention to 'Hasidism in Medieval Germany',[38] a Jewish religious movement in the Rhineland and Northern France,[39] which shows several

---

36. Louis Dupré, 'The Mystical Knowledge of the Self and its Philosophical Significance', *IPQ* 14 (1974) 495–511;511: 'The ultimate message of the [Christian] mystic about the nature of selfhood is that the self is *essentially* more than a mere self, that transcendence belongs to its nature as much as the act through which it is immanent to itself, and that a total failure on the mind's part to realize this transcendence reduces the self to *less* than itself. The direct awareness of the transcendent self underlying the flux and periodic discontinuities of the ordinary forms of self-consciousness constitutes a significant experience on which our philosophy has not yet sufficiently reflected in the past'.

37 Alexander Altmann, *Studies in Religious Philosophy and Mysticism* (London, 1969) 1–40: 'The Delphic maxim in medieval Islam and Judaism'. Two sayings based on the Delphic oracle are attributed to Muhammed. The first, quoted by Ibn Sina (Avicenna), reads: 'He who knows himself knows the Lord'. The second: 'He among you who knows himself best knows his Lord best'. Al Ghazali's *Mishkât al-Anwâr* quotes a version which is even closer to Genesis in the Hebrew Scriptures: 'Allah created Adam in the image of the Merciful One' (p.8). Altmann asserts (p.3) that from Islam the concepts of self-knowledge leading to the knowledge of God passed into medieval Judaism; he goes on (leaving the Christian interpretation aside) to explain the spiritual and mystical interpretations and applications of it in medieval Islam and Judaism.

38 Gershom Scholem, *Major Trends in Jewish Mysticism*, 8th ed. (New York, 1974) 80–118.

39 Since Belgium connected both these countries, it could not but attract Jewish communities, particularly to the thriving cloth industry at that time. There is, to my knowledge, no systematic study on Jewish spirituality in Belgium in the twelfth and thirteenth centuries. See, however, K.A. Smelik, ed., *Jodendom. Bibliografie over het Jodendom en Israel voor het Nederlandse taalgebied* (The Hague, 1983), which could not be consulted in this study. Additional information could be gleaned from Caesarius of Heisterbach and similar writers. Notorious is the case of a Jewish girl Catherine whose parents moved, probably from Cologne, to Leuven in 1215, when she was five years old; three years later she joined the nearby Cistercian nuns of Vrouwenpark, creating a heated debate. See Roisin, *L'Hagiographie*, 65–66, and Emile Brouette, 'La cistercienne Cathérine de Louvain fut-elle abbesse de Parc-les-Dames?', *AB* 78 (1960) 84–91. Hadewijch mentions a Jewish Sarah who lived near Cologne. She became a Christian when she was sixteen and had several mystical experiences (VM, *Visioenen*, 1: 186, ll.141–62]

similarities to the contemporary movement of the *mulieres reli-giosae.*[40]

When Etienne Gilson's study of *The Mystical Theology of Saint Bernard* first appeared in English, [41] the publishers used as frontispiece a picture of a cadaver in an advanced state of decom-position with the Greek subscription of the Delphic oracle, 'Know thyself'. Impressive as this representation may be, it is neverthe-less misleading, for self-knowledge presented under this form of human mortality focuses attention in a striking way on one limited aspect of the much more comprehensive 'know thyself'. One of the Greek formulations of a number of other and older myths in the Middle East and India [42] is the Delphic oracle which comes to us in its oldest form in the Homeric hymn to Apollo.[43] Whatever the mythical origins of the 'know thyself', a long historical development encompasses its understanding and expla-nation. Classical Greek and Latin literature offer a great number of interpretations.[44]

---

40 Scholem, *Major Trends,* 127. The statement by Güdeman (p.84) that 'similar causes produced similar effects' is unfortunately not elaborated upon, at least not here. Some Jewish scholars posit a connection between Christian mysticism of that period and the Hasidic movement. Hasidic means 'the devout', a title also given to the Christian *mulieres religiosae,* in both cases on religious grounds. See also J.B. P[orion], *Hadewijch: Lettres spirituelles. Béat-rice de Nazareth: Sept degrés d'amour* (Geneva, 1972) 297–310: 'Le mouve-ment extatique chez les Juifs contemporains', and G. Vadja, *L'Amour de Dieu dans la théologie juive du moyen-âge* (Paris, 1957).

41 ET by A.H.C. Downes (London, 1940).

42 Joseph Fontenrose, *Python. A Study of Delphic Myth and its Origin* (Berkeley-Los Angeles-London: University of California Press, 1959, first paperback edition, 1980) 465: 'The Apollo-Pytho myth and the Zeus-Typhon myth are two closely related expressions of a single antecedent myth, itself a member of a myth-family that ranged over most of Europe and Asia'.

43 Joseph Fonterose, *The Delphic Oracle. Its Responses and Operations with a Catalogue of Responses* (Berkeley-Los Angeles-London, 1978) 294.

44 Pierre Courcelle, '"Nosce teipsum", du Bas-Empire au Haut Moyen-Age. L'Héritage profane et les développements chrétiens' [henceforth cited as *Nosce teipsum*], *Settimana di Studi del Centro italiano di studi nell 'alto medievo,* Spoleto 9 (1962) 165–95, and the more extensive work by the same author, *Connais-toi toi-même: de Socrate à Saint Bernard* (Paris, 1974–75) 3 vols. The famous oracle, if genuine, is unclear. When the oracle answered the question: 'What is best for man?', the actual response may have been: 'Know your

There is little doubt that the Christian use of the maxim 'know thyself' borrowed heavily from the classical writings, combining them with biblical teaching expressed by the Greek and Latin Fathers of the Church. For St. Ambrose, followed by several others, the Delphic oracle originated not from Apollo, but from Moses and Solomon. Bernard, Richard, John of Salisbury, the writer of the *Vita antiqua* of William, and others said explicitly that the 'know thyself' came down from heaven, [45] and in some sense it had.

Bernard, following St. Paul and Augustine, took the greatest care to underline the universal obligation for everyone to come through self-knowledge to the knowledge of God.[46] Attaining self-knowledge is not merely a fancy that one may indulge in or not. 'If you do not know yourself', said Bernard, 'you are like a building without a foundation; you raise not a structure, but a ruin'.[47] Without self-knowledge, contact with God is out of the question: If a man is not yet capable of seeing himself, 'in vain does he direct the eye of his heart toward God'.[48] Self-knowledge reveals to man that he is a reality which is of necessity relational. Human self-knowledge is the awareness of being not a completely autonomous agent, but the creation of a higher agent, of a creator whose being is Being. Just as nothing can exist without

---

place in the world', 'Know that you are a man', 'Know your true self', among other possible interpretations. (Fontenrose, *The Delphic Oracle*, 294 and 304). A (pagan) Greek understanding interpreted the saying as 'Know thyself that thou may'st know that thou are not a god but only a mortal' (A.J. Festugière, *L'Idéal religieux des Grecs et l'Evangile* [Paris, 1932] 232, 24). The gods are superior to man precisely because they are immortal, whereas man is by definition mortal; A.J. Festugière, *Contemplation et vie contemplative selon Platon*, 3rd edition (Paris, 1967) 255.

45 Courcelle, *Nosce teipsum*, 281 and 291, n.12

46 Dil 2.6; SBOp 3: 124, 'Proinde inexcusabilis est omnis etiam infidelis, si non diligit Dominum Deum suum toto corde, tota anima, tota virtute sua'. For an overview of the importance of self-knowledge among Cistercians, see Anna Maiorino Tuozzi, *La conoscenza di sè nella scuola cistercense* (Naples, 1976).

47 Csi 2.3.6; SBOp 3: 414, 'Si te nescieris, eris similis aedificanti sine fundamento, ruinam, non structuram faciens'.

48 Richard, *Benjamin minor.* 71; PL 196: 51C, 'Frustra cordis oculum erigit ad videndum Deum, qui nondum idoneus est ad videndum seipsum'. Richard echoes here Augustine's *De Trinitate* 10.9.12; PL 42:980.

him, so God cannot exist without himself: he, God, exists for himself, he exists for all.[49] William presents God as saying: 'Know yourself for you are my image, thus you can know me whose image you are and you will find me within you'. William continues the exhortation by adding: 'Strive to hold him ever in your memory, to know him through love, and to love him by knowing him'. [50]

Humankind is thus in a particularly privileged situation, for God wrote the law of his love on the human heart. God loves man in such a way that man generates his own love out of his need and capacity to reach the goal to which he is created and called.[51] On the one hand, out of the necessity inherent in his createdness man is obliged to love God, and on the other, out of the freedom deeply engrained in his human nature, he simultaneously chooses to give priority to this love.[52] This is man's incomparable greatness which comes from his God-given qualities of intellect and freedom.[53] This is man's greatest dignity and highest calling: it makes him genuinely precious.[54] Through deepened self-knowledge, man becomes aware of both his greatness and his limitations, of how at the same time he is wonderful and miser-

49 Bernard, Csi 5.6.13; SBOp 3: 477: 'Quid autem Deus? Sine quo nihil est. Tam nihil esse sine ipso, quam nec ipse sine se potest: ipse sibi, ipse omnibus est...suum ipsius est et omnium esse'.

50 Cant, PL 180: 494A. 'Cognosce te, quia imago mea es, et sic poteris nosse me, cujus imago es...satage eum jugiter habere in memoria, et amando intelligere, et intelligendo amare'. See also Dominic Monti, 'The Way Within: Grace in the Mystical Theology of William of Saint-Thierry', *Citeaux* 26 (1975) 31–47; and Jean-Marie Déchanet,'Les fondements et les bases de la spiritualité bernardine', *Citeaux* 4 (1953) 292–313; 297, n.32.

51 Marie Madeleine Davy, 'Le rôle de la connaissance de soi dans l'Ecole Cistercienne du XIIe siècle', *VS* 64 (1984) 118–41. For Bernard in particular, see Pacifique Delfgaauw, *Saint Bernard. Maître de l'amour divin* (Diss., Rome, 1952) 131–32. [Henceforth cited as *Saint Bernard.*]

52 Bernard, SC 83.4; SBOp 2: 301; 'Cum amat Deus, non aliud vult, quam amari: quique non ad aliud amat nisi ut ametur'.

53 Delfgaauw, *Saint Bernard*, 151–7.

54 William, Cant, PL 180: 494C. 'O imago, recognoscere dignitatem tuam, refulget in te auctoris effigies...pretiosa res est'. William follows here Ambrose's *Expositio in Ps. 118*, sermo 10.10; PL 15:1333A, rather than Plotinus, as has been shown by David N. Bell, 'Greek, Plotinus and the Education of William of St. Thierry', *Citeaux* 30 (1979) 242–3.

able.[55] The common source for the writers we have mentioned was Augustine. In his *'Noverim me, noverim Te'*, Gerard Verbeke has detected four different interpretations, all coming down to the statement that self-knowledge is indispensable for any knowledge of God just as, reciprocally, knowledge of God is required for genuine self-knowledge.[56] Augustine's saying, which goes back to his mentor, Ambrose of Milan, has been called a complete program, pre-eminently a prayer, the shortest and most perfect prayer. [57]

Self-knowledge was in fact one of the dominant themes in Western spirituality at the time the *mulieres religiosae* movement flourished. We hear then 'a great deal about "the self", not expressed in that abstract way, but in such terms as "knowing oneself","descending into oneself", or "considering oneself"'.[58] As heirs of that tradition the *mulieres religiosae* were eager to arrive at self-knowledge. Some examples can be found in their biographies and writings. Alice of Schaarbeek's biography mentions that through her understanding of Scripture, she developed a reverential fear of God and thus became rooted in *vera sua cognitione*, which could be translated as rootedness in her true identity or, even better, in the knowledge of her true

---

55 Richard, *De statu interioris hominis.*, PL 196: 1122D. 'Mirabile sane, imo et miserabile'.

56 Gerard Verbeke, 'Connaissance de soi et connaissance de Dieu chez saint Augustin', *Augustiana* 4 (1954) 495–515; 495–7.

57 Colin Morris, *The Discovery of the Individual 1050–1200* (London, 1972; Harper paperback, New York-San Francisco-London, 1973) 65. This was often expressed in a personal way, even when writers like Aelred of Rievaulx made wide use of Augustine and Bernard. See A. Maiorino, 'La "connaissance de soi" chez Aelred de Rievaulx', *RAM* 44 (1970) 145–60. Caroline Walker Bynum, *Jesus as Mother. Studies in the Spirituality of the High Middle Ages* (Berkeley-Los Angeles-London, 1982) examined anew the discovery of the individual (82–109) and concludes (107–08): 'Not only is it possible to specify something of the particular nature of the twelfth-century culture by the phrase "discovery of self"; it is possible to delineate the period more precisely when "discovery of self" is coupled with and understood also in the context of "discovery of model of behavior" and "discovery of consciously chosen community"'.

58 Courcelle, *Nosce teipsum*, 282.

self.[59] Beatrice of Nazareth frequently reverts to her desire for full (70,81), fuller (46,28; 105,4; 124,99), greater (66,36), total and complete self-knowledge (120,5). Hadewijch too shows acquaintance with the Apollonian 'know thyself'.[60] For them, self-knowledge did not imply self-centeredness. Embued as they were with a Christian approach to self-knowledge, they could not consider the self simply as an end in itself, since it is necessarily relational.

As a creature, man [61] is by that state related to all the rest of

---

59 *AA SS* June 2: 478,3: 'radicatur in vera sui cognitione'.

60 Reynaert, *Beeldspraak*, 90.

61 There is little doubt that women have been shortchanged in Jewish and Christian writings about the relation of God with humankind. The modern trend in the West to equalize women and men is, or at least should be, a successful attempt to restore the balance between the genders without falling into excesses. Phyllis Trible, for instance, said in 'Depatriarchalizing in Biblical Interpretation', *Journal of the American Academy of Religion*, 41 (1973) 30–44, that in the Old Testament Yahweh is portrayed neither as a 'he' nor a 'she'. Her paper called forth a reply by John W. Miller, 'Depatriarchalizing God in Biblical Interpretation: A Critique', *CBQ* 48 (1986) 609–16. Miller argues that Yahweh is certainly not presented as a mother, though in several passages he is spoken of in a mother*like* way. Men and women are made to God's image and likeness, and the term *Adam* encompasses both sexes. For some remarks on Miller's paper, see Mark S. Smith, 'God Male and Female in the Old Testament: Yahweh and His "asherah"' *TS* 48 (1987) 340, n.25 with bibliography. In the Christian tradition it should be said, God is understood as one God who is One in three Persons, the second becoming incarnate, born of a human mother without a human father. As a human being, Christ was a man, not a woman, which had the advantage, first, of making him acceptable as a teacher and a preacher in the male-dominated society in which he was born; secondly, of removing an unavoidable confusion and misinterpretation of his being simultaneously God and man. His human mother could all too easily have been considered a goddess. No mariologist did or could accept such a title, whatever might have been the tendency to enhance the splendor of the Theotókos, the Mother of God. The Latin *homo*, the Teutonic *Mensch* or *mensch* (today spelled *mens* in the Low Countries), encompasses both sexes; the English language does not have an equivalent expression. To be as complete as possible, we should note that Christian writers have at time emphasized the superiority of the masculine sex. Ida Lewis' biographer, for instance, says (*AA SS* Oct. 13: 109,6) that she persevered in her struggles *viriliter*, manfully, just as Ida of Leuven's biographer (*AA SS* April 2: 159, 3) mentions that the devil was upset because she did not behave in the manner of a woman, *muliebriter*. Biographers, however, could be excused for using such expressions, which they took over from the mentors of the *mulieres religiosae*. English puts us at a disadvantage since it has no term

creation. Knowing that he is neither the maker nor the master of creation, he knows—or should know—that he has no right to be the exploiter or spoiler of created reality but has the responsibility of being its steward.[62] What has been called 'contempt for the world' (*contemptus mundi*) in the Middle Ages should not be understood (apart from a few exceptions) as disdain or scorn,[63] for these *contemptores* generally felt a keen sense of stewardship and of great delight in the beauty of the world. They saw the world as a reflection of God's beauty, and sensed their own innate connaturality with the loveliness of creation.[64] One has only to

that includes both sexes, and the use of (s)he is a poor substitute. The use of the masculine noun or pronoun in these pages has in no way an exclusive or predominant meaning, certainly not in speaking of the *mulieres religiosae*. To remind the reader of this remark the noun *mensch* will at times be added to the term *man*, when the *mulieres religiosae* themselves, their mentors, or their biographers use the word *man*.

62 Robert Javelet, *Image et Ressemblance au douzième siècle* (Paris, 1967) 2 vols. [henceforth cited as *Image*], 1: 246–7.

63 In his publication, *La doctrine du Mépris du Monde* (Leuven-Paris, 1963–64), and in his response to Francesco Lazzari's objections, 'Méthode et conditionnement', *RAM* 40 (1964) 412–92 , Robert Bultot has a rather narrow view of the *comptemptus mundi*, to which the *RAM* tried to bring a more open view in several articles by Réginald Grégoire, Jean Claude Guy and Francesco Lazarri (RAM 41 [1965] 237–304).In 'Cosmologie et "contemptus mundi" ' ('*Sapientiae Doctrina'. Mélanges ...offerts à Dom Hildebrand Bascour*), (Leuven, 1980) 1–23, Bultot objected also that N. Max Wildiers (*Wereldbeeld en Teologie. Van de Middeleeuwen tot Nu*, 2nd ed., [Antwerp-Amsterdam, 1977, ET by Paul Dumphy, *The Theologian and his Universe. Theology and Cosmology from the Middle Ages to the Present*, New York, 1982]) neglected to treat *contemptus mundi* adequately as Bultot sees it. Wildiers' theme has been reformulated by Jean Delumeau, *Le péché et la peur. La culpabilisation en Occident (XIIIe-XVIIIe siècles)*, (Paris, 1983). This very well documented book also keeps looking at the 'world' or rather at *contemptus mundi* from a negative point of view. If the author had balanced his book by another about the positive aspects of the concept, he would undoubtedly have produced a highly interesting and helpful work. His second chapter, for instance, 'Du mépris du monde aux dances macabres' (44–97) states the truth, but not the whole truth. One could as well speak about 'contempt for the world' by writing a chapter 'Du mépris du monde aux drugs', or simply by referring to what newspapers report daily about modern expressions of *contemptus mundi*. For a more balanced view, see M.D. Chenu, *Nature, Man and Society in the Twelfth Century*, ET by Jerome Taylor and Lester Little (Chicago-London, 1968): 'Nature and man', 1–48.

64 Roisin, *L'Hagiographie*, 162; Mens, *Oorsprong*,107–8, n.21–22. For Hadewijch, see the nuanced interpretation of Reynaert, *Beeldspraak*, 269–72.

read the writings and biographies of the *mulieres religiosae* to grasp their appreciation of the 'world' and of all creatures.[65] When they insisted on detachment from the world, they did so not because they disdained creation, but because they realized the consequences of their divine calling and the resulting demands of superior values.[66] As for the 'world' in the sense of other human beings living on the same planet, they felt a genuine and deep concern for them. Their biographies are full of examples of their aid to needy individuals and attention to the social problems of their time.

Occasionally one encounters in the biographies the expression *sibimetipsi vilescere*, a saying of Bernard, [67] frequently repeated by others in words to like effect. It would be an error to interpret Bernard's words as preaching contempt or hatred for oneself. The knowledge and experience of man's greatness and his limitations, the discrepancy between his nobility as man and the inconsistency of his human condition with its pains, uncertainties, and

---

65 For references to the three Idas, Lutgard, Beatrice, and Alice of Schaarbeek, see R. De Ganck, 'The Cistercian nuns', *CSt* 5 (1970) 118. For Hadewijch see VM, *Brieven*, 1: 136, and *ibid.*, 1: 244, ll. 61–62. The text concerns a general statement by Hadewijch without specifications.

66 Roger of Caen, *De contemptu mundi*, PL 158: 703C. See Javelet, *Image*, 2: 214, n.29. A striking example is given by Patrick Catry, 'Amour du monde et amour de Dieu chez saint Grégoire le Grand', *StM* 15 (1973) 253–75. See further David Bell, 'Love and Charity in the Commentary on the Song of Songs of Thomas the Cistercian', *Citeaux* 28 (1977) 253–7.

67 Hum 1.2; SBOp 3:17. See R.A. Gauthier, *Magnanimité. L'Idéal de la grandeur dans la philosophie païenne et dans la théologie chrétienne*, Bibliothèque Thomiste 28 (Paris, 1951) 439–40: 'Néant de la créature et grandeur des dons de Dieu selon saint Bernard': 'Il faut attendre jusqu'au XIIe siècle et jusqu'à saint Bernard pour trouver en Occident une doctrine techniquement élaborée de l'union de l'humilité et de la magnanimité, encore que cette doctrine soit le point d'aboutissement de la théologie augustinienne. L'homme est à la fois, petit et grand...voilà ce qu'accomplit dans le coeur des élus le privilège de la grace divine: ni l'humilité ne les fait pusillanimes, ni la magnanimité ne les fait arrogants'. The two verses (p.485, n.1) attributed to Malachy of Armagh (d. 1148 in Clairvaux), and cherished during the Middle Ages, express the two 'faces' of the *sibimetipsi vilescere*:

Spernere mundum, spernere sese, spernere nullum,
Spernere se sperni, quatuor haec bona sunt...

(To despise the world, to despise oneself, to despise nobody, to despise being despised, these four are good).

worries led Bernard to a realistic appraisal of human frailty. The *sibimetipsi vilescere*, despising oneself, is synonymous with distrusting oneself, recognizing that man's standing lies not in himself or in his achievements, but in his hope and trust in God.[68] Reliance on God entails a certain nobility and one does not despise one's own nobility, which William, following Gregory of Nyssa, called man's kingliness.[69] If these spiritual masters did not wish to be primarily of the world or for the world, they nevertheless experienced the painful reality of being in the world, as Ambrose expressed it in a theme further developed by Bernard, William, Hugh and Richard. [70]

Navigating the waves of the human condition, the *mulieres religiosae* took self-knowledge as their compass. Daily and sharply they experienced their human condition with its joys but also with its shortcomings originating from impotence, ignorance and forgetfulness, the three sources of sin or of omission they so much dreaded. This aspect of their asceticism is often described in Beatrice's *Vita*. Temptation, too, was part of the debt to be paid to the human condition (175,94). It was a rod of correction, a divine testing (167,45), a gift from God by which one should be trained through struggle (143,45). Or as Hadewijch was told one day by the Lord in a vision: 'Since you are a man (*mensch*= human being) bear all the miseries proper to the human condition, save sin alone'.[71]

Sin was for these medieval Christians not merely a fault, an act committed against an external rule, but an estrangement from their true selves and from God, insofar as sin is a deviation from

---

68 Roger Baron, *Hugues de Saint-Victor, La contemplation et ses espèces* (Tournai-Paris, 1955) 46: 'Seipsum contempsit qui non in propriis, nec in scientia, sed in solo Deo sperat et confidit'.

69 Nat corp, PL 180:717B. Here William follows Gregory of Nyssa's *On the Making of Man*. Richard used the same expression; see Reynaert, *Beeldspraak*, 367–68, n.8a.

70 See Gilson, *Mystical Theology*, 232, n.90.

71 Vision 1, VM, *Visioenen*, 1: 30, l. 350: 'Na dien dattu mensche best, Soe leve ellendech als mensche'. *Ibid.*, 31, l.357:'Maer ghevoelt v mensche in allen dien ghebreken die ter menscheit behoren sonder sonde allene'. (But feel yourself as man in all the hardships proper to the human condition, except sin alone).

an internal law, the law of God's love.[72] They feared not only the stain of sin, but even 'possible falls and consent to sins of some kind or other because of the excessive depravity of the senses and the instability of the will' (269,76). Sin was felt as a laceration, a deformation, a woundedness, a tear. It meant therefore alienation and separation from the One who is All and was their All.

They experienced, moreover, that man in his life on earth is a pilgrim in a foreign land (_terra aliena_) on his way to his real home, his fatherland (_patria_)—common themes in religious literature from ancient times on. We will meet this aspect later again, and need not to insist on it now. The acquaintance of the _mulieres religiosae_ with the human condition was part of their self-knowledge. They expressed it from the heart, engaged as they were on a thorough following of Christ who taught them the price they would have to pay for a safe return 'home'.

These women were no less alert in detecting and amending whatever might hinder their growth. In the _Vitae_ and writings of the _mulieres religiosae_ we can see that their search for God called for ongoing self-presence and interiorization. 'To meet your God, there is no need to cross the seas, to penetrate the clouds, to cross the Alps. Enter deeply within yourself,' says Bernard.[73] 'Avoid all dispersion in the multiplicity of the world,' adds William.[74]

The _mulieres religiosae_ labored patiently and perseveringly to make themselves freer of the selfish self and freer for the true God-oriented self. With the help of self-knowledge they learned to enter into themselves, as Hugh expressed it,[75] and to achieve a healthy interiorization: a persistent solicitude for interiority culminating at the core of their being in its God-relatedness. This

---

72 Javelet, _Image_, 1: 379.

73 Adv 1.10; SBOp 4: 168. 'Non te oportet, o homo, maria transfretare, non penetrare nubes, non transalpinare necesse est'. He paraphrases here Dt 30: 12–14, as did Augustine in his _Confessions_ 10.8.15, and Gregory of Nyssa in his homily 2.2 on _In Cant_.1,8.

74 Ep frat 1.5.13; PL 184: 316D: 'Non ambiens multiplicari in saeculo' [ET: CF 12:28].

75 _De vanitate mundi_, PL 176: 715B: 'Ascendere ergo ad Deum hoc est intrare ad semetipsum, et non solum ad se intrare, sed ineffabili quodam modo in intimis etiam seipsum transire. Qui ergo seipsum, ut ita dicam, interius intrans et intrinsecus penetrans transcendit, ille veraciter ad Deum ascendit'.

interiorization was directed toward an encounter in the depths of the heart with the beloved Lord and God, for it is in the heart that the encounter of man and God takes place.

This stress on introspection and interiorization should not mislead us. The *mulieres religiosae* and their mentors were well aware of the need for equilibrium in their spiritual ascent. Their interiorization was healthy enough not to get mired down in this interiority or intoxicated by self-centeredness and selfishness, but to move beyond narcissism to a higher or deeper Reality. The 'know thyself' taught them to strike a balance between what we might call today an inferiority and a superiority complex, appreciating themselves realistically, without prizing or despising themselves, and keeping an equal distance between presumption and despair.[76] They strove with demanding intensity and exacting fidelity to enter deeply into themselves by means of a progressive application to meditation and contemplation (terms frequently used interchangeably), unremitting studiousness, unflagging love for neighbor, an urgent desire for conversion and purity of heart. They yearned for the restoration of the divine image, and with a constantly growing longing for a fathomless union with God, as the *Vitae* and the writings of Hadewijch and Beatrice abundantly reveal. At each stage of their ascent they had to surrender humbly to God's activity within themselves and be crucified by the stringent demands of his purifying love.

---

76 Courcelle, *Nosce teipsum*, 295.

CHAPTER THREE

THE CREATOR AND CREATION

I N SPEAKING OF SELF-KNOWLEDGE, we stated that this is of
necessity relational. The inward movement meets a downward one in its contact with all that the self encounters in its
creaturely surroundings.Both the inward and the downward point
upward to the absolute Being, who gives to the self its meaning
and finality. For the *mulieres religiosae* God was the deepest
center and the ultimate goal of all that exists. Their attention and
application to self-knowledge brought them to the realization of
the Supreme Being's allness and to a clearer perception of what
creation meant and pointed to: their own creation in God's image
and likeness. The following sections will therefore speak about
God as God and as Creator, about creation and about its jewel:
man himself.

THE ONE GOD

The *mulieres religiosae* understood God to be the undisputed
origin of the relationship they had with him. Drawing on Scripture, Hadewijch [1] and Beatrice [2] explicitly said so. More impor-
tantly they all said it by the way they lived, as is clearly shown in

---

1 Reynaert, *Beeldspraak*, 403–23.
2 *Vita*, 85, 17–52.

the extant biographies.[3] They were not faced, as we are today, with questions about God arising from developments in technology, human sciences, and the conquest of the macrocosm and the microcosm. Nor were they greatly concerned with having their faith supported by metaphysical, psychological or sociological considerations. To talk about projection or a possibly self-made need for the numinous would be out of place because they knew themselves and knew God in the context of a God-man and a man-God relation set in motion by the Absolute. God is transcendent and his transcendence spilled over, so to speak, into their faith because of his self-disclosure in the Scriptures and in the deeds by which he stepped into our human history.[4]

Knowledge typically leads to possession of, and power over, what is known. Such knowledge, however, contrasts sharply with knowledge of God. Knowledge of God, as the Scriptures speak of it, is not an abstract knowledge, for God can be known only as a mystery at once transcendent, supremely sublime, inexpressibly holy, totally other than all we know, and at the same time immanent, present, caring, saving, loving. God is rather apprehended than comprehended, to be talked to than to be talked about. Before God, man's proper stance is one of loving reverence, for by his self-knowledge he knows deeply that he is only a creature. He can express his reverence by opening himself up to accept and respond to the self-revelation and self-communication

---

3 Roisin, *L'Hagiographie*, 35 and 186; for Ida of Nivelles, see *Quinque*, 207; – Ida Lewis, *AA SS* Oct. 13: 113, 18; – Ida of Leuven, *AA SS* April 2: 160 and 188; – Alice of Schaarbeek, *AA SS* June 2: 478.

4 All *Vitae* are replete with biblical references and reminiscences, not merely because of the custom of that time to spice this kind of literature with an abundance of citations, but more because the God-oriented people one meets in these biographies nourished their spiritual lives on Scripture. The reading of those *Vitae* is utterly convincing. A citation from Beatrice's *Vita* (85,18) confirms this observation: 'She was zealous to form all her actions and affections, within and without, according to the counsel of the Scriptures. Daily with all her might she sought in the vast field of the Scriptures what was or could be profitable to her passage through life'. In this regard she was very much in line with her Cistercian mentors: Bernard, William, Guerric of Igny, Aelred of Rievaulx, Gilbert of Hoyland and others. See P. Dumontier, *Saint Bernard et la Bible* (Bruges-Paris, 1953) 38–39.

of a God who comes to him as a friend (Ex 33:11), who loves him and expects to be loved in return. This relationship of reverence and love is already expressed through observance of the decalogue, the ethical dialogue of right living in the presence of the holy God who entered with man into a covenant of faithfulness. The Hebrew Scriptures, what we call the Old Testament, provide the basis of Judaic monotheism. The initial dialogue between Yahweh and Moses made it plain that Yahweh is 'I am who am' or 'I am the one who is present' (Ex 3:14). This stresses his distance and at the same time his nearness, his transcendence and immanence, and suggests what he, Yahweh, wished, in fact, for his people.[5]

The 'Good News' of the New Testament, that the God of Israel is a trinitarian God, is not explicitly mentioned in the Hebrew Bible. In fact, one finds in Genesis and Isaiah only a few hints, discernible in the light of the combined Old and New Testaments.[6] Though the *mulieres religiosae* did not have at hand the scientific works we have at our disposal,[7] they had not the slightest doubt that the single, monotheistic, undivided and indivisible God of the Old Testament is the selfsame monotheistic God of the New Testament. This is, for instance, what Bernard explicitly affirmed in his book *De consideratione*. There he dialogued with his former monk, Pope Eugenius III:

> Hence Boethius says of God: 'This is truly one in which there is no number, in which there is nothing beyond that

---

5 Henry Renckens, *The Religion of Israel*, ET by N.B. Smith (New York, 1966) 97–139: 'The God of Israel'.

6 Bertrand de Margerie, *La Trinité chrétienne dans l'Histoire*, Théologie Historique 31 (Paris, 1975), particularly 21–89: 'De Yahweh au Dieu Père, Fils et Saint-Esprit'. See also Fr. Taymans d'Eypernon, *Le mystère primordial. La Trinité dans sa vivante Image*, Museum Lessianum, section théologique 41 (Brussels-Paris, 1950) 16–35:'Simple rappel des données de la Révélation'.

7 H. Kleindienst, G. Quell, E. Stauffer, K. Kuhn: *Theos*, in *TDNT*, ET by G. Bromiley (Grand Rapids, MI, 1966) vol.3: 65–139; Karl Rahner, 'Theos in the New Testament', *Theological Investigations*, vol.1, ET by C. Ernst (London-Baltimore, 1961) 79–148, to name only two of the many publications on this subject.

which it is'.... Compare to this one everything that can be
called one, and the latter will not be one. But God is Trinity.
What then? Do we destroy what has been said about the
Unity because we introduce Trinity? No, but we establish
what this Unity is. We say Father, we say Son, we say Holy
Spirit, but we speak not of three Gods, but one.... You say:
'But I have something which I can number and something I
cannot: the substance is one, the persons three. What is
marvelous, or what is obscure in this?'. Nothing, if persons
are thought of separate from the substance. But now since
the three persons are the one substance, and the one substance the three persons, who can deny that the number is
there? Truly they are three. But who can number them? For
truly they are one. If you think this an easy explanation, tell
me what you have enumerated when you speak of three.
Natures? There is [only] one. Substance? there is [only] one.
Deities? There is [only] one. You say, 'I number not these
but the persons'. And are they [the three persons] not that
one nature, that one essence, that one substance, that one
divinity?[8]

William said the same thing, but more simply: 'In the Trinity
which is God, those who are three are very truly one, and they are

---

8 Csi 5.7.17; SBOp 3: 481: Hinc de eo Boethius [*De Trinitate;* PL 64:
1250C]: Hoc vere unum, in quo nullus est numerus, nullum in eo aliud praeter id
quod est.... Compare huic uni omne quod unum dici potest, et unum non erit.
Trinitas est tamen Deus. Quid ergo? Destruimus quod dictum est de unitate quia
inducimus trinitatem? Non; sed statuimus unitatem. Dicimus Patrem, dicimus
Filium, dicimus Spiritum Sanctum, non tamen tres Deos, sed unum...'Sed
habeo', inquis, 'quid numerum et quid non numerum: substantia una est, personae tres sunt'. Quid mirum, vel obscurum in hoc? —'Nihil, si personae
seorsum a substantia cogitentur. Nunc vero cum tres illae personae illa substantia sint, et illa una substantia tres illae personae, quis numerum negat? Nam vere
tres sunt. Quis numeret tamen? Nam vere unum sunt. Aut si tu facile explicatu id
putas, dicendo tres, dicito quid numerasti? Naturas? Una est. Essentia? Una est.
Substantia? Una est. Deitas? Una est.'—'Non haec, sed personas numero',
inquis.—'Quae non sint illa una natura, illa una essentia, illa una substantia, illa
una divinitas?' Bernard's text is reminiscent of the so-called Athanasian creed.
See John N. Kelly, *Early Christian Doctrines* [henceforth cited as *Doctrines*],
2nd ed. (London, 1960) 273.

not three gods but one God of one nature and the same essence. Predication of one essence implies perfect unity'.[9] Jesus himself sharpened this monotheistic confession.[10] The New Testament is the'Good News' precisely because the dimensions of God's love for humankind and of God's call to human beings to love him in response have been immensely expanded beyond all expectations and dreams. God's self-revelation in the New Testament disclosed something of his own oneness to be thought of, believed in, responded to and to be shared in by all.

The *mulieres religiosae* movement, with its intense orientation toward God and his love, knew existentially that the demands of love go deeper than the commands of law. This relationship of love starts with God, not with man, and arrives at its summit through the action of God and through man's response. God made man precisely to enable him to converse with him, to draw him into a personal relationship with an absolutely free God who gave man his own freedom. The love of the supremely free God does not force human freedom nor does it prevent a loving response, since real love includes this choice made in freedom. If human freedom is profoundest risk, it is also highest gift: the very much cherished 'nobility' the *mulieres religiosae* spoke of so appreciatively. Living up to God's love is a tremendous responsibility, requiring a correlative self-giving to God in a love which can be negated, ignored, poorly or happily fulfilled. This self-giving in love to the other is not two independent one-sided relationships but a mutual giving, indeed, a union in love. This is how the *mulieres religiosae* regarded the meaning and value of their personal being, call, and responsibility. Some of them were to go to the very limit in the extremely painful process of gaining themselves by losing themselves in the infinite abyss of the loving God. Only in this self-giving love would they, remaining within their own createdness, be allowed to come closer to the Transcendent and arrive by his grace at a mystical union

---

9 Aenig, PL 180: 412C; CF 9: 63–64: 'In Trinitate vero quae Deus est, qui tres sunt verissime unum sunt; et non tres dii, sed unus Deus sunt, unius naturae, ejusdem essentiae. Unius essentiae praedicatio perfectam concludit unitatem'.
10 Stauffer, *TDNT* 3: 102.

with the same transcendent God whose being is timeless and tireless love.[11]

In and through the incarnation of God's Word or Son Christianity's basic mystery of God as Trinity became known. In this section we shall speak of God, not as One, but as Trinity, even if such an attempt seems to be absurd.[12] The Bible itself does not use the terms 'trinity', 'essence', or 'persons'. God is more than a concept, whether of a person or of a substance. God as concept is not identical with God as Being. God is Somebody in relation to himself (*ad intra*) and in relation to his creation (*ad extra*). It may be difficult to come to some apprehension of who and what the Absolute is.[13] Even supported by revelation and faith, theologians

---

11 'In his divine simplicity, God cannot become smaller or greater, or change in any way, for he is infinite'. Augustine made this remark in his commentary *In Joh. Evangelium*, PL 35: 1383. See also Étienne Gilson, 'L'Infinité divine chez saint Augustin', *AM* 1:569–74. Bernard used Augustine's text in his Div 60.1; SBOp 6/1:291.

12 Robin Attfield, 'The Lord is God: there is no other', *RSt* 13 (1977) 73–84: 'No sense can be made of the claim that God is three persons in one substance'(84).

13 Leo Scheffczyk, *SM* 2: 389–90: 'God is not an indigent and dependent being. He has in himself a movement of love, independently of any relation to the world and in itself. But this is only possible between persons. And so the recognition of God in his essence as love, independently of the world, leads to the assumption that there are personal relations within God, which constitute the mystery of the Trinity. Of course it is only possible to make this conceptual connection on the basis of a positive, divine revelation of the three persons in God, such as is found in the history of salvation. The New Testament above all makes it clear that God's being in its relation to the world and as bestowing salvation finds its perfect revelation in Jesus Christ the Son of the Father, and that this revelation becomes in the Holy Spirit a permanent reality in the world which lays hold of man and fills him. Thus the revelation-event itself exhibits a personal linking of God's action with the unoriginated abyss of love in the Father, the perfect generation of this love in the Son, and its spiritual interiorization and its perpetual actualization in the Holy Spirit.... Unless anchored in firm faith in an immanent Trinity of three essentially equal persons, redemption could only be regarded as an appearance of the one God'. For a short theological overview of the Trinity, see Hugo Rahner, 'Dreifaltigkeit', *LThK*, 3: col. 548–54, or Karl Rahner, *SM* 6: 295–303.

took generations a to make this seemingly contradictory affirmation of one God who is Trinity of Persons to some extent understandable and acceptable. In its struggle against Arianism, the first Ecumenical Council at Nicaea (325) did not speak of 'One God in three Persons', but simply of God the Father Almighty, and one Lord Jesus Christ, and the Holy Spirit.[14] Theological thinking, particularly that of the Cappadocian Fathers, focused on the terms *ousia* and *hypostasis*, *ousia* meaning God's simplicity and indivisibility in his essence or substance common to the Father and the Son, and *hypostasis* referring always to the Person(s).[15] Nicaea expounded the divinity of the Son,[16] and Constantinople I (381) the divinity of the Holy Spirit,[17] while in the West Augustine elaborated the Latin formulation of the Trinity's unity, and the *filioque*,[18] the statement that the Spirit proceeds 'from the Father *and the Son*' which was introduced in the creed in the sixth century.[19] The Greek Fathers were not entirely happy with their own terminology,[20] nor were Augustine and some others wholly satisfied with the Latin terminology.[21] Theo-

14 Kelly, *Doctrines*, 232.
15 Ignacio Ortiz de Urbina, *Nicée et Constantinople*, Histoire des Conciles Oecuméniques, G.Dumeige ed., vol.1 (Paris, 1963) 67–92.
16 Kelly, *Doctrines*, 231–37.
17 *Ibid.*, 255–63; Werner Jaeger, *Gregor von Nyssa's Lehre vom Heiligen Geist*, H.Dörries ed. (Leiden, 1966) 180–222.
18 Kelly, *Doctrines*, 272–73. For the doctrinal aspect of the *filoque*, see B. Schultze, 'Zum Ursprung des Filioque', *CXP* 84,(1982) 5–18; for the historical aspect, see Philip Hughes, *The Church in Crisis. History of the Twelve Great Councils* (London, 1963) 143–50. God the Father did not become Father in the incarnation of the Son which is, in fact, only the manifestation of what he is from all eternity. In his excellent paper 'Het geheim van God: Drie personen, een natuur' [God's secret: three persons, one nature], *Bÿdragen* 18 (1957) 243–59, C. Strätter made this prefectly clear, showing also the compatibility of the stand taken by the Greek and Latin branches of Christianity.
19 Ortiz de Urbina, *Nicée et Constantinople*, 198–99. Beatrice of Nazareth uses it a few times, albeit not verbatim: 164, 61; 217, 92.
20 Kelly, *Doctrines*, 267–68.
21 *Ibid.*, 272–78; Étienne Gilson, *Introduction à l'étude de Saint Augustin*, 3rd ed., Etudes de philosophie médiévale [henceforth cited as *Introduction*], (Paris, 1949) 97–98; R. Vanneste, 'Over de betekenis van enkele abstracta in de taal van Hadewijch' [henceforth *Abstracta*], *Studia Germanica* 1 (1959) 9–95; 29–30.

logians of the twentieth century are understandably still dissatisfied.[22] The difficulty stems in the first place from the transcendence of a God who cannot be conceptualized by our human faculties. Secondly, it remains difficult to combine in thought the existence of a God who is one in essence and at the same time three in Persons. If God is to be God, the supreme and infinitely perfect Being, he cannot be so without being infinite love. Love, however, implies relations. If God were one Person, he would be infinitely self-love and consequently neither true love nor the true God as he showed himself to be. To come to some understanding, a distinction made by William could be of help:

> The Father, Son and Holy Spirit exist consubstantially; but the Father exists principally, not principally as if pre-eminently, or with primacy of time or dignity, but of origin. God the Father is, so to speak (*quasi*), the font and source of the divinity.[23]

Starting from this distinction, and keeping in mind that God is not a God who evolves into a trinity, but one God who *is* Trinity, one could put William's insight in this simple way: The Father sees the fullness of his infinite perfection, which he acknowledges. This acknowledgment is called the Word or the Son. When the Father and the Son see each other infinitely perfect and lovable, they cannot but acknowledge and express their mutual appreciation. This mutual expression of their appre-

---

22 To name a few: Karl Rahner, 'Remarks on the Dogmatic Treatise De Trinitate', *Theological Investigations*, vol.4, ET by K. Smyth (Baltimore-London, 1966) 77–102; J.A. Bracke, 'The Holy Trinity as a Community of Divine Persons', *HJ* 15 (1974) 166–82; Piet Schoonenberg,'Continuïteit en herinterpretatie der Drieëenheidsleer', *TT* 14 (1974) 54–72.

23 Aenig, PL 180: 435C and 436A; cf. CF 9: 108–09: 'Etenim consubstantialiter sunt Pater, Filius et Spiritus Sanctus; sed principaliter Pater, non principaliter quasi praecipue, vel principalitate aliqua seu temporis seu dignitatis, sed originis. Est enim Pater quasi fons quidam et origo divinitatis'. William's explanation excludes any subordinationism, i.e. he does not make the Son or the Holy Spirit dependent on or inferior to the Father. They are all three completely equal, and in relation to creation they are one principle.

ciation is the Holy Spirit who is therefore called the bond of love between the Father and the Son, or, as the mentors of the *mulieres religiosae* called him, their kiss. No one of the three is anterior or posterior, more or less perfect than the others. They love one another continually from all eternity and into all eternity.

If one wishes to have a more theological description of the One who is Trinity, Albert Deblaere's description, which needs attentive reading and reflection, seems appropriate:

> The Persons are one single Being or one single Essence. The Paternity is completely turned toward the Son: the Son toward the Father. Each Person loses himself totally in the Being of the other Person, is turned toward the other Person. The unique Being which they are, is and becomes always the Being of the other Person, without becoming the other Person. The unique Being is received from one Person as the Being of that Person, and the selfsame Being is given or returned to the other Person as his own Being. Being is the ground of the Persons. It is and remains one unique Being, God himself.
>
> The trinitarian love is a *personal* love, *viz.* between Persons (not between Beings). As a result the love between the Father and the Son is a Person: the Holy Spirit. As Being, this Spirit is and possesses one and the same divine Being as the two other Persons. He differs in nothing as to what the Father gives to the Son and what the Son returns to his Father. This being totally lost in the Being as the Being of the other Person is the supreme moment of the divine Beatitude, the experience of the Unity of the God-Love. It is the engulfment of the Persons in the Being, in *their* essential Unity.[24]

---

24 Albert Deblaere in a seminar given to the theological faculty of the Flemish Jesuits in Leuven-Heverlee (1964–66). The French text is quoted by Joseph Alaerts in his paper 'La terminologie "essentielle" dans *Die Gheestelike Brulocht* et *Dat Rijcke der Ghelieven*' [of John of Ruusbroec], *OGE* 49 (1975) 337–65; 344–45.

In his *Aenigma fidei*, which is really his *De Trinitate*, William
expresses the being of the One God who is Trinity thus:

> The essence is the Father, the essence is the Son, the essence
> is the Holy Spirit, and yet they are not three essences, but
> one essence.... The Father is always Father; the Son always
> Son, and the Holy Spirit always Holy Spirit. Thus, they are
> one in substance, but distinct in person and name.[25]

It should be evident that the *mulieres religiosae* knew the
formulation of the fourth Lateran Council (1215).[26] Hadewijch
expressed this trinitarian belief in a correct but personal way. A
careful study has shown that she knew very well the exact
meaning of essence, nature and substance,[27] and had a good grasp
of the theology of her time.[28] The way she wrote about the Trinity
in prose and poems, is proof of the Trinity's centrality in her

---

25 Aenig, PL 180: 411C and 421B; CF 9: 67 and 80: 'Essentia est Pater,
essentia est Filius, essentia Spiritus Sanctus; sed tamen non tres essentiae, sed
una essentia....Pater semper est Pater, Filius semper Filius, Spiritus Sanctus
semper Spiritus sanctus. Itaque substantia unum sunt, personis ac nominibus
distinguuntur'.

26 'We firmly believe and confess without reservation that there is only one
true God, eternal, infinite (*immensus*) and unchangeable, incomprehensible,
almighty and ineffable, the Father, the Son and the Holy Spirit: three persons
indeed but one essence, substance or nature entirely simple. The Father is from
no one, the Son from the Father only, and the Holy Spirit equally from both
(*pariter ab utroque*). Without beginning, always, and without end, the Father
begets, the Son is born and the Holy Spirit proceeds. They are of the same
substance (*consubstantialiter*) and fully equal, equally almighty and equally
eternal. [They are] the one principle of the universe, the creator of all things,
visible and invisible, spiritual and corporeal, who by His almighty power from
the beginning of time made at once (*simul*) out of nothing both orders of
creatures, the spiritual and the corporeal, that is, the angelic and the earthly, and
then (*deinde*) the human creature, who as it were shares in both orders, being
composed of spirit and body...' The full Latin text has been published by Cl.
Leonardi, *Conciliorum Oecumenorum Decreta* (Freiburg/Br., 1962) 163–247 ;
the ET is taken from J.Neunerand J.Dupuis, *The Christian Faith in the Doctrinal
Documents of the Catholic Church* (Westminster, Md., 1975) 15–16. See the
comments of B. de Margerie, *La Trinité chrétienne dans l'Histoire*, 194–96.

27 Vanneste, *Abstracta*, 19–32.

28 *Ibid.*, 24, n.1.

spirituality and mystical life.[29] In relation to the Trinity Beatrice too speaks clearly about 'the distinction of persons, the unity of the divine essence' (164,62), 'the difference of the persons existing in the one essence of the eternal divine Majesty' (217,93).[30] Ida Lewis had a good understanding of Augustine's writings about the ineffable unity of the Trinity (*de illa ineffabili Trinitatis unitate dixit mirabilissima*), but when she realized in a conversation that her talk was going over the head of her interlocutor, she shifted to Christ's humanity.[31] They all followed Augustine, as did William,[32] but they were not mere copyists. God is a 'unique unity',[33] Three-in-One,[34] three Persons in one sole Being.[35].

By saying that in this life God is best known by unknowing, William was echoing an old and well-established tradition—a tradition which may be witnessed in Augustine,[36] as in Dionysius the Areopagite, though the latter spoke of it in a more refined and elaborate manner. This has led some scholars to suggest that

---

29 Reynaert, *Beeldspraak*, 84–88; 144–50; 237–41 in particular, though the whole book illustrates it.

30 In the absence of a systematic study, may it suffice to refer to these two passages in her *Vita*: 164, 62 and 217, 93. Her biography tells us that she used 'books on the Holy Trinity of which she kept a supply at hand' (213,12).

31 *AA SS* Oct. 13: 114,21; 122,50.

32 William, Aenig, PL 180: 397B–440D. This is William's treatise on the Trinity, and has as its chief source Augustine's *De Trinitate*. See John D. Anderson, *The Enigma of Faith*, CF 9: 16–24. 'Trinity itself is not in one God, but the Trinity is God; and God is not in the Trinity, but God is the Trinity' ('Nec in uno Deo est Trinitas, sed Trinitas ipsa Deus est; nec Deus est in Trinitate, sed Deus ipsa Trinitas est'): PL 180: 434C; CF 9,105.

33 Bernard, Csi 5.8.19; SBOp 3: 483: ' Unice unum'.

34 J.E.Sullivan, *The Image of God. The Doctrine of S.Augustine and its Influence* [henceforth cited as *The Image*], (Dubuque, IA, 1963) 93.

35 Hadewijch; VM, *Mengeldichten*, 82, l. 124.

36 Med 7; PL 180: 22D: 'In hac vita Deus melius nesciendo scitur'. For Augustine, see David N.Bell, *The Image and Likeness. The Augustinian Spirituality of William of St.Thierry*. This work is a shortened version of the author's doctoral dissertation (Oxford, 1975) published by Cistercian Publications, Kalamazoo, MI, CS 78, 1984 [henceforth cited as *The Image*]). I am grateful to Dr. Bell for very kindly providing me with a photocopy of the book prior to its publication.

William was directly dependent on pseudo-Dionysius, but recent studies have called this hypothesis seriously into question.[37] The *mulieres religiosae* seem not to have been influenced directly by Dionysius. No specialized study has yet been made of this subject and a statement that they too 'breathed some Dionysian air',[38] is too general to be acceptable without more investigation. Dionysius had influence both in the East,[39] and in the West, where he became widely accepted by such theologians and mystics as Hugh, Albert the Great, Thomas Aquinas, Meister Eckhart, and John of the Cross.[40] This does not mean that Dionysius' theories, particularly his mysticism, have not been questioned.[41] If Dionysius did reach or could have reached the *mulieres religiosae*, it would have been through their mentors.[42] A thorough study by Bernard McGinn [43] shows how little impressed the Cistercians were by Dionysius' complicated system, with the exception of Isaac of Stella, Garnier of Rochefort,[44] and, we may

---

37 For references, see below, notes 43 and 47. Dionysius' concepts about the divine impenetrable darkness, the equivalent of God's absolute, inaccessible and unknowable transcendence, and the way man nevertheless arrives at union with God, need not be explained here. For an excellent treatment of Dionysius' writings, doctrine, and bibliography, see R. Roques, *DSp* 2: 246–86, and by the same author: 'Contemplation, extase et ténèbres chez le Pseudo-Denys', *ibid.*, 2: 1885–1911.

38 Mens, *Oosprong*, 139–40.

39 Policarp Sherwood and André Rayez, *DSp* 3: 286–318.

40 André Rayez, *DSp* 3: 318–429. Interestingly, no mention is made of Teresa of Avila.

41 Jan Vanneste, 'La théologie mystique du Pseudo-Denys l'Aréopagite', *Studia Patristica* vol.5 (Berlin, 1962) 401–15; *Id.*, 'Is the mysticism of Pseudo-Dionysius genuine?', *IPQ* 3 (1963) 286–303; Endre von Ivánka, *Plato Christianus* (Einsiedeln, 1964) 285–88.

42 *DSp* 3: 318–29. The influence of Dionysius on Thomas Gallus (d.1246), who wrote commentaries on several Dionysian writings between 1238 and 1244, or of Bonaventure and Hugh of Balma is probably too late to have had an impact on the leading *mulieres religiosae* of the first half of the thirteenth century. See von Ivánka, *Plato Christianus*, 352–53; Maurice de Gandillac, 'Note sur le 13e siècle', *DSp* 3: 357, and Robert Javelet, 'Thomas Gallus et Richard de Saint-Victor mystiques', *RTAM* 29 (1962) 206–33; 30 (1963) 89–121.

43 Bernard McGinn, 'Pseudo-Dionysius and the early Cistercians', *One Yet Two. Monastic Tradition East and West*, Basil Pennington ed., CS 26 (Kalamazoo, MI, 1976) 200–41.

44 Garnier, abbot of Clairvaux (1186–93), had a good grasp of Dionysius' ideas and took some of them in his own teaching. See M.D. Chenu, 'Erigène à

add, Alan of Lille, who entered Citeaux as a 'fin de carrière' and can barely be called a Cistercian writer. The School of Chartres and the Victorines were much more dionysian. Hugh, in particular wrote a *Commentary on the Celestial Hierarchy* of Dionysius in which he augustinianized many of the Areopagite's concepts. Richard, Hugh's disciple and successor, evidently knew Dionysius and used him, but much less. His *De Trinitate* shows no trace of dionysian concepts or the usual dionysian stress on darkness.[45]

It has been claimed that William was influenced by John Scot Eriugena who translated into Latin some works of Gregory of Nyssa, Maximus the Confessor and of Dionysius the Areopagite. Between 862 and 866, John Scot Eriugena wrote commentaries on Dionysius' works and published his own *De divisione naturae*, based on Dionysius.[46] The alleged Dionysian-Eriugenan influence on William, however, has been challenged recently by scholars who have closely checked the supposed similarities.[47]

　　　　　•

Citeaux', *La Philosophie et ses problèmes,* Festschrift R. Jolivet (Paris, 1960) 99–107. Garnier is the only Cistercian considered in this study. Chenu notes (p.106) that 'pour le reste, il [Garnier] demeure dans la ligne de saint Augustin et dans le climat de saint Bernard'.

45 Gervais Dumeige, *DSp* 3: 327. See also A.M. Ethier, *Le "De Trinitate" de Richard de Saint-Victor* (Paris-Ottawa, 1939).

46 Eriugena's translations and works were known and used particularly in theological schools (D.N. Bell, *Citeaux* 33 [1982] 8), and about the end of the twelfth century by heterodox movements (Henry Bett, *Johannes Scotus Eriugena. A Study in Medieval Philosophy* [NewYork, 1964] 174). 'Infected' *Florilegia* were also available. See G. Mathon, 'Un florilège érigénien à l'abbaye de Saint-Amand au temps d'Hucbald', *RTAM* 20 (1953) 302–11, and J. Marenbon, 'A Florilegium from the *Periphyseon*, *RTAM* 47 (1980) 271–77. It is possible that William knew Eriugena through *florilegia* rather than in Eriugena's treatise *De divisione naturae* itself (Bell, *The Image,* 127, n.10.) Eriugena's treatise was condemned in 1210 and 1215. See Aimé Forest, 'La synthèse de Jean Scot Erigène', *Histoire de l'Eglise,* A. Fliche and V. Martin, eds., Vol. 13, (Paris, 1965) 9–32; 13.

47 David Bell studied carefully the relations between 'William of St. Thierry and John Scot Eriugena', *Citeaux* 33 (1982) 5–28. As for the 'Greek sources' of William, see John Anderson, 'The use of Greek sources by William of St. Thierry, especially in the *Enigma fidei*', in *One Yet Two,* CS 29: 242–53; E. Rozanne Elder, 'William of St.Thierry and the Greek Fathers: Evidence from Christology', CS 29: 254–66; D.N. Bell, 'Greek, Plotinus and the Education of William of St.Thierry', *Citeaux* 30 (1979) 221–48; Id., 'The Alleged Greek

Most probably, William knew no Greek, although he could have known some translations, certainly Gregory of Nyssa's *De imagine*, but he remained an Augustinian with his own personal stamp.[48] That the *mulieres religiosae* experienced God's incomprehensibility and darkness as much as anyone else is only natural. As women with a spiritual longing of great intensity they burned with an insatiable desire for God. Striving with all their natural capacities and aided by God's grace, they tried to 'reconquer' original purity of heart, freedom from all sinfulness, love for neighbor and for God and union with him. In the ups and downs inherent in such an endeavor they inevitably experienced darkness in the deferment of their aspirations, while the light of the blissful but fleeting experiences of God's presence only increased their craving for him. This exquisite and painful purification found expression in Hadewijch,[49] and in Beatrice,[50] who even spoke of the 'burden of heavenly delights' (202,48). Similar expressions are found in the various *vitae*.

Despite the periods of darkness through which the more advanced *mulieres religiosae* had to go as part of their all-demanding ascent to God, they considered the experience not, as did Dionysius the Areopagite, a blinding light resulting in utter darkness, but as the medium through which God revealed himself and his love.[51] This is true of Hadewijch,[52] of Beatrice,[53] and of

---

Sources of William of St.Thierry', *Noble Piety and Reformed Monasticism*, E.R. Elder, ed., CS 65 (Kalamazoo, MI, 1981) 109–22. It is unlikely that J.Scot Eriugena influenced the *mulieres religiosae*. For Hadewijch in particular, see J. Reynaert, *Beeldspraak*, 157.

48 See Bell, in 'Greek, Plotinus and the Education of William of St.Thierry', *Citeaux* 30 (1979) 221–48; 248: 'main conclusions'.

49 VM, *Brieven*, 2: 103; Reynaert, *Beeldspraak*, 59 and 73.

50 Herman Vekeman, '*Vita Beatricis* en *Seuen Manieren van Minne*. Een vergelijkende studie', *OGE* 46 (1972) 3–54; 33.

51 In this they were in accordance with their Cistercian mentors. See Paul Verdeyen, 'La Théologie Mystique de Guillaume de Saint-Thierry', *OGE* 53 (1979) 361: 'Guillaume et tous les auteurs cisterciens, s'éloignent du Pseudo-Denys par leur conception lumineuse de l'unité d'esprit'.

52 Reynaert, *Beeldspraak*, 55–79: 'Lichtmetaforiek'.

53 We lack a synthetic study of Beatrice. See, however, the many places in her *Vita* where light is stressed.

the others as well. One example among many comes from Ida of Nivelles' biographer who commented: 'It is not incredible that God who is the highest light of all lights, made her interiorly alight by his wonderful light'.[54] What the most fervent *mulieres religiosae* were doing was in accord with the mystical theology of William, who said: 'Is there something in God that can be perceived? Indeed there is, if you desire only that which you are capable of attaining'.[55] Their desire stretched them to the limit. Beatrice, for instance,

could never stop her desire to investigate, could never withdraw from the search. In season and out of season she took it upon herself to comprehend the incomprehensible' (214, 33), 'not rashly like some who seek things too high for them and search into what is deeper than their understanding, but with humble heart, devout mind and fervent love' (213,8). She 'fixed her contemplative gaze on the incomprehensible essence of the divinity' (236,32) 'unattainable to earthly intellects' (223,34).

In other words she tried the impossible, because she was so deeply attracted by the impossible. Likewise Ida of Nivelles one day, during the celebration of the Eucharist, had a vision of the Trinity through which she received great consolation. But she was unable to put into words the divine and inscrutable mystery she had gazed upon.[56] Hadewijch, in her turn, described the

---

54 *Quinque*, 266: 'Non incredibile [est] Deum qui est summum lumen luminorum lumine suo mirabili dilectam suam interius... luminosam reddidisse'.

55 Aenig, PL 180: 397D: 'Estne ergo in Deo quod percipi potest? Est plane, si modo hoc velis quod possis' [ET: CF 9:36].

56 *Quinque*, 271: 'Dum missa celebraretur Sanctissimam Trinitatem conspexerat. In hac autem visione plenam consolationem recepit, nec tamen omnino effari potuit divinum illud et inscrutabile mysterium quod intuebatur'. According to Ernst Benz, *Die Vision. Erfahrungsformen und Bilderwelt* [henceforth *Die Vision*], (Stuttgart, 1969) 493–94, visions of the Trinity are uncommon: 'Unter den mannigfaltigen visionären Erfahrungen der christlichen Seher finden sich nur wenige Visionen der göttlichen Dreieinigkeit'.

unattainable through spatial metaphorical interpretations of the divine 'dimensions' and paradoxes.[57]

However unattainable the incomprehensible mystery of God might be to human reason, it is not a completely locked and sealed gate. As William said in one of his meditations:

> But when and how and as far as the Holy Spirit wills, it controls the believing mind, so that something of what you [God] are may be seen by those who in their prayers and contemplation have gone beyond all that you are not, although they do not see you as you are. Nevertheless this understanding serves to soothe the loving spirit, for there is clearly nothing in it of that which you are not and, although it is not wholly what you are, it is not different from that Reality.[58]

The available biographies confirm the women's strong desire to obtain through prayer and meditation at least a glimpse, or better an experience, of the One who is Trinity. One of Ida of Nivelles' meditations was on the holy and undivided Trinity. She esteemed whatever delight she got from resting in this holy contemplation more than any other.[59] Her biography mentions that the monastic custom of bowing at the *Gloria Patri*, while crossing her arms over the knees signified embracing the Blessed Trinity.[60] She also told about a special enlightenment, expressing it not in theological but in experiential terms:

---

57 Hadewijch, Letter 22. See Reynaert, *Beeldspraak*, 231–56; 237.

58 Med 3.11; PL 180: 214C; CF 3: 108: 'Sed sensum fidelem sic quando, et quantum, et quomodo vult Spiritus sanctus, perstringit; ut orantes te vel contemplantes supergressi nonnumquam omne quod tu non es, videant aliquatenus te, qui es, quamvis non videant te sicut es; sed tamen medium quid devotae mentis demulceat intuitum, quod constet nec de eis esse, quae tu non es; nec, etsi non sit omnino totum quod es, alienum tamen esse, ab eo quod es.'

59 *Quinque*, 277: 'Octava ejus fuit contemplatio circa sanctam et individuam Trinitatem... in ejus sancta speculatione quiescere, quoddam gaudium omni gaudio excellentius reputabat'.

60 *Quinque*, 207: 'Cum Gloria Patri cantatur a monachis et monialibus, cancellatis brachiis inclinantur, per quod congrue significare dicebat quod monachi et moniales, sic agente, beatam Trinitatem debent amplexari'.

One day I was in the infirmary because of some illness and because of a strong and insatiable desire for the Trinity. My heart grew passionate within me, and a light—not consuming but illuminating and inflaming—began to glow within me. And behold, suddenly a man with a venerable countenance and covered with a cloak shining as white as manna, stood in front of me. Out of his mouth flowed a liquor looking delightfully delectable. This man looked at me with gracious familiarity and said: 'Oh, my very dear, though you are inexperienced, you greatly desire to know and to savor the ineffable knowledge of my divinity. To fulfil the burning desire of your soul, I very gladly will pour to the full into your heart the most tasty honeycomb of my divinity'. Thereupon he took the liquor emanating from his mouth and instilled it into my mouth. At once the depth of my soul became enlightened with such divinely sweet knowledge that from that day on and ever since I had such a knowledge of the Blessed Trinity as was given me to know.[61]

Before entering the cistercian monastery of Roosendaal, Ida of Leuven composed for her personal use some 'hours' she prayed in honor of the holy and undivided Trinity.[62] These few instances suggest that in the nuns' relation to the Trinity more was involved than reason. In this matter, reason has to be supported by faith in response to God's self-revelation and self-communication.

---

61 *Quinque*, 254–55; 'Ecce subito astitit mihi vir quidam venerabilis quidam, clamide candidissima circumamictus; de cujus ore manabat liquor quidem aspectu delectabilis, qui candidus tamquam manna esse videbatur. Cumque idem vir, gratiosa quadam familiaritate me intueretur, dixit mihi: "Tu desiderasti vehementer, o charissima mea, cognoscere et sapere, inexperta licet ineffabilem meae divinitatis notitiam, et ego libentissime, ut ardentissimum animae tuae desiderium adimpleatur, super omnia sapidissimum divinitatis meae favum cordi tuo ad cumulum instillabo"'. Statim tanta dulcedine et cognitione divina illustrata est interius animae meae, quod a die illa et deinceps, quantum mihi scire concessum est, beatae Trinitatis agnitionem consecuta sum'. The image Ida used is not attractive, nor is it meant to be attractive. The idea behind this image is the profound intimacy between Ida and the divinity as Trinity.

62 *AA SS* April 2: 164: 'Speciales quasdam horas affectione praecipua quotidie decantaret, in honore sanctae et individuae Trinitatis'.

William called reason supported by faith *ratio fidei*, the reasoning of faith.[63] A recent commentator gives the following description of this expression which occurs no less than twenty-two times in the treatise *Aenigma fidei*:

> *Ratio fidei* is an expression of a reconciliation of the tension between faith and reason. This phrase expresses a view of faith which subordinates reason to faith, but not in an anti-intellectual, or repressive way. Reason is not rejected; no hint is given of 'blind faith'. What is meant is a *ratio* which investigates and scrutinizes the content of *fides*, but with certain limitations which are imposed by the very nature of that faith: mystery.[64]

Thus William could affirm: 'Nowhere in this life is the Divinity better grasped by the human understanding than in what is understood to be more incomprehensible: that is, in the preaching of the Trinity'.[65] For his part, Bernard, in response to his own question, what is God?, answered that God is unknowable, and that in relation to himself, he alone knows.[66] In her turn, Hadewijch wrote in her *Mengeldicht* 16 that the Trinity is a mystery transcending all human comprehension:

> Living water is her [Love's] name
> Truly appropriate after that of dew.
> This flowing forth and flowing back
> Of one into the other and mutual permeation,
> Surpasses mind and understanding
> Above comprehension and above expression
> Of human creatures.[67]

---

63 Aenig, PL 180: 414B–418A; CF 9: 67–74.
64 John D. Anderson, Introduction to *The Enigma of Faith*, CF 9:22.
65 Aenig, PL 180: 426C: 'Nusquam in hac vita divinitas melius humano intellectu comprehenditur, quam in eo quo magis incomprehensibilis esse intelligitur: hoc est in praedicatione Trinitatis'.
66 Csi 5.11.24; SBOp 3: 486: 'Quid est ergo Deus?... Quod ad se, ipse novit'.(What is God?...What he is to himself, he alone knows).
67 VM, *Mengeldichten*, 82, ll. 127–133. The *dew*, according to Reynaert's quite acceptable interpretation, refers to the oneness within the Trinity

Beatrice was no less convinced of the ineffable mystery of the Trinity (164,58; 214,37; 217,88). Their contemporary, the beguine Mechtild of Magdeburg (1202–82), who spent her last twelve years as a Cistercian in Helfta, followed in this both Hadewijch and Beatrice.[68] The same conviction has been quoted in regard to Ida of Nivelles.[69]

The veil of this trinitarian mystery has been partially lifted by the author of 1 Jn 4:8: 'For God is love'. This phrase led to the assumption that there are personal love-relationships within God. Bernard affirmed it explicitly: 'What else maintains that supreme and unutterable unity in the highest and most blessed Trinity if not love? Love is God's life'.[70] Richard was insistent in his *De Trinitate* that if God is love, then the Trinity is implicated.[71] Bernard's resounding formula that 'Love triumphs over God'[72] was echoed by Richard, 'Love in an unconquerable strength which prevails even over the Unconquerable himself',[73] and by Hadewijch, 'Love has vanquished the Divinity in its own nature'.[74]

For the *mulieres religiosae* and their mentors, love is the law of God as Trinity: 'Love is a law, the law of the Lord, which in a

---

(*Beeldspraak*, 136), while the two following verses speak of the interpersonal relations of the divine Persons (144).

68 Hans Neumann, 'Mechtild von Magdeburg und die Mittelniederländische Frauenmystik', *Medieval German Studies. Festschrift für Frederic Norman* (London, 1965) 231–46; 236–38, where the author suggests that Mechtild could have come in contact with the writings of Hadewijch and Beatrice through an intermediary copy in Low-German.

69 See above, note 56.

70 Dil 12.5; SBOp 3: 149: 'Quid vero de summa et beata illa Trinitate summam et ineffabilem illam conservat unitatem nisi charitas? Ipse ex ea vivit'.

71 Gaston Salet, *Richard de Saint-Victor. La Trinité*, SCh 63 (Paris, 1959) 511, q.v. caritas. On p.43, Salet handles the objection that could be made against Richard that his reasoning is a syllogism. See also A.M. Ethier. *Le "De Trinitate" de Richard de Saint-Victor* (Paris-Ottawa, 1939).

72 SC 64.10; SBOp 2: 171: 'Triumphat de Deo amor'.

73 *De gradibus charitatis*, PL 196: 1196A: 'O insuperabilis virtus charitas, quae ipsum quoque insuperabilem superasti'.

74 Letter 20. Love 'vainc la Déité dans sa propre nature', J.B.P[orion], *Hadewijch, Lettres spirtuelles*, 162. This translation is closer to the original text: 'si [Minne] hevet de godheit bedwongen in hare nature' (VM, *Brieven*, 1: 173, l. 103) and less open to misinterpretation than the ET.

certain way holds and brings together the Trinity' said Bernard.[75]
So did Richard,[76] an unidentified Yvo,[77] Hadewijch,[78] and Beatrice.[79] But 'Love is from God'as well (1 Jn 4:7), or as Bernard put
it: 'It is rightly said that love is God and a gift from God'.[80] In the
self-communication of God to man, especially through the incarnation of the Son and by his redemption, love becomes the bond,
the link between God and man. Ida of Nivelles' biographer
expressed this interconnection of love by writing metaphorically
that Ida's 'soul adhered to the Trinity with the lime of love'.[81] It
is, as it were, with the two arms of understanding and love, said
Bernard, that God can be 'embraced and grasped'.[82] Love as gift
from God becomes the soul's medium of sight: 'When there is
love, there is an eye', as Richard put it.[83] Love is a form of
understanding, *amor ipse intellectus est*, as William would say,[84]

---

75 Dil 12.35; SBOp 3:149: 'Lex est ergo, et lex Domini, quae Trinitatem in
unitate quodammodo cohibet et colligat'.

76 *De Trinitate*, 3.11; PL 196: 923A–B: 'Vides ergo quomodo charitatis
consummatio personarum Trinitatem requirit, sine qua omnino in plenitudinis
suae integritate subsistere nequit'.

77 Gervais Dumeige, *Yves. Epître à Séverin sur la charité*, Textes philosophiques du Moyen Age 3 (Paris, 1955) 85. This work, henceforth cited as *Yves*.
Epître, although for a long time attributed to Richard, was written by an
unidentifiable Yvo, who borrowed copiously from Bernard: 'L'opuscule est *du*
saint Bernard, mais non *de* saint Bernard ' (Dumeige, 23): this work is *of*
Bernard, but not *by* Bernard.

78 Reynaert, *Beeldspraak*, 43–46.

79 Vekeman, '*Vita Beatricis* en *Seuen Manieren van Minne*', OGE 46 (1972)
41.

80 Dil 12.35; SBOp 3:149: 'Dicitur ergo recte caritas, et Deus, et Dei
Donum'.

81 *Quinque*, 271: 'Anima ejus Trinitati glutino amoris impressaerat'. Hadewijch too knew this glutinum-motive (Reynaert, *Beeldspraak*, 51–53) as did
Augustine and Bernard (*ibid.*, 53, n.57), Jerome and Thomas the Cistercian
(Bell, *Citeaux* 18 [1977] 262) and many others. For the translation of *glutinum*
as lime, see below, chapter XVI, note 48.

82 Ep.18.3; SBOp 7:68: 'quasi duabus animae brachiis, intellectu videlicet et
amore...amplectitur et comprehenditur Deus'. Bernard used the metaphor of a
kiss in other contexts, particularly in his Sermons on the Song of Songs.

83 *Benjamin minor*, 13; PL 196: 10A: 'Ubi amor, ibi oculus'. In fact, this was
a popular proverb; Thierry of Chartres used it (see B. Hauréau, *Notices et
extraits de quelques MSS latins de la B.N.* [Paris, 1890] 1: 53); it appears also in
Baldwin of Ford (PL 204:572A) and Adam of Perseigne (PL 211: 596D).

84 Jean Marie Déchanet, '*Amor ipse intellectus est*'. La doctrine de l'amour
chez Guillaume de Saint-Thierry', RMAL 1 (1945) 349–74.

or, love is knowledge, *amor notitia est*, an expression more often used by Gregory the Great, Bernard, Richard and many others.[85] At the same time the texts avoid a cyclopean outlook as though love were all eye and nothing else, for they speak of the complementarity of reason and love. Hadewijch, borrowing from William,[86] says:

> Reason cannot see God except in what he is not, love rests not except in what he is..., the two, however, are of great mutual help one to the other; for reason instructs love, and love enlightens reason. When reason abandons itself to love's wish, and love consents to be forced and held within the bounds of reason, they can accomplish a very great work.[87]

Enlightened reason instructs the soul about the infinite distance between God and herself, and thereby cuts off pride. Reason convinces her of the need to be free of all that is not God and readily open to the purifying sufferings implied in loving God above all else.[88] Beatrice, in her ascent to God, often had recourse to reason (68,40; 69,67; 112,21; 181,185; 204,71). Both reason and love played their mutual roles. Alice of Schaarbeek's biographer noticed that 'what she conceived by knowledge, she exerted herself to bring to birth through love'.[89] Taken together, reason and love constitute the two eyes of the soul, as William,[90]

---

85 For several references, see R. Javelet, 'Intelligence et amour chez les auteurs spirituels du XIIe siècle', *RAM* 37 (1961) 273–90; 429–50; and Bell, *The Image*, 211–12 and notes.

86 Nat am 21; PL 184: 393A: 'Sunt autem duo oculi in hoc visu...amor et ratio'. See also Paul Verdeyen, 'Les deux yeux de l'âme', *OGE* 51 (1977) 355–58.

87 Hadewijch, Letter 18, VM, *Brieven*, 1: 155, ll. 82–98. For the apparent contradiction between love and reason, see Porion, *Lettres spirituelles*, 29–30, and Bernard Spaapen, *OGE* 44 (1970) 118.

88 Stanzas 6–15 of Hadewijch's *Poems in Stanzas* refer to this relation between love and reason: VM, *Strophische Gedichten*, 195–97, ll. 31–90.

89 *AA SS* June 2: 478,5: 'Per amorem parturire satagebat, quod per cognitionem antea conceperat'.

90 Nat am 8.21; PL 184: 393A.

Hadewijch,[91] and Beatrice[92] put it. Love enjoys priority for, as Hugh commented, 'God is more loved than understood; love draws near and enters, whereas knowledge remains outside'.[93] Where rational knowledge cannot reach, love can. Yet, neither may dismiss the other. Both intellect and heart are needed and they complement each other.

It was their love for the Trinity that induced the *mulieres religiosae* to live this mystery. And this loving and living are equivalent to experiential knowledge.[94] In the sense of this experienced 'familiarity', Ida Lewis was called the *triclinium Deitatis*, the dining room of the Godhead.[95] The mystery of the Trinity as a loving God 'is soothing to the pious; it stirs them up and urges them on to seek God's face always'.[96] And Bernard, William's friend, was no less interested—as can be expected—in knowing by experience that:

> there are...spiritual persons who serve him [God] faithfully and with confidence, speaking with him as a man speaks with his friend, and whose consciences bear witness to his glory. But who these are is known only to God, and if you desire to be among them, then hear what sort of people you should be. I say this, not as one who knows it by experience, but as one who desires to do so. Show me a soul which loves nothing but God, and what is to be loved for God's sake, to

---

91 Letter 18, VM, *Brieven*, 1: 159, l. 175. See Reynaert, *Beeldspraak*, 58–60.

92 Herman Vekeman, *Seuen Manieren van Minne. Lexicografisch Onderzoek* [henceforth cited: *Lexicografisch Onderzoek*]. Unpublished dissertation in two volumes (Leuven, 1967) 1:158.

93 *Commentarium in Hierarchiam Caelestem*, PL 175: 1058D: 'Plus enim diligitur quam intelligitur, et intrat dilectio et appropinquat, ubi scientia foris est'.

94 Vanneste, *Abstracta*, 12.

95 *AA SS* Oct. 13: 110,12. In classical Latin, *triclinium* meant the dining room with its couches. Beatrice of Zwijveke referred to Our Lady as *Triclinium Trinitatis*, a title already given to her by Hugh. See L. Reypens, 'Nog een dertiendeeuwse mystieke Cisterciënsernon', *OGE* 23 (1949) 244.

96 William, Aenig; PL 180: 426C: 'Hoc est aenigma fidei...blandum piis, ad excitandos eos et provocandos quaerere faciem ejus semper'.

whom to live is Christ, and of whom this has been true for a long time now; who in work and leisure alike endeavors to keep God before his eyes, and walks humbly with the Lord his God; who desires that his will may be one with the will of God, and who has been given the grace to do these things. Show me a soul like this, and I will not deny that she is worthy of the Bridegroom's care, of the regard of God's Majesty, of his sovereign favor, and of the attention of his governance.[97]

This discussion of the Trinity brings us to the center of the spiritual life of the *mulieres religiosae* and their mystical attainments. Bernard's eloquence was unrestrained in describing the dynamic development of such a life:

> *Ita est*, and so it is: the love of God gives birth to the love of the soul for God (*amor Dei amorem animae parit*), and his surpassing affection fills the soul with affection, and his concern evokes concern. For when the soul can once perceive the glory of God without a veil, it is compelled by some affinity of nature to be conformed to it, and be transformed to its very image.[98]

Ita est, and so it is: to live and to love the Trinity is to be conformed to it; to be conformed to it is to have restored again the image and likeness in which man was originally created, but now in its even more brilliant christian dimension, to be readied for the ultimate transformation to which Bernard pointed.

CREATION

Man finds himself in a creation in which he is central. At first glance, the matter looks quite simple, but it is not so. The complexity, however, is one not of intricacy but of exceptional

---

97 SC 69.1; SBOp 2: 202.
98 SC 69.7; SBOp 2: 206.

richness. The infinite, ineffable God has to some extent lifted the veil of his true identity which is love. Out of love he created man and invited him to a love-relation that never ends. Scripture and subsequent tradition have expressed this vocation by saying that man is created to God's image and likeness. After a short introduction about creation in general, we will consider man's creation both from the Creator's and from the creature's side, including the extensive dowry man received when he came into being on earth.

Creation of Man's Habitat.

The *mulieres religiosae* knew nothing of light years, galaxies, and nuclear fission, but their ignorance of the universe and its capacities was balanced by their awareness of the world they lived in. They seem to have had a greater sensitivity to creation and a deeper appreciation of the Creator than do moderns, spared as they were the continual waves of information which wash over us from the mass-communication media. Their notions of the cosmos were those of their own time, not of ours. Similarly, no one can expect the *mulieres religiosae* to have been versed in twentieth-century hermeneutics, exegesis or comparative religion. They accepted the traditions handed down by the Bible, the Fathers of the Church, and their own mentors, but they felt free to express them in their own way.

The Creator.

The first of the two scriptural creation-narratives, in Genesis 1–2:4, written, as we know now, by the priestly author, speaks of the world as resulting from God's action. 'God said...called...made...saw...blessed',[99] 'so that what was not would be'.[100] The *mulieres religiosae* likewise looked at creation not in scientific, but in religious, terms. Creation pointed in the first place at

---

99 Gerhard von Rad, *Genesis*, ET by J.H. Marks (London, 1961) 61–65: 'Notes on the priestly account of creation'.
100 Hugh, PL 176:183C: 'Quo factum est ut essent que non erant'.

the Creator, so supreme that by comparison whatever is not God is non-being.[101] God is the uncreated Being; as William said:

> He alone should be said truly to be, who is unchangeable from eternity; for him, to be is what he is. And what he is he always is; and just as he is, so he is always. He does not possess in himself the possibility not to be what he is, because he does not possess in himself the possibility to be what he is not. And what he is is not preceded by a beginning, is not brought to an end by a conclusion, does not pass through time, is not contained in space, is not changed by age. Nothing is lacking there because everything is in him; nothing is excluded because nothing is outside of him.[102]

Nothing exists without God, the Creator; that is, the Holy Trinity.[103] The three persons create not separately, but conjointly.[104] No creature, not even Christ's humanity, escapes this trinitarian principle of co-creation.[105] In the *vitae* and writings of some *mulieres religiosae* the Divinity or God as Trinity is often called Creator; the Father or Christ is also addressed as Creator, but never in an exclusive way.[106]

---

101 Bernard, Csi 5.6.13; SBOp 3: 477: 'Nonne in comparatione hujus quidquid hoc non est, iudicas potius non esse quam esse'.

102 Aenig; PL 180: 420C; CF 19: 79–80: 'Solus quippe vere esse dicendum est, qui ab aeterno incommunicabiliter est, et hoc est ei esse, quod est; et quod est, semper est; et sicut est, sic semper est. Non in se habet posse non esse, quod est; quia nec in se habet posse esse, quod non est; et quod sic est, non initio praevenitur, non fine claudatur, non temporibus volvitur, non locis continetur, non aetatibus variatur. Nihil ibi deest, quia totum in eo est; nihil superest, quia nihil extra eum est'.

103 William, Nat corp 2; PL 184: 722B: 'Nihil sine creatore Deo, scilicet Sancta Trinitate existit'.

104 William, Aenig; PL 180: 425D: 'Non tres sunt creatores, sed unus creator'.

105 Bernard, Nat 2.4; SBOp 4: 254: 'Cum prima ex duobus [body and soul] facta sit, secunda iam coniunctio [with God's Word in the incarnation] ex hoc ipso ad sacramentum accedere Trinitatis'. Or as Ida of Nivelles expressed it (*Quinque*, 271): 'Cum Trinitas non sit incarnata...tantum easdem personas incarnationi Domini cooperantes'.

106 Beatrice referred to God as 'the uncreated Good', or 'the eternal true God' (75, 70; 217, 108; 263, 15; 264, 37; 266, 73); or as 'the divinity' (173, 69);

God is infinitely above everything, and he is the principle through which all creatures sprang into being.[107] He is their maker,[108] the craftsman,[109] the one cause (*principium*) of all that is.[110] He is the Lord and Creator of everything,[111] he created all things.[112] By the act of creating he is not diminished or increased, nor is he subject to any change.[113] He can in no way be identified with his creation,[114] which came forth neither by emanation nor from any material source.[115] The Creator created with a purpose, not merely for the sake of creating.[116] He did it not out of necessity, cupidity, curiosity or vanity, but out of the abundance of his goodness.[117] The dynamism and vitality of God's creative action originates from his love and invites a free response from man, and, above all from the crown of the whole of his creation, his Son made man.[118].

---

or as 'Father' (223, 36). Christ is also referred to as 'Creator' by Beatrice (92, 29; 101) and by Ida of Leuven's biographer: *AA SS* April 2: 171, 5; 172, 6–7; 174, 14–15; 179, 29; 180, 34;184, 8.

107 William, Aenig; PL 180: 425C: 'Prima et principalis ejus [creaturae] essentia et veritas existendi, quae in Deo est, et Deus est'.

108 Bernard, SC 4.4; SBOp 1: 20: 'Ipse factor eorum'.

109 Bernard, Nat 2.1; SBOp 4: 252: 'artifex'.

110 William, Contem 10.22; PL 184: 379B: 'Unum te omnium principium'.

111 *Quinque*, 215: 'Dominus et Creator universorum'.

112 Hadewijch, VM, *Strophishe Gedichten*, 26, l.25: 'God die ghemaecte alle dinghe'.

113 Bernard, Div 60.1; SBOp 6/1: 290: 'Nec minui potest, nec augeri, aut aliquo modo variari'.

114 B.L. De Raeymaeker, *The Philosophy of Being*, 2nd ed., ET by E. Ziegelmeier (St.Louis, MO-London, 1957) 286: 'The fundamental cause, completely independent, is the perfectly adequate reason of everything, both from the point of view of efficiency and from those of finality and exemplarity. God, the Creator, is the Cause absolutely free'.

115 Bernard, SC 4.4; SBOp 1: 20: 'Ipse factor eorum, sed causale, non materiale'.

116 Bernard, I Nov 5. 3–4; SBOp 5: 319: See Alberic Altermatt, 'Die Christologie Bernhards von Clairvaux', *AC* 33 (1977) 31–32: 'Die Schöpfung: Offenbarung von Gottes Macht, Güte und Weisheit'.

117 Isaac of Stella, *Sermo* 25; PL 194: 1772B: 'Nec necessitate...nec cupiditate...nec curiositate...nec vanitate...sed gratuita voluntate'.

118 On Hugh, see Robert Javelet, 'Image de Dieu et nature au XIIe siècle', *La filosofia della natura nel Medioevo. Atti del III Congresso internazionale di filosofia medioevale* (Milan, 1964) 290–91; -Richard, *Benjamin major*; PL 196: 70C–D; -Bernard, Pent 3.3; SBOp 5:172; -Aelred, C. H. Talbot, ed., *Sermones*

Creation.

In their great variety creatures are numerous, useful, and beautiful. These three qualities are the lineaments of the Trinity as power, wisdom, and kindness.[119] What has been created by a good God cannot be other than good.[120] If creatures are beautiful, it is because their Creator is supremely and unchangeably beautiful.[121]

Creation affords some idea of the Creator,[122] and leads man, by the hand as it were (*manuductio*), toward the Creator.[123] Creation is a book in which anyone who wills to do so can read of God's wisdom.[124] Hadewijch's sensitivity to nature is graphically expressed in her *Poems in Stanzas*. Nearly all of them begin with a reference to seasons, weather, plants, trees, grass, flowers, birds, valleys and other natural phenomena. Each was used as an introduction to what she wanted to say about *Minne*, love of and love for God.[125] Ida of Nivelles, looking at the beauty around her,

---

inediti B.Aelredi Abbatis Rievallensis [henceforth cited as *Sermones inediti*], (Rome, 1952) 107–08.

119 Alberic Altermatt, 'Die Christologie Bernhards von Clairvaux', see above, n.116.

120 Bernard, Gra 6.19; SBOp 3: 180: 'A bono Deo non potuit creari nisi bona'.

121 Aelred, *Spec car* 1. 2; in *Aelredi Rievallensis opera omnia*, Anselm Hoste and C.H. Talbot, eds., CCCM vol. 1 (Turnhout, 1971) 14: 'Quoniam ipso a quo sunt, summe et incommutabiliter pulcher est, pulchra sunt omnia'.

122 William, Ep frat; PL 184: 318A: 'In hoc quod notum est Dei, manifestum est illis. In hoc aestimatur de creatura Creator'.

123 Hugh, *Expositio in Hierarchiam coelestem* 2; PL 175: 948A: 'Quorum manuductio mens humana utitur...ut dirigatur'. Hugh is here depending on Eriugena. See H. Weisweiler, 'Die Ps.-Dionysiuskommentare "In Coelestem Hierarchiam" des Scotus Eriugena und Hugos von St. Viktor', *RTAM* 19 (1952) 26–47; 36.

124 Bernard, Div 9.1; SBOp 6/1: 118: 'Velut communis quidem liber et catena ligatus sensibilis mundus iste, ut in eo sapientiam Dei legat quicumque voluerit'.

125 In writing her Poems in Stanzas (*Strofische Gedichten*), Hadewijch did not merely invent the form of those poems. She followed mostly the trouvères of the North of France, though the troubadours of Provence and the German Minnesinger are not absent. In one form or another such poems begin with a tribute to nature which is supposed to create an atmosphere for what is to follow. The poets usually make a reference to spring, and Hadewijch is no exception. But to limit Hadewijch's Poems in Stanzas only to the literary forms of her time

could not but shed tears, so deeply moved was she and so grateful for the goodness and wisdom of the Creator which shone through his creation.[126] The Creator's wisdom was particularly perceptible to medieval persons in the order within creation. Each creature has, in orderly fashion, its proper place, time and manner within the universe.[127]

---

would not do justice to her as a genius in the written Flemish vernacular. Moreover, she used these forms of poetic expression, including the beginning stanza(s) related to nature, in the religious context of her culture and her own spiritual journey, which is part of the *mulieres religiosae* movement. See E. Rombouts and N. De Paepe, *Hadewijch. Strofische Gedichten* (Zwolle, 1961) 23–28. J. Reynaert too spoke extensively of Hadewijch's relation to nature in *Beeldspraak*, 259–91: 'De natuurlijke wereld'. The same topic has been amply and thoroughly treated by Frank Willaert in his study, *De poëtica van Hadewijch in de Strofische Gedichten* (Utrecht, 1984; henceforth cited: *De poëtica van Hadewijch*): ' Het exordium in de Strofische Gedichten', 88–135; 'Vreugde en verdriet [and equivalent expressions] in de Strofische Gedichten', 135–224; 'Het slot in de strofische gedichten, 224–39. See also Marieke J. Van Baest, *'Fiere herte doelt na minnen gronde'. De fierhied als kernmoment in het zelfverstaan van Hadewijch* [henceforth: *De fierheid als kernmoment van...Hadewijch*], (Tilburg, 1984) 65–69.

126 *Quinque*, 276: '...Interdum memor esset operum Dei, et aspiceret creaturas quas fecit Dominus...vix eas sine lacrymarum effusione poterat intueri, quin ex creatura bonitatem et sapientiam Creatoris conspiciens'. To ask whether Ida were an environmentalist would be an inappropriate question to put to her time. Moreover, the fact that nature's beauty reminded her of its source and originator shows how this natural beauty pointed primarily to God the beautifier, not to man the modifier.

127 Aelred, *Spec car* 2.4; *CCCM*, 1: 14–15: 'Sunt ergo [omnia] bona per naturam, pulchra per speciem, bene ordinata ad ipsus universitatis decorem'. Aelred, in fact, follows Augustine; see Gilson, *Introduction*, 280–81. Bernard says it in his own masterly way: 'Look first of all, at the creation, distribution and composition of things: what great power is shown in their creation, what wisdom in their distribution, what goodness in their composition. In creation you can see how much has been made, and with what power is has all been made so great. By their distribution you can see how wisely everything has been placed. By their composition you can see how benignly the highest has been combined with the lowest, with a charity as lovable as it is wonderful'. The translation is taken from Leo Hickey, *Saint Bernard. The Nativity* (Chicago-Dublin-London, 1959) 24. The Latin version comes from V Nat 3.8; SBOp 4: 217. Christine Mohrmann stresses the rhythmical structure of the Latin text; see SBOp 2: xxvii:

Et primo quidem intuere
creationem, positionem et dispositionem rerum:
quanta sit videlicet in creatione potentia,
quanta in positione sapientia,

Ida of Nivelles saw visible and corporeal creatures as so many steps by which one ascends with admiration to the Creator, realizing how wonderful, praiseworthy and lovable he has shown himself to be in them.[128] And all this beauty and order is in the service of man,[129] made for him and created to serve him.[130] Man in his turn should express his creaturely existence by loving his Creator, the whole of mankind and all other creatures in an appropriate way, 'ready for all virtues in which Love is honored, without any other intention than to render Love her proper place in man, and in all creatures according to their indebtedness'.[131] In a flowery style Beatrice said: 'just as love unceasingly embraces God, the Creator of all, with outstretched arms, so [the soul] should incline to the needs of creatures, loving good and bad alike, and should extend itself with a generous embrace even to irrational creatures'.[132] And so she did. As her biographer mentions (242,33) in a scene not unlike some of

---

in compositione quanta benignitas.
In creatione
vide quam multa et quam magna potenter creata sunt,
in positione
quam sapienter cuncta locata sunt,
in compositione
quam benigne suprema et infima connexa sunt,
tam amabili
quam admirabili
caritate

128 *Quinque*, 206: 'Ex eo quod de imo respiciebat in laudem Creatoris assumens in omnibus operibus suis, mirabilem, laudabilem et amabilem reperierat'.

129 Aelred, *Spec car, CCCM* 1: 15: 'Irrationabili itemque insensibili creaturae quis modus aptior, quam ut illorum [hominum] saluti subserviant'.

130 Bernard, SC 21.6; SBOp 1: 126: 'Cui ad serviendum creata fuere'.

131 Hadewijch, Letter 6, VM, *Brieven*, 1: 169, ll. 371–74.

132 *Vita*, 265,15. The *Quinque prudentes virgines* do not use the term *microcosmos* to designate man in relation to the *macrocosmos*, the universe, as was so often done in their time. See M.D.Chenu, *Nature, Man and Society*, 24–27; Bernard McGinn, *The Golden Chain. A Study in the Theological Anthropology of Isaac of Stella*, CS 15 (Washington D.C.: Cistercian Publications, 1972) 122–33, and the bibliography mentioned in these publications. The iconographic illustration of this theme is presented by Aldegundis Fürkötter and Angela Carlevaris in their publication of Hildegard of Bingen's *Scivias, CCCM* 43–43A (Turnhout 1978) 2 vols; and by Gérard Cames, *Allégories et symboles dans l'Hortus deliciarum* (Leiden, 1971) 11–15.

Francis of Assisi's *fioretti*: 'wild birds and small woodland fowl sometimes flew to her from their hiding places in the groves, and sat on her lap very tamely, fluttering sweetly up against her. By their novel and unusual joy in fluttering up to her, they showed that this specially-chosen servant of God was wholly lacking that harshness which little animals and birds of that kind naturally fear in other human beings'.

The Creation of the Human Body.

According to the Yahvist account in the second creation-narrative (Gn 2:4b–25) 'man' and animals were formed out of the ground or soil. Unique to this story is the play on words in one verse (Gn 2:7) which declares that 'man' (*adam*, a collective noun) derives from *adama*, the ground; that he was made out of the dust (meaning here clay) of the ground, and that God blew into his nostrils the breath of life, making him a living being. The solemnity of the formula contrasts with the simple 'formed out of the ground' that is predicated of the other animals in Gn 2:19.[133] At first reading this seems to say that creation occurred in two stages: first the body and then the life-giving spirit. Gregory of Nyssa,[134] and Augustine[135] interpreted it otherwise, as did most twelfth-century authors.[136] In Bernard's view, creation in two steps is logical rather than chronological:

> The clay was already created in the beginning when God created heaven and earth, but the spirit does not share this common condition but has its own particular origin. The latter was not created with the matter, but breathed into

---

133 Bruce Vawter, *On Genesis. A New Reading* (Garden City, NY, 1977) 66–67; Richard J. Clifford, 'The Hebrew Scriptures and the Theology of Creation', *TS* 46 (1985) 607–23.

134 Walther Völker, *Gregor von Nyssa as Mystiker*, [henceforth: *Gregor von Nyssa*], (Wiesbaden, 1955) 59. Gregory refused to accept the view of Plato and Origen that the soul pre-existed before it 'descended' into the body. See Jérome Gaïth, *La conception de la liberté chez Grégoire de Nysse* [henceforth cited: *La conception de la liberté*], Études de philosophie médiévale 43 (Paris, 1953) 95 and 110.

135 Augustine, *De Trinitate* 12.15.24; PL 42: 1011–12.

136 Javelet, *Image*, 1: 115.

matter with a certain unique excellence. Acknowledge your dignity, man, acknowledge the glory of your human condition. You have a material body, but it is appropriate that he who was established over the whole mass of created reality should be partly similar to it. However, you have something loftier; you do not deserve to be compared and made equal with the other creatures. Body and soul are joined and united in you: the first fashioned, the latter in-spirited.[137]

Man's excellence can be seen even in the upright posture of his body: 'by gazing heavenward [man] shows his imperial and royal dignity, indicating his dominion over all downward looking creatures'.[138]

The body is the garment of flesh,[139] the host of the soul.[140] When someone dies, the body returns to the earth from which it was taken.[141] This provides good reason for humility, which derives from *humus*, the Latin of *adama*. Beatrice, among many others, 'saw matters for humility offered to her consideration because the lowliness of earth...indicated that she was trampling underfoot at every moment that which she was and in the future would become' (107,29). Her simple, sober statement is quite different from some morbidly excessive expressions of the same reality in the later Middle Ages.[142] The pre-scholastics were neither pessimists nor Manichaeans.[143] They knew that after man

---

137 Bernard, Nat 2.1; SBOp 4: 251–52. See also A. Van den Bosch, 'Présupposés à la Christologie Bernardine', *Citeaux* 9 (1958) 5–8.

138 William, Nat corp 2; PL 180: 714B: 'Erecta hominis figura ad coelum extensa, et sursum aspiciens, imperialem regalemque dignitatem animae rationalis significat'. See Mayeul Cappuyns, 'Le "De imagine" de Grégoire de Nysse traduit par Jean Scot Erigène', *RTAM* 33 (1965) 212; this theme became widely accepted.

139 Ida of Leuven, *AA SS* April 2: 178, 26: 'carnis tunica'.

140 Bernard, Adv 6.4; SBOp 4: 193: 'Anima apud te [corpus] est hospitata'.

141 William, Nat am 44; PL 184: 407A: 'Pondus suum unumquodque defert in locum suum; corpus in terram de qua assumptum est'.

142 Étienne Delaruelle, *La piété populaire au Moyen Age* (Turin, 1975) 437–64: 'La vie religieuse dans le pays de langue française à la fin du XVe siècle; 457–59: memento mei, dances macabres et triomphes de la mort, artes moriendi; see also J. Delumeau, *Le péché et la peur* (see above, Chapter Two, n.63) 44–97.

143 Javelet, *Image*, 1: 225.

had become a self-centered victim of his sin and his body had become rebellious, the ascent to God was still possible, but not without discipline of the inner and the outer man. William insisted that due care should be given the body so that it would not rebel or grow wanton, but it should nevertheless be disciplined in such a way that it is able to serve, for it has been given to the spirit to serve it.[144] Bernard too spoke of the natural necessity of loving the body in an orderly fashion.[145]

Beatrice herself, 'carefully suppressed and brought to nothing the illicit movements of evil pleasures, and daily adorned her general self-restraint with fresh flowers of virtues' (85,25). Her biographer praised her because she taught her body, that 'frail house of the outer man' (159,70), to obey her spirit (29,116). The ascetical efforts of the *mulieres religiosae* to subject the body to the leading of the spirit had to do not so much with 'the flesh' as with their aspiration toward a virtuous, holy life. The tensions they experienced in their practices were related to their view that life on earth was only temporary. Their sometimes burning desire to be dissolved and freed from the body resulted from their ready orientation toward real and everlasting life in union with God. The instances when they look disparagingly at the body reflect this higher aspiration.

The Creation of Man.

In the priestly creation narrative only man is presented as a conscious creature.[146] His creaturely consciousness mirrors in some fashion that supreme Consciousness with whom he can dialogue.[147] Gregory of Nyssa observed that God's immanence in his creation became conscious and personal in

---

144 Ep frat 1.18; PL 184: 320C; SCh 223:200, 74: 'Ideoque durius quidem tractandum est corpus ne rebellet, ne insolescat, sic tamen ut servire sufficiat, quia ad serviendum spiritui datum est'.

145 QH 10.3; SBOp 4: 445: 'Diligat anima carnem suam, sed multo magis suam ipsius animam servet'.

146 After man's creation, God said not only—as he did in relation to the preceding stages of creation—that he saw that it was good, but that it was *very* good (Gn 1:31).

147 Vawter, *On Genesis*, 57.

man.[148] God made man's humanity.[149] That is why, for the mentors of the *mulieres religiosae*, 'the Victorines and the Cistercians, discussion of the nature of the soul, classification of its powers, and the manner of its union with the body was important, as this provided the foundation for the theory of the destiny of man as the image and likeness of God'.[150] In his body man is already a distinguished creature, and because his body is informed by a conscious soul, man is great.[151] Bernard addressed the body directly to congratulate it for housing so noble a guest, a very noble guest indeed.[152] Man's spirit was created with an acute ability to perceive what is good. William noted that the human spirit with its active nature excelled every material object, shone brighter than all material light, and was greater in dignity because it was the image of its Creator and capable of reason.[153] This is not a trivial observation, but an intentional stress on man's created dignity. Ida of Leuven[154] and Beatrice (55,38; 173,69; 217,107; 226,81) each spoke of God as *her* Creator; and Abundus of Villers called God 'the Lord of our life'.[155] They realized very well that their creation would lead through redemption to consummation, to everlasting union with God as intended by him and desired by them.

---

148 Gaïth, *La conception de la liberté*, 35.
149 The prologue of Ida Lewis' biography (*AA SS* Oct., 13: 107, 1) states that God, the lover of men, is the one from whom, and out of whom, and by whom man's intellect, mind, and reason were produced, are and remain ('Nihil dubium est quin humanator hominum, a quo et ex quo et per quem intellectus et mens et ratio perducuntur, et sunt, et permanent').
150 Bernard McGinn, Introduction to *Three Treatises on Man. A Cistercian Anthropology*, CS 24 (Kalamazoo, MI, 1977) 20.
151 Bernard, QH 14.1; SBOp 4: 469: 'Secundum corpus egregiam creaturam...magna res est homo'. See also O. Schaffner, 'Die "nobilis creatura" des hl. Bernhards von Clairvaux', *GL* 23 (1950) 43–53.
152 Adv 6.3; SBOp 4: 192: 'Nobilem hospitem habes, o caro, nobilem valde'. Ida Lewis used the same expression, saying in *AA SS* Oct. 13: 122, 50, that the soul is the body's guest: 'hospes corporis'.
153 Ep frat 2.2.4; PL 184: 340C; SCh 223: 308, 199: 'Spiritus enim hominis in appetitu boni, subtilis et efficacius naturae conditus, et in arce creatricis sapientiae, omni corpore melior, omni etiam luce corporea lucidior ac dignior ob imaginem Creatoris, et capacitatem rationis'.
154 *AA SS* April 2: 171, 5; 172, 6–7; 174, 14; 180, 34.
155 A. Frenken, 'Vita Abundi', *Citeaux* 10 (1959) 19, l. 7.

At the command of the unifier of things, earthen clay and the spirit of life became intimately bonded.[156] There is a natural unity between body and soul,[157] a native unity whereby soul and flesh give birth to one man.[158] In a letter, Hadewijch sums up in a single sentence several of these pervasive themes:

> When you descend the mountain, you must walk erect, that is, although you must at times come down to the level of supplying your needs and feel the exigencies of your body, you must nevertheless keep your desires lifted up to God.[159]

Man resembles the Creator, for his spirit enjoys a certain ubiquity in relation to the body, just as God is actively and totally present in the whole of his creation.[160] The ontological distance between the infinite God and created man remains the same: only God, 'the Holy Trinity...is what it possesses and what it is always and unchangeably'.[161] The smallness of the creature can in no way be compared with the lofty greatness of the Creator, said Ida Lewis' biographer.[162] Or, as Hadewijch expressed it simply: 'God is God, and man is man'.[163]

---

156 Bernard, Nat 2.1; SBOp 4: 252: 'Qualis artifex, qualis unitor rerum, ad cuius nutum sic conglutinentur sibi limus terrae et spiritus vitae'.

157 Bernard, Div 84.1; SBOp 6/1: 320: 'Unitas naturalis est inter corpus et animam'.

158 Bernard, Csi 5.8.18; SBOp 3: 482: 'Et est nativa [unitas], qua anima et caro unus nascitur homo'.

159 Letter 15; VM, *Brieven*, 1: 128, ll. 97–101.

160 William, Ep frat 2.3.16: PL 184, CD; SCh 223: 350, 260: 'Sicut ubique est Deus, et ubique totus est in creatura sua, sic et in corpore suo omnis vivens anima'. This theme is already found in Augustine and Claudianus Mamertus. See McGinn, *Three treasises on Man*, CF 24: 42.

161 Bernard, SC 85.5; SBOp 2: 280–81: 'Sola summa et increata natura, quae est Trinitas Deus,...quod habet est, et quod est, semper et uno modo est'.

162 *AA SS* Oct. 13: 121, 48: 'Modicitas creaturae, comparari non praevalet excelsae magnitudini Creatoris'.

163 Letter 28; VM, *Brieven*, 1: 238, l. 231: 'Jc sach gode god ende den mensche mensche'. The authenticity of this letter is questioned by J. Reynaert, *Beeldspraak*, 425–27; *Id.*, 'Attributie-problemen in verband met de "Brieven van Hadewijch"', *OGE* 49 (1975) 225–47; 225–38; and maintained by F. Willaert, 'Is Hadewijch de auteur van de XXVIIIe Brief?', *OGE* 54 (1980) 26–38. Authentically Hadewijch or not, the statement that God is God and man

MAN AND HIS CREATOR

The creation of man's habitat and of man himself was by no means God's last creative word. As a 'reasonable animal' man outranks all other visible creatures, the stewardship of which is entrusted to him. Both his own constitution and his responsibility as steward point to a relationship with the Creator more intimate than anything his creatureliness could expect.

The Archetype of the Image.

The Greek and the Latin Fathers were in agreement that the first person within the Trinity is the 'font and source of divinity'.[164] Gregory of Nyssa applied the term 'archetype' to the Father in relation to the Son.[165] The Father is the archetype of whom the

---

[only] man is in line with Gregory of Nyssa's repeatedly affirmed teaching: it is impossible for man to have an adequate understanding of God; he never will be able to cross the frontier of being mere man. See W. Völker, *Gregor von Nyssa*, 36: 'Der Mensch mit seiner Erkentniss kann niemals die Grenzen überschreiten, die ihm durch sein Mensch sein gezogen sind'. See also R.E. Heine, *Perfection in the Virtuous Life. A Study in the Relationship Between Edification and Polemical Theology in Gregory of Nyssa's 'De Vita Moysi'*, Patristic Monograph Series 2 (Cambridge, MA, 1975) 49–50: A 'basic distinction that Gregory sees between God and man, the uncreated and created [is] a distinction which has its roots in the problem that all things pertaining to man are characterized by mutability, while God is immutable'. This was also pointed out by Norbert De Paepe, *Hadewijch. Strofische Gedichten*, 162. The reference on p.161 to Hadewijch's sixth letter, wherein she differs, according to De Paepe, from Bernard and William in relation to 'original sin', seems to refer to a not yet acquired participation in God's beatitude. If this is the case, Hadewijch is in line with Gregory of Nyssa, not unknown to her (Bernard Spaapen, 'Hadewijch en het vijfde visioen', *OGE* 45 [1971] 143–55), and that would make a difference. In this connection, see Roger Leys, *L'Image de Dieu chez Saint Grégoire de Nysse. Esquisse d'une doctrine*, Museum Lessianum, Section théologique 49 (Brussels-Paris, 1951; henceforth cited: *L'Image de Dieu*) 39: 'Grégoire ne pense pas la relation du fini à l'Infini selon la catégorie aristotélicienne de cause et d'effet mais selon celle, platonicienne, de participation, laquelle pose devant l'esprit, entre le fini qu'il appréhende et l'Infini qu'il pressent, la relation médiatrice d'image à exemplaire'.

164 See above, n. 23.

165 See David L. Balás, *Methousia Theou. Man's Participation in God's Perfection According to Saint Gregory of Nyssa* [henceforth cited: *Man's Participation*], Studia Anselmiana 55 (Rome, 1966) 70, n.115, where several references are listed.

Son is properly said to be not in his image, but his Image,[166] the only perfect,[167], the pre-eminent Image.[168]

The archetype of creation—and this without beginning, from all eternity—is the Father's Son, his Image, the first form (*forma prima*) as Augustine called it,[169] which conceals in Itself the prototypes or 'ideas' of all creatures.[170] When the Father creates, he does it according to his Word, his Idea, called *noūs*, the mind, in Greek.[171] For Augustine and his followers the Father's Word and Image are not an abstract idea but a person, who as archetype contains in himself the reasonable causes of all things. In this sense Hadewijch related in one of her visions that

'I saw him whom I sought. His Countenance revealed itself

---

166 Gilson, *Introduction*, 277; - on Hugh, *Adnotationes in Pentateuch* 7; PL 196: 37CD; – on William, Nat am 11. 34; PL 184: 402B.

167 Richard, *De Trinitate* 6.11; PL 196: 975B: 'Solus Dei Filius imago Patris dicitur'.

168 Bernard, SC 80.3; SBOp 2: 278: 'Imago non parum eminet'.

169 *De Trinitate* 8.10.14; PL 42: 960C. See also, Charles Couturier, 'La structure métaphysique de l'homme d'après saint Augustin,' *AM*: 1: 543–50; 544. More augustinian references are listed by Henri de Lubac, *The Mystery of the Supernatural*, ET by R. Sheed (London-New York, 1967) 303, n.49, and by D.N. Bell, 'The vision of the world and the archetypes in the Latin spirituality of the Middle Ages', *AHDL* 44 (1977) 16, n.51. Many twelfth-century authors admit with Augustine that the Word, the Father's Image, is the archetype of creation; see Javelet, *Image*, 1: 114.

170 Vladimir Lossky, *The Mystical Theology of the Eastern Church* (rpt Crestwood, NY, 1976) 131: 'In the tradition of the Eastern Church... the image of God is the ordering of the human person toward its Archetype'. On how the twelfth-century authors in the West viewed this archetype, see Javelet, *Image*, 1: 102–10. The term 'Archetype' does not have here the same meaning as it has for Carl Jung. For misleading uses of 'Archetype' in a theological context, see Anthony Baxter, 'The term 'archetype' and its application to Jesus Christ', *HJ* 25 (1984) 19–38.

171 In his Adv Abl; PL 180: 270CD, William opposes Abelard to Plato who, when questioned about the origin of all things, admitted man's ignorance and referred to the mind of the supreme God in whom are contained the original and reasonable causes (*rationales causae*) of all things. The Platonic School of Chartres followed instead the Greek view by calling the *noūs* the archetype of creation. Bernard McGinn explains in 'Isaac of Stella and the Divine Nature', *AC* 29 (1973) 3–56; 37–42, how Isaac was influenced at this point by Chartres.

with such clarity that I recognized in it all the countenances and all forms that ever existed and ever shall exist'.[172]

Beatrice also examined 'the very causes of things flowing from the fountain of eternal justice,... unattainable by earthly intellects' (223,83). Master Hildebrand, likely a monk from Himmerod in the Rhineland writing in the last part of the thirteenth century, said to Christ: 'In you all that is from you and all that is out of you will, through you, be given out to be seen'.[173] As Paul wrote: 'God's Son is the image of the unseen God and the firstborn of all creatures, for in him were created all things in heaven and on earth, everything visible and invisible' (Col 1:15–16a). This statement, connected with other biblical passages, led to deductions of great importance.[174] Because man is made by and according to God's uncreated Image,[175] and because this Image became man, man's relationship to God took on the quality of an even more intimate alliance between them, with all the implications this contains. Not only is man directed toward his own archetype, but he shares in the directedness of the Word

---

172 Vision 6; VM, *Visioenen*, 1: 67, ll. 43–44.

173 *Contemp*; PL 180: 1691–2: 'In te quidquid est a te, videre dabitur per te...et omne quod est ex te'. Bell called attention to this text in his study , 'The vision of the world', (see above, n.169) p.12. In a final remark (p. 31, n.132) Bell writes that Hildebrand was a man 'born a century too late—a pre-scholastic 'spirituel' in a scholastic world'. Given the *mulieres religiosae* in his neighborhood I would be inclined to cut 'a century' down to, perhaps, a half century.

174 Isaac of Stella, *Sermo* 9; PL 194: 1719C expressed it metaphorically: 'God's word is a book twice written, once inside and once outside. In the first the Father wrote from all eternity everything once and for all. From this book was transcribed into the second, i.e. the rational mind, all that can be read therein. The latter book is the image of the first' (without being a photocopy!).

175 Robert Javelet, 'La Réintroduction de la liberté dans les notions d'image et de ressemblance, conçus comme dynamisme' [henceforth cited *La Réintroduction*], in *Miscellanea Medievalia: Der Begriff der Repräsentation im Mittelalter. Stellvertretung, Symbol, Zeichen, Bild*, A. Zimmermann ed. (Berlin-New York, 1971) 1–34; 24: 'Le Verbe, en tant qu'Image, est lui-même relation, un 'ad' [toward] vers le Père, et l'âme qui n'est pas même image, mais simplement un 'ad' vers Lui, participe à son élan vers l'Archétype' [of the Word toward the Father].

toward his Father, the supreme Archetype.[176] Through Christ, the incomprehensible God made his invisibility visible in human form, showing that man's origin and his goal were wedded to God's love, the very essence of his Being.

The Greek Fathers maintained that man is God's image through the mediation of the incarnate Word.[177] According to Gregory of Nyssa man is made in the image, not, as we would expect, of God, but of Christ,[178] who shows us the way we should follow in our ascent to God. In order to follow Christ, man should by his free will yield to grace.[179] Augustine conceived the created image in man not as something static and abstract, but as operative, active,[180] and immediate,[181] indicating that man has to affirm that image by clinging to his God,[182] and by striving toward union with him with the help and grace of God's Son-made-man.[183] Though Bernard exhorted his monks to recognize 'more fully the soul's origin',[184] he added little to the consideration of God or Christ as archetype. His attention went mostly to Christ as God's Word, the soul's Bridegroom, the basis of his mystical theology.[185]

176 André Feuillet, 'La Création de l'Univers d'après l'Epître aux Colossiens (1:16a)', *NTS* 12 (1966) 1–9; 7: 'Le Christ incréé est comme le miroir dans lequel Dieu lui-même a contemplé le plan de l'univers lorsqu'il a créé'.

177 J. Kirchmeyer, 'L'Eglise grecque... L'Archétype de l'image', *DSp* 6: 814–15: 'An expression that covered divergent explanations'.

178. Leys, *L'Image de Dieu*, 95 and 124–25. Stressing God's ineffable incomprehensibility, Gregory's polemics with the Eunomians compelled him to speak of Christ as the mediating exemplar of man as image, for only in Christ did the archetypal God become apparent.

179. Leys, *L'Image de Dieu*, 139; W. Völker, *Gregor von Nyssa*, 45 and 49–50. Völker (73) pointed out that Gregory's presentation at this point appears only in his *De hominis opificio*.

180 Sullivan, *The Image of God*, 50.

181 *Diversae Quaestiones* 51.2; PL 42: 33: 'nulla interposita creatura'.

182 *De Trinitate* 12.11.16; PL 42: 1006–7.

183 Augustine's trinitarian theology, which is more a theological spirituality, is also based on his interpretation of Gn 1:26. It is a God speaking in the plural as Trinity, who is the source and cause of man's existence (*De Trinitate* 12.6.6.; PL 42: 1001). Augustine looking at man, used his psychological analogies to find there an analogical trinity of the Trinity, of which more below.

184 SC 81.1; SBOp 2: 284: 'anima suam plenius agnoscat originem'.

185 Delfgaauw, *Saint Bernard*, 165, n.75, where some references are collected.

All three of these Fathers of the Church stressed that man is not God's equal image as the Son is, but that he shares in the Son's divinity to some extent, i.e. by participation.[186] This may also be what Beatrice had in mind when she wrote that 'Christ modeled her soul in his own image and informed it most fittingly with a certain proportionality' (166,28), that is, through participation.

Beatrice reminded herself frequently that she was made in the image of God (108,34; 236,40), or of the Divinity (124,84), of Christ (136,65; 166,28) or to God's image and likeness (121,34). Hadewijch in one of her letters recommended that somebody dear to her, 'follow your being in which God created you'.[187] Using augustinian terms, she wrote in a poem apparently addressed to some acquaintance: 'I pray the Holy Trinity...as it honored you with its image'.[188] As far as it is possible for the *mulieres religiosae* to touch us through their biographies and writings, they seem to have realized that their being made in God's image called for an existential relationship by means of a living and loving response, or as William, addressing God, put it: 'We were created for you by yourself'.[189]

Man's Pre-existence in his Archetype.

The entire range of created reality in time and space existed from all eternity in the mind of the Creator. As Hugh stated: 'From within God knows everything that is, and was, and will be. He has no need to know anything from without'.[190] God's Word did not begin to be the archetype of creation with the act of creating. Quite the reverse. All existing things existed from the beginning in the infinite mind of the maker. They were there, moreover, in a way that was yet more perfect, because they existed yet more

---

186 On Gregory of Nyssa, see Leys, *L'Image de Dieu*, 47–49 and 125; – on Augustine, *De Trinit*ate 7.3.5; PL 42: 938; – on Hugh, *Adnotationes in Penteteuch*. 7; PL 175: 37CD; – on Bernard, SC 80.3; SBOp 2: 278; SC 81.4; SBOp 2: 286; – on William, Nat corp, PL 180: 717C.

187 Letter 6; VM, *Brieven*, 1: 62, ll. 191–92.

188 *Poems in Couplets*, VM, *Mengeldichten*, 27, ll. 5 and 7.

189 Med 1.3; PL 180: 206A: 'Ad te a te creati sumus'. More texts of William referring to pre-existence can be found in D. N. Bell, *The Image*, 91.

190 *De Sacramentis* 1.2.15; PL 176: 212.

truly in the Word, sharing in the eternal and immutable.[191] Isaac of Stella echoed Augustine when he wrote:

> In the Word, the archetype, all things exist not only by an eternal present prescience but also potentially, for the Word of God is source, that is, the examplar of all things which are or can be. Whatever would come into actual existence existed eternally in the mind and the will of the Word, where they were more truly than before their creation, together with the infinity of things never yet created.[192]

In a direct address to God, William speaks in the same vein:

> Your foreknowledge, o my God, is one thing with your wisdom, which is with you from all eternity, and so would it have been with you, had never a creature existed. It is the eternal ground of all that happens in time, and by that same foreknowledge all creatures come to be in their own time. And yet creation was never in the future in regard to you, for life was in your consubstantial Word, who made all that was made. In him was life, as it was to be in the future, exactly as it was to be, because life was in him.[193]

We would say that God's temporal plan is clearly distinguished from his ideal plan, but terminological precision is not always the hallmark of pre-scholastic writers. When 'from the beginning', *ab initio*, is used, it can mean pre-existence, predestination, and even the original state of creation. This last meaning applies to Beat

---

191 Augustine, *De Genesi ad litteram* 5.15.33; PL 34: 332–33: 'Et utique ibi meliora ubi veriora, ubi aeterna et incommutabilia'.

192 *Sermo* 24; PL 194: 1769C and 1769B. For Isaac's contribution to this subject, see McGinn, 'Isaac of Stella and Divine Nature', *AC* 29 (1973) 40–42. Some similar texts from Augustine, Scot Eriugena, Anselm of Canterbury, Hugh, Richard and Achard of St Victor are listed by G. Salet, *Richard de Saint-Victor. La Trinité*, SCh 63 (Paris, 1959) 475–76: *ab aeterno*.

193 Med 1; PL 180: 206B; CF 3:91, whence this translation is taken. John Hick's questions made in regard to 'What is Man ?' in his *Death and Life*, 2nd ed. (London, 1985) 35–54, do not match the positive statements made by Hugh, Isaac, and William.

rice's use of *ab initio* in two passages (124,84; 236,42), while in 174,87 it refers to predestination,[194] as it does in the biography of her friend, Ida of Nivelles.[195] In her eleventh vision, Hadewijch saw symbolically 'the perfection of her original image, while her created nature was [here] still growing toward it',[196] and in her first vision Christ said to her: 'Stand erect, for you are standing erect in me from all eternity, in total conformity and without guilt'.[197]

The Archetype and Man's Predestination.

At this point we must narrow our attention from the pre-existence of all things to focus on man, who 'surpasses the whole of creation as a revelation of God, for he is made to the image and likeness of God'.[198] The relation of the divine archetype to man is unique, for they exist for one another: the archetype calls forth its image, which reflects back and aspires toward its archetype. Man's pre-existence flows into his predestination. Yet, this does not happen necessarily. Both poles of the relationship are free agents, and the created being is inevitably vulnerable, often even unpredictable, in his choosing.[199]

---

194 Beatrice's biography speaks about her place in heaven which she looked at in an ecstasy, and to which she would be admitted when she died. The Latin text (174, 87) has the confusing expression: 'locum a Deo sibi perpetualiter ab initio praeparatum'.

195 Ida's biography mentions that her place in glory had been shown to her, the place which God had prepared for her from the beginning of the world: *Quinque*, 289: 'Dixit quia locum gloriae quem Dominus ab origine mundi in praemium praeparaverat eidem in coelo ostendisset'.

196 Herman Vekeman, *Visoenenboek van Hadewijch* (Nijmegen-Bruges, 1980) 133 .

197 Vekeman, *Visioenenboek*, 41, 1. 341; B. Spaapen, 'Hadewijch en het vijfde visioen', *OGE* 44 (1970) 131.

198 Thomas (of Perseigne), using the words of Hugh. See David Bell, 'The Commentary on the Song of Songs of Thomas the Cistercian and his Conception of the Image of God', *Citeaux* 28 (1977) 17–18.

199 Augustine wrestled for more than thirty years with this problem. At the end of his life he came to the conclusion that 'those marked out by God for salvation are infallibly saved. Their number is predetermined from eternity. God does not positively reject the rest, but permits them to assign themselves to perdition because of their sins'. See J.M. Dalmau, '*Praedestinatio, electio* en el libro 'De praedestinatione Sanctorum', *AM* 1: 127–36; Henri Rondet, *SM* 5: 88,

For the pre-scholastics, predestination did not include predetermination. They admitted only that man is predetermined to exist, first in God's mind, and then in historical time, without human request.[200] On the one hand lies God's absolute sovereignty, and on the other, man's freedom of choice, which can vacillate one way or the other, opening or closing itself to God's grace.[201] Predestination means 'that one, who could perish, will not perish'. The predestined, looked at *sensu divino* (i.e. apart from his predestination) can perish, but looked at *sensu concreto* (i.e. as predestined) he cannot perish.[202] It is in this sense that Ida of Leuven said of a Franciscan that he was elected beforehand, prior to time.[203] Through Christ, man-as-image received an invitation

---

referring to Augustine's *De Correptione et gratia, De praedestinatione sanctorum,* and *De dono perseverantiae,* PL 44 and 45. In the end, says Gilson, *Introduction,* 204, 'le dernier mot d'Augustin sur cet obscur problème est un aveu d'ignorance'.

200 Javelet, *Image,* 1: 118–24: 'Predestination'. Bernard, for instance, paid less attention to the 'discriminatory' aspects of predestination, stressing rather God's eternal love. See Van den Bosch, 'Le Mystère de l'Incarnation chez saint Bernard', *Citeaux* 10 (1959) 173.

201 Cistercian writers usually put great stress on man's freedom: man can turn his back or his heart to grace. Bernard, Gra 1.2; SBOp 3: 166: 'Tolle liberum arbitrium, non erit quod salvetur; tolle gratiam, non erit unde salvetur'. Praedestination grows into justification, but even if man has little to say in praedestination, which is grace as sheer gift, he is personally involved in his justification, which includes grace-in-action, and consequently his own choice. See also Bernard's I Nov 4.4; SBOp 5: 317: 'Non habeo quod mihi in praedestinatione attribuam, sive vocatione. Non sane ab opere justificationis alienus sum: operatur et illud gratia, sed plane mecum'. Man's freedom can impede or realize his predestination, of which grace is preparation and effect: William, Exp.Rm 5; PL 180: 640C. Or as L. Scheffczyk (*SM* 2: 388) put it: 'The freedom inherent in divine love cannot nullify the decision of freedom even in man and the sinner, but can only keep on inviting it afresh. The mystery of the loss of the goal of beatitude cannot be attributed to the lack or lessening of divine love for particular human beings, but only to a love which always respects created freedom and which bears and tolerates the sinner's self-hardening'.

202 Isaac of Stella, *Sermo* 34; PL 194: 1803 AB: 'Qui praedestinatus est, perire potest per mutabilitatem naturae, sed non peribit, propter praedestinationem gratiae'.

203 *AA SS* April 2: 185,14: 'ante saecula tempora praeelectus est'.

to respond to God's creative love.[204] 'Ah', wrote Hadewijch to a
mulier religiosa under her direction, 'may you grow up according
to your dignity, to which you were called by God from all
eternity',[205] and 'to which we are called and chosen in his
[Christ's] predestination, in which he had us foreseen from all
eternity'.[206]

According to William, predestination is preparation for
grace,[207] and when grace is accepted and rightly responded to,
predestination presents no great problem:

> If one is not ungrateful, he will realize that as God's image
> he is foreknown, predestined, pre-elected and known. God's
> foreknowledge of you refers to his goodness, his predestina-
> tion is his goodness already in action, election the work [of
> salvation] itself, knowledge the seal of his grace.[208]

William was speaking in the context of sinful man, but the
shining star in man's clouded sky is God's goodness and love.
God's foreknowledge points, in fact, to its ultimate realization,
the knowledge of the victory of his grace, which William calls the
seal of grace. Between the two lies man's response. Making man
a free person, free to consent to his will, God made him—

---

204 Stephan Otto, *Gottes Ebenbild in Geschichtlichkeit* [henceforth cited:
Gottes Ebenbild], (Munich-Paderborn-Vienna, 1964) 22: 'Bildsein' und 'Ant-
wortsein' sind synomym...Gott erschafft nicht einen Menschen, damit er ihm
antworten könnte, sondern Gott schafft den Menschen, damit er ihm antworte.
Das erhellt schon daraus, dass wir auf Christus hin erschaffen sind, der selber
Antwort an den Vater ist. Christus, das Bild des Vaters, ist nach biblischer
Aussage auch das Urbild, dem der Mensch gleichbildlich werden soll. This
renders well Gregory of Nyssa's idea: 'L'Image n'existe pas pour elle-même,
mais elle est orientée toute entière vers la "manifestation" de l'archétype'. See
Leys, *L'Image de Dieu*, 27.
205 Letter 19; VM, *Brieven*, 1: 164, ll. 37–38.
206 Letter 6; VM, *Brieven* 1: 68, ll. 341–42.
207 Exp. Rm 5; PL 180: 604A: 'Praedestinatio est gratiae praeparatio'.
208 William, Cant; PL 180: 494D: 'Si ingrata non es, quod praescita es, quod
praedestinata, quod praeelecta, quod cognita. Praescientia enim Dei de te, ejus
circa te bonitas est; praedestinatio jam operans bonitas; electio opus ipsum,
cognitio signaculum gratiae'.

according to Bernard—his collaborator,[209] or, to use a modern expression, his partner.

Man can refuse, as Ida of Leuven was aware,[210] and as Beatrice perceived in a vision (216,82). The possibility of perishing is a consequence of our nature; that we do not perish is God's province. But if man perishes, as Isaac of Stella says, he does so by his own fault and, as a consequence, by God's judgment.[211] God never predestines anyone to perdition. It is the obdurate sinner who excludes himself forever from any love-relation with God. By doing so he rejects God in his Godhead and goodness, and by the same token rejects his own true self. That obdurate choice is called reprobation or hell. In a prayer William said to God: 'I think that hell can no hold greater torment than the impossibility of seeing you'.[212] Beatrice challenged the Lord when she addressed him directly in a soliloquy:

> O just and merciful Lord, terrible and very strong, if it is pleasing in your sight that I should sink for no reason into the depth of hell...I willingly consent to your good-pleasure, but I shall bear the eternal separation from you most grievously as surpassing all the horrendous tortures of hell. And even if this is necessary, never shall I stain with the foulness of any mortal sin this wretched soul of mine,

---

209 Gra 14.51; SBOp 3: 203: 'Coadiutorem fecit, cum fecit volentem, hoc est suae voluntati consentientem'.

210 *AA SS* April 2: 174,13: a local tyrant 'omnium vitiorum genere deformatam in se repraesentando sui creatoris imaginem'.

211 *Sermo* 34; PL 194: 1803A: 'Nam posse perire, naturae nostrae; non perire, suae misericordiae. Perire autem nostrae est culpae ac justitiae suae' [Dei].

212 Med 8; PL 180: 231D: 'Non puto in inferno majus esse tormentum, quam tua visione carere'. Something similar is said by the anonymous author of the *Tractatus de interiori domo*, PL 184: 532B: 'Not to see God and to miss his bliss, which man could have obtained, is greater than all other punishments of hell'. This treatise is a compilation of excerpts mostly taken from Bernard. See Philippe Delhaye, 'Dans le sillage de S.Bernard. Trois petits traités', *Citeaux* 5 (1954) 92–105; 96–100. An older text goes back to Guibert of Nogent (d.1121); see J. Reynaert, *Beeldspraak*, 168–69.

created to your image and likeness, even if I have to fight till my heart breaks. But in the day of judgment when you come to judge the living and the dead, I shall offer it to you clean and immaculate, by your grace. And if even then you condemn it to be eternally punished, I shall obey your judgment, humbly consenting and acquiescing.[213]

This is obviously a paradoxical and hyperbolic statement. Not Beatrice's logic, but her heart did the talking here. To be separated from her Beloved was hell to her, both in this life (97,127; 222,17) and in the next.

For the *mulieres religiosae* 'eternal bliss' lay not in a vague future. It meant union with God and a participation in Christ's sonship. Paul's statement that we are to become 'adopted children' of God through Christ (Eph 1:5; Rm 8:29–30 and similar texts) pointed to the ultimate unfolding of the depths of God's love for man,[214] so frequently sounded by Bernard,[215] and William:

God loved us first not with an affective love, but an effective love, since before the ages he predestined us to be adopted sons and in the time of his good-pleasure he poured out his love in our hearts through the Holy Spirit. For, the Eternal loves no one temporally, and he who is unchangeable is not subject to affections. The Spirit of the Lord fills the earth with the goodness of his omnipotence, and bathes all things in the great richness of his superabundant grace

---

213 *Vita*, 146, 29.

214 Bernard, Ded 7; SBOp 5: 393. In regard to this text, Delfgaauw (*Saint Bernard*, 163, n.52) remarks: 'Pour la pensée bernardine, c'est précisément la prédestination, révélée dans la justification qui nous découvre d'emblée notre vraie grandeur: la filiation divine. See also Maur Standaert, 'La doctrine de l'image chez St Bernard, *ETL* 23 (1947) 104.

215 SC 21.6–7; SBOp 1: 125–26; SC 23.15; SBOp 1:149; SC 25.7–8; SBOp 1:167–68; SC 27.7; SBOp 1:186. According to A. Van den Bosch, 'Le mystère de l'Incarnation chez saint Bernard', *Citeaux* 10 (1959) 173,: 'L'amour éternel de Dieu est bien le sens ordinaire de la prédestination des hommes chez saint Bernard'. See above, n. 200.

according to the capacity and measure of each, so that each might take its proper place and willingly remain there.[216]

From all what we have seen so far, and apart from any special insight that some *mulieres religiosae* may have had about pre-existence, predestination, and their own creation, we realize how conscious these women were that the process of salvation began with God's love and would be crowned in proportion to their own loving response. Because of their human condition they could not presume to be able to complete this circle, and this uncertainty caused them some anxiety. Hence their eagerness to receive confirmation that their name was written in the 'book of life' (Rev 21:27). Ida of Nivelles gave one of her sisters the assurance of knowing through a private revelation that her name was in the book of life,[217] and Ida's biographer mentions that one day she was allowed to read the names of many persons in this book.[218] Alice of Schaarbeek, already a leper and segregated from her community, told her maid that her name was written in 'the book of the living'.[219] Beatrice too knew positively that her name was inscribed in the book of life (170,22; 173,61), just as Bernard spoke of his monks as 'having their names recorded in the book of predestination'.[220] Because this final reckoning was held to be all important, such an assurance was highly appreciated. Bartholomew, Beatrice's father, knew it of himself (14,118) and of

---

216 Aenig, PL 180: 440B; CF 9: 116, from which the translation is taken. On the basis of the only twelfth-century manuscript of the *Aenigma*, Charleville 114, John Anderson says that because God is unchangeable, he is not subject to the changing affections man is so familiar with. See also the study of Wolfgang Zwingmann in *Citeaux* 18 (1967) 5–37; 192–226, on *affectus* as used by William to refer to man's affection for God, not to God's for man. Speaking about a few of the most outstanding among the hundreds and hundreds of unknown *mulieres religiosae*, we could recall a saying of William: 'the Holy Spirit bathes all things in the great richness of his superabundant grace according to the capacity and measure of each one'.

217 *Quinque*, 218: 'Certissime [scio] nomen tuum scriptum esse in libro vitae'.

218 *Quinque*, 243–44: 'Liber quem videbat erat liber vitae. Et cum coepisset in eo legere, invenit multarum nomina personarum scripta'.

219 *AA SS* June 2: 481,28: 'Liber viventium'.

220 Asc 2.5; SBOp 5:129: 'Nomina in libro praedestinationis annotata'.

all his children of both sexes (14,121); this is, at least, what the biographer says. As for Beatrice herself, Ida of Nivelles asked of and received from the Lord a sign that her friend Beatrice would be saved.[221] Ida of Leuven also received the Lord's assurance of her salvation for all eternity.[222]

We might think that private revelations would have been enough for these women, but no sooner had the first question been solved than they asked another: why me? Beatrice, 'recollecting herself in her self-knowledge began to ask the Lord why he had chosen her for so lofty a summit' (171,25). After the assurance that he had done so for his own sake and for the sake of his holy name, the Lord gave her three proofs, all leading her to 'walk with continuous steps of virtue through things both sweet and bitter, harsh and smooth' (171,43). Beatrice could also have found the answer in Bernard, who maintained that no one who loves God should have doubts about being loved by God.[223] This conviction was echoed by Hadewijch: 'The sign that anyone possesses grace is a holy life. The sign of predestination is the pure and genuine impulse by which the heart is borne, in living confidence and unspeakable desires, toward God's honor and toward what benefits the incomprehensible divine sublimity'.[224]

We would be very unkind to the *mulieres religiosae* if we were to conclude from this that their interest lay in their own predestination and their search for God was merely self-seeking. If that were the case, they would not deserve to be called *mulieres religiosae*, or even professed Christians. Their sense of solidarity with all mankind, their concern for other people, and their constant readiness to be of service were proof against self-

---

221 *Quinque*, 212: 'Certum salvationis ejus mihi signum ostende'.

222 *AA SS* April 2: 178,26: 'de salute sua perpetua certam a Domino sententiam' [accepit].

223 Ep 107.8; SBOp 7:273: 'audi de praedestinatione...nemo itaque se amari diffidat, qui iam amat'.

224 Letter 6; VM, *Brieven*, 1; 68, ll. 344–49. In her eleventh vision, she 'understood that, since her childhood, God had drawn her to himself alone', (VM, *Visioenen* 1: 115, ll. 86–88). See also *Poem in Stanzas* 12, 1; VM, *Strophische Gedichten*, 157, ll. 3–4; where she speaks of 'the noble hearts, chosen to bear the yoke, the chains of love', a reference to predestination.

centeredness. There is no special need to belabor this point: the extant biographies and writings speak for themselves. These texts, in their honesty, also show that not all *mulieres religiosae* were as deeply committed to this way of life as were the more outstanding among them. We are dealing here with human, and diverse, persons.

Beatrice's biographer assures us that 'with a wonderful charity she used to desire that all those whom the Lord had called to the heritage of the saints by eternal predestination, should be able to understand the mysteries of Sacred Scripture by which they could be formed to right living' (86,49). When in trouble, she fled for help to Sacred Scripture where she found 'many consoling things...about the election of the Gentiles and the eternal predestination of the faithful, and immediately she was greatly rekindled by the fire of devotion' (154,53). Predestination was not merely a private, personal thing, but had both individual and collective dimensions which these devout women often had on their mind and in their heart. As Hadewijch once wrote:

> God grant success to those who strive
> To please the will of Love,
> Who for her sake gladly receive
> Great burdens with heavy weights,
> And who always endure much on her account
> Of which they judge Love worthy.
> I truly wished they should yet behold
> The wonders of Love's wisdom.[225]

---

225 *Poem 32 in Stanzas*, VM, *Strophische Gedichten*, 209, ll. 65–72.

CHAPTER FOUR

MAN CREATED TO
GOD'S IMAGE AND LIKENESS

MAN'S CREATED BEAUTY and his eminence among all other visible creatures did not make him merely the jewel and the responsible steward of creation. This place of primacy was given to him from the beginning as the appropriate expression of a uniquely all-surpassing greatness: that he was, as man, created to God's image and likeness.

Traditionally the statement of Gn 1:26 that man was created to the image and likeness of God has been taken to mean that 'no identity of God and man can or should be asserted but only a similarity'.[1] Patristic and subsequent exegesis strongly argued the impossibility of any identity. But before the *mulieres religiosae*'s time the interpretation of those biblical terms and their mutual relation had gone through a Greek and then a Latin translation, and their interpretation had taken a great variety of shades within a common conviction: image and likeness refer to the spiritual life, i.e. our spiritual relation with God.[2] Man's creation by God out of love brings him so near to God and gives him such a godly affinity, a nobility, and a God likeness that man can with God's

---

1 H.D. Preuss, *TDOT*, G.J. Botterneck and H. Ringgren eds., ET by J.T. Willis and G.W. Bromiley (Grand Rapids, MI, 1978) vol.3: 259.

2 For a short overview on the evolution of the meaning of image and likeness through the centuries, see Javelet, *Image*, 1: xix–xxiii.

help and grace come to share eternally in the bliss of God himself. The many elements included in the notions of image and likeness led to an abundant unfolding of their content.[3] Our perfection consists not in what we have in common with the whole of creation, but in what distinguishes us from the created order and assimilates us to the Creator. All the Fathers of the Church, both East and West, agree in seeing a primordial correspondence between our being and that of God in the fact that we have been created to his image and likeness.[4] The numerous descriptions they have left do not always make easy reading and understanding, for they often looked at image and likeness from different angles. They certainly pointed to 'something divine in man',[5] a discovery which was not altogether new.[6] A survey of the interpretation of God's image and likeness by Gregory of Nyssa and Augustine, two prominent Fathers, and by twelfth-century mentors does not seem to be out of place here,[7] since the *mulieres religiosae* built on the foundations laid down by them.

GREGORY OF NYSSA AND AUGUSTINE

When Gregory seems to distinguish sometimes between image and likeness, he means not that they are distinct, but rather that

---

3 Robert Javelet, *Psychologie des auteurs spirituels du XIIe siècle* (originally published in *RSR*), (Strasbourg, 1959; henceforth cited as *Psychologie*) 95–104.

4 Vl. Lossky, *The Mystical Theology*, 114.

5 Javelet, *Image*, 1: 110.

6 Mircea Eliade. *A History of Religious Ideas*, vol.I: *From the Stone Age to Eleusinian Mysteries*, ET by W.Trask (Chicago, 1978) 59–62 and 391–92: 'Man before his gods'.

7 By no means does the selection of Gregory of Nyssa and Augustine suggest that they were the only Fathers of the Church among the mentors of the *mulieres religiosae*. Their influence has, however, been more fully investigated than that of others, such as Ambrose of Milan or Gregory the Great, who affected them too. The lack of monographs on the latter in relation to their position to man's creation to God's image and likeness, and the limited scope of Beatrice's context regretfully do not allow us to take them into consideration here. The interest of Cistercians in Ambrose and Gregory the Great should not be underestimated. See Jean Baptiste Auberger, *L'Unanimité cistercienne primitive: Mythe ou réalité?* (Achel, 1986) q.v. Ambroise and Grégoire. [This publication is henceforth cited as *L'Unanimité cistercienne*].

they are two aspects of one reality.[8] Both terms are, in fact, so intimately connected that they coincide and could be said to be synonymous.[9] Reason, freedom and love make up man's image and likeness, and give him an affinity with God. The image invites and urges us toward participation in the divine perfections which are God essentially.[10] Holding the image and likeness together is up to fragile man.[11] He can with God's help choose to be faithful to himself and to his God by responding in love or he can turn his back to God's grace. In the latter case he dishonors the respect God has for his freedom, and disowns God. In one way he loses the image, in another he retains it now smeared and obscured.[12] Forfeiting the likeness, however, he scatters his dignity and loses the privileges connected with it, especially that of immortality, mastery of the passions (*apatheia*), and virtuousness.

And this is what happened.[13] Man opted for his 'garments of skin', *viz.* his human condition in a corrupted and mortal state, without the benefits inherent in the likeness.[14] In the abundance of his infinite love, the immutable God did not renounce his eagerness to be engaged in a love-relationship with man.[15] He knew all along what would happen to paradisiacal

---

8 Hans von Balthasar, *Présence et pensée. Essai sur la philosophie religieuse de Grégoire de Nysse* (Paris, 1942; henceforth cited as *Présence et pensée*) 88–89; Leys, *L'Image de Dieu*, 116.

9 Jean Daniélou, *Platonisme et Théologie mystique. Essai sur la doctrine spirituelle de saint Grégoire de Nysse*, Théologie 2 [henceforth cited as *Platonisme*], (Paris, 1944) 52; J. Gaïth, *La conception de la liberté*, 45.

10 W. Völker, *Gregor von Nyssa*, 67; D. Balás, *Man's Participation*, 141–42.

11 J. Daniélou, *Platonisme*, 64–65, to be completed by D. Balás, *Man's participation*, 149, n.47, and E. von Ivánka, *Plato Christianus*, 175–77.

12 Balás, *Man's Participation*, 149: 'Insofar as man's nature (rationality and freedom) and its essential ordination to the sharing of divine perfections could not be lost, the image remained and was only covered by sin; but insofar as the image included also the further partaking of divine goodness, of which man was now deprived [by his free refusal], the image of God was destroyed'.

13 Gregory relates to this event the propagation of the human race, not anymore in an 'angelic' but in a 'bestial' way. See E. Corsini, 'Plérôme humain et plérôme cosmique chez Grégoire de Nysse', *Ecriture et culture philosophique dans la pensée de Grégoire de Nysse*, Colloque de Chevetogne 1969, M. Harl, ed. (Leiden, 1971) 111–26; 115.

14 Daniélou, *Platonisme*, 31 and 64–65.

15 Völker, *Gregor von Nyssa*, 45.

man.[16] To remedy the disorder of his obscured image he gave man the means of washing away the dirt which besmirched that image.[17] He made the incomprehensibility of his Being and the infinite immensity of his love comprehensible to some extent through the incarnation of his Son.[18] Through the example of his own human life, Christ showed man the way of return to God. He enlightened man through his teachings, incorporated him in himself through baptism, and strengthened him by the Eucharist and the other sacraments.[19] Divine grace, always available through the Holy Spirit, enabled man to follow Christ amid the vicissitudes of his journey on earth through the demanding practice of all the virtues.[20] Man can, if he gives heed to his nostalgia for his lost original glory,[21] recover the splendor of his original purity, liberty and nobility, and by the same token he can realize his potential for likeness,[22] a goal that some *mulieres religiosae* were intensely eager to attain. The incarnation of God's Son means moreover that man can share in the Sonship of Christ, who became his brother, and can live forever his relationship with God in the intimacy of an adopted son of God, his *Abba*.[23]

For Augustine, image and likeness were connected without being co-extensive: 'Wherever there is image, by that very fact

16 von Balthasar, *Présence et pensée*, 43.

17 Daniélou, *Platonisme*, 64–65.

18 Völker, *Gregor von Nyssa*, 54; Daniélou, *Platonisme*, 58.

19 Balás, *Man's Participation*, 97 and 152.

20 Leys, *L'Image de Dieu*, 70; Völker, *Gregor von Nyssa*, 57 and 71; Balás, *Man's Participation*, 161.

21 Daniélou, *Platonisme*, 90–93.

22 Leys, *L'Image de Dieu*, 115–19; Daniélou, *Platonisme*, 65; For Gregory's comparison of this state with the 'angelic life', see Colomba García, *Paradis et vie angélique*, translated from the Spanish by S. Caron (Paris, 1961) 30–31.

23 Völker, *Gregor von Nyssa*, 52. Thanks to Christ and in cooperation with grace, man can acquire *apatheia* and *parrhesia*. The latter term indicates that shame and fear as consequences of sin are overcome and man's familiarity with God restored. By sharing in Christ's divine sonship this familiarity becomes very intimate (Daniélou, *Platonisme*, 110–23, confirmed by W. Völker, *Gregor von Nyssa*, 238). The very intimate relationship resembles not that between a servant and his master, but that between a son and his father on the level of love and frankness. Beatrice and Hadewijch would later express *parrhesia* by using the term: *coene*, bold.

there is also likeness',[24] but the reverse is not true.[25] The only earthly creature which is formed in God's image is the rational human being, and this image is dependent upon the operation of the inseparable psychological trinity: memory, understanding and will/love.[26] 'The most true honor of man is the image and likeness of God, which is not preserved except in relation to him by whom it is impressed'.[27]

The statement that man is made to the image and likeness of God indicates that he is *not* God's true and perfect Image and Likeness' that is the Son.[28] Instead, man possesses a direct latent participatory communion with God, and also is required to do something about his capacity to actualize this participation.[29] Augustine did not systematically work out a theory of participation because he found it so obvious: the image in man is so called because man *has* the capacity for participation in God.[30] Likeness is the actualization of this potential participation, 'a drawing near to God, which is to become like him, whereas to withdraw is to become unlike him'.[31] In this process God is always present to man, who himself becomes present to God whenever he welcomes him, not in the future, but already here and now, at all times. For this reason Augustine opposed those who dissociated the notion of image and likeness and held that man was created only in God's image and that likeness was reserved until after the

---

24 J.E. Sullivan, *The Image*, 11.

25 Gerhard B. Ladner, 'St. Augustine's Conception of Man to the Image of God', *AM* 2: 867–78; 873–74; D.N. Bell, *The Image*, 36, and the same author's 'Esse, Vivere, Intelligere: The Noetic Triad and the Image of God', *RTAM* 52 (1985) 5–43.

26 Herman Somers, 'Image de Dieu et illumination divine. Sources historiques et élaboration augustinienne, *AM* 1: 450–62; S. Otto, *Gottes Ebenbildlichkeit*, 89–93; Isabel Bochet, *Saint Augustin et le désir de Dieu* [henceforth cited: *Augustin et le désir de Dieu*], (Paris, 1983) 203–04.

27 Augustine, *De Trinitate* 12.6.7; PL 42: 1005. See J.E. Sullivan, *The Image*, 50, from which the translation is taken.

28 Augustine, *De Genesi imperfectus liber* 61; PL 34: 244.

29 Bell, *The Image*, 39.

30 Augustine, *De Trinitate* 14.18.11; PL 42:1044. Javelet, *Image*, 1: 451 expressed this by saying that the image is 'arched' toward God. See also von Ivánka, *Plato Christianus*, 202–05.

31 Augustine, *De Trinitate* 7.6.12; PL 42: 946.

resurrection. As *imago facta*, a created image, man is always related to and aspires toward the *Imago genita*, God's begotten Image, his Son, through whom participation is possible.[32] Image and likeness apply to all human beings; Augustine rejected the opinion that women were not made to God's image and likeness equally with men.[33]

To be able to respond to his God-given, realizable vocation, man as a rational being was necessarily equipped with freedom of choice, without which there could be no love-relation.[34] But man failed to use his freedom rightly and thus lost God's likeness almost entirely. He deformed the image which always remains, however sinful an individual may be. Although capable of deforming himself, man was not, however, equally able to recover and reform himself all by himself.[35] But God would not let his loving plan be thwarted; he did more than put man back on the right track. In Augustine's thought we do not simply regain the blessed and illuminated state of Adam before the fall; through the incarnation God himself undertook the process of healing the wounded man.[36] He renewed him in a way befitting his own infinite love and glory: by an enormous enlargement of man's capacity for sharing in the divinity, through a sharing in the sonship of God's Son.

Unlike his formation, man's re-formation was to be very painful for all of his life.[37] The difficulties result no less from the resistance of the human person to outgrow the restrictions of his self-centered tendencies than from the demand to let himself be

---

32 Bell, *The Image*, 53.

33 Augustine, *De Trinitate* 12.7.9; PL 42: 1003: 'Human nature itself, which is complete in both sexes, has been made to the image of God, and does not exclude the woman from being understood as the image of God'; see also *De Genesi ad litteram* 11:42, 58; PL 44: 452–53; J.E. Sullivan, *The Image*, 49, and C.W. Wolfskeel, 'Some Remarks with Regard to Augustine's Conception of Man as the Image of God', *Vigiliae Christianae* 30 (1976) 63–71.

34 M. Huftier, 'Libre arbitre, liberté et péché chez saint Augustin', *RTAM* 33 (1966) 187–286; 218–23.

35 Augustine, *De Trinitate* 14.16.22; PL 42: 1053.

36 References are given in Bell's *The Image*, 62, n.175. See also I. Bochet, *Augustin et le désir de Dieu*, 342–48.

37 Gilson, *Introduction*, 221.

drawn freely into a loving following of Christ.[38] But when man is willing, image and likeness come together harmoniously in the soul's final deification. This participation in divine life is given by the Father, through the Son and effected by the Holy Spirit, who is not only gift, but also the communion of man with God, just as he is the communion in unity of the Trinity within Itself.[39] The vocation of man's soul to the unity of image and likeness is achieved through participation in the trinitarian life.[40]

Gregory and Augustine approached the notions of image and likeness somewhat differently, faced as they were with different circumstances, often of a polemic character.[41] They were of a different temperament and were influenced not only by common sources, but by diverse contemporary writers. On the subject of image and likeness, they both perceived that image means a capacity for participation in God, and likeness the actualization of it.[42] For both, the original creation of man to God's image and

---

38 Otto, *Gottes Ebenbildlichkeit*, 22.

39 Bell, *The Image*, 62.

40 Javelet, *La Réintroduction*, 10–11; Bochet, *Augustin et le désir de Dieu*, 215.

41 For Gregory, see John Quasten's short overview in vol.3 of his *Patrology* (Utrecht-Antwerp, 1960) 257–60, and M. Van Parijs, 'Exégèse et théologie dans les livres contre Eunome de Grégoire de Nysse: Textes scripturaires controversés et élaboration théologique', *Ecriture et culture philosophique dans la pensée de Grégoire de Nysse* (see above n.13) 169–93. For Augustine's problems with Donatism and Pelagianism, see W.H. Frend, *The Donatist Church* (Oxford, 1952) 227–43: 'St. Augustine and the Donatists'; Robert F.Evans, *Pelagius: Inquiries and Reappraisals* (London, 1968) 66–89: 'On Augustine and Pelagius'. For a short overview of the differences between the Greek and Latin branches of Christianity in relation to the Image, see Louis Dupré, *The Common Life* (New York, 1984) 9–19.

42 Some authors speak of two stages in relation to Augustine's teaching about image: a virtual image as capacity for God, and an actualized image (e.g. A.Solignac, *DSp* 7: 1421). Likewise likeness can be looked at as the ascent toward the realized likeness, a likeness on its way, *in via*, and the likeness as perfect vision, not possible on earth in a mortal body, but only possible after the resurrection, which is of such a nature that the body does not in any way conflict with the ultimate perfection of man (J.E. Sullivan, *The Image*, 12 and 68). The usefulness of the two-stage image depends on one's point of view. When and where the image becomes perfected, then and there the likeness progresses toward its perfection. In the end both converge as the finalized image and the full-blown likeness.

likeness has a rich and varied content, crowned by an unexpected and undeserved enhancement through the incarnation of God's Son, the open gate for a close and intimate proximity and kinship with God.

IMAGE AND LIKENESS IN THE TWELFTH CENTURY

The twelfth century witnessed the emergence of a specialized interest in theology. The 'professional theologians', the *magistri*, showed a pronounced tendency toward abstract, speculative thinking, even to the point of going beyond the *auctoritates* of old, the tradition drawn mostly from the Fathers of the Church.[43] Monastic thinkers were usually more concerned with human experience than with philosophical speculation. They favored a spiritual and mystical interpretation born of Scriptural and patristic reading which accentuated personal experience. This is particularly obvious in their numerous commentaries on the *Song of Songs* where they stress the bridal relationship between God's Word and the individual soul.[44] There was also an 'in-between' group of writers who were members neither of the great schools of Laon, Paris, and Chartres, nor of the school of the Augustinian Regular Canons of St. Victor in Paris, nor affiliated with monastic milieux.[45] But all these three groups were influenced by Augustinian or pseudo-augustinian writings and by the growing accessibility of Greek thought, whether in the original Greek or, more often, in translation. It was a time of renewal in intellectual activity and revitalized spirituality, part of the 'twelfth-century Renaissance'.

Given the variety of writers and teachers with their various audiences and interests at a time before attention was paid to an

---

43 Joseph de Ghellinck, *L'Essor de la littérature latine au Moyen-Age*, 2nd edition (Brussels-Bruges, 1954; henceforth cited: *L'Essor*) 33–108: 'Le groupe scolaire'; M.D. Chenu, *Nature, Man, and Society in the Twelfth-Century*, 270–309.

44 For the characteristics of monastic theology, see Jean Leclercq, *The Love of Learning and the Desire for God*, ET by C.Misrahi (London-New York, 1978) 233–86.

45 de Ghellinck, *L'Essor*, 109–72: 'En marge des groupes scolaires'.

exact terminology, the fluidity of the notions of image and likeness which were used, juxtaposed, opposed, compounded in various ways is not amazing.[46] Relating man to God the Trinity or to
the Son as Exemplar, 'image' was referred to knowledge, rationality, *magnitudo* or greatness, natural gifts, *rectitudo* or uprightness. All these dissimilarities notwithstanding, the common
element was the assertion of a vital spirituality. The disparity of
all those writers does not permit classification in schools; the
Cistercians are the exception because most of them followed
Bernard[47] and, we may add, William.

In the thought of Hugh of St. Victor (d.1141), image was
related to reason, likeness to love.[48] The wrong choice of the first
man did not annihilate the image but perverted it. It still cries out
with hope for restoration. The re-ordering toward God is set in
motion by grace and made a reality by the practice of virtues.[49]
Hugh sometimes assimilated image and likeness,[50] but elsewhere
he distinguished 'in the image' from 'in the likeness', the latter
pointing toward deification.[51] In fact, he has a whole string of
distinctions, but in the end he saw likeness in virtues, drawing
man's steps toward the eminent and all-ruling Majesty.[52] Thanks
to the incarnation of God's Son and the salvation brought about
by him, man arrives at the contemplation of God by which he
finally participates in God's beatitude.[53]

Though Hugh is generally accepted as the greatest theologian
of St. Victor,[54] it was Richard, a Scot (d.1171), who seems to

46 Javelet, *Image*, 1: 212–24, ends his survey with the remark that 'durant
tout ce XIIe siècle les compilateurs et les auteurs fidèles à la tradition des
"auctoritates", particulièrement saint Augustin, ont répété, déformé, adapté,
aggloméré, fondu ou confondu les distinctions reçues, en [les] usant selon leurs
besoins'.
47 Javelet, *Image*, 1: 224.
48 *De Sacramentis* 1.6.2; PL 176: 264CD.
49 *Didascalion* 1.9; PL 176: 747A.
50 *In Eccliasten Homiliae* 2; PL 175: 141D.
51 *Expositio in Hierarchiam coelestem* 4; PL 175: 998C, and passim.
52 *Ibid.*, 1; PL 175: 926A.
53 *Ibid.*, 7; PL: 175: 1055B. Hugh integrates the theories of Dionysius the
Areopagite in his synthesis here.
54 Roger Baron, 'L'Influence de Hugues de Saint-Victor', *RTAM* 22 (1955)
56–71.

have appealed more to the *mulieres religiosae*. He often speaks about the image and likeness in his *Benjamins*[55] and his *Four Degrees of Vehement Charity*.[56] Following, as he usually does, his master Hugh, Richard states that God made man in his image in accordance with reason; in his likeness in accordance with love. Reason pursues truth, likeness the virtues.[57] In his *De statu interioris hominis*,[58] Richard departs from Hugh, however, to take over Bernard's stress on free choice, integrating it in his own synthesis.[59] There is an existential dynamism in the image, a thrust toward its perfection, the likeness. Free choice relates to both image and likeness and determines man's final outcome.[60] 'When one looks into the human heart to find in man what is formed in God's image and likeness, he will meet the free and reasonable choice'.[61] It is the rational person who is free and his freedom of choice is the image of the divine Image Itself.[62] The harmonious tandem freedom-reason manifests another: freedom-love, of which the image is the principle. The deepest meaning of man's creation in God's image and likeness is that God and man are both free. They can enter into a love-relationship initiated and fulfilled by Him who is love, and responded to by man through freedom of choice.

But man did not live up to the potentiality of his free choice.He could lose his initial power (*potestas pristina*) to live up to his call, but having failed to do so, he can never regain it all by

---

55 PL 196: 1–202.

56 Gervais Dumeige, *Ives. Epître à Séverin sur la Charité*. Richard de Saint-Victor. *Les quatre degrés de la violente charité* [henceforth cited: *Yvo, Epître*, and *Les quatre degrés*], Textes philosophiques du Moyen Age 3 (Paris, 1955). The adjective 'violent' (p.101) is not in the original, but was not improperly added in the fifteenth-century manuscripts.

57 Javelet, *Psychologie*, 114–15. For the right understanding of the relationship between likeness and virtues, see Henri de Lubac, *The Mystery of the Supernatural* [henceforth cited: *The Supernatural*], ET by R. Sheed (London-New York, 1967) 127.

58 PL 196: 1117–58.

59 Javelet, *La Réintroduction*, 29: 'Si Bernard est le réinventeur de la liberté, Richard est l'inventeur de la personne humaine'.

60 Javelet, *La Réintroduction*, 27–29.

61 *De Statu* 1.14; PL 196: 1126C.

62 *Ibid.*, 1.3; PL 196: 1118D.

himself.[63] As a consequence he suffers a painful conflict, a life-long grappling to integrate the resistance and obstacles inherent in his human condition.[64] Man is still master of his free choice. His healing can come about if he wills it, but only if he asks for help from him who made the promise.[65] 'O happy fault of Adam, *felix culpa*', wrote Richard in his *Liber de Verbo incarnato*.[66] 'God's Son became man, God's Likeness took on the likeness of fallen man',[67] thus giving him the chance to cooperate in the restoration of the image and the realization of the likeness.[68]

The impressive interest the Cistercians had in this image and likeness can be seen in the several treatises *On the Soul*, they wrote. To know oneself meant to know in what sense one is made to God's image and likeness. Modern parlance calls it theological anthropology. Geoffrey Webb rightly observed that the interest in *De anima* was not 'a special Cistercian province',[69] but it was certainly very important to them. In the last twenty years this has become more and more evident.[70] Bernard did not write a

---

63 *Ibid.*, 1.15; PL 196: 1127C.

64 *Benjamin major* 4.13; PL 196: 149D. Book four of *Ben maj* insists more on the human efforts needed to become a balanced person. because it is easier to indulge than to renounce.

65 *De Statu* 3.8; PL 196: 1158B.

66 *De Verbo* 8; PL 196: 1003B.

67 *Ibid.*, 10, PL 196: 1006AB.

68 *De Statu* 3.8; PL 196: 1160AB.

69 Geoffrey Webb, *An Introduction to the Cistercian De anima*, (London, 1962) 6.

70 M.D. Chenu, *'Spiritus*, le vocabulaire de l'âme au XIIe siècle', *Revue des Sciences philosophiques et théologiques*, 41 (1957) 209–32, particularly 210–11. Of importance is the introduction by Bernard McGinn to the publication of *Three Treatises*, CF 24:1–100, particularly 'The Meaning of the Cistercian Treatises on the Soul', 75–93. CF 24 contains the ET of William's *The Nature of the Body and the Soul* by Benjamin Clark (101–52), Isaac of Stella's *Letter on the Soul* by B. McGinn (153–77) and of the anonymous *Treatise on the Spirit and the Soul* by Erasmo Leiva and Benedicta Ward (179–288). While William and Isaac wrote their own works, the treatise *On the Spirit and the Soul* is a compilation written by an unidentified Cistercian between 1162 and 1191. Its original two first parts, chapters 1–50, were known by Alan of Lille, Albert the Great, Bonaventure, and Thomas Aquinas. McGinn has discussed the problem of the authorship (neither Augustine nor Alcher of Clairvaux) and the context of the treatise (CF 24: 63–74). Gaetano Raciti—cited by McGinn—is correct when he denies the authorship to the oft-credited Alcher of Clairvaux ('L'Autore del

special treatise *On the Soul*, though his *On Grace and Free Choice* comes close to it.[71]Cistercian treatises *On the Soul* have no better defined terminology than those of their contemporaries.[72] Though the following list of Cistercian writings *De anima* is not complete, it is sufficient to indicate what prominence the white monks gave to anthropology. Image and its concomitant likeness were central for Bernard,[73] William,[74] Aelred,[75] and Isaac of Stella,[76] to name only these four. For the purpose of the

---

"De Spiritu et anima"', in *Rivista di Filosofia Neo-Scholastica*, 53 (1961) 392–94], but his hypothetical attribution to Peter Comestor does not stand the tests of Leo Norpoth. Had Raciti and McGinn been able to consult Norpoth's philosophical dissertation (Munich 1924), which was later published as a *Festschrift: Der Pseudo-augustinische Traktat: De Spiritu et Anima. Erstmals gedruckt und anstelle einer Festschrift dem Autor zu seinem 70. Geburtstag am 14. April 1971 überreicht* (Cologne-Bochum, 1971), they would have been spared much time and energy. This extensive and thorough study confirms McGinn's conclusions. Norporth is of the opinion that chapters 51–65 are not original, but were added at the beginning of the thirteenth century by somebody else (p.35).

71 ET by Daniel O'Donovan (51–111) with an introduction by Bernard McGinn (3–50), CF 19 (Kalamazoo, MI, 1977; reissued as *On Grace and Free Choice*, CF 19A, 1989).

72 Bernard has discordant views of the image; see Maur Standaert,'La doctrine de l'image chez S.Bernard', *ETL* 23 (1947) 70–129. Bernard admitted it himself (SC 81.11; SBOp2: 291: 'diversa...non adversa'). William was not always too concerned about the philosophical exactitude of his terminology (Bell, *The Image*, 154–55 and n.126]. Aelred has an 'undulating and diverse vocabulary (Amédée Hallier, *Un éducateur monastique: Aelred de Rievaulx* [henceforth cited as *Un éducateur*; Paris, 1959] 94). The more philosophical Isaac of Stella shows little interest in giving definitions for the simple reason that philosophical definitions cannot capture its true essence (McGinn, *Three Treatises*, 61). The treatise *On the Spirit and the Soul* has a number of definitions, but these are taken from every possible source and juxtaposed with no thought of the possibility of contradiction (McGinn, *Three Treatises*, 74). Thomas the Cistercian is 'not that different from other Cistercians but his terminology is more difficult to work with' (Bell, *Citeaux* 28 [1977] 21).

73 Gilson, *The Mystical Theology*, 118; P. Delfgaauw, *Saint Bernard*, 146.

74 Jean-Marie Déchanet, *Oeuvres choisies de Guillaume de Saint-Thierry* (Paris, 1943) 253; Odo Brooke, 'The Trinitarian Aspect of the Ascent of the Soul to God in the Theology of William of St.Thierry', *RTAM* 26 (1959) 87–88 [reprinted in *Studies in Monastic Theology*, CS 37 (Kalamazoo, MI, 1980) 12–13].

75 Hallier, *Un éducateur*, 30.

76 McGinn, *Three Treatises*, 60.

context of the *mulieres religiosae*, one need only pay attention to the two most influential of them all: William and Bernard.

WILLIAM OF SAINT THIERRY

The soul (*anima*) is incorporeal and imparts life to the body. When this soul is viewed from its intellectual side William calls it *animus* or rational soul.[77] The *anima* is capable of reason, the *animus* possesses it.[78] William explains the peculiarity of the rational soul (*animus*) in his treatise *The Nature of the Body and the Soul*. The soul finds itself the link between God and the body: 'because it is unlike any body since it is made to the image of God, nevertheless, it cannot be equated with God; although it has its beginning from him, it is not made out of him or descended from him'.[79] Yet despite the dissimilarity, the *animus* is, must be, and remains capable of God,[80] and enjoys an affinity of nature with God. 'God, being the fullness of all good, made man to his image...therefore in that he [man] is capable of the fullness of all good, the image is like to its Exemplar'.[81] As Odo Brooke has pointed out, the image is a dynamic force impelling the soul toward its perfection in the likeness.[82] Brooke's statement is according to a competent scholar, 'a true and accurate presentation of William's mystical theology'.[83]

---

77 *Anima* is the soul as the center of activity in the sensible, while *animus* is the same soul as the center of intellectual activity (Javelet, *Psychologie*, 50), a distinction already found in Augustine (Sullivan, *The Image*, 46). William generally uses *spiritus*, *animus* and *mens* interchangeably when speaking of the rational soul (Bell, *The Image*, 96, n.35). Sometimes he writes *anima* when he has *animus* in mind, but in such cases the context generally clarifies what he means.

78 Ep frat 2.4; PL 184: 340C; SCh 223: 306, 198: 'Anima est res incorporea, rationis capax.... Quae ubi perfectae rationis incipit esse, non tantum capax, sed et particeps'.

79 PL 180: 722D; CF 24: 148. Here and elsewhere the citations in English are taken from the ET in CF 24: 103–52.

80 Bell, *The Image*, 100–01.

81 Nat corp, PL 180: 717C; CF 24: 138.

82 Cited by Bell, *The Image*, 102 and expressed in a slightly different wording in Brooke's 'The Trinitarian Aspect', *RTAM* 26 (1959) 98.

83 Bell, *The Image*, 102.

However dynamic and impelling a force the image might be, it is not of itself the realization of this capacity. Image and likeness have to do with a person invited to a love-relationship with a loving God, and love cannot be forced. A free choice and consent are needed, and at this point man is faced with a competition between his *anima* and *animus*.[84] If man chooses to respect and consent to the impelling force of the image, 'he is enabled to understand that he both can and should cleave to him whose image he is'.[85] In this case the *animus* rules the body, while its 'better part' (namely its memory, understanding and will/love) chooses always to dwell where it knows it has received all that it is and has.[86] But if man gives priority to his *anima*, he becomes unreasonable and his animality gains the upper hand. He reduces his ability to activate the capacity inherent in the image.

This potentiality (*posse*) to thrust himself toward his fulfillment, however, cannot be shaken off, for the image itself is there to stay, whatever man does.[87] Talking to God, William said:

> You created me to your image and placed me in your paradise ...I fled paradise and in exchange for the place you gave me, I found a sewer and submerged myself there. I kept the seal of your face...always, but by my actions I rejected it'.[88]

---

84 Cant; PL 180: 494D; SCh 82, 166: 'Adesto [anima] ergo tota tibi, et tota te utere ad cognoscendum te, et cujus imago sis; ad discernendum et intelligendum quid sis, quid possis in eo cujus imago es. Sta in gradu tuo, ne succumbas, ne degeneres': Be wholly present to yourself, and employ yourself wholly in knowing yourself and knowing whose image you are, and likewise in discerning and understanding what you are and what you can do in him whose image you are. Stand in your rank; be not overcome, be not dishonored'.

85 Ep frat 2 5; PL 184: 341–42: 'Et per hoc quod imago Dei est, intelligibile ei fit, et se posse et debere inhaerere ei cujus imago est'. William follows here Gregory of Nyssa. See M. Cappuyns, 'Le "De imagine" de Grégoire de Nysse traduit par Jean Scot Erigène', *RTAM* 32 (1965) 234. The two texts are juxtaposed in Déchanet's *Aux sources de la spiritualité de Guillaume de Saint-Thierry* (Paris, 1944) 43–44.

86 Ep frat 2.5; PL 184: 342A.

87 Several references are listed in Bell's *The Image*, 110, n.92.

88 Med 9.6: PL 180: 233D. This metaphor appears also in Basil's *Ad adolescentes* and in Gregory of Nyssa's *De virginitate*. See Pierre Courcelle,

By sinning 'we fell from God into ourselves, and from ourselves beneath ourselves into such an abyss of unlikeness that there is no hope left'.[89] But only seemingly so. First, man is presented from within with a continual demand to turn back to his Maker.[90] Secondly, the Son of God

> bowed his heavens and came down. He made of himself somebody who should be among us and like to us, so that we might grasp him and resemble him in order to be raised up by him: thus the constant remembrance of this mystery would be a constant remedy'.[91]

By referring to the rational soul's 'better part', William shifts from the ontological to the spiritual level which characterizes his *Golden Epistle*.[92] 'For this end alone were we created and do we

---

'Tradition néo-platonicienne et traditions chrétiennes de la "région de dissemblance" ', *AHDL* 24 (1958) 5–33; 15, n.2.

89 Cant, PL 180: 502A; SCh 82: 200,83: 'Conditi sane ad imaginem et similitudinem Creatoris, cecideramus a Deo in nos per peccatum, et a nobis infra nos, in tantum profundum dissimilitudinis ut nulla esset spes'.

90 Med 1.3; PL 180: 206A: 'Ad te a te creati sumus, et ad te conversio nostra': We were created for you and by you, and toward you our face is set.

91 Cant, PL 180: 502A; SCh 82: 200,83: 'Filius Dei...inclinavit coelos suos et descendit, et fecit de semetipso quiddam in nobis, quod simile esset nobis, quod apprehenderemus; et simile sibi, per quod levaremur: cujus mysterii continua memoria, continua esset medicina'.

92 Javelet, *La Réintroduction*, 15. It would be surprising if Bernard had not known about William's *Golden Epistle* addressed to the Carthusians of Mont-Dieu in 1145. According to a legend Bernard visited this house personally (Déchanet, *Lettre aux Frères du Mont-Dieu*, SCh 223: 84–86; Volker Honemann, *Die 'Epistola ad fratres de Monte Dei' des Wilhelms von Saint-Thierry. Lateinische Überlieferung und mittelalterliche Übersetzungen* [henceforth cited: *Die 'Epistola'*], Münchener Texte und Untersuchungen zur deutschen Literatur des Mittelalters 61 [Zurich-Munich, 1978] 171). Bernard was certainly acquainted with this Carthusian house where he was remembered down the centuries (André Wilmart, *Auteurs spirituels et textes dévots du Moyen Age latin* [Paris 1932, rpt Paris, 1971, henceforth cited: *Auteurs spirituels*], 251, n.3, and J. Leclercq, 'Autour de la correspondance de S.Bernard', *'Sapientiae Doctrina'* *offerts à Dom Hildebrand Bascour* [Leuven 1980] 185–98; 192). Bernard was very friendly with prior Gervais of Mont-Dieu (1150–59/60), at whose request he wrote his letter 290 (SBOp 8: 207) to cardinal Hugh, the former Cistercian abbot of Trois-Fontaines. Though William wrote to prior Haymo of Mont-Dieu

live, to be like God, for we are created to his image'.[93] It is
by, i.e. by following, Christ who is the way that the likeness
becomes restored.[94] God's love, the Holy Spirit, activates man's
animus, and gives him the full ability to be perfectly integrated

---

in 1145, telling him that he could dispose of the *Golden Epistle* as he saw fit,
even burning it [SCh 223: 141, 14]. It became, in fact, widespread and avidly
copied [Honemann, *Die 'Epistola*, 163–215]. In a manuscript of the second half
of the twelfth century from Himmerod (a foundation from Clairvaux), this
Epistola is said to be the work of Bernard [André Wilmart, *Auteurs spirituels*,
251], an attribution which prevailed from the thirteenth century on in the
majority of the extant manuscripts. In 1156 a manuscript in the Cistercian abbey
of Pontigny (which contains a sermon of Anselm of Canterbury as a third book
of the *Epistola* [SCh 223: 53–55] attributes the three books to Guigo I, the
Carthusian [Wilmart, *Auteurs spirituels*, 253]. Wilmart corrected this false
attribution to Guigo [*Auteurs spirituels*, 248–60], and Déchanet was able to cut
the Gordian knot of the centuries-old attribution to Bernard ('Études critiques du
texte de la lettre aux Frères du Mont-Dieu', *Scriptorium* 6 [1952] 196–212; 8
[1954] 236–71). In his editions of the works of Bernard (1667 and 1690) Jean
Mabillon (d.1709) concluded that the attribution of the *Golden Epistle* to
William made by Bertand Tissier in the fourth volume of his *Bibliotheca Patrum
Cisterciensium* (Bellefontaine, 1662) was correct (Jean Leclercq, 'La préhistoire
de l'édition de Mabillon', *AC* 9 [1953] 202–25—noting particularly Tissier's
letter to L. d'Alchery, Mabillon's collaborator). Massuet, who in 1719 published
Mabillon's third edition argued that the attribution in the Pontigny manuscript to
Guigo was correct. Unfortunately, Migne, in PL 184, reproduced Massuet's
Admonitio, thus continuing the confusion over the real author. It is worth noting
that a manuscript from Anchin, written about 1165 in three volumes (Douai
372), has a nearly complete collection of Bernard's writings, including William's
De contemplando Deo and his *De natura et dignitate amoris* which are
attributed to Bernard (Jean Leclercq, 'La plus ancienne collection d'oeuvres de
Saint Bernard', *AC* 9 [1953] 124–33). It is surprising to see Paul Verdeyen
imply that William purposely gave the manuscripts of his writings to the
Carthusians to save them from being subsumed under Bernard's name. See his
'La Théologie mystique de Guillaume de Saint-Thierry', *OGE* 52 (1978) 260,
where he speaks of: 'le geste inattendu de Guillaume, qui à la fin de sa vie, a
confié ses oeuvres non pas à ses frères cisterciens mais à ses amis Chartreux du
Mont-Dieu. Il n'est pas impossible que Guillaume, prévoyant que sa propre
théologie mystique serait noyée dans les flots de la marée bernardine ait cherché
un abri sûr pour les oeuvres dont il était, sans doute, le premier à connaître
l'originalité'.
    93 Ep frat 2.16; PL 184: 348C; *SCh* 223: 350, 259: 'Propter hoc enim solum
creati sumus et vivimus, ut Deo similes simus, cum ad Dei imaginem creati
simus'. See also, Aiden Nichols, *The Art of God Incarnate. Theology and Image
in Christian Tradition* (London-New York, 1980) 142–49.
    94 William explains it extensively in Ep frat 2.18; PL 184: 350AB.

into the dynamic process of deification.[95] Then, and only then, has man's *anima* become truly *animus*, for it 'becomes good insofar as it already loves its good' [God], and without God it could be neither good nor *animus*.[96] Dedicating himself to a virtuous life in fidelity to his *animus*, and striving toward the realization of his capacity for participation, man approaches what has been called William's third likeness. The first is the natural likeness by which the soul's ubiquity in the body corresponds to God's ubiquity in his creation. The second likeness is closer to God 'inasmuch as it is freely willed. It consists in the virtues and inspires the soul as it were to imitate the greatness of the Supreme Good by the greatness of its virtue'.[97] This likeness was described above in the state in which the *animus* wills what God wills: 'to will what God wills is already to be like God'.[98] The third likeness is *unitas spiritus*, unity of spirit,[99] the inability to will anything but what God wills.[100] Man's liberty of choice has then become a liberty of fidelity, the culmination of human perfection, here on earth.[101].

BERNARD OF CLAIRVAUX

The genial and outgoing Bernard and the deep but rather withdrawn William were good friends.[102] Their friendship meant

---

95 Javelet, *La Réintroduction*, 13–20. William himself prefers to speak of *deificus*: being made Godlike.

96 Ep Frat 2.16; PL 184:341A; SCh 223: 310, 201 'et fit animus et bonus animus'.

97 *Ibid.*, PL 184: 348D.

98 *Ibid.*, 2.15; PL 184: 348B; 'velle quae vult Deus, hoc jam Deo similem esse est'.

99 Gilson, *The Mystical Theology*, 127: 'Unity of spirit is a unity, first of all, which is no more than the unity of two spirits...the perfect accord of their structures and lives. The true nature of this unity is expressed unequivocally in the word 'likeness'. The only way in which one spirit can become another without ceasing to be itself, is by way of perfect resemblance to this other'.

100 Ep frat 2.15; PL 184: 348B: 'ut non possit velle nisi quod Deus vult'. See also *ibid.*, PL 184: 349A.

101 Gilson, *The Mystical Theology*, 212–14; Bell, *The Image*, 146; Javelet, *La Réintroduction*, 18–20.

102 Jean-Marie Déchanet, *William of St.Thierry. The Man and his Work*, ET by R. Strachan CS 10 (Spencer, MA: Cistercian Publications, 1972) 24–33.

closeness, not dependency. By sharing their writings,[103] they inevitably influenced one another.[104] Fluid as the terminology might be,[105] the content is much more important, and it is here that we see the fruit of their mutual support.

'God, he who is who he is, not what he is',[106] does not so much

---

103 It was Bernard who, according to Déchanet (SCh 82: 10, n.2) stirred in William the desire to write his own *Exposition on the Song of Songs* in a symbolic or 'a moral sense', as William himself called it (PL 180: 476A), meaning as a song of union between the soul and God. (Jean Leclercq,'Etudes sur Saint Bernard et le texte de ses écrits', *AC* 9 [1953] 117). William almost certainly influenced Bernard in re-ordering his view on the image and likeness in his SC 80–82 (Javelet, *La Réintroduction*, 24). That William shared his writings with Bernard is confirmed by Déchanet (CS 10: 103) and Jacques Hourlier (CF 3: 17). For Bernard's use of some of William's writings, see David N. Bell's introduction to *The Nature and Dignity of Love*, CF 30 (Kalamazoo, MI, 1981) 26–27. It should be obvious that both cooperated in their writings about Abelard. Much more could be said about this interchange, but what has been mentioned is sufficient for our purpose.

104 Gilson, *The Mystical Theology* 239, n.178: 'Each doctrine [of William and Bernard] reaches the same conclusions and leaves enough room for all the essentials of the other, but each travels by its own particular road'. The references given by Gilson could be multiplied, but there is no compelling need to do so here.

105 In his introduction of *Bernhard von Clairvaux. Mönch und Mystiker*, Internationales Bernhardskongress Mainz, 1953 (Wiesbaden, 1955), Joseph Lortz, the editor, pointed out that modern authors have added to the ensuing confusion (xvi-xlii). He rightly regrets that no further clarifying studies were made to complement that of Vladimir Lossky, 'Études sur la terminologie de Saint Bernard', *Archivum latinitatis Medii Aevi* 17 (1942) 79–96. Maur Standaert, in his meticulous, already mentioned study, 'La doctrine de l'image' *ETL* 23 (1947) 102–04, detected four different doctrines about image, but all of them holding the notion of man as *capax Dei*. Wilhelm Hiss came to the same conclusion (*Die Anthropologie in der Theologie Bernhards von Clairvaux*. Quellen zur Geschichte des Philosophy 7, P. Wilpert ed. [Berlin, 1964] 77). Of particular interest is Ulrich Köpf, *Religiöse Erfahrung in der Theologie Bernhards von Clairvaux* [henceforth cited as *Religiöse Erfahrung*], Beiträge zur historischen Theologie 61, J.Wallmann ed. (Tübingen, 1980) 78. Our major objection to Köpf's section on image and likeness (71–81) is that he interprets Bernard from a sixteenth-century Lutheran point of view, while Bernard and his contemporaries—and this applies as well to the pre-scholastic *mulieres religiosae*—enjoyed greater flexibility in their theology and philosophy than did the polarized theologians of the sixteenth century. This is often overlooked (and not by Köpf alone), and confirms the comment by Lortz.

106 Csi 5.7.16; SBOp 3:480: 'Est qui est, non quae est'.

possess love but rather is love.[107] Because God wanted a human love-partner, he made man to his image and likeness.[108] Bernard's greatest concern was to bring the soul to a deep consciousness of her dignity as a free being made to God's image, which gives her an intimate relationship, affinity and propinquity with the Word, God's Son and Image.[109] As Robert Javelet pointed out, one of Bernard's important contributions to the concept of image was his re-introduction of metaphysical liberty. By giving metaphysical consistency to man's liberty, he identified it with person, a being dissimilar to God and capable of measuring himself with him.[110] Bernard is very outspoken about image-liberty-likeness in his treatise *On Grace and Free Choice*.[111] While God has metaphysical liberty by nature, a human person has it as an indefectible gift, inborn in his nature and thus natural.[112] Liberty is inalienable; it cannot be divided or split,[113] and always remains.[114] Man cannot lose it, even if he chooses to do so, because he simply cannot dispose of his person, whatever he does or wherever he is.

A rational soul does three things for the body: it vivifies it, sensitizes it and directs it. Only when it fails in its directive function will it be held accountable.[115] The mind is the seat of the

---

107 SC 59.1; SBOp 2: 136: 'quia non amorem tam habet quam hoc est ipse'.

108 See Köpf, *Religiöse Erfahrung*, 72, for Bernard himself; and W. Hiss, *Die Anthropologie*, 67, n.3, for his 'auctoritates', the tradition.

109 Ded 2.2; SBOp 5: 376: 'Non capit eum nisi imago sua. Anima capax illius est, quae nimirum ad ejus imaginem est creata': only the image gets hold of God, for she alone is capable of it, doubtless because she is made to his image.

110 Javelet, *La Réintroduction*, 21.

111 *On Grace and Free choice*, CF 19: 51–111, which should not be read without a prior reading of McGinn's introduction, *ibid.*, 3–50.

112 Gra 3.6; SBOp 3: 170: 'Pro sui ingenita libertate aut dissentire sibi, aut praeter se in aliquo consentire, nulla vi, nulla cogitur necessitate'.

113 Ann 1.7; SBOp 5: 19: 'Ego divinam arbitror esse imaginem, quae nimirum non assuta, sed insita atque ipsi impressa naturae, dividi scindique non potest'.

114 If not taken from Gregory of Nyssa, this interpretation is close to Gregory's. See Daniélou, *Platonisme*, 115–16.

115 Div 84.1; SBOp 6/1: 325 : 'habet anima tria facere in corpore: vivificare, sanctificare, regere... Sin autem tentatori victa succubuit, hoc illi ad peccatum reputatur'.

free will, and this free will is in God's image.[116] It is in this free will, more accurately in this free choice, *liberum arbitrium*, that man is faced with his responsibility as a human person: to accept or to reject God's invitation to a love-relationship. This is the risk God had to take if he desired love in return, because free choice is the indispensable prerequisite of love. God is *sui juris*, infinitely free and absolutely independent.to make God's image within him bloom into the fullness of likeness, man needed to be, not absolutely independent as God is, but independent under God. Man's independence was such that he could not go astray without willing it, just as he could not be made to stay on the right path against his will.[117] 'Free choice takes its name from that freedom only by which the will is free to judge itself either to be good if it consents to good, or to be bad if it consents to bad. In either case free will knows it has willed when it is certain of having consented'.[118]

What God is looking for is not an imposed but a loving response to his love, a response arising from man's own choice.[119] This is what Bernard called freedom from necessity or constraint, the root of dialogue in love between God and man. To make clear how important this free choice is, Bernard explained what is involved in it: will, reason, judgment and consent.[120] Through its consent to God, freewill is self-actualizing, self-determining.[121]

---

116 Both Augustine and Bernard place the image in man's spiritual nature, but while Augustine prefers to seek it in intellectual cognition, Bernard places it in the will, especially in the free choice. See Gilson, *The Mystical Theology*, 46 and his *The Spirit of Medieval Philosophy* (New York, 1940) 210–13.
117 Gra 11.36; SBOp 3: 191. For a more detailed presentation, see Maur Standaert, 'Le principe de l'ordination dans la théologie spirituelle de Saint Bernard', *Coll* 8 (1946) 178–216: 'ordination par consentement', 197–205.
118 Gra 4.11; SBOp 3: 173.
119 Div 26.2; SBOp 6/1: 194. William seems here to have joined Bernard. See R. Javelet, *La Réintroduction*, 16.
120 Gra 2.3–4; SBOp 3: 167–69.
121 Aimé Forest, 'Das Erlebniss des consensus voluntatis beim heiligen Bernhard', *Bernhard von Clairvaux. Mönch und Mystiker*, J.Lortz, ed., 120–27; 121.

To show how God's image, located in the free choice, is the starting point in the process toward likeness, Bernard distinguished three states of freedom. The first is freedom from necessity related to his freedom of choice. The second is freedom from sin, also called liberty of grace or liberty of counsel; it helps the will, which is oppressed but not suppressed,[122] to choose what is good, i.e. what God wills. This is a time- and energy-consuming re-ordering of man toward God and a growth in love: a demanding striving toward virtuousness.[123] The third is freedom from misery (liberty of enjoyment or liberty of glory) which releases the will from all corruption and from the constraining consequences of sin. Positively stated, it is the delightful fruition which is reserved for the real life in heaven, and is sometimes and for short moments relished in ecstasy.[124] Despite his capability for happiness man made the enormous mistake of willing what his *own* will willed, using, Bernard said, reason against reason.[125] In line with Scripture and the whole patristic tradition, Bernard acknowledged that human sinfulness goes back to Adam.[126]

---

122 Gra 4.12; SBOp 3: 174.
123 Gra 4.12; SBOp 3: 175; CF 19: 68: It is the equivalent of 'Thy kingdom come', coming 'closer to God by degrees in actual and virtuous striving, and, daily more and more gradually extending its bounds. It does so in those whose interior self is renewed from day to day with God's help'.
124 Gra 5.15; SBOp 3: 177; CF 19: 71: 'Those who with Mary have chosen the better part...take joy (*fruuntur*) in freedom of enjoyment [Bernard's third freedom], rarely however, and fleetingly' [during ecstasies]. Ulrich Faust, 'Bernhards "Liber de gratia et libero arbitrio"'. Bedeutung, Quellen und Einfluss', *Analecta Monastica*. Studia monastica 50 (Rome, 1962) 35–51; 42, confirms the findings of G.Bavaud, 'Les rapports de la grace et du libre arbitre. Un dialogue entre saint Bernard, saint Thomas d'Aquin et Calvin', *Verbum caro* 14 (1960) 328–38, and cites John Calvin (*Institution Chrétienne* [1560] 2.2, ed. Benoit [Paris, 1957] 29) as saying: 'Je reçoys volontiers cette distinction'.
125 V Nat 4.9; SBOp 4: 226: 'superbus vero et cum ratione, et contra rationem'. See also Adv 1.2; SBOp 4: 162.
126 Adv 1.4; SBOp 4: 163–64; IV HM,6; SBOp 5:60, etc. In the then still open question of Mary's immaculate conception, Bernard held that Mary was conceived in sinfulness, but sanctified in her mother's womb, before her birth (Ep.147,7; SBOp 7: 392). It comes as no surprise that U. Köpf in his remarkable study *Religiöse Erfahrung* stresses the point that Bernard did not find a satisfactory answer to the question how man can 'in a strange and twisty way' (SC 81.7; SBOp 2: 288), or 'in a strange and evil way' (SC 81,9; SBOp 2: 289) enslave himself to sin. Adam is, according to Köpf, more a prototype of earthly man

Original sin itself is for Bernard 'clearly another matter'.[127] Before his fall, Adam had the first of Bernard's three freedoms, a free choice which he retained after the fall. The other two freedoms admit of two degrees: one higher and one lower. Liberty from sin on the higher level means not being able to sin; at the lower, being able not to sin. Liberty of misery on the higher level means not to be able to be disturbed in enjoyment; at the lower level, being able not to be disturbed. The root of Adam's troubles lay in the fact that, although he received the ability not to sin, he yet sinned because he willed it. Thus he missed the chance 'to appear the more glorious, did he not sin when he was capable of doing so'.[128] This way Adam lost liberty of sin and liberty of enjoyment on both levels, and all men likewise lost them, but because of Adam's fall, they never possessed them on the higher level. From there Bernard deduced 'that in the three freedoms is contained the image and likeness of the Creator in which we were made, and that in the freedom of choice lies the image and in the other two is contained a certain twofold likeness'.[129]

> If with the help, even in some small measure, of those two freedoms [as was Adam's case], it [free choice] was yet unable to raise itself from the good to the better, how much less chance does it stand now that it is deprived of them, of raising itself up by its own power from evil to that former level which was good.[130].... It was, indeed, able to fall by itself, but could rise up again only through the Spirit of the Lord.[131]

---

than the first cause or origin of man's sinful condition. Bernard McGinn (CF 19: 45–48) shows briefly how close to and yet how distant from Bernard's teaching was from that of Luther. See also Gilson, *The Mystical Theology*, 223–24, n.38.

127 Gra 2.5; SBOp 3: 169. 'excepto sane per omnia originali peccato quod aliam constat habere rationem'.

128 *Ibid.*, 7.21–23; SBOp 3: 181–83; CF 19: 78–80.

129 *Ibid.*, 9.28–29; SBOp 3: 185–86; CF 19: 84. See McGinn in his *Introduction* to CF 19: 21–27.

130 *Ibid.*, 8.25; SBOp 3: 184; CF 129: 82.

131 *Ibid.*, 6.23; SBOp 3: 183; CF 19: 80: 'By his will alone, man fell into the pit of sin; but he cannot climb out by his will alone, even if he wishes, he cannot

God's Word, his Son, saw to it that although man had been tricked by the devil's wickedness to strive to become 'like God', he would still profit from Christ's love. And thus—as Bernard has God's Son to say—'I come and show myself so that whoever would be envious of me, whoever would try to imitate me, this emulation would be attributed to him as good'.[132] Therefore, 'that Form came to which free choice was to be conformed, because in order for it to regain its original form, it had to be reformed by that out of which it had been formed'.[133] Christ came to free man's will not from necessity—Bernard argued—but from sin.[134] 'Free choice constitutes us willers; grace, willers of good.[135] This, however, should be well understood:

What was begun by [creative] grace alone, is completed by [saving] grace and free choice together, in such a way that they contribute to each other new achievement not singly but jointly; not by turns but simultaneously. It is not as if grace did half the work and free choice the other; but each does the whole work, according to its peculiar contribution. Grace does the whole work and so does free choice—with this one qualification: that whereas the whole is done *in* free choice, the whole is done *of* grace.[136]

The situation of the first man is also ours: by free choice we have still to choose and we do so freely:

Take away free choice and there is nothing to be saved. Take away grace and there is no means of saving. Without

---

not sin'. *Ibid.*, 10,35; SBOp 3: 190; CF 19: 90: 'To rise up again he needs the Spirit of the Lord'.
   132 Adv 1.4; SBOp 4: 164. William expresses it in the same way: Nat am 11.34; PL 184: 401B.
   133 Gra 10.33; SBOp 3: 189; CF 19: 89.
   134 *Ibid.*, 3.7; SBOp 3: 171; CF 19: 63.
   135 *Ibid.*, 6.16; SBOp 3: 178; CF 19: 72.
   136 *Ibid.*, 14.47; SBOp 3: 200; CF 19: 106.

the two combined this work cannot be done.... God is the author of salvation, the free willing faculty merely capable of receiving it. What therefore is given by God alone to free choice alone, can no more happen without the recipient's consent than without the bestower's grace...for to consent is to be saved.[137]

Consenting to the Word and his efficient grace,[138] man—like the prodigal son—leaves the foreign country, the land of unlikeness,[139] and goes back to his homeland,[140] the land of likeness.[141]It is in this return that man accomplishes the purpose of his creation: 'No one seeks you [God], unless he already found you'.[142]

In his sermons *On the Song of Songs*, Bernard speaks of the mystical relationships that exist between the Word and the soul, the Bridegroom and the bride.[143] In sermons 80–82, however,

---

137 *Ibid.*, 1.2; SBOp 3: 166–67; CF 19: 54–55.

138 SC 85.1; SBOp 2: 308.

139 'The land of unlikeness' is a theme which goes back to Augustine. See a.o. Pierre Courcelle, 'Tradition néo-platonicienne (see above n.88) . *Id.*, 'Témoignages nouveaux "de la region de dissemblance"', *Bibliothèque de l'Ecole des chartes* 118 (1960) 20–36, with further additions by R. Javelet, *Image*, 2, 239–43. J.M. Déchanet, 'Les fondements et les bases de la spiritualité Bernardine', *Citeaux* 4 (1953) 292–313; 297, made the observation that for Bernard, *regio dissimilitudinis* does not necessarily imply the idea of the fall: 'C'est tout simplement la condition terrestre par opposition au ciel'. J.B. Auberger, *L'Unanimité Cistercienne*, 302–03, suggests that 'perhaps' William passed the expression 'land of unlikeness' on to Bernard.

140 Par 1.7; SBOp 6/2: 267.

141 Javelet, *Image*, 1: 191.

142 Dil 22; SBOp 3: 137: 'Nemo quaerere te valet, nisi prius invenerit'.

143 In line with the tradition and particularly with Origen, Bernard also speaks about the nuptial relations between the Word and the Church. See Helmut Riedlinger, *Die Makellosigkeit der Kirche in den lateinischen Hoheliedskommentaren des Mittelalters* [henceforth cited: *Die Makellosigkeit*], Beiträge zur Geschichte der Philosophie und Theologie des Mittelalters 38, Part 3, A.M. Landgraf ed. (Münster/W, 1958) 155–67. In the preface of his commentary on the Song of Songs (PL 180: 476A), William states modestly that he does 'not presume to treat of the other deeper mysteries which the Song of Songs contains with regard to Christ and the Church', but that he 'will restrain himself... and touch lightly in a certain moral sense in regard to the Bridegroom and the bride, Christ and the Christian soul'. For a fuller account on William in this matter, see Riedlinger, *Die Makellosigkeit*, 167–69.

we hear another bell.[144] Without mentioning liberty or grace, Bernard stresses that the soul is made *to* the image and the likeness of the Word. Between the two there is a kinship: the one is the Image of God and the other is made to that Image. The Image, the Word, has greatness and uprightness and these are one with him, because he has them by filiation and consubstantiality. Man has greatness and uprightness too, but as created endowments. The soul is great in proportion to its capacity for the eternal, and upright in proportion to its desire for heavenly things.[145] It always retains its greatness, but when its uprightness has been damaged it limps.[146] What Bernard had attributed twenty years earlier to liberty is here attributed to uprightness. This substitution could cause confusion, were we unaware that the older Bernard approached image and likeness from another point of view.

In his eighty-first sermon *On the Song of Songs*, Bernard tackles the problem of likeness, describing it as threefold. It consists in simplicity, immortality and free choice and is, as before, still oriented toward the spiritual embrace of the Word. Here, however, Bernard looks not to the future, the actualization of the soul's potential, but to its origin.[147] For God, being is synonymous with being in a state of blessedness; and this is the first and purest simplicity.The soul's simplicity, on a lower plane, is to be and to live. But the soul can be raised up not only to live well, but even to live in blessedness:[148] this is an acquired

---

144 To this point, Bernard has integrated into his own doctrine a number of ideas from Augustine, as can be seen in Huftier's study, mentioned above in n.34.

145 SC 80.2–4; SBOp 2: 278–79.

146 SC 80.4; SBOp 2: 279: 'per magnitudinem, quam retentat etiam perdita rectitudine, in imagine pertransibit homo, uno quasi claudicans pede et factus filius alienus'.

147 SC 81,1; SBOp 2: 284: 'The more fully the soul recognizes its origin, the more anxious it will be to make every effort to reform what it sees in its nature to be deformed by sin, so that with God's help, it may rule itself in a way worthy of its origin, and confidently approach the Word's embraces'. This text is important for understanding the *mulieres religiosae*, as will be seen in Part Three of this work.

148 SC 81.2; SBOp 2: 285.

simplicity. God is also true, absolute, and complete immortality admitting no change or termination. The soul is immortal and in this it is similar, but not equal, to the Word, for plainly it changes in its affections. Its likeness to God has no small dignity, for it seems to resemble the Word in two respects: simplicity of essence and perpetuity of life.[149] The third likeness which enhances the soul's greatness is free choice:

> Something clearly divine which shines forth in the soul like a jewel set in gold. From it the soul derives its power of judgment,[150] and its option of choosing between good and evil, between life and death, between light and darkness and other concepts which are perceived by the soul as opposites. It is the eye of the soul, which as censor and arbiter exercises discrimination and discernment between these things, arbiter in discerning, and free in choosing.... When man sins he is dominated but by his will, not by nature, and he is not thereby deprived of the liberty which is his birthright.[151]

'I am free', says Bernard, 'because I am like God, unhappy because I am in opposition to him'.[152] The third likeness has all the characteristics of the image and the twofold resemblances described in Bernard's treatise *On Grace*. And it is at this point that he refers back to that work, acknowledging that his doctrine is now different from, but not opposed to, his earlier teaching. To clarify his position, he refers to Scripture:

> When Holy Scripture speaks of the unlikeness that has come about, it says not that the likeness has been destroyed, but concealed by something else which has been laid over it.

---

149 SC 81.5; SBOp 2: 286–87.

150 It is what we call today 'the voice of conscience'. See Gilson, *The Mystical Theology*, 50; Delfgaauw, *Saint Bernard*, 152; by Bernard himself it was called 'Christ's vicar': Hum 7.21; SBOp 3: 32.

151 SC 81.6–7; SBOp 2: 287–88.

152 SC 81.9; SBOp 2: 289: 'liber quia similis Deo, miser quia contrarius Deo'.

The soul has not, in fact, put off its original form, but has put on one foreign to it. The latter is an addition; the former has not been lost. This addition can hide the original form, but it cannot blot it out.[153]

Bernard probably borrowed this idea from Gregory of Nyssa.[154] Jean Daniélou suggests that it was William who brought Bernard in contact with Gregory's works, but who gave what to whom and when remains unclear.[155] But the similarity is striking: 'the soul is unlike God', wrote Bernard, 'and consequently unlike itself as well'.[156] The unlikeness is of a moral order and depends on man; the likeness betokens a divine order and depends on God. To be restored to the likeness in its splendor the soul has only to consent to its real nature, its inborn capacity for God, and to God's grace which is always waiting for its consent. It seems likely that William was responsible for making Bernard realize that man as image has a resemblance to his principal Exemplar, the Word, and that the resemblance is threefold, not twofold.[157] Bernard, however, was right in putting

---

153 SC 82.2; SBOp 2: 293. He cites Rm 1:21 and Lm 4:1 to state his case, adding that 'the gold [of the third likeness] has grown dim, and its pure color faded'.

154 Daniélou says that he certainly (*sûrement*) found it in Gregory (*AC* 9 [1953] 53), and Javelet, *La Réintroduction*, 27, admits as much. Daniélou's argumentation is very impressive. The ideas Bernard expresses are those of Gregory, but his biblical references in the whole of *Sermo* 82 do not mention Gn 3:7 or Gn 3:21. This, however, is not a strong argument. Whatever sources Bernard used, he wove them into his own doctrine, as U. Faust [see above n.124] has shown he did in regard to Augustine (p.47): 'Warscheinlich hat Bernhard Augustins Abhandlungen gekannt. Mit grosse Selbstständigkeit behandelt er jedoch denselben Fall und benutzt ihn, um seine eigene Auffassung darzulegen. Nirgends schreibt er einfach Augustin ab'.

155 I have no doubt that the library at Clairvaux was much better stocked than that at St. Thierry, Signy or any other Cistercian houses. It is worth noting that Bernard of Pisa, Bernard's former monk at Clairvaux, who became pope Eugene III (1148–53) asked Burgundio of Pisa to translate some works of Greek Fathers into Latin. See Roger Mols, 'Burgundio de Pise', *DHGE* 2: 1366–69. Eugene's interest could have been stimulated by Bernard through William, by Bernard alone, and even without Bernard.

156 SC 82.5; SBOp 2: 295: 'Inde anima dissimilis Deo, inde dissimilis sibi'.

157 The threefold likeness consists in simplicity, immortality and free choice; the twofold is related to liberty from sin and liberty of enjoyment. See above, the text referred to in n.124.

liberty at the start, because liberty is linked to the rational nature of the soul.[158]

At the end of sermon 82, Bernard advised his monks to think of the question 'Lord, who is like you?' in terms of difficulty, not of impossibility. For when man's unrighteousness, which has made him incapable of loving either himself or God, is overcome, 'there will be oneness of spirit, a reciprocal vision and reciprocal love....Then the soul will know as it is known and love as it is loved'.[159].

THE *MULIERES RELIGIOSAE*

This lengthy digression on man's creation to God's image and likeness has been necessary because the doctrines of these mentors formed the basis of the spirituality of all the *mulieres religiosae*, including the best known of them, sometimes called ecstatics. These positive, optimistic women realized that the whole meaning of life was to be found in God, who created them to his image and likeness.We know for certain that the most outstanding among them had this truth constantly in the consciousness of their minds, in the pulsating desire of their hearts, and in the conduct of their daily lives.This truth was for them like a diamond which they could turn around, admiring its different warm colors and its brilliant rays from whatever angle they looked at it. According to their intellectual development, emotional temperament and spiritual growth they would stress one or another or several aspects of this basic truth, as will be seen below when some of these aspects will be treated in detail. That they were formed in God's image pointed to their ennobling origin with its inherent and enabling potential for God. They chose with God's help to actualize their capacity for God into likeness to him as much as is possible on earth, and to reach never ending fullness in the true life where their union with God would be perfect and eternal.

---

158 Javelet, *Image*, 1: 197.
159 SC 82.7–8; SBOp 2: 279–80.

God was their origin and their end. God also filled the interstice between these two intimately interconnected poles, informing the whole of their lives with love. Reading the writings of Hadewijch and Beatrice makes one realize how fiercely and incessantly they strove in a spiraling struggle to bring this image and likeness together to completeness in the consuming fire of God's love for them and their ebullient love for him and for their neighbor. Both women had an admirable gift, the capacity to articulate their ideas and experiences in a rich and expressive vocabulary.

When we turn to the biographers, we must take their interpretation into consideration. Most of them wrote soon after their subjects had died. They were therefore contemporaries or near contemporaries who lived in the same atmosphere. Working with the written or oral communications at their disposal, they sometimes showed more than mere sympathy, and were occasionally inclined to overstress what they believed to be the proofs of their subject's holiness or her supernatural gifts, at a time when the extraordinary seemed almost ordinary. In their days, books of *exempla* were very much in demand viz. writings with a moralizing tendency, filled with (sometimes exaggerated) stories of persons and events.[160] This is not to say that the biographers misused

---

160 The *Exemplum* has been lately the subject of several publications: J.Berlioz, 'Le récit efficace: l' "exemplum" au service de la prédication (XIIIe-XVe siècles)', *Mélanges de l'Ecole française de Rome. Moyen Age, Temps modernes* 92 (1980) 113–46; Régis Boyer, 'An Attempt to define the typology of medieval hagiology', *Hagiography and Medieval Literature. A Symposium* (Odense, 1981) 27–36; on p. 28 he stresses that 'the very basis of hagiography is the *exemplum*, these texts have been... born of a pedagogical, edifying intention'; C. Brémond, J. de Goff, J.Cl. Schmidt, *L' "Exemplum". Typologie des sources du Moyen Age occidental* 40 (Turnhout, 1982). Examples of this genre include: the *Exordium Magnum Cisterciense*, ed. B. Griesser, Series Scriptorum S.Ordinis Cisterciensis 2 (Rome, 1961), written around 1206, or the works of Caesarius of Heisterbach, particularly his *Dialogus miraculorum*, written about 1220, (ed. J.Strange: Cologne, 1851), or those of James of Vitry (d.1240). See T.F. Crane, *The Exempla or illustrative stories from the Sermones vulgares of Jacques de Vitry* (New York 1890, rpt 1971); Goswin Frenken, *Die Exempla des Jacob von Vitry. Ein Beitrag zur Geschichte der Erzählungsliteratur des Mittelalters.*, Quellen und Untersuchungen zur lateinischen Philologie des Mittelalters, P. Lehmann, ed., Vol. 5, Part One (Munich, 1914). See also Thomas of

the information they had at hand. In fact, it would be difficult to prove that they mingled fiction with fact, even when a moralizing tendency or a special purpose are evident.[161] *Mulieres religiosae* should be taken as they were: simply religious women, i.e. Christians who tried energetically to live their faith. They were not, nor had they any desire to be theologians. They were captivated by Christ's teaching and example, and familiar with the Scriptures, a familiarity fostered and deepened by their daily liturgical worship. Through their mentors they had at their disposal a solid basis for their spirituality. Many ideas in their writings and biographies can be traced to patristic sources.

Augustine, the great master of their mentors, was undoubtedly theirs as well. Juliana of Cornillon (1193–1258), to give one example 'read with much eagerness the writings of Augustine'.[162] Gregory of Nyssa was not unknown to Hadewijch and Beatrice.[163] These women certainly knew at least some of the

---

Cantimpré's *Bonum universale de apibus* (Douai, 1605), and Henri Platelle, 'Le receuil de miracles de Thomas de Cantimpré et la vie religieuses dans les Pays-Bas et le Nord de la France au XIIIᵉ siècle', *Actes du 97ᵉ Congrès National des Sociétés savantes, Nantes 1972* (Paris, 1979) 469–98, and other publications in this same area.

161 They are sometimes accused of heing too credulous, and this is true in some cases. Stripped of their context, medieval events and mentalities present problems for us if we test them by our methods of modern criticism.All too often we miss too many needed bits of information to have a complete report. On their part, modern scholars can slip to skepticism, for it is tempting to dismiss the so-called 'faits merveilleux', Healthy suggestions have been proposed by Peter Dinzelbacher, 'Körperliche und seelische Vorbedingungen religiöser Träume und Visionen', *I Sogni nel Medioevo, Seminario internazionale. Rome, 2–4 ottobre 1983* (Rome, 1984) 57–86.

162 To Augustine's authentic writings should be added the many pseudo-augustinian works circulating under his name at the time. For Juliana of Cornillon, see her biography (*AA SS* April 1:444, 6 [English translation by Barbara Newman, *The Life of Juliana of Mont Cornillon* (Toronto: Peregrina Press, 1989)—ed.]. Other *mulieres religiosae* could be added; for example, Ida Lewis, *AA SS* Oct. 13: 122,52.

163. Spaapen, 'Hadewijch en het vijfde visioen', *OGE* 45 (1971) 143–55. Hadewijch may have read Yvo's *Epître*, mentioned above, n. 56. The *Letter* found its way into another (this time apocryphally bernardine) work, the *Libellus seu Tractatus de Charitate* (PL 184:585–636) to which Vekeman found references in Beatrice's treatise (Vekeman, '"Minne" in "Seven manieren van Minne" van Beatrijs van Nazareth', *Citeaux* 19 [1968] 296). Yvo's *Epître*

writings of their favorite mentors: Richard,[164] William,[165] and Bernard.[166] This does not of itself mean that the *mulieres religiosae* read or heard read *all* the works of their mentors. There were enough *florilegia* or anthologies,[167] *legendaria*[168] and theological or spiritual compilations in circulation[169] to bring them into indirect contact with their masters.

It is not less significant that, within the framework of their tradition, the *mulieres religiosae* took the same freedom as did their mentors. They expressed their insights and experiences very personally, as they found it expedient. And when they did so, they did it well. Their spiritual life was a sharing in the common good at a personal level. As far as the Cistercian nuns are concerned, examples of their fidelity to detailed prescriptions of community

---

makes up the first part of the *Tractatus de charitate*, and it is to this part that Vekeman's citations refer, as Spaapen observed in *OGE* 45 (1971) 137, n. 26.

164. Hadewijch, for example, copied without saying so, as was usual in her day, a passage from Richard's *Explicatio in Cantica canticorum*. See J. M. Schalij, 'Richard van St. Victor en Hadewijch's 10de brief', *TNTL* 62 (1943) 219–28.

165. Hadewijch likewise integrated a passage from William's *De natura et dignitate amoris* in her Letter 18. See Van Mierlo, 'Hadewijch en Willem van St-Thierry', *OGE* 3 (1929) 45–59, and Verdeyen, 'De invloed van Willem van St. Thierry op Hadewijch en Ruusbroec', *OGE* 51 (1977) 3–19. Hadewijch probably knew the treatise as a work of Bernard.

166. This is so evident that one need only point to Juliana of Cornillon, who is said to have known by heart more than twenty of his sermons on the Song of Songs (*AA SS* April: 444,6, and 451, 26).

167 Each chapter of de Ghellinck's *L'Essor* refers to some anthologies in various fields of knowledge, from theology to history, poetry, and love-lyric.

168 *Legendaria*, like the *Speculum historiale* (1244–55) of Vincent of Beauvais, are usually summarized biographies of saints and are to be distinguished from biographies and hagiographies. For an overview of this rather complicated matter, see Guy Philippart, 'L'edition médiévale des légendiers latins dans le cadre d'une hagiographie générale', *Hagiography and Medieval Literature* (see above, n. 160) 127–65.

169 Among them *De spiritu et anima*, of which Norpoth (pp. 229–35) lists nearly one hundred manuscripts in his publication (cited above, n. 70). Of the voluminous compilation on the Song of Songs by Thomas the Cistercian, at least sixty manuscripts are known to exist. See Bell, 'The Commentary...of Thomas the Cistercian', *Citeaux* 28 (1977) 3.

life could be gathered with little effort,[170] and their biographies show at the same time how uniquely personal each was. This applies also to other *mulieres religiosae*. The movement was far from demanding a de-personalizing collectivity.

Some, like Beatrice, repeatedly spoke about being made to God's image and likeness (138,165; 146,36; 247,32), or about being in God's image, without referring explicitly to the term likeness (94,62; 197,42) or they would consider likeness in the state of its origin or its restoration through Christ's sufferings;[171] or they would speak about the likeness without any mention of the image, as happened sometimes, but not always, with Hadewijch.[172]

Their mentors often accentuated the need for a virtuous life to undergird growth toward likeness. The *mulieres religiosae* applied themselves to the path of an ascetical and virtuous life with their whole heart, mind and strength, without need for exhortation. A disciplined life is part of any genuine, deeply spiritual life of whatever form, however different the circumstances of life or culture may be. The *mulieres religiosae* reflect the preoccupation of the Christian thirteenth-century. Hence their strong desire to go back to man's original state of sinless openness toward God, re-echoing what William had said earlier.[173] Beatrice expressed this several times in her *Vita* (121,34; 197,41; 236,41) and in her treatise:

> to serve the Lord faithfully, to follow him vigorously and to love him truly, actively drawn to attain and to remain in that purity, liberty and nobility in which it [the soul] was made

---

170 A general overview occurs in Roisin, *L'Hagiographie*, 91–105. For Beatrice in particular, see 24, 17; 49, 6; 67, 22; 122, 27; 231, 67.

171 Ida of Leuven, *AA SS* April 2: 179, 31: 'Non es tu, illa quam...meo sanguine...fugato pristinae deformitatis omnique foeditatis obstaculo reparavi?'; *ibid.*, 188, 25: 'Tam electa, tam nobilis, tam a primo creationis suae origine perfectissima creatura'.

172 De Paepe, *Hadewijch. Strofische Gedichten*, 162. In her *Poems in Couplets*, she makes an explicit reference to the image. See VM, *Mengeldichten*, 27, ll. 5 and 7: 'I pray to the Holy Trinity...as it honored you with its image'.

173 See above, nn. 90–91.

by its Creator to his image and likeness which the soul must intensely love and preserve.[174]

Hadewijch too saw this recovery of man's original state as indispensable to a love-relationship with God intended by the Creator and made possible through Christ. As she wrote in her sixth letter: 'By his divine power and his human justice God's Son lifted and drew us up to our first dignity, to our liberty, in which we were created and loved'.[175] What Bernard had said: 'no one can seek you [God] unless he has found you',[176] seems to resonate in Hadewijch's same letter when she speaks about the human condition:

> You and I, have not yet become what we are, and have not grasped what we have, and still remain so far from what is ours. We must, without sparing, love all for all; and learn intrepidly the perfect life of Love, who has urged on both of us to her work'.[177]

A virtuous life, marked by 'works of love', is the way to union with God: the *unitas spiritus*, the unity of spirit that the mentors of the *mulieres religiosae* so frequently mentioned. This was the goal continually and most earnestly aimed at by such women as Beatrice (162,31; 193,30; 236,40), Ida of Nivelles,[178] Alice of Schaarbeek,[179] and Ida Lewis.[180] In Hadewijch's words: 'This is always its [a loving heart's] desire and prayer, to be in oneness of love, as we read in the Song of Songs: "Dilectus meus mihi et ego illi" [Sg 2:16 :'My Beloved to me and I to Him']. Thus in the one will shall there be a single meeting of unitive love'.[181] In these and similar texts they all said the same thing, but they

---

174 R-VM, *Seven manieren*, 1–2, ll. 13–18.
175 VM, *Brieven*, 1:68, ll. 338–40.
176 Dil 22; SBOp 3:137: 'Nemo quaerere te valet, nisi quis prius invenerit.'
177 Letter 6; VM, *Brieven*, 1:55, ll. 30–35.
178 *Quinque*, 271: 'ut spiritus ejus unus cum Domino spiritus efficeretur'.
179 *AA SS* June 2: 482, 31: 'anima ejus quasi amicta Deitate'.
180 *AA SS* Oct. 13: 121, 48: 'Unio cum spiritu Dei et virginis [Idae]'.
181 Letter 13, VM, *Brieven*, 1: 113–14, ll. 11–12.

worded it according to their taste, their point of view and the pull of their desire.

The *mulieres religiosae* seem not to have been worried about their or their mentors' inconsistencies in terminology. A lack of precise terminology is not without its dangers, but we today, in a post-scholastic world, need to realize that by overstressing precision we can also drain the vitality from the content. A text from Alice of Schaarbeek's biography might illustrate how a flexible terminology could in the thirteenth-century capture the substantial meaning of image and likeness:

> Interiorly she glowed by clinging to God's image which she bore in her heart, while exteriorly she tried all the time to be consciously present to it in her behavior and conduct'.[182]

The *locus* of the image here is the heart.[183] The'glowing, clinging all the time, trying to be present' belong to the traditionally accepted vocabulary. The opposition between interior and exterior is not so much an opposition as a comparison. As the consciousness of being made to God's image penetrated ever more deeply into Alice's heart, it permeated her exterior behavior as well. In this case virtuous exterior conduct is equivalent to striving toward likeness, as is clear from the string of practiced virtues following the quoted text of the biography.

The realization that God created man to his image and likeness was taken by the *mulieres religiosae* as a demonstration of how far God went to meet them and to invite them to a love-relationship with himself. Striving to actualize the potential of the image through a virtuous life, they made their free response visible by following Christ, the God-Man. To God's gift of himself to them, they reciprocated with the gift, the total gift, of themselves to him.

---

182 *AA SS* June 2: 478,4: 'Intus Dei imagini, quam in corde gessit adhaerendo nituit; cujus foris conspectui omni hora, gestu et habitu se praesentare studuit'.

183 This is compatible with Augustine, for whom 'the word heart (*cor*) is a poetic equivalent of the word *anima*, soul' (de Lubac, *The Supernatural*, 84, n. 27). See also, Anton Maxsein, '''Philosophia cordis'' bei Augustinus', *AM* 1: 357–71; and E. de la Peza, *El significado de 'Cor' en San Augustin* (Paris, 1962).

CHAPTER FIVE

FACETS OF THE IMAGE
AND LIKENESS

N O MATTER WHERE THE MENTORS of the *mulieres religiosae* located God's image and likeness in man, it always had to do with man's rationality,[1] the great gift whereby he stands in a special relationship with God, in whose image he is made. 'For it is by him [God] and for him that the rational spirit was created in order that its inclination might be toward him...and that as long as its life here lasts, it may approach as nearly and as truly as possible to him by the resemblance from which it retreated only by dissimilarity'.[2]

This spirituality always has both God and man in view. The experience of the human condition can seem hopeless as long as one looks only at the human side. But there is always God's side, too, without which the human remains incomplete. 'As long as I am with you [God], I am also with myself; I am no longer with

---

1 Völker, *Gregor von Nyssa*, 88: 'Es ist das, was den Menschen überhaupt erst zum Menschen macht'. Rationality, like so many other terms, does not necessarily cover the same meaning as this term has in modern times.

2 William, Ep frat 2.5; PL 184: 341; SCh 223: 314,208: 'Ab ipso enim ad ipsum conditus est rationalis animus, ut ad ipsum sit conversio ejus... hoc est ut quamdiu hic vivitur, quam proprius potest accedat ad eum similitudine, a quo sola receditur dissimilitudine'.

myself when I am not with you'.[3] And in this too the *mulieres religiosae* followed their mentors.

ANALOGICAL IMPLICATIONS OF THE IMAGE AND LIKENESS

God's own essence is and forever remains impenetrably transcendent and unknowable to man. Only the attributes 'around it', only descriptions of the divine operations 'descending on us' can be known. Gregory of Nyssa wanting to define man's true nature started from the concept of God, in whose image man was made,[4] and taught that creation provides the only analogical knowledge of God man can attain through his own faculties.[5]

Augustine, by contrast, convinced that the rational mind is capable of becoming like God by participation,[6] moved from the ontological to the psychological level, to see what he could find out about his Maker. Theorizing that rationality depends upon the inseparable operation of memory, understanding and will, Augustine realized that man not only has the capability of being like God, but can also catch a glimpse of the operations of the Trinity within Itself.[7] When he treated this theme in *Sermo* 52, he maintained that the Father is not memory, the Son is not understanding, the will is not the Holy Spirit.[8] In his treatise *On the Trinity*, however, he took a further step to maintain that the three faculties '*can* be equated separately to some small extent with the Father, Son and Holy Spirit',[9] 'keeping in mind that the three faculties are of one man, not one man, whereas the three Persons of the Trinity are of one God and are one God'.[10] Augustine used

---

3 Med 2.1; PL 180: 208C: 'Quamdiu sum tecum, sum etiam mecum; non sum autem mecum, quamdiu non sum tecum'.

4 Vl. Lossky, *Orthodox Theology*, 120.

5 Völker, *Gregor von Nyssa*, 35–40; Daniélou, *Platonisme*, 149.

6 *De Trinitate* 12.7.12; PL 42: 1004–05.

7 Gilson, *Introduction*, 288; Klaus Winkler, 'La théorie augustinienne de la mémoire à son point de départ' *AM* 1: 511–19; Bell, *The Image*, 18.

8 *Sermo* 52.23; PL 38: 364.

9 *De Trinitate* 15.23.43: PL 42: 1090. To warn against a too explicit equation, Augustine qualifies his statement by adding *principaliter* (chiefly) or *proprie* (particularly): *De Trinitate* 15.17.28; PL 42: 1080.

10 Javelet, *Image*, 1: 208; Bell, *The Image*, 18–22.

the psychology of the three faculties as a springboard for an analogical knowledge of the Trinity.[11] Medieval writers showed far less concern with relating man's three major faculties to the Persons of the Trinity.[12] In one place, for instance, Bernard has the three faculties flowing from God to man: 'The God who is truth is the source of the first of these gifts [here reason] ; the God who is love, of the second [the will]; the God who is all-powerful, of the third [the memory]',[13] thus expressing his view that truth refers particularly to the Son, love to the Holy Spirit, and memory to the Father. In another place he states that at creation, the Trinity made a created trinity: memory, reason and will.[14] Well aware of what he was saying, he added the caution: 'In doing so, however, we must beware of excluding either the Father or the Son or the Holy Spirit from any of these communications, lest the distinction of Persons diminish the divine fullness proper to each of them, or their perfection be so understood as to annul the personal properties'.[15] For William the three faculties 'are not just a convenient similarity, a simple psychological parallel, but something which exists in and by direct ontological participation in its source, and which therefore

---

11 *Confessiones* 9.4.10; PL 32: 174. See J.E. Sullivan, *The Image*, 104. The question whether Augustine intended his psychological image of memory, understanding and love as a metaphor or as an analogy proper is still being discussed. See O. Brooke, 'The Trinitarian Aspect', *RTAM* 26 (1959) 95, and D.N. Bell, *The Image*, 44, where he says that when Augustine speaks of *imago Trinitatis*, 'he presents us with a trinitarian analogy of the three inseparably distinct factors in unified operation'. Bernard too speaks of the *imago Trinitatis*, but very seldom; see Standaert, 'La doctrine de l'image chez saint Bernard', *ETL* 23 (1947) 100.

12 Javelet, *Image*, 1: 280; Bell, *The Image*, 142.

13 SC 1.6; SBOp 1: 58.

14 Div 45.6; SBOp 6/1: 265.

15 *Ibid.* That 'chaque personne s'approprie la réformation de chacune de ces facultés' [Javelet, *Psychologie*, 56] is correct in the sense that it is Bernard who assigns a particular faculty to a particular person. He is talking about God's concern for man's return from the land of unlikeness to the resemblance to God, who is Trinity.

expresses in some real degree the principle of which it is the image'.[16] In his work *On the Nature of the Soul*, William writes:

As in that Trinity, the Father is the one who begets, the Son the one who is begotten, and the Holy Spirit the one who proceeds from them both, so reason is begotten from memory and from both memory and reason proceeds the will. So that the rational soul created in man may adhere to God, the Father claims the memory for himself, the Son the reason, and the Holy Spirit, who proceeds from both, claims the will proceeding from both.[17]

'The image being what it is', a modern scholar comments, 'must reveal its model, and although the picture would be remote... there must still remain a true figure for those who wish to seek it'.[18] A similar doctrine about the faculties, not always expressed in the same sequence or in exactly the same terms,[19] can be found in Aelred,[20] Isaac of Stella,[21] Thomas the Cistercian,[22] Hugh,[23] and Richard.[24] Threefold formulas can easily be found in the writings of medieval authors.[25] Alan of Lille (d.1203) spoke of

16 Gilson, *The Mystical Theology*, 203–04; Bell, *The Image*, 139–40.

17 William, Nat am, PL 184: 382CD. Many more quotations could be added. It may suffice to refer to Augustine (I. Bochet, *Augustin et le désir de Dieu*, 377–78); – Hugh, *De tribus diebus*, PL 176: 833;- Richard, *De Trinitate* 5.20; PL 196: 963C; – William, Aenig, PL 180:412C;- Bernard, V Nat 4.9; SBOp 4: 227; Csi 5.8.18; SBOp 3: 482.

18 Bell, *The Image*, 142, points out that the distinction between William and Augustine is 'surely only a distinction in degree, not in kind'.

19 *Id.*, 'The Commentary... of Thomas the Cistercian', *Cîteaux* 28 (1977) 11; Bell has elaborated at some length on the 'Augustinian, Bernardine and Abelardian-Victorine traditions' in this regard.

20 Hallier, *Un éducateur*, 72–73; Marie Anne Mayeski, *Ailred of Rievaulx (1109–1167) and the Spiritual Life: A Study of the Influence of Anthropology on Theology*, (Dissertation, New York, 1974; University Microfilms, Ann Arbor, MI, 1974) 53–65.

21 George Boswell Burch, trans., *The Steps of Humility* (Notre Dame, 1963) 265–66.

22 Bell, 'The Commentary...of Thomas the Cistercian', *Cîteaux* 28 (1977) 11–21.

23 Javelet, *Psychologie*, 100–03.

24 Javelet, *Image*, 1: 128; and *Psychologie*, 98–100.

25 Javelet, *Image*, 2: 161–64, n. 243, lists a number of them, obviously without the intention of being complete.

a'multiplicity of ternaries',[26] but most of them are not important enough to merit attention here.[27] The available sources of the *mulieres religiosae* movement show clearly how important a place the Trinity had in their spirituality and mysticism, yet it is worth noticing that trinitarian analogies are not very frequent. They can be found in some biographies, especially where the biographer, not his subject, speaks about such analogies. Examples occur in the biography of Ida Lewis,[28] and in that of William of Brussels, the former abbot of Villers (1221-37) and supporter of the *mulieres religiosae*.[29] As can be expected, Beatrice is more explicit in speaking about the faculties common to the three Persons, though separately attributed to them. Her biography claims that 'illuminated more abundantly by divine light, Beatrice knew that all things are and subsist by the power of God the Father, are governed by the wisdom of the Son, and subsist preserved by the mercy of the Holy Spirit'.[30] In her first Letter, Hadewijch too wrote clearly of God's attributes on the trinitarian level. Giving advice to a correspondent she said:

> Learn to contemplate what God is: how he [the Son] is Truth in which everything is manifested, and Goodness [the Holy Spirit] overflowing with all wealth, and Totality [the Father] replete with all virtues. It is for these three names [attributes

---

26 Marie-Thérèse d'Alverny, *Alain de Lille*. *Textes inédits* [henceforth cited: *Alain de Lille*], Études de psychologie médiévale 42 (Paris, 1965) 255.

27 Sullivan, *The Image*, 87: 'Augustine finds trinitarian reflections everywhere, as is evident from the sheer number of trinitarian formulae in his work'. Javelet (*Image*, 1: 61) classifies Augustine's triades in two categories: the first composed of the ones related to man himself, the second including the 'trinities' related to God.

28 *AA SS* Oct.13: 107,1: '[Deus] a quo et ex quo et per quem intellectus et mens et ratio perducuntur'.

29 Martene and Durand, *Thesaurus* 3, 1283: 'Liber primus de gestibus abbatum villariensium', caput v.

30 *Vita*, 223, 36. Vekeman in his *Lexicografisch Onderzoek*, 2: 385, states that it remains an open question if Beatrice saw an analogical relation between the activity of the psychological faculties and God's intratrinitarian life. Though he admits the possibility, he is inclined to answer in the negative.

common to all three] that the *Sanctus* (holy) is sung three times in heaven, because these three names comprehend in their unique essence (*Wesen*) all the virtues, whatever may be the particular works of the three distinct attributes.[31]

Whenever the *mulieres religiosae* showed an interest in trinitarian analogies, they did so to treat them as exemplary structures assisting the spiritual ascent of the soul toward its completion.[32] Hadewijch is perhaps the most explicit of them all. For her the three faculties were a reflection of the Trinity, and aim at union with God.

> I pray the Holy Trinity
> Through its grace and for the sake of its goodness,
> As it honored you with its image
>
> If you live with *reason* in truth,
> You enlighten all your labor;
> So your *will* is pleased to love well
>
> And then your *memory* becomes valiant,
> and in it shall reign glory
> And likewise confidence with fidelity
> That it may contemplate its God to the full.[33]

---

31 VM, *Brieven*, 1: 17, ll. 25–32.

32 Spaapen, 'Hadewijch en het vijfde visioen', *OGE* 44 (1970) 361.

33 The fourth Poem in Couplets, VM, *Mengeldichten*, 27, ll. 5–8; 15–17; 21–24. Albert Brounts expressed his reservations about Hadewijch's presentation in his posthumously published study by R. Lievens: 'Hadewijchs eerste ontwerp van de wezensmystiek (Br.xvii)', *HL* 17 (1972) 5–57, especially 38–39 and 45–46. Hadewijch's sentence: 'between God and the blissful soul that has become God with God, there exists a spiritual *caritate* [friendship]', (Letter 28; VM, *Brieven*, 1: 234, ll. 121–22) can, indeed, have an unorthodox ring, if taken out of context. For the rectification of Brounts' interpretation, see Vekeman, 'Hadewijch. Een interpretatie van de Brieven I, II, XXVIII, XXIX als dokumenten over de strijd rond de wezensmystiek', *TNTL* 90 (1975) 337–66; 356–57.

Beatrice gave thanks to God for the natural gifts of memory, reason, and understanding (*intellectus*),[34] given her when God created her to his own image.[35]

The three faculties are not only related to the three divine persons, but together they are called a created trinity by Bernard,[36] William,[37] and others.[38] Hadewijch too was of the opinion that the three faculties are our trinity: 'Keep your trinity well ordered in you', she wrote to a friend,[39] And some writers simply identified the soul with the three faculties.[40]

ATTENDING MEMORY

In the tradition of the Fathers of East and West, the twelfth century held that God the Father is, so to speak, the font and

---

34 *Vita*, 94,62. There is no way of stating exactly the source from which Beatrice or the biographer took the term *intellectus*, often used by Cistercian and Victorine writers, who frequently considered *intellectus* a form of love. See Javelet, 'Intelligence et amour chez les auteurs spirituels du XIIe siècle', *RAM* 37 (1961) 273–98; 183–88: 'amor ipse est intellectus', and Zwingmann, 'Affectus illuminati amoris. Über das Offenbarwerden der Gnade und die Erfahrung von Gottes beseligender Gegenwart', *Citeaux* 18 (1967)193–226, particularly 206–15.

35 Here and in 197, 42, she speaks of the image without mentioning the likeness, though in several other places, when referring to the same thing, she mentions both image and likeness. Another example of how a correct understanding of the *mulieres religiosae* and their mentors does not yield much scope to strictly literalist interpretation.

36 Div 45.1; SBOp 6/1: 262: '[anima rationalis] quae in eo praefert vestigium quoddam illius summae Trinitatis, quod ex memoria, ratione et voluntate consistit'.

37 Nat am; PL 184: 382C: 'In ejus quasi quadam arce vim memorialem collocavit, ut Creatoris semper potentiam et bonitatem memoraret: statimque et sine aliquo morae interstitio, memoria de se genuit rationem: et memoria et ratio de se protulerunt voluntatem'.

38 For example, Godfrey of St Victor [d.1194] (Bell, 'The Commentary...of Thomas the Cistercian', *Citeaux* 28 [1977] 17) and Alan of Lille (M-T. d'Alverny, *Alain de Lille*, 257).

39 Poem 4 in Couplets; VM, *Mengeldichten*, 30, l. 105: 'Dus hout v drievuldicheit in ghereke'. See also R. Vanneste, *Abstracta*, 84.

40 Bernard, Conv 6.11; SBOp 4: 84, and SC 11.5; SBOp 1:57; – William, Nat am; PL 184: 382CD; the treatise *De spiritu et anima* in several places. See McGinn, *Three Treatises*, 69–70, where he discusses the 'texts of Augustine himself', which are at best ambiguous. But later patristic and carolingian sources

source of the divinity.[41] In some cases, as in Hadewijch's Letter 22, memory is attributed to the Son, not to the Father.[42] Though the attribution of the memory to the Father was commonly accepted by her twelfth-century mentors, she did not—regrettably—explain in this case why she attributed the memory to the Son.[43] Bernard assigned the memory to the Father as 'an unfailing fountain'.[44] So did William who said: 'God established, as it were, in the apse, the summit of the soul,[45] the power of memory'.[46] It is here that the Father has his couch (*cubat*), at that secret point where resides the latent remembrance of his goodness and power...the most deeply graven trait of his image, that which evokes all the other [faculties] and enables us to make ourselves like him.[47]

This is what Vanneste seems to refer to when he says that for Hadewijch the memory is the seat or couch of the contemplation of God.[48] Hadewijch herself spoke of an *armariolum*, a little

---

making explicit one side of Augustine's thought, clearly affirmed such an identity. To this opinion the Cistercians form a unanimous witness to the traditional doctrine of identification'.

41 William, Aenig, PL 180: 435D: 'Quasi fons quidam et origo divinitatis'. See also P. Verdeyen, 'La Théologie mystique de Guillaume de Saint-Thierry', *OGE* 52 (1978) 160.

42 VM, *Brieven*, 1: 193, l. 139.

43 Vanneste, *Abstracta*, 85–86.

44 SC 11.6; SBOp 1: 58: 'Fons indeficiens'.

45 He calls it *caput animae*: Nat am 2,3; PL 184: 382CD.

46 For references to the created trinity, with memory as the first faculty attributed to the Father, see above the text referred to in n.17 of this Chapter. See further W. Zwingmann, 'Ex affectu mentis. Über die Vollkommenheit menschlichen Handelns und menschlicher Hingabe nach Wilhelm von St.Thierry', *Citeaux* 18 (1967) 5–37; 19–21: 'Das *Schema* mens-ratio-voluntas'.

47 Nat am 2,3; PL 184: 382CD. In reference to this passage Gilson (*The Mystical Theology*, 204) adds the observation that 'it is hardly necessary to insist on this genesis of the faculties of the soul. It determines once and for all the conditions of their legitimate exercise...that of a reason that knows naught but God, of a will that tends to naught but God, because the memory whence they proceed is filled with nothing but the remembrance of God'.

48 Vanneste, *Abstracta*, 84.

cupboard where precious things are kept.[49] Bernard called it 'the stomach of the soul',[50] Richard, 'the innermost secrecy or fold of the mind,[51] and Beatrice the 'basket of memory' (24,24; 103,67). In our modern age, some might refer to this as religious consciousness.

This memory is not to be confused with any actual recollection of things past. It concerns not remembering,[52] but being present to the present, or more accurately, being present to the Presence.[53] 'If you are with me in your mind', William has God say to him, 'there will I sit down with you at table, and there will I feed you'.[54] The introversion of memory (not as remembrance) allows a human being to find his own secret, to discover that he exists in relation to God whom he thus approaches.[55] This is what Hadewijch said,[56] and Beatrice also thought (157,32; 237,48), along with many others. According to Ida of Nivelles' biographer 'by adhering to God, she drew God within her and she was wholly drawn into him'.[57] Ida Lewis 'had God always in her mind', and was 'always longing to contemplate the sublimity of heaven'.[58] Alice of Schaarbeek did not 'allow mundane things to enter the

---

49 Here, her love. See J. Reynaert, *Beeldspraak*, 244–45. Alan of Lille too spoke of the 'memoria in armariolo recordationis'. See M-T. d'Alverny, *Alain de Lille*, 257.

50 SC 36.4; SBOp 2:6: 'stomachus animae'.

51 *Benjamin major* 5.2; PL 196: 170B: 'intimum mentis sinum'.

52 It is permanently present in the memory: 'perenni memoriae retinetur'; Dumeige, *Richard, Les quatre degrés*, 133, l. 2.

53 Gilson, *Introduction*, 139.

54 Cant, PL 180: 494A: 'In mente tua, si fueris mecum, ibi cubabo tecum, et inde pascam tibi'.

55 Javelet, *Image*, 1: 393. See also, Louis Dupré, *The Deeper Life: An Introduction to Christian Mysticism* (New York, 1981) 25–29.

56 Letter 20; VM, *Brieven* 1: 174, ll. 116–22: 'Love renders [man's] memory so unified that he can no longer think of saints, or of man, or of heaven, or of earth, or of angels, or of himself, or of God, but only of *Minne* (Love) who has taken possession of him in an ever-new presence'. To Vanneste (*Abtstracta*, 60), the presence spoken of relates to Bernard's saying (Pre 20.60; SBOp 3: 293): 'Who loves the Lord is present to him inasmuch as he loves; to the measure he loves less, to that extent he is absent'.

57 *Quinque*, 247: 'Deo adhaerens, Deum in se trahebat et a Deo in Deum trahebatur'.

58 *AA SS* Oct. 13: 120,40: 'semper meditans ea quae Dei sunt'; *ibid.*, 121,45: 'et avida coelorum celsitudinem contemplari'.

inner shrine of her heart,...interiorly open and at leisure for divine meditation'. Stricken with leprosy 'she saw it as an excellent way to be freer to be at leisure (*vacare*) with God alone, and to dwell within the chamber of her mind, for the Lord desired to remain there with her and to inebriate his spouse with the sweetness of his fragrance'.[59] Ida of Leuven:

> under the guidance of Christ and his Paraclete, progressed so much in the school of contemplation, that to whatever places she went or in whatever occupation she was involved, simultaneous contemplation was ever there. And however extraordinary it might seem, she was always equally prepared to prolong this contemplative service, not rarely or alternately as usually happens, but during the whole span of day and night, at each moment of time.[60]

Ida of Nivelles contemplated 'God's inexhaustible and marvelous goodness, not merely because of the blessings he bestowed or because of his wonderful creation, but primarily because he is within himself ineffably good'.[61] As Beatrice 'could scarcely ever recall her bodily eyes from looking upward' (157,33), so Ida of Leuven had 'her open eyes always turned toward the sky'.[62] Their eyes followed where their memory went. They could apply to themselves Bernard's saying:'my eye is my memory'.[63]

Even if we were to take into consideration biographers' tendency to paint their subjects in vivid colors, it is evident that a number of these *mulieres religiosae* were exceptionally open, gifted and committed.[64] Those who enjoyed keeping their

---

59 *AA SS* June 2: 479,12; 478,4; 479,9.

60 *AA SS* April 2: 186,16.

61 *Quinque*, 276. Ida seems to echo a sentence from William in his third meditation: PL 180: 213B.

62 *AA SS* April 2: 171,23: 'ut nihil terrenis sapiens vel advertens, apertis oculis in coelum semper intenderet'.

63 OS 5.5; SBOp 5: 364: 'oculus meus, memoria mea'.

64 Some of Beatrice's sisters in her own community, who were 'not similarly affected... called her crazy for constantly looking at the sky with upturned gaze'

memory directed toward God were said *diem festum agere*, 'to celebrate a holiday or feastday with the Lord'.[65] Cognizant of the teachings of the Bible and of their mentors, and moved by their own awareness of the various implications of being made to God's image and likeness, the *mulieres religiosae* became living witnesses of what it meant to be created by God and for God. This acute awareness could not but express itself in their behavior.

NOBILITY, DIGNITY, PURITY

For the *mulieres religiosae* trinitarian analogies and attentive memory were not intellectual approaches. They pointed toward a vital link between an infinitely perfect God and a creature made by him to share in his life and the beatitude of his love.

Beatrice spoke of 'the nobility of the uncreated Good' (249, 116), and Hadewijch of 'God's incomprehensible nobility',[66] while Ida Lewis called him the 'noble Beloved'.[67] His dignity was generally spoken of as 'divine Majesty',[68] or similar expressions, while verbs like 'to glorify' indicated that 'honor and reverence' (93,48)are his due.

It is because man was created to the image and likeness of this God that the *mulieres religiosae* had so great an appreciation of human nobility, dignity and purity.[69] These gifts were seen as indications of God's love for them, obliging them to love him in return, and to respect and love all people as God's people.

(157, 37), thus indicating that not all the *mulieres religiosae* were of the same mind, as can be expected in any movement.

65 Ida of Nivelles, *Quinque*, 223, 247, 258, 259, 265. The same celebration (*diem festum celebrare*) is mentioned in the biographies of Mary of Oignies, Lutgard and Juliana Cornillon. See A. Mens, *Oorsprong*, 230, n.29. This expression, which is also mentioned by Richard (Dumeige, *Les quatre degrés*, 165, l. 19) is, in fact, taken from Ps 75:11.

66 Letter 6; VM, *Brieven*, 1: 68, l. 348.

67 *AA SS* Oct. 13: 177,33: 'dilectus nobilis'.

68 Examples in Beatrice's *Vita*: 40,63; 92,35; 93,48; 101,8; 126,28; 199,65; 223,30.

69 It is evident that this kind of purity must not be confused with chastity or with sexual purity in the modern sense. It simply is the purity inherent in man's primordial creation to God's image and likeness.

Without love for neighbor, their love for God could never be noble, worthy and pure. Just as God's love is all-inclusive, so had theirs to be.this does not mean that all persons are endowed with the same degree of nobility, dignity and purity. God's measure of predilection is not the same for all, nor does each person equally respond to God's initiative. As Hadewijch mentioned, 'God's riches are manifold and all his children are filled with delight, though one more than another'.[70] 'Many gifts are distributed by the Lord in different ways to different people' (123,63) some of whom are more fervent and others more negligent.[71]

The terms nobility, dignity and purity, though not radically distinct, are neither equivalent nor synonymous. At times they are used adjectivally to stress the importance of one or the other attributes. Generally speaking, nobility is related to the image, and purity to the likeness, while dignity flows from the former and points to the latter. But all three, each in its own way, aspired to the recovery of man's primordial state, that he might be enabled to re-echo more freely and clearly the resounding affirmation of God's love.

Nobility

God, who is incomprehensible Nobility, made man noble by creating him in his image and likeness as a preparation for everlasting union with himself.[72] 'It is from there [God's love], as its birthplace, that man has his lineage of eminent nobility',[73] and it is up to man's nobility to live nobly and lovingly as befits his high descent.[74] Words such as lofty, worthy, distinguished, point

---

70 Letter 28; VM, *Brieven*, 1: 236, ll. 185–86.

71 Ida of Nivelles, *Quinque*, 244: 'quidam velocius, quidam morosius'.

72 See Ernst Benz, 'Über den Adel in der deutschen Mystik', *Deutsche Vierteljahrschrift für Literaturwissenschaften und Geistesgeschichte* 14 (1936) 505–55. Though this paper has chiefly Germany in view, this 'nobility' applies elsewhere as well.

73 William, Nat am 2.3; PL 184: 382B: 'Nec debet latere de amore, de quo agimus, quibus ortus sit natalibus, qua nobilitatis linea insignis habeatur; vel quo oriundus loco. Primum igitur ejus nativitatis locus Deus est. Ibi natus, ibi alitus, ibi provectus'.

74 Hadewijch, Letter 28; VM, *Brieven*, 1: 254, ll.70–71: 'To live worthily according to the noble Trinity, as is fitting'. In his study 'Hadewijchs "Hoghe

to the illustrious degree of man's nobility,[75] which deserves to be perfected in a love of extraordinary quality: the *unitas spiritus*, unity of spirit. Ida of Leuven stood in awe of a creature so noble since its creation, from the moment it came into existence.[76] Similarly, Hadewijch exclaimed: 'O soul, creature, such a noble being',[77] and(in the plural): 'O free, noble and highborn souls, called and chosen'.[78] Ida of Leuven's biographer spoke of 'the rational soul made by God as an elegant excellency provided with excellent elegance'.[79]

As a gift from God, nobility requires from man more than mere appreciation. An effective cooperation can show that so great an endowment is truly valued:

> For I understand from the nobility of my soul
> That in suffering for sublime Love, I conquer.
> I will therefore gladly surrender myself

Geslachte" (*Hoogheid en devotie in de Middeleeuwse Maatschappij, Handelingen van het wetenschappelijk colloquium te Brussel, 21–24 oktober 1981*, J.D. Janssens, ed. [Brussels, 1982] 156–73), Reynaert pointed out that in whatever way Hadewijch was influenced by courtly poetry, her 'nobility' seems to refer, not so much to her ancestry—as is often assumed—as to her nobility as a person created to God's image and likeness, re-created by Christ, in order to reach union with God. Reynaert confirms an observation made by P. Dinzelbacher (*Vision*, 224), that in Hadewijch's time, spiritual nobility refers to man deified in Christ, rather than to one's social station: 'Auch für den Mystiker ist der "Adel des in Christus vergotteten Menschen" wichtig, nicht der soziale Stand'. See also Benz' study, mentioned above in n. 72. Wilhelm Breuer, however, is still of the opinion that Hadewijch belonged to the nobility. See his study: 'Mystik als alternative Lebensform. Das 37. Strophische Gedicht der Suster Hadewijch', in *Zeitschrift für deutsche Philologie*, Vol. 103 (1984) 103–15; 110.

75 Delfgaauw, *Saint Bernard*, 143.

76 *AA SS* April 2: 188,25, which recalls Richard's exclamation about 'this noble, indeed, most noble creature made in God's image', *Ben maj*, PL 196: 109A.

77 E. Rombauts and N. De Paepe, *Hadewijch. Strofische Gedichten*, 256–57: Poem 36,6. Vanneste (*Abstracta*, 47) showed that 'edele figuere' means being (*wezen*).

78 VM, *Strophische Gedichten*, 29, l. 37.

79 *AA SS* April 2: 188,25: 'animae rationalis elegantem excellentiam et excellentem elegantiam cognoscit'.

In pain, in repose, in dying, in living
For I know the command of lofty fidelity.[80]

What these writers desired so vehemently[81] was the alliance and fusion of nobilities. They were conscious of the need to give a free consent to all the requirements of a love that was noble enough to be proportionate to God's love. As Beatrice saw the need for doing justice to her nobility by a free consent to God in 'noble liberty' (*edele vriheit*),[82] so Hadewijch advised a friend to 'conform wisely and valiantly, as one undaunted, to all that is meet to you, and act in all things according to your free nobility (*vrie edelheit*)'.[83]

God's nobility and their own demanded that they do their utmost to attain as closely as possible the state in which man was initially created, to be able to fulfill the longing of their shared nobility for mutual union.[84] For Beatrice, Hadewijch and so many other *mulieres religiosae*, nobility tugged at man's capacity for participation in God.[85] In her *Seven Manieren* Beatrice asserts

---

80 VM, *Strophische Gedichten*, 29, ll. 10–14.

81 Desire as a noun and as a verb is so frequently used in the biographies, and is of such an importance in the writings of Hadewijch and Beatrice, that references are simply superfluous.

82 R-VM, *Seven manieren*, 14, l. 18.

83 Letter 18; VM, *Brieven*, 1: 152, ll. 10–12.

84 See the texts quoted above in Chapter IV, nn. 82 and 94. Bernard referred to the image in a similar fashion: SC 25.7; SBOp 1:167; 'Their [those who strive toward saintliness] attention is fixed on improving and adorning the inward self that is made to the image of God, and is renewed day by day. For they are certain that nothing can be more pleasing to God than his image, when restored to its original beauty. Hence all their glory is within, not without'.

85 The twelfth century had the flexibility to accept two ways of looking at man's nobility and the miseries of his human condition, both stressed by Augustine; M. Huftier, 'Libre arbitre, liberté et péché chez saint Augustin', *RTAM* 33 (1966) 245 and 275–79. The first preferred to look at man's limitations as inherent in all created beings, while the second looked instead at man's ungratefulness for the gifts originally received and his mistreatment of God's love because of his self-centered pride; Javelet, *Image*, 1: 249. Hadewijch is in tune with the first (De Paepe, *Hadewijch. Strofische Gedichten*, 161–62), while Beatrice followed Bernard, William and many others in the second trend. This difference of accentuation is not a plain opposition, for it depends on the approach to man's need of restoration, setting the image in the right direction for the pursuit of a restored likeness.

'that the soul with all its diligence and with great longing and all possible ingenuity, strives to reject and avoid whatever can impede or harm it in this matter'.[86]

Dignity

The soul's nobility gives it its dignity, a technical term for honor.[87] Equivalents of dignity are adornment (*decus*) or beauty (*decor*).

Aimé Forest has stated that 'Bernard always had this *one* intention in mind: to bring into consciousness the soul's dignity as the image of God'.[88] Bernard himself,[89] William,[90] Richard,[91] and some compilers,[92] often stressed this same conviction in their own words. Beatrice too 'noticed attentively the natural beauty (*decor*) of soul which she had received from the impressed likeness of the eternal Godhead, when God created her to his image and likeness' (121,32). Alice of Schaarbeek is said to have glowed when adhering to God's image,[93] as we noted earlier, and Hadewijch advised a friend 'to be attentive and exert herself in accordance with God's dignity'.[94]

---

86 The original text has 'so pijnt si hare', (R-VM, *Seven manieren*, 5, 1. 36), indicating generous efforts to eliminate from the heart all that could obstruct or hinder growth toward likeness.

87 Javelet, *Image*, 1: 248. In many cases it refers to Ps 48:13: 'homo cum in honore esset, non intellexit'. This sentence was often used by the mentors of the *mulieres religiosae*, as, for example, Bernard in Div 42.2: SBOp 6/1: 256.

88 A. Forest, 'Das Erlebniss des consensus voluntatis beim heiligen Bernhard', *Bernhard von Clairvaux*, Joseph Lortz ed., 120: 'Immer hat der heilige Bernhard *ein* Vorhaben: der Seele ihre Würde zum Bewusstsein bringen, die Würde von Gottes Abbild'.

89 Nat 2.1; SBOp 4: 252: 'Acknowledge, man, your dignity'.

90 Nat corp 2; PL 180: 717A: 'See and embrace, o man, the dignity of your nature'; Cant, PL 180: 494C: 'O image of God, recognize your dignity, let the effigy of your Creator shine forth in you'.

91 *Benjamin major* 13; PL 196: 123A: 'I beseech you, man, know your God; think about the excellent nature of your soul made by God in his image and likeness'; *De eruditione* 22; PL 196: 1268A: 'Appreciate, if you can, the sublimity of your God'.

92 As the anonymous author—probably a Cistercian—of the *Meditationes piisssimae* 39; PL 184: 547C: 'Understand your dignity, noble creature'.

93 *AA SS* June 2: 478,5: 'Intus imagini, quam in corde gessit, adhaerendo nituit'.

94 Letter 24; VM, *Brieven*, 1: 213, 1. 108.

The *mulieres religiosae* were well aware that their innate human dignity was not always manifest. Beatrice began 'to notice... that the natural beauty of soul... was not a little disfigured' (121,34), and avoided discouragement through the conviction that the loving Lord who created her to his image and likeness 'does not will the death of the sinner but that he be converted and live' (138,166).

Bernard—and he was no exception—often listed the most obvious defects of the human condition in order to make a psychological impact, before showing how incomparably relative they were when seen in the perspective of the *anteriora*, the sublime things to come:

> Even amid the fluctuating events and inevitable shortcomings of this giddy world you will ensure for yourself a life of durable stability, provided you are renewed and reformed according to the glorious and original plan of the eternal God. In him—unlike anybody else—there is no such thing as alteration, no shadow of change.... Living thus this noble creature, made to the image and likeness of his Creator, indicates that even now he is re-acquiring the dignity of that primordial honor, since he deems it unworthy to be conformed to a world that is waning.[95]

The *anteriora* refer to the thrust toward union with the transcendent prototype, through a progressive conformation. This patristic interpretation of Philippians 3:13, goes back to Origen, Basil the Great, and Gregory of Nyssa,[96] and is not infrequently used by some *mulieres religiosae*,[97] and their mentors.[98]

The dignity of the primal honor can be re-acquired; as William stated: 'man *can* recover his natural dignity and likeness'.[99] This

---

95 Bernard, SC 21.6; SBOp 1: 125.
96 Javelet, *Image*, 1: 116.
97 Occurrences in Beatrice's *Vita*, 39,56; 166,41; 197,35.
98 For example, by Bernard (SC 49.7; SBOp 2, 72), and William in his Spec fid, PL 180: 367B.
99 Ep frat 6.15; PL 184: 318A: 'In auxilio recuperandae dignitatis, et conservandae similitudinis'.

recovery is made possible by God's Son, Jesus Christ: the fact that God sent his Son as man is a further indication of human dignity.[100] Christ's grace provided men with all they need for this recovery, 'while they are still unable to gaze into the brightness of the Majesty of your [Christ's] divinity'.[101] Honored with nobility and dignity as God's image, and provided with Christ's grace, man now can and should do all he can to free himself from sin so that he can be restored to his primal dignity.[102] Hadewijch realized that human freedom opened the door to a mystical union with God.[103] Beatrice gave the impression that she had come close to this union. In her *Seven Manieren* she wrote that'when the soul is in this state, all things seem small, and everything which pertains to love's dignity seems easy to do or to omit, to tolerate or to bear'.[104] What the soul's dignity meant is pointedly expressed by Hadewijch:

Soul is a being that can be beheld by God and by which, again, God can be beheld. Soul is also a being that wishes to please God; it maintains a worthy state of being as long as it has not fallen beneath anything that is alien to it, and less than the soul's own dignity. If it maintains this worthy state, the soul is a bottomless abyss in which God suffices to himself ever finding in her his own delight, as the soul, for its part, ever does in him.[105]

---

100 Bernard, Adv 1.7: SBOp 4: 166: 'Propter nos venit [Christus]. Mirae quaerentis Dei dignatio, magna dignitas hominis sic quaesiti'.

101 William, Med 10.4: PL 180: 236A: 'Non sufficientes adhuc intueri in claritatem illam divinae majestatis tuae'.

102 References to Hadewijch, Beatrice and some of their mentors in Reynaert, *Beeldspraak*, 390–91, and Javelet, *Image*, 1: 247; 'La dignité de l'image de Dieu consiste surtout pour les cisterciens dans *la liberté de l'homme, la liberté libérée*'.

103 Reynaert, *Beeldspraak*, 442.

104 R-VM, *Seven Manieren*, 24, ll. 15–18.

105 Letter 18; VM, *Brieven*, 1: 154, ll. 64–72. This remarkable text reverberates with sentences of Bernard's SC 83, 7–8; SBOp 2: 297–98, and reminds us of a saying by William: 'You [God] love yourself in us, and us in yourself, when we love you through you'. Contem 11; PL 184: 375A; See also J. Van Mierlo, 'Hadewijch en Willem van St. Thierry, *OGE* 3 (1929) 455–59; 457. Hadewijch's text refers also to noble pride, see below n.137.

PURITY

Of the trio—nobility, dignity, and purity,—the last seems to move
closest toward resemblance or likeness. The attributes of God the
Father, as God and Father, are 'pure Divinity'.[106] God is the
source of purity,[107] 'the supreme and uncircumscribed Pure One,
and only the pure can arrive at him'.[108] He is 'supreme Purity'
(248,93) and 'purity is taught by Love (*Minne*)'. Man's love
'works and strives only for purity and sublimity and for supreme
nobility, as Love itself is such in its very nature; Love teaches this
activity to those who cultivate Love'.[109]

Purity as a noun, pure as an adjective, or purify as a verb can
evidently be used in many combinations. The footnote references,
far from being comprehensive, offer only sample instances.[110]
Purity is occasionally expressed by other words with a similar
meaning,[111] or is intensified in the superlative. From the beginning (124,84; 236,42) the soul was created in purity (123,75;
124,84; 197,41), in most noble purity (121,35). Ida of Leuven,
'gazing in the light of the divine clarity...wondered how it was

---

106 Hadewijch, Letter 17; VM, *Brieven*, 1: 140, ll. 22–23.

107 Evangelos Konstantinou, *Die Tugendlehre Gregors von Nyssa im Ver-
hältnis zu der Antik-Philosophischen und Jüdisch-Christlichen Tradition*
[henceforth cited: *Die Tugendlehre Gregors*], (Würzburg, 1966) 141: 'Gott ist
für Gregor die Quelle der Apathie, die Reinheit'.

108 Bernard, SC 5.8; SBOp 1: 25: 'Haec summo atque incircumscripto
Spiritui, qui solus... purus capitur a puris'.

109 Beatrice, R-VM, *Seven manieren*, 7, ll. 59–64. In her treatise Beatrice
connects purity with nobility six times, each time purity taking precedence
(Vekeman, *Lexicografisch Onderzoek*, 2:193). God is love but love is not
necessarily only God. *Minne* will be spoken of below in Chapter XV.

110 Love can be said to be pure (Hadewijch, vision 11, VM, *Visioenen*, 1:
117, l.122, and Letter 23, VM, *Brieven*, 1: 206, l. 5). Beatrice tried to recover
purity of heart (42, 12; 191,151; 197,38); or purity of heart and body, meaning
purity in its totality, without any hindrance coming from the bodily senses
(131,30), or purity of nature (123,75; 124,82), or—as Hadewijch—purity of
genuine intention (Letter 6, VM, *Brieven*, 1: 67, l. 310), or purity of humility
(vision 1, VM, *Visioenen*, 1: 13, l. 42), or purity of obedience (Letter 2, VM,
Brieven, 1: 31, l. 166).

111 Ida of Nivelles avoided polluting the neatness (*munditia*) of her heart
(*Quinque*, 206); Beatrice was intent on keeping her mind and affections (94,73),
or her body and soul unpolluted (138, 168), while the biographer and Alice of
Schaarbeek herself were against any defilement (*AA SS* June 2: 477,1; 478,3).

possible for such a noble and, from the beginning of its creation, a most perfect creature to be induced, drawn or impelled into consenting to sin'.[112] The experience of the actual human condition taught the *mulieres religiosae* that they no longer enjoyed the purity in which humanity was created. When invited by the creating, trinitarian God to enter into union with him, 'this seemed not to be enough for man, and so he fell',[113] indicating that—misusing his freedom as their mentors had said—he desired to be independent (*sui juris*), not under God, but autonomous. Being in such a predicament, the *mulieres religiosae* had first to face the reality: Beatrice looked at the general miseries of the human condition of which the first 'is the miserable and harsh inclination of the human race to commit sin, which not even an infant one day old can avoid'.[114] Beatrice, without going into details, examined her use of the gifts she has received from God, and she

perceived right away many bramble bushes of negligence thriving on her neglect of divine graces, which she could not see before, because her heart was blinded. She began to notice that the natural beauty of soul which she had received from the impressed likeness of the eternal Godhead, when he created her to his image and likeness, was not a little disfigured, because she was drawn away and enticed by

112 *AA SS* April 2: 188, 25.
113 Letter 30; VM, *Brieven*, 1: 254, ll. 61–62. How Hadewijch experienced the human condition has been pointedly stressed by De Paepe in his *Hadewijch. Strofische Gedichten*, 161–63, and n.113. To say that Hadewijch does not speak about the fall and the land of unlikeness, the *regio dissimilitudinis*, can be true of her *Strofische Gedichten*, but is not as evident in her other writings. Even if she concentrated on the experiences rather than on the 'cause' of man's historical condition, in Letter 30 (VM, *Brieven*, 1: 254, ll. 72–76), she is in agreement with her mentors, who also stigmatized man's pride for choosing to be autonomous as God or against God, and refusing to be independent, yet under God.
114 *Vita*, 102, 26. The reference to 'an infant one day old' could come from Walter Daniel. See his *Epistola ad Mauricium*, 76 ('nemo mundus a peccato, nec infans cuius est unius diei uita super terram); F.M. Powicke, *Walter Daniel's Life of Ailred, Abbot of Rievaulx* (London, 1950). The sentence evidently refers to original sin. See Rm 5:12, and Bernard's IV HM 6; SBOp 5:60.

contrary affections, and neglected therefore... the noble purity of soul as she had received it from God.[115]

Any kind of sin and imperfection was a stain on the purity of the heart yearning for purification. In her first vision, Hadewijch saw a tree with many branches, and the third of the middlemost of them symbolized purity. In a sentence which shows what a fine psychologist she was, she wrote that she understood that this branch signified:

remaining pure of all stain in spirit, in desire and in the soul [so] that no baseness may penetrate there by error, haughtiness, vainglory, despair, or excessive hope of what one does not possess, and that one may not fall into joy over possessing something, or grief over lacking something, or into emotional attractions.[116]

Beatrice was determined 'to fight and to resist to death, rather than bear on her soul the infectious virus of even one mortal sin of whatever kind' (133,73). Christ himself urged Hadewijch 'to live in all hardships proper to the human condition, except sin'.[117]

The possibility of sinning seems to have been, at least partially, responsible for the desire of the *mulieres religiosae* to regain their primordial purity. To focus on one example: Beatrice found it 'extremely necessary to learn to conform herself wholly to the pursuit of rectitude and to exert herself moreover in that limpid purity, according to the grace given her by God from the beginning'.[118] The recovering of primordial purity is evidently not a small step, nor the last. Beatrice had to follow up the desire for recovery with 'the reformation of her capacities and virtues':

Proceeding along the line of purity and beauty, she did not draw back from the path of virtuous progress until she

---

115 *Vita*, 121, 29.
116 VM, *Visioenen*, 1: 18–19, ll. 144–51.
117 Vision one; VM, *Visioenen*, 1: 31, ll. 357–59.
118 *Vita*, 124, 82.

reached that perfection...in which she walked, going from virtue to virtue, with equal promptness of purity, her mind enlightened with truth.[119]

The laborious efforts to recover the lost or disfigured resemblance, to bring it toward its perfection on earth and its completion in the life to come, was often exhausting enough to provoke psychosomatic side effects. The biographies abound in examples.

The purity at which the *mulieres religiosae* aimed had to be total and free from any adulteration. One day, Ida of Leuven complained to the Lord that she was still deprived of the 'love of fruition', and had to be content with 'love of desire'. And she received from God the admonition not to be so anxious and perturbed about fruition : 'when she was filthy and deformed, he fell in love with her, cleansed her from her filth and healed her disfigurement'.[120] Having tasted during several raptures the sweetness of fruition, Ida had become inordinately desirous of such experiences and was in danger of seeking them, rather than the One who grants them.[121] Hadewijch expressed pointedly how pure love for God is supposed to be, when she wrote: 'Love thus exclusively for holy Love (*Minne*), out of pure love, not because of the satisfaction you might find by communing with love in devout exercises, but in order to devote yourself to God himself'.[122] In order to be totally pure in heart at the moment of her death, Ida Lewis asked the Lord that she might be completely purified, disentangled from any obstacles, able to take up her residence in the mansion of her Beloved.[123] In a letter

---

119 *Vita*, 124, 85. This is another way of saying that she put God's image within her or her capacity for participation in God into active and progressive motion toward likeness.

120 *AA SS* April 2: 179, 31. According to the biographer 'love of fruition' is reserved for heaven, while 'love of desire' is the insatiable love experienced on earth.

121 William warned against the danger of seeking raptures. See Bell, *The Image*, 304–06.

122 Letter 23; VM, *Brieven*, 1: 206, ll. 5–7.

123 *AA SS* Oct. 13: 112,14: 'Suspirans... ut absque purgatorio posset ad gaudia [caelestia] pervenire... nullatenus die vel unico tardaretur'.

Hadewijch exhorted a friend of hers: 'Have your eyes fixed with plain, exclusive purity [on the Lord], never henceforth to regard anything else'.[124] Beatrice, of whom we possess autobiographical information wrote in her treatise that the soul 'experienced a certain divine power and a clean purity...a gentle intimacy with our Lord and a nearness to God'; (Beatrice, in fact, is speaking here about herself in the third person).[125] Her biography gives us even more outspoken information: 'When she had been in office as prioress for a long time,[126] she knew [in a rapture] that she had arrived at that pristine purity and liberty of her spirit, at that clarity in which she had been created from the beginning' (236,45).

Beatrice's *Vita* and her treatise on love offer all one needs to realize how demanding is the call to the mystical life, if one would restore, or better, help restore in oneself the original nobility, dignity and purity one was created in 'from the beginning'. 'Like gold proved in fire, receiving its natural sheen from the blaze, so with her heart's recovery of total purity,...Beatrice passed into the liberty of the children of God'.[127]

THE SEAL

In their feudal society the *mulieres religiosae* were familiar with seals stamped on or attached to any official or important document to authenticate it. The five biographies in Chrysostomus

---

124 Letter 24; VM, *Brieven*, 1: 211, ll. 64–66. 'Plain' means the total purification (*puerlike*) of one's consciousness. See R. Vanneste, *Abstracta*, 87. Gregory of Nyssa (*De oratione dominica* 3; PG 44: 1154C) said nearly the same thing according to a passage cited in Latin by W. Hiss, *Die Anthropologie Bernhards von Clairvaux*, 79, n.35.

125 R-VM, *Seven manieren*, 24, ll. 20–24. Nearness (*nakenisse*) can mean propinquity with God, but could also express a closeness as the result of an experiential knowledge of God (*na kenisse*). It is difficult to express in a Latin or English or any translation what a dense vernacular text contains, least of all after the passage of seven centuries.

126 *Vita*, 234, 4. She was prioress from 1237 till 1268.

127 It seems worth noting that in *Vita*, 191, 153 and 236, 41, purity and liberty are mentioned together, bringing Beatrice 'into a certain delightful refreshment, being made purer than gold and more resplendent than any crystal'.

Henriquez' *Quinque prudentes virgines* contain no explicit use of the term coin,[128] nor do they refer to an image engraved or chiseled in the human soul,[129] or a 'representation',[130] much less of the brand placed on cattle to identify their owner. Like Bernard, the biographers seem to have had a preference for a seal, relating it to the image and likeness.[131] Sharing in the nobility and dignity of God, persons were sealed not as things or objects, but as subjects, as souls on which he had impressed the seal of his image and likeness. Occasionally they would refer to God's image and likeness impressed on them at their creation or regenerated in their baptism. When Beatrice had gone through a painful purification,

> she felt herself abiding in the same purity of heart which anyone receives when he is washed free from the infection of all sins in the baptismal font, or when in its creation God impressed and infused the grace of purity in the soul, forming in it his image' (197,41).

More important is the use of the seal in relation to the image moving toward fuller participation in the likeness, wherein the volition of the will is involved. In bridal mysticism the love

---

128 'Moneta Christi homo est, ibi imago Christi', said Augustine in his *Sermo* 90.10 (PL 38: 566]: man is like a coin, bearing in accordance with a centuries-old custom the image of the ruler (here Christ).

129 'Engraven image' (*insculpta*) is used by Rupert of Deutz (before 1070–1129), a Benedictine monk once at Liège and an acquaintance of William, in his *Liber de divinis officiis* (Hrabanus Haacke, *Ruperti Tuitensis Liber de divinis officiis*, CCCM 7 [Turnhout, 1967] 228). William's friendship did not impede him from objecting (PL 180: 341–44) to certain ideas put forward by Rupert in this same work in relation to the Eucharist). See John Van Engen, 'Rupert of Deutz and William of St. Thierry', *RBén* 93 (1983) 327–36.

130 This term is used in the pseudo-Bernardine treatise *Meditationes piissimae* (see above, n. 92), which shows some influences of the treatise *De spiritu et anima*. As Wilmart noted (*Auteurs spirituels*, 183, n.1) the two treatises are nearly contemporary.

131 D.H. Williams, 'The Seal in Cistercian Usage with Special Reference to Wales', *Mélanges Anselme Dimier*, vol.1, part 3 (Artois, France:Pupillon, 1983) 249–57. See, for instance, Bernard, Nat 2.3; SBOp 4: 253: 'Man, created to God's image and likeness, was thus authenticated with God's seal': divino munita sigillo ad imaginem quippe et similitudinem creavit [Deus] hominem'.

motive is the uniting bond between God and the soul, a reference
to the likeness. When the Lord appeared one day to Beatrice, he
proposed to her a compact to remain united.

> She pledged willingly to keep such a salutary covenant....It
> seemed to her that he, the Lord of all consolation and mercy,
> pressed her soul wholly to himself in the sweetest of
> embraces; and just as the soft wax pressed with the seal,
> shows forth the seal's character in itself, so the divine Spirit
> modeled her soul accordingly to his own image, and con-
> formed it most fittingly to his own likeness.[132]

Hadewijch called this bond of love 'the seal of love'. In a
vision she was told that previously she fell down before the
Countenance [of God's Son] and like any ordinary soul she had to
acknowledge the inaccessibility of his Majesty. But when she
stood up and contemplated his Countenance, she saw herself a
perfect, veritable bride, marked with the seal of love.[133] In a
passage of Ida of Nivelles' biography, the seal is related to the
Trinity and love: for some days 'whenever the Eucharist was
celebrated, she experienced the presence of the Blessed Trinity'.
She said that 'as an impression with a seal keeps the image of the
seal, so her soul was impressed with the lime of a very ardent
love, so that her soul became one spirit with the Lord',[134] a clear
reference to the likeness to God.

In whatever way image and likeness are distinct, there were
some *mulieres religiosae* who, consenting to the activity of God's

---

132 *Vita*, 166, 24. This text seems to have been influenced by Bernard (SC
83.1–3; SBOp 2: 298–99), who spoke of the alliance between the soul as bride
and Christ, by whose image it sees itself honored, and in whose likeness it
knows itself made glorious, reformed by him and conformed to him in love.

133 Vision 12; VM, *Visioenen*, 1: 133, ll. 165–69. A few lines before the
quoted text, Hadewijch spoke of the bride wearing a brooch which meant
symbolically 'the divine seal evidencing that she had experiential knowledge of
the undivided divine Unity', *ibid.*, 132, ll. 142–45.

134 *Quinque*, 271. Ida is here in accordance with Achard of St.Victor
(d.1170–71), who follows Augustine. See Jean Chatillon, *Théologie, Spiritualité
et Métaphysique dans l'oeuvre oratoire d'Achard de Saint-Victor*, Études de
Philosophie médiévale, 58, E. Gilson, ed. (Paris, 1969) 156–57.

grace, went deeply enough through laborious purifications of the heart to be united with the all-demanding love of God. The seal of the image becomes co-extensive with the seal of love, *viz.* the seal of likeness. In such situations the image's capacity for participation has grown into an image capacitated to effectively participate—as far as possible on earth—in God as he essentially is: Love.

NOBLE PRIDE: *FIERHEID*

The nobility, dignity and purity of the soul, the 'seal' of himself which God impressed on them, made some of the *mulieres religiosae* speak of an important 'natural good', which they called *fierheid*, which can best be translated as noble pride. By it

> the soul seeks, loves and pursues things better and more sublime than itself. Through the use of reasonable judgment it transcends what is frail and slippery, and detests and spurns all the incentives of vice springing from the root of the opposite sort of pride.[135]

But there is a still more positive aspect to noble pride: 'a subtleness of spirit by which it clings more firmly and more promptly in simple desire to the supreme Good'.[136] *Fierheid* is a gratefully accepted and cherished condition of God's relatedness to man and man's to God, a taste of the Absolute, proudly opposed to the experience of the limiting human conditions. As Hadewijch expressed it in a sentence to a friend under her guidance:

> If you wish to follow your being in which God created you, you must in noble-mindedness spare no pains. In stout-

---

135 *Vita*, 122, 39. This rather negative aspect of *fierheid* is reminiscent of William: 'Withdraw from things which are beneath you. They are less formed, less beautiful than you are. Come up to the Form [God's Son] that gives form so that you may be more beautiful': Nat corp, PL 180: 721D.

136 *Vita*, 122, 50. This seems to refer to William's sentence which follows the one just quoted: 'Constantly unite yourself to this Form, for you will receive more from its beauty, the more the natural tendency (*pondus*) of love presses you to this Form'.

hearted noble pride you will not permit yourself to fail, but valiantly and at all costs lay hold to the best part—I mean the great totality of God—as your own good.[137]

These references—there are several more—are sufficient to give an idea of what noble pride meant to these writers: how a small human creature was made to stretch itself toward the Incomprehensible, its unreachableness notwithstanding, and to realize in all simplicity how uplifting and inexpressibly great such a God-given *fierheid* is.[138]

---

137 Letter 6; VM, *Brieven*, 1: 62, ll. 191–96.

138 For a more extensive study of noble pride, see Marcel Brauns, 'Over fierheid in de religieuze beleving', first published in *Bijdragen* 6 (1943–45) 185–246; 7 (1946) 73–139, and later in one volume, *Fierheid in de Religieuze Beleving* (Bruges, 1959). M.J. Van Baest, whose entire dissertation concerns *fierheid* ('fiere herte doelt na minnen gronde') has a whole chapter (133–74) on 'De fiere theologie van Hadewijch', a 'noble pride' primarily based on being made to God's image and likeness.

CHAPTER SIX

NATURAL AND
GRATUITOUS GIFTS

GRACE IS GOD'S SELF-COMMUNICATION TO MAN. The East,[1] the patristic age[2] and the medieval West knew nothing about 'pure nature'[3] In reality, man does not have much choice in this matter. He finds himself in a God-man relationship gratuitously established by God at his creation. If he refuses or rejects it, he falls into a man-*pecus*, a man-beast relation. This is explicitly stated by Gregory of Nyssa,[4] Augustine,[5] and the twelfth-century mentors of the *mulieres religiosae*,

---

1 Vladimir Lossky, *Mystical Theology*, 101 and 126, to refer to this one work among so many.

2 Augustine in particular. See Sullivan, *The Image*, 53; Xavier Léon-Dufour, 'Grâce et liberté chez S.Augustin', *RSR* 33 (1946) 126–63; 148: 'Pour bien comprendre S.Augustin, il faut résister à la temptation de solidifier le pseudo-concept de 'nature pure' en une réalité subsistant en dehors de la grâce'.

3 At least not before the sixteenth century when Cajetan (1468–1534) and Suarez (1548–1617) wrote about Thomas Aquinas' teaching of 'pure nature'. Their theory was, in fact, a misinterpretation of what Thomas wrote on this subject. According to Yves Congar, to speak about pure nature would have been for Thomas himself contradictory, since for him, pure nature is nature considered in itself, independently of all references to God. See de Lubac, *The Supernatural*, 8–16.

4 Daniélou, *Platonisme*, 79–88.

5 *De Trinitate* 1.11.6; PL 42: 1008: 'pervenit [homo] ad similitudinem pecoris'.

each of them applying his own nuances.[6] There is no neutral zone, no man-man equation. It is either God or beast. Man came into being through God's creative act, without any *debitum naturae, viz.* with no suggestion of any demand prior to what God laid on the man he created. Ida of Leuven's biography does speak about a *debitum naturae*, but this is quite a different obligation, one that man brought upon himself. It is 'the common debt of nature'[7] which he pays when he dies. Man cannot hold God in his debt, as owing some debit due to himself.[8] His creation is a free gift from God, endowing him with an openness for more to come.[9] From the start man received his existence as an undeserved and gratuitously given grace, his coming into being to God's image and likeness. This grace may be called natural, because this is the way man came into existence from the beginning, *ab initio,* by God's creating grace.[10]

GIFTS AND GRACES.

The distinction between natural and gratuitous graces was commonly used, particularly at the end of the twelfth century.[11]

---

6 Hugh, *In Ecclesiasten Homiliae* 18; PL 175: 249B; – Richard, *De Emmanuele* 1.11; PL 196: 618D; – Bernard, SC 24.6; SBOp 1: 158; SC 82.5; SBOp 2:296; – William, Cant; PL 180:503C, – Aelred, Spec car 1.2; PL 195: 507B; – Isaac of Stella, *Sermo* 2; PL 194: 1695C; – Thomas the Cistercian, *In Cant* 4; PL 206: 249A; – Alan of Lille: M.T. d'Alverny, *Alain de Lille,* 304.

7 *AA SS* April 2: 187,20: 'commune naturae debitum'. Hadewijch also said that by dying, Christ paid the debt of human nature. Letter 6; VM, *Brieven,* 1: 58, ll. 112–13.

8 If there is any debt it is one owed to God who, as Hadewijch wrote, gave 'us grace to live worthily according to the noble Trinity, as is fitting'. Letter 30; VM, *Brieven,* 1: 254, ll. 68–71.

9 K. Rahner, *Theological Investigations* 4, 'Nature and grace', 165–88; 183– 84: 'The basic essence of man, his nature as such openness (transcendence) can be perfectly well established. The initial elements of such fulfilment are already present: the experience of infinite longings, of radical optimism, of unquenchable discontent, of the torment of the insufficiency of everything attainable, of the radical protest against death, the experience of being confronted with an absolute love precisely where it is lethally incomprehensible and seems to be silent and aloof, the experience of radical guilt and of a still abiding hope, etc'.

10 Hugh, *De Sacramentis* 1.6.17; PL 176: 273C; – Bernard, Gra 6.16; SBOp 3: 178; – William, Cant 22; PL 180: 480B.

11 Alan of Lille related the natural gifts to the image, and the gratuitous to the likeness, as did the pseudo-Bernardine *De praecipuis mysteriis nostrae*

Beatrice listed some of 'the natural and gratuitous gifts' or graces with which she had been endowed by her Creator.[12] Since her *Vita* is so explicit in this matter, a closer look at what she had to say about this matter seems indicated. She described what the natural gifts were and how she had to turn them to her advantage.

They included her natural faculties of memory, reason and *intellectus* (94,63), and qualities such as the natural beauty (*decor*) of her soul (121,31); her most noble purity (121,35); her noble pride as a creature made to God's image and likeness (122,39); subtlety of spirit through which the soul usually advances in the contemplation of heavenly things (122,48); keenness of spirit through which the soul clings more firmly and more promptly in simple desire for the Supreme Good (122,50); natural simplicity which walks more freely and without injury amid the various stumbling blocks of the world as it is more devoid and ignorant of the curious investigations of different matters (122,46); innate severity which by its own nature always detests and attacks every kind of vice, acting in accordance with the norms of justice in everything, lest it exceed the bounds of equity in its motives, or plunge over a precipice if reasonable judgment is clouded (122,52). On the contrary this natural good respects the norms of justice. It is peace-loving, quiet tranquillity of heart. Out of desire for peace, it inflicts its own troubles on no one else and even bears others' injuries with calmness (122,57). Very many other goods also exist, such as generosity, liberality, ability, affability and many like things (123,61).[13]

In the biographies, particularly in Beatrice's, these goods (*bona*) are often called grants (*data*) and gifts (*dona*), benefits or favors (*beneficia*). The terms are so freely used that they cannot be directly linked to the influence of any particular source,

---

religionis, PL 184: 773–74, and several others, some of them contemporaries of the *mulieres religiosae* movement. See Javelet, *Image*, 2: 192, n.443, explaining the diversity of opinions at the end of the twelfth century.

12 *Vita*, 93, 58; 121, 26.

13 The natural goods enumerated by Beatrice sound much like William's requirements for an *animus*, see above, pp. 103-107.

whether Hugh, the Cistercian bishop Otto of Freising (d.1158) or Gilbert of Hoyland (d.1172).[14] The God-given natural goods are the preliminary basis planned by God for his full self-communication to man. It is he who desired to have man as partner in a love-relation, to the extent that a creature is capable of entering by participation into an endless union with an absolute and infinite God. This is the teaching of Gregory of Nyssa,[15] Augustine,[16] and the twelfth-century mentors of the *mulieres religiosae*, Cistercians and Victorines alike.[17] Sometimes the gratuitous gifts were described as superadded (*superadditum*).[18] Beatrice expressed the vastness of the gratuitous gifts in dense sentences with a meaning much deeper than a quick glance conveys: She grasped through their singular magnitude that greater abundance of the graces divinely given her. In addition to what she had received with all Christians—namely the title of Christianity (94,67) and baptism, 'the bath of regeneration' (94,68)—she recalled the gratuitous gifts she personally had received (and listed in 94,69; 171,38; 208,7). She reflected upon the incarnation of the Lord, Jesus Christ, the work of her salvation and his work of Redemption (95,87). She copiously thanked the

---

14 Gilbert tried unsuccessfully to complete the unfinished commentary of Bernard on the Song of Songs, and he gave clear-cut definitions of grants and gifts (*data et dona*). For references to the three mentioned authors, see de Lubac, *The Supernatural*, 117.

15 Leys, *L'Image de Dieu*, 97–106; E. Konstantinou, *Die Tugendlehre Gregors*, 93, 106 and 152.

16 Sullivan, *The Image*, 51–53. For Augustine, 'It is because he wills us to be one day with him that God wills us to "to be"', for that, in the full metaphysical sense of the phrase, is our only *raison d'être*'. This conclusion, arrived at by Gilson, is cited by de Lubac, *The Supernatural*, 125.

17 J. Lortz, *Bernhard von Clairvaux*, xxxvi: 'Das natürliche gilt noch als ein Element, das darauf hingeordnet ist, in das Übernatürliche einzugehen'; Javelet, *Image*, 1: 323–27, and his *Psychologie*, 17: 'Le surnaturel est naturel à l'homme, non pas qu'il soit de même nature... mais parce que, en fait, la destinée de l'homme se joue par rapport à Dieu'.

18 In pre–scholastic thought, natural gifts are not seen in opposition to the supernatural gifts in the modern sense, but as capacity evolving toward fulness in participation. See Javelet, *Image*, 1: 327–43. See also de Lubac, 'La rencontre de *superadditum* et *supernaturale* dans la théologie médiévale', *RMAL* 1 (1945) 27–34.

divine liberality...especially for the health-giving Sacrament of his body and blood (95,99).

In this pre-scholastic period we should not expect the neat classifications of later times. For the *mulieres religiosae*, as for their mentors, grace originated with God who is infinite love. They saw God dispensing freely according to his own good will the grace which embraced both predestination by him and the free response in love from man. Without entirely neglecting classifications, they seem to have been primarily interested in experiencing God's graces and desiring them with vehement vigor and 'violent' striving as it behooves human beings loved so much by such a loving God. The desire they felt came from God and tended toward him, becoming a 'burning desire', burning to be faithful when unfulfilled, and burning yet more when filled to enlarge its capacity to be fulfilled still more by love for a God who is infinitely fulfilled in himself and who is for man a never-ending fulfillment.

A text from Bernard, a prominent but certainly not the only influential mentor of the *mulieres religiosae*, written to his former monk, pope Eugene III, allows us to capture the richness and vastness of God' grace.

> God alone can never be sought in vain, even when he cannot be found. For what is God?.... That which is to the universe, the end; to the elect, salvation;...[he is] omnipotent will, benevolent virtue, eternal light, unchangeable reason, supreme blessedness; he creates souls to share in himself, vivifies them that they may experience him, causes them to desire him (*afficiens ad appetendum*), enlarges them to receive him (*dilatans ad capiendum*), justifies them that they may deserve him; he inflames them with zeal, brings them to fruition, enlightens them with knowledge, preserves them to immortality, fills them with happiness, surrounds them with security.[19]

---

19 Csi 5.11.24; SBOp 3: 486–87.

Many *mulieres religiosae* were experientially acquainted with this process. Beatrice's biography allows more insight into how she and others looked at God's grace. At seventeen, still very young, she hoped for a while,[20] 'to acquire by exterior labor the grace that is freely given, and to buy with the price of bodily acts the gift which is priceless' (67,25). But she learned her lesson:

Wonderfully animated in spirit she felt herself entirely strengthened by a new and unusual fortitude and spiritual constancy which she would have to follow willy-nilly, wherever it led. By the Lord's gift she received then such an illuminated spiritual insight, that with strengthened discretion and increased powers of reason, she knew with infallible judgment the way of truth in which she would have to proceed henceforth, and would judge subtly between good and evil, profane and useful. Then indeed by her subtlety of spirit she saw clearly how foolish she had aspired to obtain the supreme free gifts by exchange and repayment. Now she knew and understood that the Lord's gifts, according to the etymology of the name, are distributed by him to whom and how and when he wills, without reward or recompense; they are distributed freely without the venality of a pact by him who gives abundantly and without restraint.... She obliged herself by a voluntary promise never in the future to presume that she would attain the gift of divine grace by her own efforts. From that time on she intended to serve the works of virtue with a stronger desire, and she strove to convert to the improvement of life her wandering thoughts and the itch to act and to speak. And lest she receive the grace of God in vain, she promised with a firm purpose that she would conform herself to the divine good-pleasure.[21]

Beatrice spoke of habitual grace in terms of 'divine Majesty', which accentuates the giver rather than the gift, for the gift of the

---

20 *Vita*, 62, 67: from Easter till 14 September 1217.
21 *Vita*, 68, 33: Some parts of these excerpts are reminiscent of William's saying that grace is freely given 'anterior to all our good merits': Exp Rm; PL

giver is the giver himself. For Beatrice, as for all the *mulieres religiosae* for that matter, habitual grace was so magnificent and so greatly appreciated because of the greatness and magnificence of the 'uncreated Good' (196,14). Grace is, in fact, the divine Majesty, the supreme and incomprehensible God whose self-communication to man is a peerless gift.

Habitual grace for Beatrice meant the gaze (92,35), the eye (101,8), the sight (93,49; 106,26; 126,28), the presence of divine Majesty,[22] who looks not down upon but looking across at the one he chose to create as his partner in a love-relationship. On the advice of Ida of Nivelles, Beatrice applied herself to make her heart a fitting receptacle and dwelling place for God's presence (50,49; 51,81; 92,40). She evidently became even increasingly aware of the presence of the divine Majesty during her several ecstasies.[23] There are passages in which majesty and presence do not strictly refer to the habitual grace of God's present Majesty,[24] but these exceptions are clear from the context.

Having received baptism (194,40) and sharing in redemption (147,58), Beatrice tried hard to please the divine Majesty in all circumstances (97,129; 199,65), taking good care of natural and gratuitous gifts (103,58). Since God's divine glance penetrates everything hidden in the conscience (106,20), she tried on the one hand to be worthy of what she had received (90,61), and on the

---

180: 623C. Similarly Bernard said in Pasc 2.7: SBOp 5:98: 'What shall we give him in return for his grace, who has need of nothing and possesses all? Grace is given gratis; even when it is bought, it is bought without payment, for the thing we give for it is, by the giving, the better kept for ourselves. The three spices of the mind must be bought with the coin of our own will. And when we part with that, we do not lose it, rather gain enormously; indeed we make a good exchange when that which was our own is held in common, for to will the common good is charity, and charity is kind and rejoices not in iniquity. And the three spices that the mind must buy are compassion, zeal for righteousness, and the spirit of discretion'. The ET is taken fron *Saint Bernard. On the Christian Year*, translated by a Religous CSMV (London, 1954) 95–96.

22 *Vita*, 40, 63; 73, 11 (which Reypens, *Vita*, 59, n.1 suggests is equivalent to confirmation in grace); 90, 61; 120, 18; 127, 52; 132, 62; 206, 10.

23 *Vita*, 55, 37; 149, 80; 159, 77; 165, 7; 172, 53; 174, 86; 193, 29; 213, 18; 217, 93; 223, 89; 236, 30. The succession and frequency in time deserve to be noticed.

24 For example: *Vita*, 40, 61; 96, 117; 109, 50; 113, 49; 128, 58.

other to apply herself to a virtuous life.[25] She was prepared to avoid sin at all costs,[26] to fight till her heart should break (146,38).

Here we come in touch with the 'actual grace', given to an individual in his personal situation. This special gift (124,83) is a divine favor,[27] showing the goodness, kindness or mercy of God[28] stressed from beginning to end in Beatrice's biography; it is in accordance with his good-pleasure and her needs that God infuses or inspires such grace.[29]

Beatrice referred to actual grace as divine visitations.[30] These require steadfast vigilance and demanding efforts if she is to be faithful to them.[31] In the last part of her biography she is said to have become physically and psychically strong enough to carry the burden (*pondus*) of such divine visitations.[32] The light of grace[33] made her anticipate grace, (73,13; 103,61) which she felt strengthened her,[34] particularly when she prayed[35] or was tested

---

25 *Vita*, 85, 27; 91, 19; 104, 73; 106, 25; 110, 59; 114, 71; 118, 6; 124, 91; 133, 87; 149, 97; 154, 41; 166, 51; 174, 85; 196, 4; 199, 67.

26 *Vita*, 40, 61; 43, 47; 130, 14; 139, 185; 169, 80; 186, 62.

27 As in *Vita*, 6, 59; 19, 62; 50, 38; 52, 104; 64, 50; 67, 23; 85, 17; 92, 39; 118, 7; 124, 93; 131, 41; 143, 48; 199, 70; 201, 25; 213, 18; 217, 106. The biographies of Ida of Nivelles (*Quinque*, 282) and of Ida of Leuven, *AA SS* April 2: 172, 2, speak similarly.

28 *Vita*, 47, 50; 64, 102; 73, 14; 81, 35; 98, 140; 124, 83; 133, 79; 137, 138; 148, 77; 170, 22; 180, 157; 186, 62; 192, 14; 208, 11.

29 *Vita*, 53, 117; 62, 104; 64, 101; 65, 11; 66, 36; 70, 89; 74, 24; 84, 94; 90, 69; 200, 4; 201, 25 , as also in the case of Ida of Nivelles: *Quinque*, 282.

30 *Vita*, 53, 114; 73, 16; 81, 43; 90, 68; 94, 76; 165, 11; 188, 84; 189, 112; 208, 13.

31 *Vita*, 51, 54: Ida of Nivelles had warned Beatrice that her glory in heaven would not come automatically but would depend on her faithfulness to grace: 'If only you will take care to use well his sweet gifts of grace in this world, he will multiply the glory of the world to come'.

32 *Vita*, 202, 51. Ida Lewis had a similar overwhelming experience, *AA SS* Oct. 13: 116, 31, as did Ida of Leuven, *AA SS* April 2:171, 2.

33 *Vita*, 52, 91; 62, 72; 66, 36; 163, 56; this was also experienced by Ida of Leuven, *AA SS* April 2: 170, 45; Ida of Nivelles, *Quinque*, 250 and of course by Hadewijch. See Reynaert, *Beeldspraak*, 58–64.

34 *Vita*, 29, 117; 64, 102; 65, 6; 70, 89; 98, 140; 123, 69; 124, 93; 155, 66; 201, 25; 208, 9. See also Ida Lewis, *AA SS* Oct. 13: 163, 12.

35 *Vita*, 68, 44; 123, 75; 137, 138; 137, 158; 141, 32; 143, 48; 155, 61. Scripture is also mentioned (86, 44; 137, 142) as are the liturgy, the divine office or the common prayers said or more often sung in choir.

by temptations or torpor to be purified by them.³⁶ Fearing care-
lessness (90,63) and neglect (123,74), she stressed her endeavors
(*industria*) and zeal (*studium*) at obtaining the needed grace so
often that her biographer referred to it in one place as her 'usual
zeal' (*studio solito*) 'to take the right-hand way, that is, the way of
improvement'(168,63).

This way of improvement included the experience of what
William called 'hidden grace',³⁷ the feeling of being desolate, as
if God's grace had been withdrawn from her.³⁸ But she knew too
that grace was given to make her agreeable to God³⁹ by doing his
will in accordance with his good-pleasure.⁴⁰ For only with God's
grace could she arrive at 'stability of spirit and heart' (226,86),
and remain imperturbably anchored in the love of her God.

All this could, on the other hand, be seen as self-centeredness.
But grace given, accepted or rejected, is not merely an individual
affair. God sees and loves man collectively as well as individually. What he gives to an individual has also social and collective
dimensions.⁴¹ Grasping the meaning of grace, Beatrice knew
about the implied sharing, and she shared.⁴²

Often one finds expressed in the writings and biographies of
the better-known *mulieres religiosae* their awareness of what man
meant to God and God to man. For that reason, Beatrice, like
many others would repeatedly express her thanksgiving (*gratiarum actio*) to the giver of all graces. The following two citations,
chosen from an abundance of similar texts, give an idea of how

---

36 *Vita*, 46, 36; 66, 35; 75, 66; 91, 17; 104, 80; 126, 35; 139, 181;143, 46;
148, 74; 149, 92; 155, 66; 169, 92.
37 Cant 786; PL 180: 499D: 'occulta gratia'.
38 *Vita*, 131, 41; 135, 113; 139, 179; 141, 19; 143, 45; 145, 19, etc.
39 Later, technically called *gratia gratum faciens*.
40 *Vita*, 86, 58; 69, 63; 71, 7; 72, 39; 91, 9; 91, 11; 96, 108; 97, 125; 130, 6;
130, 26; 146, 30; 164, 71; 166, 33; 166, 40; 180, 169; 192, 12; 196, 7; 199, 62;
205, 87; 212, 89; 217, 108; 218, 113; 222, 7; 226, 93; 228, 19; 264, 27.
41 Beatrice did not know the expression '*gratia gratis data*', as used later in
theological terminology to indicate that grace is so gratuitously given to an
individual that it has to be freely shared with others, if it is to keep its value. The
same could be said of Hadewijch. See Letter 18; VM, *Brieven*, 1: 154, ll. 58–60.
42 *Vita*, 6, 72; 49, 55; 86, 54; 102, 22; 108, 35; 112, 33; 123, 68; 127, 54; 154,
53; 199, 71; 218, 124; 221, 65; 224, 55; 263, 4; 268, 100.

her heart vibrated with thanksgiving. 'As time succeeded time, she continued constantly in offering the Lord worship in the temple of her heart' (89,53).

Recognizing God's gracious gifts, she praised the giver of every grace, singing the hymn *Te Deum laudamus* to the divine Trinity as a special act of praise. From then on [she] remained in a fuller knowledge of herself and served the Lord with a more abundant supply of goods, both gratuitous and natural, in purity of conscience and sweetness of heart.[43]

God's actual plan to have man (*mensch*) as his partner in a love-relation is and remains written into man's being and cannot be undone by the human misuse of his freedom. This misuse, as the patristic and twelfth-century mentors of the *mulieres religiosae* pointed out,[44] even opened up perspectives of gratuitous gifts, immensely excelling the original human condition: sharing in Christ's divine Sonship, giving the union of God and man new and more intimate dimensions. The movement from creation toward restoration or reformation and consummation,[45] became a classical triad.[46] The closer one comes to the primordial state, the more sin and all that is offensive to God is discarded, and this action opens up the flowering of both the natural and gratuitous gifts according to God's plan from all eternity, *ab initio*.[47] Hence

---

43 *Vita*, 124, 95.

44 See above, Chapter IV.

45 Bernard, Gra 14.49; SBOp 3:201. Bernard has this succession in his Nat 2.1; SBOp 4: 251. J. Leclercq has schematized it in his 'Aspects littéraires de l'oeuvre de S.Bernard', *Cahiers de civilisation médiévale* 1 (1958) 425–50; *ibid.*, 8 (1965) 299–326, rpt in *Recueil d'Études sur Saint Bernard et ses Écrits*, Storia e Letteratura 114 (Rome, 1969) vol.3: 13–104; 64.

46 Javelet, *Image*, 1: 337 and 343: 'La grâce est l'action de Dieu, découpée par les auteurs spirituels selon ses opérations successives: création, restauration, consommation'.

47 This restoration 'has to be thoroughly understood because it forms, so to, speak, the bed-rock of all the Cistercian mysticism. It is from this point that the soul sets out *ut amplexus Verbi fidenter accedat*, and confidently approaches the Word's embraces'; Gilson, *The Mystical Theology*, 54. See Bernard, SC 81.; SBOp 2:284.

the *mulieres religiosae*'s high appreciation of grace, which flows from the redemption by God's incarnate Son and is diffused by the Holy Spirit.[48] Without going into an unnecessarily full consideration of Christology and Pneumatology, a limited look at a few *mulieres religiosae* helps illustrate this aspect.[49]

---

48 They were not speculatively concerned about the question whether the incarnation would have taken place if primordial man had not turned away from God by going his own way. This question, which later divided the scholastic Thomists and Scotists, has been treated by Gustave Martelet, 'Sur le motif de l'Incarnation', in *Problèmes de Christologie*, H.Bouëssé and J. Latour eds. (Bruges-Paris, 1965) 35–80: 'Les deux éléments [the incarnation and our divinization by adoption] qui ne sont pas séparés, ne sont pas nécessairement identiques et... l'incarnation qui n'exclut pas la rédemption se rapporte d'abord à l'adoption'. See also James Mc Envoy, 'The absolute Predestination of Christ in the Theology of Robert Grosseteste', *Sapientiae doctrina*. Mélanges H.Bascour, 212–30. Mc Envoy based his study on Grosseteste's text published (with some errors) by Dominic Unger, 'Robert Grosseteste, bishop of Lincoln (1235–53): On the reason for the Incarnation', *Franciscan Studies* 16 (1956) 1 ?6. Of particular interest is the interesting book *Why Jesus Christ?* by J. B. Carol, (Manassas, Va.1986).

49 This aspect is connected with the question of God's immutability and emotionality. Some philosophers hold that God is without emotions; this can be seen in Louis De Raeymaeker, *The Philosophy of Being*, 206 and 308–16 (ET by E. Ziegelmeier, St Louis-London, 1957²); or in R. Jolivet, *The God of Reason*, ET by M. Pontifex (London, 1959) 83–86; 96–99. However, William E. Mann, defending God's immutability ('Simplicity and Immutability', *IPQ* 23 [1983] 267–76) acknowledges that this immutability 'has drawn fire from virtually every philosopher who considered it'. K. Rahner, who approached this topic theologically, had necessarily to turn to God's self-revelation in Christ. 'The incarnation leading to the 'foolishness' of the cross is part of God's plans from all eternity. He desired so much to have man as a love partner that through the incarnation he gave man the chance to share by free consent in the Sonship of his own and only Son. God's immutability within himself can, at the same time, become something 'in another', *viz.* his Image becoming man. (Karl Rahner, 'On the Theology of the Incarnation', *Theological Investigations*, vol.4: 105–20; 114). Or as he says elsewhere: 'The existentially personal and active character of God's behaviour, in contrast to some fixed metaphysical attributes of his essence, is just as clear when he is called *good, merciful, loving*, and so on.... Properly and precisely, we know *who* God is, not from ourselves and the world, but only by the activity in history of a free and living God, through which he showed us who he wished to be to us'. See K. Rahner, 'Theos in the New Testament', *Theological Investigations*, vol.1: 79–148; 114–116.

THE GRACE OF CHRIST

Beatrice, aware that 'by no preceding merits of hers had she gained so lofty a prerogative of grace, asked the Lord why he had written her name with his own merciful hand in the Book of Life' (171,22) and she was told by him: 'for my sake and for the sake of my holy name I poured out this flood of my graces upon you, and do not try to see any other cause for this matter than the simple evidence proceeding from my good will' (171,32). Christ also pointed out to Ida of Leuven the gratuitousness of his love (*amore gratuito*) for her: 'With no preceding or any apparent indications that she deserved it, he fell in love with her'.[50]

In the biographies, such expressions as 'with the help of Christ's grace' or 'with the help of the Lord's grace' occur frequently, usually related to difficulties to be faced. In some cases grace is identified with Christ. A monk asked the famous Arnulph of Brussels (d.1228), a laybrother in Villers, to pray for him and to send him the Lord (*mitte mihi Dominum*), *viz.* a special experience of grace. When he received it he could not stop weeping for joy for one hour. Through Arnulph's prayers some Cistercian nuns of Robermont (Liège) had the same experience.[51] Receiving the visit of the Lord [in the Eucharist], Ida of Nivelles became so overwhelmed 'by divine grace descending to the depths of her soul through the aqueduct of love that for some time she could not move'.[52]

Grace is not a luxury to be dealt with as one pleases. As Hadewijch wrote in one of her letters: 'every man should be observant of the grace he has and cooperate wisely with it. For the graces of the Lord...lay obligations on man. If he works with his

---

50 *AA SS* April 2: 179,31: 'amore gratuito nullisque praecedentibus aut apparentibus in te meritis, adamavi'.

51 *AA SS* June 7: 622,29: 'ruptae sunt cataractae capitis ejus, et ab oculis ejus tanta lacrymarum inundatio erupit, quod impetu earum, etsi voluisset, retinere non potuit.... Simili modo quibusdam monialibus Roberti-Montis gratiam Domini praedixit affuturam, et quemadmodum praedixerat, ita accidisse'.

52 *Quinque*, 250: 'per aquae ductum amoris in animam ejus descendente imbuta est ut...diutius a loco eodem moveri non posset'.

grace, he pleases God; but if he does not do so, he becomes culpable'.[53] Beatrice expressed in her way the same warning:

Whatever anyone receives from the grace of Christ, according to the measure of his giving, let him remember that he will be the more severely punished for the talent received, unless he turns it to the praise of him from whom he received it, and uses it for his own and his neighbor's needs, according to grace given him and working in him.[54]

The parables of the talents (Mt 25:14–30 and par.) which Beatrice referred to in this quotation were also used by many others, Hadewijch among them: 'It is needful that he whom God has set up as a merchant to trade with his goods should be wise and so guard his grace that it may remain with him'.[55] The five biographies of Henriquez's *Quinque prudentes virgines* confirm Bernard's saying that 'to seek the Word is to consent by his grace to his grace'.[56] Hadewijch expressed it in her own personal way:

Anyone who is ever without grace must pray to God for grace; he who is in grace must pray to God that he may preserve it. For as often as a man allows that good of the Lord to diminish and does not augment it, so often does he forfeit it all and challenges God's goodness. This is why one reads about the bride in the Song of Songs that she sought her bridegroom not only with desire but with wisdom; and when she has found him she was no less careful to hold him. This is what every wise soul should do when stirred by love. She should continually increase her grace with desire and

---

53 Letter 10; VM, *Brieven*, 1: 90, ll. 83–88.
54 *Vita*, 123, 65.
55 Letter 10; VM, *Brieven*, 1: 91, ll. 93–95.
56 SC 85.1; PL 183: 1188B: 'quaere Verbum cui consentias, ipso faciente ut consentias'. The explicative *ut consentias* does not occur in the critical edition (SBOp 2: 308, l. 11), but appears as an addition in manuscripts of the Clairvaux tradition, reprinted in Migne's PL, and explains well what is meant by *cui consentias ipso faciente*.

wisdom and carefully cultivate her field, rooting out weeds and sowing virtues; and she should build the house of a pure conscience, wherein she can worthily receive her beloved.[57]

Both God's supremacy and man's voluntary and free consent in the realm of his salvation are to be combined. The two partners are involved and neither one of them brings man adequately and effectively to his full realized destiny without the other. This collaboration encompasses man's life in all its stages. This is precisely what the *mulieres religiosae* had in their minds and in their hearts.

GRACE OF THE HOLY SPIRIT

Expressions such as 'divine spirit' or 'divine grace' do not necessarily point to the Holy Spirit,[58] unlike explicit references to the grace of the Holy Spirit. The Holy Spirit's great involvement in man's creation, in the incarnation of the Word and in man's regeneration and consummation or glorification has been variously expressed.[59] As far as man is concerned, the Holy Spirit involved in this process, is not inevitably and necessarily, the Spirit as the substantial love of the Father and the Son (as he is within the Trinity), but the Spirit as gift, or in our human terms, our participation in him.[60] On this gift depends man's journey to his destiny: 'To become, not God, but what God is, that is to say, man becomes through grace what God is by nature'.[61] It is this

---

57 Letter 10; VM, *Brieven*, 1: 91, ll. 97–112. The passage about the bride reflects some ideas of Richard, *In Cantica canticorum explicatio* 6; PL 196: 423B.

58 Beatrice, for example. See *Vita*, 118, 7; 124, 83; 200, 10; 213, 18; 215, 47.-Hadewijch, Letter 5; VM, *Brieven*, 1: 43, l. 5.- Ida of Nivelles, *Quinque*, 216.

59 Javelet, *Image*, 1: 321: 'Avec toutes les nuances qui s'imposent d'auteur à auteur, on peut affirmer que tous croient à cette mission du Saint-Esprit qui est d'assurer la présence de Dieu parmi les créatures, *temporellement par l'Incarnation, spirtuellement par l'infusion de la grâce, éternellement par la glorification*'. The italiziced words are quoted from Thomas the Cistercian, *Cant*, 9; PL 206: 617C.

60 Bell, *The Image*, 137–43.

61 William. Ep frat 2.16; PL 184: 396B; SCh 223: 354, 263:'fieri meretur homo Dei, non Deus, sed tamen quod est Deus: homo ex gratia quod Deus ex natura'.

destiny which gives meaning and purpose, direction and worth-
whileness to man's short-lived stay on earth.

As Richard wrote, 'Our mother is the grace of the Holy Spirit,
who regenerates us spiritually'.[62] This supposed man's cooperation. Graced as he is by the Holy Spirit, man's only way 'to grace'
this Spirit is to respond to his grace. Grace is never given to be
spent fruitlessly. According to his biographer, Gobert of Aspre-
mont (1189–1263)—a nobleman and crusader who, probably in
1237, became a monk in Villers after he had met a beguine in
Nivelles[63]—received the gift of the Holy Spirit and behaved well
in the monastic life through this gift.[64] This is the expression of
theological thinking in ordinary daily living.

Beatrice's *Vita* calls the Holy Spirit the leader (*dux*) in her
process toward consummation. As a small child she experienced
his direction,[65] and later in her life, around 1234, it was said that

> thinking over and subtly debating within herself about
> knowing, attaining and enjoying at the same time the
> supreme and uncreated Good, she was rapt in ecstasy... and
> there, under the guidance of the grace of the Holy Spirit, she
> explored many secret mysteries concerning earthly and
> heavenly things.[66]

To put it briefly, she was 'in the school of the Holy Spirit',[67] the Spirit of whom Ida of Nivelles was also said to be a

---

62 Cant 6; PL 196: 422A: 'Mater nostra est gratia Spiritus, quae spiritualiter
nos regenerat'. This mother-theme is also found in the preface of Arnuph of
Brussels' biography [*AA SS* June 7:608,2]: mother grace, *mater gratia*.

63 Roisin, *L'Hagiographie*, 39.

64 As the biographer pointed out (Martene and Durand, *Thesaurus*,
3: 1323A), a good work is brought forth by the gift, not the gift by the good
work: 'opus ex dono est, non donum ex opere. Accepit pius Gobertus Sancti
Spiritus donum, et per hoc operatus est bonum'.

65 *Vita*, 19, 67: 'She understood'—says the biographer—'the meaning (of the
psalter which she knew by heart when she was five years old) under the
direction of the grace of the Holy Spirit': *sola Spiritus Sancti duce gratia*.

66 *Vita*, 223, 39: 'duce gratia Spiritus Sancti'; – Ida of Leuven, *AA SS* April 2:
186, 16: 'informante se Christi suique Paracliti magisterio'.

67 *Vita*, 60, 11: 'In schola Spiritus Sancti', an expression that can be found in
Bernard's Pent 3.5: SBOp 5: 173.

pupil.[68] On one occasion, the same Ida asked Christ for an 'increase of the grace of the Holy Spirit'. [69] When the Holy Spirit is said to reside (92,44: *habitare*) or to take up his residence in man,[70] this most frequently refers to an actual grace given by the Holy Spirit to man on his way toward the recovery of the lost resemblance. When the Holy Spirit visits,[71] he often does so suddenly and unexpectedly (*repente*). On such occasions a great and sudden enlightenment is not uncommon. In a flash of lightning, Hadewijch had a mystical experience of enlightenment followed by a thunderclap, the latter indicating to her the limitations of the human condition, and subsequently the inadequacy of the finite in reaching the infinite.[72] Beatrice's biography says that 'the grace of the Holy Spirit was suddenly present, enlightening her intellect, coming like a flash of lightning from heaven' (86,40). Intent to know more about the Trinity... 'it happened that the light of heavenly truth flowed like lightning into her opened heart' (213,6). But when she believed she was able to grasp this mystery, it disappeared 'like lightning leaving the searcher's intention frustrated of her desire'.[73]

The sudden eruption of the Holy Spirit into someone's inner life can be expressed in terms of breathing. One day, Ida of Nivelles, listening to a sermon preached in Flemish, a language

---

68 *Quinque*, 255: 'discipula Spiritus Sancti'.
69 *Ibid.*, 211: 'augmentare Spiritus Sancti gratiam in me'.
70 *Vita*, 130, 6. The Holy Spirit had set up his dwelling place (*mansio*) in her mind. Ida of Leuven spoke of the receptacle and abode (*vas et habitaculum*) of the Holy Spirit (*AA SS* April 2:185, 14). This could sometimes, but by no means always, be understood as habitual grace related to the Holy Spirit.
71 Beatrice: *Vita*, 161, 68; – Ida of Nivelles, *Quinque*, 270:'magnifica Sancti Spiritus visitatio'.
72 Letter 30; VM, *Brieven*, 1: 258, ll. 155–64. The lightning is an ancient term used to express enlightment. J. Reynaert (*Beeldspraak*, 185) refers to alchemy, in which lightning signified a sudden rapture and illumination, at least according to Carl Jung. Reynaert (*Beeldspraak*, 74, n. 99) gives also two references to lightning, one of Richard and one of Bernard.
73 *Vita*, 214, 39. The 'frustration of her desire' in its mystical context is another way of expressing what Hadewijch called the thunder, a comparison Ruusbroec took over. See J. Reynaert, 'Ruusbroec en Hadewijch', *OGE* 55 (1981) 208–09.

she did not yet understand,[74] was suddenly gripped by the Holy Spirit and could not restrain her tears because the Holy Spirit was blowing in her soul.[75] Of Ida Lewis too it is said that 'under his breathing' she talked marvelously about the ineffable Unity of the Trinity.[76]

Sent to restore God's likeness in man, the Holy Spirit demonstrates (125,12), shows (125,67), makes known (199,67), illuminates,[77] reveals,[78] inspires (213,20; 215,74), stimulates,[79] and sends messages to his dedicated *mulieres religiosae*[80]: all verbs indicating the dynamic activity of the Holy Spirit.

His grace, however, is delicate,[81] and requires great docility.[82] When she was fifteen, Beatrice asked the Holy Spirit in devout prayers 'to order and to moderate the intimate affections of her heart' (43,46). The Spirit of discipline (92,42) whose ways are definitely not man's ways, 'invited her again not to rest but to labor, and showed her by his grace a new form of living by which to govern herself and to acquire a richer income of divine graces by trading with virtues'.[83] Following the Holy Spirit's counsel in everything she swerved 'neither to the right nor to the left from the path of truth which he showed her' (130,7), even when for

---

74 Albert d'Haenens, is of the opinion that Ida's family could have moved earlier from the Flemish-speaking part of Belgium to the French-speaking Nivelles, which would explain why she was called *Teutonica*. See A. d'Haenens, 'Femmes excédentaires et vocation religieuse. Le cas d'Ide de Nivelles (1200–1231)', in *Hommages à la Wallonie. Festschrift* honoring M.A. Arnould and P. Ruelle (Brussels, 1981) 217–34; 220.
75 *Quinque*, 206: 'flante Spiritu Sancto'.
76 *AA SS* Oct. 13: 114, 21: 'efflata Spiritu Sancto'.
77 *Vita*, 86, 39; 223, 87; – Ida of Nivelles, *Quinque*, 270.
78 To Beatrice: *Vita*, 174, 81; 217, 96; 217, 111. To Ida of Nivelles, *Vita*, 50, 46 and *Quinque*, 240 and 242.
79 Ida of Leuven, *AA SS* April 2: 174, 13: 'instigante se gratia Spiritus Sancti'.
80 To Beatrice 'now by secret suggestions, now by nightly revelation' (*Vita*, 199,65) – Hadewijch, Letter 3; VM, *Brieven*, 1: 34, l. 38.
81 *Vita*, 92, 42, meaning that it cannot stand anything sinful.
82 Ida of Leuven, *AA SS* April 2: 185, 14: 'si quidem a gratia sibi concessa non excederit'.
83 *Vita*, 125,10. One encounters the expression 'moving from virtue to virtue' (*de virtute in virtutem*) in all the biographies of *mulieres religiosae*, as well as in the writings of their mentors.

three years (139,180) she was swayed by temptations, fear, despair, without any perceptible visitations of the Holy Spirit. She had to rely on her faith and her hope and trust in God's promise, fleeing 'for help to the consoling bosom of Sacred Scripture' (154,49).

Beatrice herself does not speak of the seven gifts of the Holy Spirit,[84] mentioned in the hymn *Veni Sancte Spiritus*, attributed by an anonymous English Cistercian to Stephen Langton, archbishop of Canterbury (d.1228) who was quite familiar with the Cistercians.[85] The twelfth century showed a great interest in the gifts of the Holy Spirit, because of their importance in the realization of God's plan for man.[86] Not surprisingly some *mulieres religiosae*—Ida of Nivelles,[87] Hadewijch,[88] and Ida of Leuven[89] —explicitly expressed their eagerness to receive the seven gifts.

LIBERATING GRACE

Never regretting or repenting his unchangeable plans, God always respects man's metaphysical freedom, since he created

---

84 The Hebrew text enumerates six gifts, using twice the same word 'fear', which can express both piety and fear (Is 11:1). The Greek and the Vulgate made the number seven by adding verse 3a and translating the same Hebrew word by 'piety' and 'fear' in the second and third verses. See *TDNT* 9: 201–02.

85 Wilmart, *Auteurs spirituels*, 37–45: 'L'hymne et la séquence du Saint-Esprit'. This hymn refers to the gifts of the Holy Spirit which appear in Rv 3:1 as seven. They were already the topic of Drogo, a Benedictine monk of Saint-Nicaise in Reims (where William first became a monk) and later cardinal (d.1137), who wrote a small treatise *De septiformi gratia Spiritus Sancti*, taken from some sermons *De diversis* of Bernard. See J. Leclercq, 'Drogon et Saint Bernard', *RBén* 63 (1953) 11–31, rpt in Leclercq's *Recueil d'Études sur Saint Bernard et ses Écrits*, Storia a Letteratura 92 (Rome, 1962) 90–103.

86 Odon Lottin, *Psychologie et morale aux XIIe et XIIIe siècles* 3/1: 329–456 ('Les dons du Saint Esprit au XIIe siècle) and 6: 27–92 ('Le traité d'Alain de Lille sur les vertus, les vices et les dons du Saint Esprit'), (Leuven-Gembloux, 1949).

87 *Quinque*, 269–70.'Desideravit aliquando beata Ida, septem Spiritus Sancti donis interius illustrari'.

88 Vision one; VM, *Visioenen*, 1: 30, 1.354 and the thirteenth vision, *ibid.*, 1: 149, 1.179.

89 *AA SS* April 2: 160,10: 'Septiformis in se Spiritus gratiam infundendo, per singulas dies attenderet augmentari'.

him to his image and likeness.[90] Man himself is in a totally different situation.[91] His liberty is the possibility of self-determination, not of absolute autonomy. By his liberty he can consciously and freely ratify his creaturely condition and his call to union with God. If he does so, he affirms both God and himself; otherwise, he disavows God and abuses his liberty.[92] In accordance with God's plans, man's creation cannot but be directed toward its consummation although now by way of restoration, *viz*, through grace which is offered for no other purpose. If conflict or failure arise, they cannot be attributed to grace, since it is grace which empowers man to recapture his liberty. At this point the Cistercians and the Victorines,[93] followed by the *mulieres religiosae*, are in accord with the patristic tradition, particularly with Gregory of Nyssa,[94] and with Augustine.[95]

What is particularly striking about some of the *mulieres religiosae* is their profound desire to be freed from all obstacles to the love of God, and unhindered by anything that could diminish their liberty or hold it captive. In this sense one could speak of

90 Bernard, Gra 4.9; SBOp 3: 173: 'Freedom from necessity [or of choice] belongs alike to God and to every rational creation, good and bad'; – Richard, *De Statu interioris hominis* 1.3: PL 196: 1118D: 'Man, created in God's image and likeness has freedom of choice which is not and cannot be dominated (*dominium non patitur*). To do violence to it is unbecoming for God and impossible for a creature'.

91 Scheffczyk, *SM* 2: 387–88: 'The God who reveals himself in the history of the Covenant as Lord does not entail man's tutelage and enslavement. He reveals man's vocation to a partnership in which equality of rights does not indeed prevail, but in which man, precisely by his awareness of infinite distance, experiences his own greatness which consists in transcending himself towards the infinity of God... It is seen to point to a transcendental, living dependence which is the ground which makes human freedom and dignity possible and makes man, as God's mandatory in the empirical domain of this world, grow to his full stature as a creature'.

92 Huftier, 'Libre arbitre...', *RTAM*, 33 (1966) 280–81. Compared to this study, John Hick's rationalization in his chapter on 'Universal salvation' in his book *Death and Eternal Life*, 2nd ed. (London, 1985) 242–61, is obscure rather than illuminating.

93 Javelet, *Psychologie*, 39–40; *Id*., 'Thomas Gallus et Richard de St.Victor mystiques', *RAM* 29 (1962) 206–33; 226.

94 Leys, *L'Image de Dieu*, 72–73; Daniélou, *Platonisme*, 85–86.

95 E. Gilson, *Introduction*, 205–14.

'freedom from', freedom with its negative connotations, as it is often understood in contemporary society.[96] In fact, what the *mulieres religiosae* feared most was not freedom, but unfreedom as they experienced it in their historical human condition. It should be noted that the biographers of some *mulieres religiosae* spoke more about the ways and means used to arrive at genuine liberty, without which there could be little talk about union with God. Biographies were written to edify, to stimulate and to show that these women were really women *religiosae*, devout women, intensely oriented toward union with God through *ascesis*, and above all through the practice of virtues and a deep prayer life. The stress on inner liberty is found occasionally in biographies, while it is frequently stressed in the writings of Beatrice, and still more so in those of Hadewijch.

A brief look at their strong desire to be totally free can help clarify their desire for liberty in the positive sense: freedom *to* love God without hindrance. The summit of liberty, the *libertas gloriae* (the liberty of glory) as it is expressed in theological terms, means being beyond the reach of evil or sin or whatever other term is used to express this unfreedom. At this stage any chance or occasion leading to unfreedom is impossible. Practically, this meant a totally unassailable response to God's love, a stage only attained once man has passed through physical death to the fullness of life and of love, the goal set by God himself when he created man to his image and likeness.

Ida of Nivelles asked to be given ever more grace that she might arrive at the glory of heaven.[97] Using a sentence from Paul (Ph 1:23) which occurs in nearly all biographies, she 'desired to

---

96 Erich Fromm, *The Fear of Freedom* (London, 1942, rpt 1966) 26–27. In this text freedom is seen explicitly in its negative sense as 'freedom from'. According to this author, Adam acting against God's command freed himself from coercion, 'the beginning of human freedom'. The *mulieres religiosae* and their mentors knew many centuries earlier that freedom is incompatible with coercion. But they certainly did not share the view that Adam's trespass, was the beginning of human freedom; quite the reverse. By misusing his inborn and God-oriented freedom of choice (*liberum arbitrium*) man became willingly self-oriented and thus unfree.

97 *Quinque*, 211: 'petit sibi augeri gratiam qua pervenire posset ad gloriam'.

be dissolved in order to be with Christ'.[98] A few days before she died she went into an ecstasy and was shown the degree of glory which God had prepared for her.[99] When she did die, one of her last utterances was to hail death for liberating her from all present and possible evil.[100] Ida Lewis was praised because she lived beautifully in accordance with grace, and at her death attained the glory of heaven.[101] A little earlier in her biography she is said to have desired to die, not in order to be free from all troubles, but to be purified by all the obstacles she had to face, integrating them into the process of her becoming. This way she became 'totally free to rush toward her Beloved and to take up her residence in the chamber of his love'.[102] Ida of Leuven considered her physical death as a liberation.[103] The context and the mystical vocabulary make it clear that she had the same liberty in mind and heart as did the other two Idas. When Alice of Schaarbeek died from her leprosy it was said—again in mystical terminology—that 'as a bride decked with necklaces and ready for the wedding, she hastened to the door of death', stripping off the 'tunic of mortality and putting on the tunic of immortality and glory'.[104]

The explicit desire to die could easily be seen as an escape from pain, sufferings and trouble. And there is no doubt that those women did, in fact, suffer pain and go through lacerating sufferings. Taken at face value and out of context, what is said about happy death or about liberation could, indeed, mean a desire to have it over with and to be free from it all. But when these

---

98 *Ibid.*, 'et ardenti desiderio coelestium affluentiam deliciarum concupiscere, ut cum Apostolo dicere possit: cupio dissolvi et esse cum Christo'.
99 *Ibid.*, 289: 'locum gloriae'.
100 *Ibid.*, 290: 'O vere beata mors, quae liberare potens es ab omnibus malis'.
101 *AA SS* Oct. 13: 124, 58: 'Laudari meritis operum non indigna, meruit ex operibus obtinere vivendo gratiam, et decedens coelorum gloriam adipisci'.
102 *Ibid.*, 112, 14: 'Postulavit ut quicquid inconveniens hac in vita contraheret... purgaretur a Deo funditus per poenitentiam in praesenti ut, cum soluto carne corporali, de praesentis vitae periculis vellet ipsius animam evocare, nullis obstaculis praepedita, cum dilecto mansionem suscipiens, ad ipsius cubiculum gaudens libere penitus evolaret'.
103 *AA SS* April 2: 180,5: 'exoravit Dominum pro sua liberatione'.
104 *AA SS* June 2: 482,32: 'Post completorium Virgo Dei, quasi sponsa ornata munilibus, et ad nuptias praeparata, ad portam mortis festinabat'.

passages are read within their context, given the meaning they had in their time and when they are listened to in their enshrining mystical terminology, then death and liberation point not to an end,[105] but to a beginning, paid for by afflictions on the physical, the psychological and the spiritual level. Readers of Alice of Schaarbeek's biography, for instance, would be very mistaken if they attributed her 'happy migration' to a desire to be freed from her then still incurable leprosy and the pain this involved, including segregation from her community. She expressed her determination most assuredly (*certissime*) to refuse to be healed if she could be. She stated explicitly—using figurative terminology—that she preferred to have God as her only visitor and be a decaying leper rather than to rule the world, provided she not be frustrated in her hope of future glory.[106] Alice's disease was a special case, but her attitude can be applied with the necessary modifications to other *mulieres religiosae* about whom we have biographical information: the liberty of glory, liberty in its highest degree, is not a liberty from, but a liberty 'for', the liberty God had destined them for from all eternity.

To follow Hadewijch and Beatrice in their full explanation of the trek toward liberty of glory would exceed the limits of the present chapter. Both described in oxymorons the burning desire of their hearts to be totally free to serve *Minne* (Love).[107] Hadewijch, speaking of herself, wrote someone who wished to fulfill all the demands of *minne* has, while still alive on earth, to

---

105 This applies to the women of the next generation of *mulieres religiosae* in Germany as well as to those considered here. See Siegfried Ringler, *Viten-und Offenbarungsliteratur in Frauenklöster des Mittelalters*, Münchener Texte und Untersuchungen zur deutschen Literatur des Mittelalters [henceforth cited: *Viten- und Offenbarungsliteratur*], (Zurich-Munich, 1980) 215: 'Es wäre ein Missverständnis, ein derartiges Herbeisehnen des Todes als Weltverneigung d.h. als Ablehnung der irdischen Wirklichkeit zu deuten'.

106 *AA SS* June 2: 479,10: 'Odoris suavitatis divinitus fit perfusa, tantis deliciis quasi paradisi voluptatibus fit repleta, quod si pristinae sanitatis optio ejus relinqueretur arbitrio, et tamen ad illam deberet sublimari gloriam, ad quam jam trahebatur, certisssime affirmabat se sanitatem refutare. Praeterea maluit in isto statu commorari, et a solo Deo visitari, quam toti mundo dominari et tamen a spe futurae gloriae non frustrari'.

107 What *minne* meant to Hadewijch and Beatrice is still debated and will be spoken of in Part III, Chapter XV. The major difficulty lies in determining if and how far *minne* is personified in their writings.

go through a rending purification equated with the agony of death.[108] Beatrice's evolution in this regard can be followed in her Vita[109] and is summarized in her *Seven manieren* where she wrote that 'it seems to the soul as if it lives while dying and dies while it feels the pain of hell'.[110] Ida Lewis' biographer speaks of her in the same vein.[111] The free, willing acceptance of such sufferings rules out the opinion that these women sought death as a freedom from suffering. Beatrice made this explicitly clear:

To desire vehemently and to be grievously impatient to be freed and to live with Christ... not for sadness about the present time, nor from fear of future troubles. Only because of holy and eternal *Minne* did she ardently and impetuously long and languish to arrive at the eternal land and its glorious fruition.[112]

A first approach of the *mulieres religiosae* to liberty was physical *ascesis*,[113] usually more evident in the early stages as described in the biographies, when youthful zeal played an active

---

108 VM, *Mengeldichten* 48, poem 10, ll. 51–52: 'Who, with love, shall remain faithful to *Minne* must enter, still living, into death'. Reynaert treated this whole process at length in *Beeldspraak* 321–32: Het doodsmotief. See also F.J. Schweitzer, *Der Freiheitsbegriff der deutchen Mystik* (Frankfurt/Main-Bonn, 1981).

109 *Vita*, 33, 48; 92, 31; 94, 79; 102, 41; 156, 23; 157, 46; 186, 61; 187, 81; 195, 65; 198, 50; 200, 16; 204, 75; 211, 65; 219, 11; 222, 6.

110 R-VM, *Seven manieren*, 12, ll. 47–49.

111 *AA SS* Oct. 13: 114, 24: 'ut prae intolerantia dicti gaudii necdum mori nec diu vivere videretur'.

112 R-VM, *Seven manieren*, 33–34, ll. 72–77; 81–87.

113 One source of asceticism in the lives of Cistercian nuns derived from the fact that it usually took some thirty years for a new foundation to attain economic stability. Exceptions were the foundations favored and well endowed by a prince such as 's Hertogendaal and Ter Kameren in the duchy of Brabant, Flines, Marquette and Bijloke in the county of Flanders. When Ida of Leuven joined the community of Roosendaal near Malines, Christ told her 'not to dread the rough austerity of the observance of the [Cistercian] Order or the penury of the place [*AA SS* April 2: 182,40]. This applies to four of Henriquez' *Quinque prudentes virgines*, particularly to Beatrice, who was sent twice to a new foundation. The leprosy of Alice of Schaarbeek, who joined Ter Kameren, was her way of suffering penury.

role, preparing the way for a more demanding, inner *ascesis*. Some biographers had a tendency to overstress the physical *ascesis* of their heroines. The one who 'translated' Beatrice's autobiography gave his personal moralizing tendencies too much free rein in this matter.[114] The focus of the *mulieres religiosae*'s *ascesis* is made evident in their longing to become free from all attachment to the body and the gamut of earthly things, when not used for or directed toward union with God. Utopian? Possibly for many people, but not for them. The intensity of their longing necessarily called for a disciplined life, *viz.* an *ascesis*, an 'orderliness' as Beatrice among others called it.[115] The frugality of life, the social services that the beguines volunteered for and their

---

114 Beatrice had poor health, as can be seen in the sixth and seventh chapters of the first book and throughout her *Vita*. The fifth chapter of the same first book on 'her penitence and mortification of the flesh' is more dependent on the first part of the biography of the famous ascetic Arnulph of Brussels (d.1228), laybrother in Villers (*AA SS* June 7: 609–16) than on Beatrice's autobiography. The biographer of Ida of Leuven, for his part, used Beatrice's biography as his model. Both Beatrice and Ida are sometimes mentioned as praying what in Beatrice's case is called 'the psalter of the Blessed Virgin'. While still an oblate in her early teens she prayed this psalter, which involved saying the *Hail Mary* one-hundred fifty times a day. At that time this prayer was limited to its first, laudatory part without the later added second, supplicatory, part. The fact that she genuflected after each *Hail Mary* is presented by the biographer as an ascetical exercise, though it was not uncommon. Caught by her mistress, Beatrice had to stop the 'burdensome practice' of the genuflections (26,55). If she were reprimanded for these multiplied genuflections, how could she have carried out, unnoticed, the manifestly excessive 'mastering of her frail body by works of penitence'(30,4), as the biographer described it in the fifth chapter? This is not to suggest that Beatrice did not practice physical ascesis, but only to indicate that she most probably was not the ascetical athlete presented by her biographer, who considered mortifications an 'edifying' touch. Ida of Leuven, still a *mulier religiosa* in her native city, for a while prayed the *Hail Mary* eleven hundred times each day, with as many genuflections (*AA SS* April 23: 261,12). This is not the only time that Ida showed an inclination toward exaggeration. In connection with the 'Marian Palter', see Andreas Heinz,'Die Zisterzienzer [Zisterzienzerinnen would be more accurate] und die Anfänge des Rosenkranzes , *AC* 33 (1977) 262–309: a group of beguines who were to become the Cistercian community of St. Thomas [Beckett] a.d.Kyll [diocese of Trier] in 1185 seem to have introduced around 1300, for their own use, the devotional prayer of the rosary.

115 Orderliness, *ordinatio* as a noun, or its related adjective, adverb or verb, occur frequently throughout her biography, as it does in the writings of Hadewijch and of their mentors.

whole lifestyle were by themselves a not altogether insignificant ascesis.[116] Cistercian nuns, even without extra ascetical practices had a hard life, as can be deduced from the many prescriptions and prohibitions of the General Chapter.[117] More important for freedom was the inner purification of the heart. Negatively, this meant freedom from egocentrism in all its ramifications and manifestations, freedom from vices,[118] sins,[119] imperfections and a whole string of psychic desires and impulses such as self-deception,[120] pride,[121] greed and competitiveness. But these could be used, as Hadewijch pointed out, for inner

---

116 McDonnell, *The Beguines*, 86–89; 148–53.

117 Legislative institutions have a built-in danger of a gradually increasing emphasis on externals, sometimes at the expense of principles and ideals. Before the end of the twelfth century this can be followed in the General Chapters' *Statuta*, and in the codifications edited by Canisius Noschitzka, 'Codex manuscriptus 31 Universitatis Labacensis (written about 1190)', *AC* 6 (1950) 1–124; Bruno Griesser, 'Die "Officia ecclesiastica Cisterciensis Ordinis" des Cod. 1171 von Trient [written in the twelfth century]', *AC* 12 (1956) 153–288; Bruno Schneider, 'Citeaux und die benediktinische Tradition', *AC* 16 (1960) 169–254; *ib.* 17 (1961) 73–114, and in B. Lucet's *La codification cistercienne*. Gerd Zimmermann stressed the fact that Cistercians and Carthusians, in order to keep uniformity in their Orders, arrived at detailed specifications (eine *Reglementierung* in den Einzelheiten) in regard to the 'cura corporum' (health care). See G. Zimmermann, *Ordensleben und Lebensstandard: Die Cura corporis in den Ordensvorschriften des Abendländischen Hochmittelalters*. Beiträge zur Geschichte des Alten Möchtums und des Benediktinerordens 32 (Münster/W, 1973) 218. The provocative study of J.B. Auberger, *L'Unanimité cistercienne* follows this Order's evolution in the twelfth century on the legislative, cultural, agricultural, architectural and spiritual levels.

118 René Wasselynck listed several of his publications on this subject in *RTAM* 35 (1968) 197, n.1, to which could be added: G. De Martel, 'Un nouveau témoin de la liste des vices au moyen âge', *RTAM* 44 (1977) 65–79. Negligence and the darkness of unconsciousness, which Beatrice called ignorance, were seen by her as vices.

119 According to Beatrice sin is a deadly poison (133,75), to which she opposed her awareness of being created to God's image and likeness (138, 165; 146, 36). For Ida of Nivelles it was a poisonous drink (*Quinque*, 273). She was so deeply grieved (*plena doloris*) by the horror of sin and the harm it did to its victims, that she vomited blood (*Quinque*, 214, 216, 221, 229, 237). This was even noted on her epitaph: *Quinque*, 242.

120 Hadewijch, for instance, lists a series of this kind in her letter 4; VM, *Brieven*, 1: 38, ll. 32–38.

121 Pride, to use an expression of Gregory the Great, is the queen of all vices. References in Wasselynck, referred to above in n. 118.

improvement: 'Man must keep himself free from sin among all vicissitudes so that he will seek his growth in all things'.[122] Instigations to sin are often attributed to the devil's ingeniousness.[123] According to her *Vita*, Beatrice was often molested by what her biographer called the devil's cunning whisperings, which proved to be counter-productive. She greatly desired to be so free at the time of her death as 'to be able to come into her Creator's presence with no obstacle of any sort' (40,61). She considered the excessive pain caused by her sickness a compensation for the pain of purgatory.[124] In November 1231 she stated in a soliloquy that she was ready to go 'through the fires of purgatory and even the torments of hell to arrive with God's help at entire purity of heart and of conscience'.[125] Her biography and

---

122 Letter 13; VM, *Brieven*, 1: 113, ll. 1–3. Others, as Beatrice (130, 13; 186, 61), for instance, said the same thing, as did Ida of Nivelles (*Quinque*, 283), Alice of Schaarbeek (*AA SS* June 2: 477, 2) and Ida Lewis (*AA SS* Oct. 13: 112, 14).

123 There is no biography in which the devil is not given deprecatory names expressing his envy of and enmity toward man. Acquainted as the *mulieres religiosae* were with the Bible, their mentors and contemporary literature, this fact comes as no surprise. Preachers and biographers had a tendency to try to keep people from sinning by inspiring fear of the devil, at a time when knowledge of man's psychological complexity was quite limited. Beatrice's biographer was very good at the technique. Ida of Nivelles' biographer, using generalities (*Quinque*, 246) tried to describe the tortures of hell. Legends and myths did the rest as can be seen in Caesarius of Heisterbach's *Dialogus miraculorum* or similar writings in which 'christianzied' non-Christian mythologies or myths which were part of the archetypal patterns of man's search for God, made at least some appearance. See Victor White, *God and the Unconscious* (London, 1952; American edition, Cleveland- New York, 1961) 188–203; Hugo Rahner, *Greek Myths and Christian Mystery*, ET by E. James (London -New York, 1963) 3–45; C.G. De Vooys, *Middelnederlandse Legenden en Exempelen* (Groningen-Amsterdam, 1976) 159–98: 'De duivel in de exempelen'.

124 *Vita*, 40, 68; 191, 134. Ida Lewis had the same desire to go, at her death, straight to heaven without passing through purgatory, *AA SS* Oct. 13:112,14.

125 *Vita*, 97, 127; 186, 59; 222, 17. 'With God's grace she would at the day of judgment offer him her soul clean and immaculate, and—she went paradoxically on—'if even then you condemn it [her soul] to be eternally punished, I shall obey your judgment, humbly consenting and acquiescing' (146, 40). A similar surrender to God's will, but in another context, is expressed in Hadewijch's letter 6; VM, *Brieven*, 1: 57, ll. 76–82.

her treatise do not mention that she had ever seen the devil,[126] nor is there any description of the 'fires of purgatory' or 'the horrendous tortures of hell'. Hadewijch was as sober about hell as Beatrice. She speaks only about 'the eternal fire of gloomy death',[127] in contrast with the conventional hair-raising descriptions of earlier times.[128]

Hadewijch knew about the fear of God that comes from experiencing the human condition,[129] from self-knowledge,[130] and from the realization of how difficult, if not impossible, it is to

---

126 Belief in the devil is not merely an expression of the credulity of the *mulieres religiosae*. To them the devil meant opposition to God, eagerness to be like God without God, the reverse of what they hoped to become. Biographies conveyed their vituperation of the devil in different ways. To the charismatic Ida of Nivelles the devil appeared under the form of a small bird (*Quinque*, 232), an ape, a dog, and 'various other ways' (*Quinque*, 234). He beat Ida Lewis over a year and a half, 'as a lion rushing toward his prey, particularly at night' (*AA SS* Oct. 13: 122,15–16). Her biogapher is careful to present this as a figure of speech at this point, but he wrote further that several devils appeared in human form and were actually (*praesentialiter*) there (*AA SS* Oct. 13: 123, 55). The devil tried to bewitch Ida of Leuven and one night appeared to her in a kind of dream or nightmare (*phantastica visio*) and fought with her (*AA SS* April 2: 160,8). She could, at times, be aware of his presence by his smell (*ibid.*, 160,7), a not uncommon 'detector' in medieval biographies and legends.

127 Letter 22; VM, *Brieven*, 1: 200, ll. 309–10.

128 Peter Dinzelbacher, 'Ida von Nijvels Brückenvision', *OGE* 52 (1978) 179–94. Ida of Nivelles' vision of the beyond (the *Jenseitsvisionen*) stays halfway between the visions of a first type—those from the sixth through the thirteenth centuries, mostly by men such as Tundall, Thurskill and others and giving quite a vivid and even sadistic description of purgatory and hell. From the end of the twelfth century on the visions are noticeably different from the earlier ones and end mystically, referring to a bridal union with the Lord, as happened to Ida (after she had a brief look at purgatory) and many others. See also Dinzelbacher's *Vision und Visionsliteratur im Mittelalter* [henceforth cited: *Vision*], Monographien zur Geschichte des Mittelalters, 23, Fr. Prinz and K. Bösl, eds. (Stuttgart, 1981) 90–105; H.J.E. Endepols, 'Bijdragen tot de eschatologische voorstellingen in de Middeleeuwen, *TNTL* 28 (1909) 49–111; 83–111; C.G. De Vooys, *Middelnederlandse Legenden en Exempelen*, 291–305. The bibliography on this topic is quite extensive and is listed in Dinzelbacher's *Vision*, 90, nn.356 and 358.

129 Letter 6: 'Man must be continually aware that noble service and suffering in exile are proper to the human condition', VM, *Brieven*,1: 57, ll. 86–88.

130 Letter 4: 'Reason knows that God must be feared, for he is great and man small'; VM, *Brieven*, 1: 38, ll. 39–40.

love God as he deserves to be loved.[131] Beatrice, timid and rather shy by nature, (21,35; 36,6) initially developed a neurotic fear of dying without having first reached the total liberty of loving God and being united with him. Though she said several times that she never committed a serious offence,[132] her biography often notes her fear of sinning or of not doing enough penance for small offenses.[133] This fear could come from an unintegrated anxiety, as we would expect in our time,[134] but seems also to have been provoked by her intense desire to be immediately united with God at her death.[135] When she was thirty-one (187,46), 'she realized that her fear sprang from a sort of pusillanimity and distrust which scarcely honored God' (169,85). 'Suddenly the Lord of mercies pierced her soul with the fire of his love as with a fiery javelin' (170,14). At that moment she received 'such a great spirit of fortitude and constancy, so strong and vehement, that she feared neither death nor sword nor any kind of torment nor any man or demon' (180,62). Freed from her fears she desired 'to immolate herself to her creator with a free heart' (180,24) and asked to suffer pain in her body and tribulations in her mind and heart. When her prayer was answered 'she honored with acts of praise and thanksgiving the mercy of the Lord, her heart's affection being the more devout as it was more free' (190,128). In this way 'she passed into the liberty of the children of God' (191,54), being 'prudent toward herself, useful to neighbor and pleasing to God' (199,72). In her treatise, written some twenty years later, one can still hear some resonances of this process, but the pitch is different. Desire for *minne* has taken over the place of fear. The psychosomatic complications her *Vita* so frequently speaks of are

---

131 Letter 4: 'The one thing always to be feared is that one does not serve *minne* sufficiently. This fear fills man with love, so strongly felt that it raises up a storm of ardent endeavor'; VM, *Brieven*, 1: 29, ll. 106–10.

132 *Vita*, 94, 73; 130, 23; 138, 168; 146, 36; 153, 33; 168, 74; 171, 38; 222, 14.

133 *Vita*, 70, 93; 101, 8; 102, 49; 110, 56; 123, 67; 130, 21; 131, 34; 146, 38; 185, 47; 186, 56; 195, 65.

134 Jerome Kroll and Roger De Ganck, 'The adolescence of a thirteenth-century visionary nun', *Psychological Medicine* 16 (1986) 745–56.

135 See above, n.124 of this Chapter.

barely mentioned. Eschatological hell yielded to the 'hell of *minne*' within her heart, so overwhelmingly and stupendously filled with an insatiable desire for *minne*, a desire as crucifying for Beatrice as it was for Hadewijch.[136]

Bodily *ascesis* and penance, however, are only the first steps 'which must necessarily precede all virtues in the way of perfection' (91,91). Striving for virtue was far more important, as all the biographies indicate. Beatrice's *Vita* clearly shows how she had to struggle with bodily *ascesis* and poor health on the one hand and with a more intense pursuit of virtue on the other. These factors worked continually in combination or in succession, until virtue, which she frequently called purity of heart, had the last word, becoming a bridge of freedom 'for'. Introspection and inwardness brought her to 'the greatest zeal in keeping her heart with all watchfulness' (42,9).

In order to rise more easily to all-embracing purity of heart, she locked up the outer shop of her senses, so to speak, and enclosed herself in the recesses of her heart. There she not only expelled the movements of illicit and harmful thoughts, but also calmed the tumult of those that were honest enough in their own way, but quite unsuitable to the purity of her heart.[137]

Virtue shines outwardly but presupposes an inward hearth, a continuous deepening and widening of consciousness. Beatrice's whole personality was mobilized in this process. She 'first inquired into her exterior acts and habits, and then scrutinized the depths of her heart with keen and subtle consideration' (120,20). She saw her struggles as a gift from God 'not that she would be tempted and succumb, but that she would be trained by them and

---

136 See Reynaert, *Beeldspraak*, 'Helle': 161–74; 162–64.
137 *Vita*, 169, 85. It dawned on her that fear and lack of trust could in no way be the answer to God's love. She perceived consciously what she had turned over and over again in her subconsciousness: that fear was Beatrice-centered, while her heart cried out all the time to be totally God-centered.

would learn to plant her footsteps in the way of virtue in the future' (143,45).

She disposed all her actions and affections interiorly and exteriorly according to reason that no part of her could be empty or idle. She ceaselessly forced her mind to serve its Creator with holy affections, her mouth to serve him in divine praises, her hand in loving works, and the other members of her body in their proper actions.[138]

As Hadewijch wrote, man, being made to God's image and likeness, is 'bound before God to acquire a knowledge of all the virtues and to learn them by exertion, questioning, study and earnest zeal'.[139] Virtue is not to be practised for its own sake or for one's own benefit, for that would be egocentricity incompatible with love for God. As she says in another Letter:

It is one's obligation to practice virtues, not in order to obtain consideration,[140] joy, or wealth, or rank, or any enjoyment in heaven and on earth, but solely out of homage to the incomparable sublimity of God who created our nature to this end and made it for his own honor and praise, and for our bliss in eternal glory.[141]

As they usually did, once they were won over by God's love, the *mulieres religiosae* tried to see everything from God's point of view. According to Hadewijch, God himself is one singular Virtue in whom all virtues are one single totality.[142] From him

---

138 *Vita*, 181, 185.
139 Hadewijch, Letter 24; VM, *Brieven*, 1: 209, ll. 19–21.
140 The *mulieres religiosae* took the wind out of vainglory's sails when they felt appreciated. Beatrice: *Vita*, 66, 36; 168, 67; 209, 34; 212, 74; 231, 68; – Ida of Nivelles, *Quinque*, 282–83; – Ida Lewis: *AA SS* Oct. 13: 118, 38; 123, 56; – Alice of Schaarbeek, *AA SS* June 2: 487,7; – Ida of Leuven, *AA SS* April 2: 160, 8; 162, 16; 187, 19;– Hadewijch, Letter 2; VM, *Brieven*, 1: 31, ll. 169–70; Letter 6, *ibid.*, 1: 61, ll. 182–84.
141 Hadewijch, Letter 6, VM, *Brieven*, 1: 67, ll. 316–23.
142 Vision one; VM, *Visioenen*, 1: 20, l. 173.

human virtues originate; to him they are directed as the concrete expressions of man's love in return for God's love. Repeating what had been said frequently in earlier generations, Ida of Nivelles's biographer called Christ 'the Lord of virtues'.[143] Alice of Schaarbeek's biographer wrote that even before she became a leper

> she subdued her body from without by hardships, and set her mind and heart from within on God's love, by which she associated herself to him (*se Deo associavit*). She became pregnant (*gravida*) with love for God, and through her discipline of body and heart she intended 'to adorn herself for her Bridegroom [Christ], uninfected by self-complacency and oriented, not to herself, but to God.[144]

Hadewijch might have had the same theme of association with God in her mind when she wrote to a friend: 'Be free and associate yourself with your Beloved'.[145] Looking in retrospect at Ida Lewis, her biographer stated that she was esteemed for her 'lovely honesty, praiseworthy maturity, gracious virtues and manners'.[146] Gracious virtues and manners do not simply come with the attentive, intensive cultivation of consciousness; this is presupposed. Motivation for it must lie deeper, as Ida Lewis herself intimated. A calligrapher and writer of manuscripts she played on the letters of her name Yda, as it was written in medieval Latin. Being a sharp letter, 'Y' stood for acuteness, 'd' for *Deus*, God in English, and 'a' for *amor* or love, so that her name meant: 'Ida has her love for God in focus'.[147]

Of all forms of unfreedom, self-will is the worst.[148] Hadewijch and Beatrice offer us the opportunity to have a closer look at

---

143 *Quinque*, 267: 'Dominus virtutum'.

144 *AA SS* June 2: 478, 4. Freedom 'from' in the service of freedom 'for' is clearly indicated in this short passage. The context makes up for the absence of more explicit terminology.

145 Letter 18; VM, *Brieven*, 1: 154, ll. 56–57.

146 *AA SS* Oct. 13: 108, 3, e.

147 *Ibid.*, 120: 40: 'Unde Yda quasi Deum acute amans ab etymolgia nominis potest dici'.

148 Gilson, *The Mystical Theology*, 95.

effective strategy in this matter. 'Those who have not come to the great countenance of omnipotent *minne* by which we live free in the midst of distress... prefer and judge it better that their will, rather than *minne*'s will, be done'.[149] Beatrice, 'aware of the instability of the will,[150] took the greatest care not to do anything contrary to the divine will' (130,26). 'For as long as her self-will—however holy, fervent and useful—reigned in her heart, she could not attain to the sublime heights of tranquillity and peace, since the remnants of her self-will were impediments' (226,56). She walked the road of virtues, the *via virtutum* (143,46), not primarily for moral perfection, but to make herself free to submit and to respond to God's love by doing his will. Consistent with her own perception and experience, Hadewijch wrote that 'whoever loves God loves his works; his works are noble virtues; therefore whoever loves God, loves virtues'.[151]

Through their direct or indirect contact with their patristic and medieval mentors, the *mulieres religiosae* realized, one way or another, that when man was created to God's image and likeness, this included the incarnation of their Archetype. God's Son himself showed them the way to freedom and love. Taking on the human condition, God's Son conformed his own will so completely to the will of his Father that, as man, he freely accepted death on a cross. This was his loving response to a loving Father, however humanly incomprehensible and even absurd this might seem to be. As Hadewijch wrote:

> This is the way the Son of God preceded us, the way of which he himself gave us knowledge and understanding when he lived as man. For the whole time he spent on earth, from its beginning to its end, he performed and accomplished in different ways the will of his Father.[152]

---

149 Hadewijch, Letter 18; VM, *Brieven*, 1: 158, ll. 150–53.
150 *Vita*, 169, 71. Hadewijch was no less concerned about this instability 'because nothing could so easily separate us from our Lord'; Letter 6, VM, *Brieven*, 1: 55, l. 38.
151 Letter 10; VM, *Brieven*, 1: 85, ll. 1–3.
152 Letter 6; VM, *Brieven*, 1: 67–68, ll. 324–30.

The immensity of Christ's love called out for an intense response to such a love by striving for virtue as Christ had done. Hadewijch, challenged in her capacity as leader of a small group of *mulieres religiosae* and criticized for her teaching,[153] was given by the Lord 'a new commandment', which she took to heart and practised faithfully:

If you wish to be like me in my humanity as you long for union with me in my divinity, you shall desire to be poor, miserable and despised by all men. You must find all kinds of grief more agreeable than all earthly satisfaction. Be in no way vexed by them, even if they are inhuman to bear. If you wish to strive after *minne* in accordance with the noble measure which my totality demands, you will have to become so estranged from people, so wretched and scorned, that you will not know where to lodge for a single night. All people will turn away from you and forsake you and no one will be disposed to accompany you in your distress and misery. For all this I will be your guarantee during the short span of life left to you, since your time [of glorification] has not yet come.[154]

This passage from Hadewijch seems to indicate that hers was an exceptional case with dire prospects. Her letters to the *mulieres religiosae* of her circle have a milder tone, showing that Hadewijch is unique among these women. Nevertheless, she admonished her friend to go the whole way in following Christ. In one of her letters she wrote: 'I entrust you by the veritable virtue and fidelity that God himself is, have continually in mind the holy virtue which God himself is and which he was in his way of living when, as man, he lived as a human being'.[155] In another she said:

---

153 This opposition seems to have come when the beguines were not yet grouped together in beguinages.
154 Vision one; VM, *Visioenen*, 1: 27–28, ll. 289–306.
155 Letter 3; VM, *Brieven*, 1: 32, ll. 1–5.

May God teach you the veritable virtue by which we render
minne the most honor and justice. May God [here Christ]
teach you that ingratiating oneness which he offered to his
Father, when as man, he lived for him undividedly and
purely. May he teach you the holy oneness he taught and
prescribed for his holy friends, who for the sake of God
rejected all alien consolation.[156]

In her sixth Letter, she advised a young friend to do what
Hadewijch herself had apparently been told in her first vision to
do.[157]

As a Cistercian nun, surrounded by the security and protection
of a well-established and, at her time, still very powerful monastic
Order,[158] Beatrice had not to face Hadewijch's isolation. But this

---

156 Letter 14; VM, *Brieven*, 1: 119–20, l.5–14.

157 The text of her sixth letter is referred to below in n.160, and the one of her
first vision in n.154 above.

158 For Citeaux' strength on the ecclesiastical and social level at that time,
see J.B. Mahn, *L'Ordre de Citeaux et son Gouvernement*, 73–169. In Beatrice's
time the opinion held by Bernard was still operative, as can be seen in Beatrice's
expression of thankfulness that the Lord had brought her to the monastery, 'the
harbor of tranquillity' (74, 71), 'the harbor of stability' (138,169), a tranquillity
and stability not found in 'the world', i.e. the profane and even the ecclesiastical
and monastic world, once they had become diseased by greed and gratification.
William spoke of 'this world' in his Cant (PL 180: 542A–543D). Gilbert of
Hoyland 'spiritualized' the city. See Lawrence Braceland, 'The Soul's Pilgrimage in the Planned City of God', *CSt* 13 (1978) 228–43. For an overview of
how the conception of the relationship between monastery and city evolved, see
Thomas Renna, 'The City in Early Cistercian Thought', *Citeaux* 34 (1983) 5–19.
On p.17 he says, for instance, that 'Cistercians are usually content to see the city
as an illustration of the way the holy soul achieves union with God'. Ida
of Nivelles saw it this way, for she called the monastery 'God's paradise'
(*Quinque*, 206). Gilson said that for Bernard the cloister is not yet *the* paradise
(*The Mystical Theology*, 91), but still *a* paradise, and not only for monks. See
Anselm Dimier, 'Mourir à Clairvaux', *Coll* 17 (1959) 272–84. Though Bernard's view of the 'city' has its own particularities (as can be seen in Renna's
study), within his own Order he seems to have developed a special concern for
the whole Order with its five principal 'mother-houses' and their filiations.
Clairvaux's own filiation amounted to 50% of all houses of men, Pontigny's to
25%, and the other 25% were shared by Citeaux, La Ferté and Morimond.
During his tenure as abbot of Clairvaux, Bernard managed to have for some time
'his' men at the head of all five principal houses: Citeaux (Guy, 1133–34;
Rainard, 1134–50), La Ferté (Bartholomew, 1124–60), Pontigny (Hugh of

could not dispense her from a painful following of Christ. The Lord reminded her of 'the vehement attraction by which I provoked you to follow me with a certain indefatigable vehemence and violence of spirit, making you walk with continuous steps of virtue through things both sweet and bitter, harsh and smooth' (171,42). She learned 'new forms of life by which to please the divine Majesty' (199, 64). 'The more sublimely she ascended the mountain of virtues after Christ and had made more progress...in the school of love, the more profoundly she entered into the valley of humility and administered by example and word to all in need, according to God's given grace' (199,67).

All of this points to a quite unrelenting endeavor for virtue.[159] Before there can be any talk of union with God, 'we must always be at the ready with new fervor: with hands ever ready for all works in which virtue is practiced, our will ready for all virtues by which *minne* is honored'.[160] To be virtuous or to 'be placed by the Lord on the promontory, the summit of virtues', as Ida of Nivelles' biography called it,[161] was what the *mulieres religiosae* were looking for.

Nor was the feminine touch missing. In her twelfth vision Hadewijch saw God's bride [Hadewijch herself] 'clad in a robe of total conformity of will by which she was always completely ready for virtues, and all that pertains thereto. The robe was adorned with all virtues, each virtue with its own symbol and its

---

Mâcon, 1114–36, who entered Citeaux with his friend Bernard at the latter's insistence), and Morimond (Walter, 1125–38). See Archdale King, *Citeaux and Her Elder Daughters* (London, 1954) 22, 110, 149, 211 and 335. Monastic 'paradises' do not seem to have existed without some politics.

159 Quietism is completely excluded as far as the *mulieres religiosae* are concerned. Becoming free through virtuousness requires long practice (Hadewijch, Letter 10; VM, *Brieven*, 1: 87, l. 33), unrelenting exercise (*Vita*, 75, 63), practised day and night (*Vita* 209,33; Hadewijch, Letter 18, VM, *Brieven*, 1: 158, l. 143), continual efforts (*Vita*, 166, 41), perseverance (Ida of Nivelles, *Quinque* ,287), and steadfastness (Hadewijch took few virtues so to heart as steadfastness; see B. Spaapen, *OGE* 44 [1970] 123), in a step by step unremitting process (Ida of Leuven, *AA SS* April 2: 170,1).

160 Hadewijch, VM, *Brieven*, 1: 69, ll. 368–72.

161 *Quinque*, 234: 'Dominus enim qui eam in summa virtutum arce locaverat'.

name written on it, making them known'.[162] In agreement with
Ida of Nivelles' request, a nun of her community who had died
six months earlier appeared to her wearing a purple robe signifying the life of martyrdom she had led in her monastic life. Her
head was adorned by a crown with four precious stones, indicating figuratively the four cardinal virtues of prudence, temperance,
fortitude and justice which she had particularly practiced during
her earthly life.[163] The main point of such visions is their symbolic intimation of the importance of virtues as unitive elements
between the bride and the Lord as Bridegroom. 'I remain a human
being who must suffer,' wrote Hadewijch, 'loving with Christ...
until *minne* growing within us into the fullness of virtues becomes
one with [that] man'.[164]

Freedom allows one to bring oneself into perfect alignment
with God. In her first vision, Hadewijch stated that she had to
'accomplish God's high will with love according to his pleasure.
Thus he [God] makes anyone who lives in this manner pleasing to
him'.[165] Beatrice spoke of 'the loftiness of mind through which
freeing herself from herself, she lifted herself up toward God's
nearing union with him as far as possible on earth'.[166]

God's totality demands all from man, and man's totality all
from God. The total freedom of the one requires the total freedom
of the other since we are dealing with love and union. For that
reason, Hadewijch advised a correspondent: 'Rise above anything

---

162 Vision 12; VM, *Visioenen*, 1: 128, ll. 58–64. According to Benz, (*Dei
Vision*, 'Das himmliche Kleid', 341–52) commenting on visions by women, a
robe is a robe, enhancing the dignty and beauty of her celestial engagement: 'In
die Visionen dieser Frauen verwandelt sich nie ein Kleid in ein Haus oder in
eine Hütte wie beim Apostel Paulus, sondern bleibt ein Kleid, das die
Empfängerin verwandelt, verjungt und zur Würdigkeit und Schönheit himm-
licher Brautschaft erhebt'.

163 *Quinque*, 219–20.

164 Letter 29; VM, *Brieven*, 1: 235–46, ll. 90–95.

165 Hadewijch, Vision one; VM, *Visioenen*, 1: 20, 168–70.

166 R-VM, *Seven manieren*, 28, l. 75. At the beginning of her sixth *maniere*
(1.2–5) she said already that 'when the Lord's bride proceeded further and
mounted higher, she experienced another manner of loving that is loftier and
gifted with greater understanding'.

that is less than God himself'.[167] In another letter she wrote: 'When the soul chooses nothing else but God and when it retains no will but lives exclusively according to his will alone, the soul is brought to naught and, by God's will, wills all that he wills'.[168] Willing what God wills, 'the soul becomes with him all that he himself is'.[169] In her first vision, Christ said to Hadewijch: 'Have at your disposal the seven gifts of my Spirit and the power and help of my Father in the perfect works of virtue by which one becomes and remains God eternally'.[170] What is meant is that she would become not God, but like God, as her mentors had taught her.

The differences in temperament and personality between them being kept in mind, Beatrice's experience illustrates Hadewijch's statement. The chronological data of Beatrice's biography allow us to follow the process of her often disturbing and painfully conflicting vicissitudes in trying to do God's will, which she usually called his good-pleasure.[171] Near the end of this struggle about 1231, she became for some time 'totally stripped of her entire will',[172] 'by which she had thus far been accustomed to

---

167 Letter 6; VM, *Brieven*, 1: 62, ll. 187–88.

168 Letter 19; VM, *Brieven*, 1: 165, ll. 54–58. In a rather Teutonic English, Ernst Arbman made the observation that 'the one-ness between the soul and God... was not experienced [by the Christian and Sufi mystics] as a vanishing, a dissolution and effacement of their own human personality or self-consciousness in God, and still less as some sort of ousting and substitution of the former by the consciousness and personality of the latter, i.e. as a possession'. See his *Ecstasy or Religious Trance* [henceforth cited: *Ecstasy*], Vol. 2 (Stockholm, 1968) 387. David Bell, 'A Doctine of Ignorance: The Annihilation of Individuality in Christian and Muslim Mysticism', *Benedictus*, CS 67, E.R. Elder ed. (Kalamazoo, MI, 1981) 30–52; 36–37, speaks of Bernard's 'virtual annihilation' [*pene annulari*: Dil 10.27; SBOp 3:143] and of other Christian and Sufi mystics (though with some reservation in regard to the latter). Arbman, (*Ecstasy*, 2: 377) expresses his opinion that this oneness between the soul and God, 'has on different but untenable grounds been contested by many representatives of modern research on the psychology of religion'.

169 Hadewijch, Letter 19; VM, *Brieven*, 1: 165, ll. 60–61.

170 VM, *Visioenen*, 1: 30–31, ll. 354–57.

171 His *beneplacitum*: *Vita*, 58, 71; 68, 58; 71, 7; 72, 39; 91, 12; 97, 121; 130, 6; 164, 7; 166, 39; 180, 169; 196, 8; 199, 62; 205, 87; 212, 88; 222, 7; 224, 47.

172 Her will was psychologically, not ontologically suspended in the sense that she did not have to *direct* her will consciously toward God's good-pleasure

govern herself' (224,43), and ended up 'by choosing neither eternal nor temporal things by the judgment of her will' (225,59). Beatrice was remarkably changed by this experience. Whereas formerly hell meant intolerable separation from God, it now appeared to her in a different light. 'She would most willingly have supported in her body the very pains of hell for a time as long as she could have arrived at the fulfillment of her desire [constantly to render homage and acceptable service to God's good-pleasure] after the fires of hell' (222,17). All fear of God's judgment was gone 'after this renunciation of self-will' (226,85). 'Her will [was] so conformed to the divine will that she would weigh in the equal balance of her will both bodily health and weakness, and would suffer both prosperity and adversity with equal love' (224,52). Or, as Hadewijch put it: 'To live truly according to the will of *minne*, is to be so perfectly one in the will of veritable *minne*, so uniquely intent on contenting her, that— even if one had another wish—one would choose or wish nothing except to desire above all what *minne* wills, no matter who is condemned or blessed by it'.[173] Beatrice did the same. 'On her scales, divine vengeance was of equal weight with the grace of consolation, and she weighed with an impartial balance the salvation of all, both those known to her and those unknown' (224,55). She 'willed that nothing be done except what God wanted. Even if she often chose by rational judgment to ask for something from the Lord, before her prayer was finished, she changed her intention, repudiated her proposed demand and very aptly ended her prayer begging that the divine good-pleasure be carried out' (225,61).

Beatrice had turned a corner. She was now in the grip of God's will and love with all the consequences this implied.[174] 'Thus

---

anymore, but was consciously *aware of her adhesion* to it. Hadewijch has a saying which, although dissimilar to Beatrice's, has some relation to it (Letter 22; VM, *Brieven*, 1:168, ll. 1–4; 6–8): 'Whoever wills to understand and know what God is in his Name and Essence, needs to belong to God, so totally indeed, that God shall be all to him, and he himself bereaved of himself.... Who therefore wills to find and know what God is in himself, let him lose himself'.

173 Letter 6; VM, *Brieven*, 1: 57, ll. 76–81.

174 Gilson, *The Mystical Theology*, 97: 'There can be no question for man of seeking [his] liberty in the refusal of all law, for even God lives by his own; but,

bearing everything with equanimity, and confiding in the great goodness of her God, and with the help of Christ's grace, she perfected for the rest of her life the work the heavenly Father had given her to do' (227,106).

Soon afterwards she heard a nun of her community reading Bernard's maxim (243,5) that 'few love themselves perfectly on account of Christ'.[175] For two days she reflected on these words with attentive meditation and 'was snatched up in ecstasy of mind' (236,30). Reflecting later on what she had seen, 'she knew the meaning of these words [of Bernard], not so much by understanding as by experience, and she loved herself perfectly on account of Christ' (237,52). Of such an experience Bernard had stated: 'I doubt if... a man ever loves himself only for God's sake. Let those who have had the experience declare it: to me, it seems impossible'.[176] Looking at Hadewijch's and Beatrice's ascent both provide evidence that grace is indeed liberating.

The biographer of Ida of Nivelles stated that he wrote in order to show 'her virtuous behavior',[177] and Ida Lewis' biographer wished to present 'this mirror of virtuous living'.[178] Alice of Schaarbeek 'grew in virtues over the years until their number surpassed her years'. The biographer added that 'God saw to it that through her virtues she would be ready to bear the affliction of leprosy by which she would be struck down... to become purified'.[179] What the biographers liked to point out was that

---

on the contrary, he must voluntarily submit himself to the only law that really liberates, since this is the very law of God, who is liberty.... What St. Bernard asks us to do is to renounce all claim to set up our own law, and to accept God's, to put our liberty on its true basis by assimilating it to God's'.

175 Dil 10.27; SBOp 3: 142: 'Nec seipsum diligat homo nisi propter Deum', not *propter Christum*, as the biographer put it.

176 Dil 15.39; SBOp 3: 153: 'nescio si... ut se scilicet homo diligat tantum propter Deum. Asserant hic ipsi qui experti sunt; mihi, fateor, impossibile videtur'.

177 In the prologue, published in *CCh* 1, 2: 222.

178 *AA SS* Oct. 13: 124, 58: 'hoc vitae speculum'.

179 *AA SS* June 2: 479, 9: 'cum ipsa virtutum augmento in annis cresceret, et tamen discretione virtutum numerum annorum superaret, volens Deus...[eam] ab omni strepitu temporali, et inquinamento saeculi penitus purgari,... morbo incurabili, lepra videlicet, ipsam graviter percussit'.

through virtues and with the help of liberating grace those women
really strove for the most intimate possible union with God here
on earth and for full and imperturbable union with him after they
had passed through the gates of physical death.
The time for becoming is now. As William says:

> Even now to the degree that we do not see him [God], we
> are unlike him.... We become more like him as we grow
> more in knowledge and love of him. To the extent that we
> see him in a closer and more intimate way (*propinquius ac
> familiarius*), we become more like him by knowing and
> loving him.[180]

Or, as a pseudo-Bernardine text says: 'the more virtuous you
are, the closer you will be to God and you will have in you a
greater likeness to your Creator'.[181] Though the terms closeness,
nearness, proximity and vicinity do not differ much and are
practically synonymous, proximity was rather seen in relation to
likeness in truth and virtue, while vicinity, also related to likeness,
lays the stress on immediacy, particularly in the area of knowledge.[182] The vicinity or nearness some texts spoke of were rather
used in reference to the dignity of beings in proportion to their
proximity to God: in paradise man was nearer to God than he is as
a sinner.[183] Beatrice spoke of seraphs as being nearer to God than
is mortal man,[184] as Hugh had said of God, angels and man.[185]
    In God there is no proximity, nearness or closeness between
the divine Persons,[186] because they are one God. Since the non-
spatial distance between the Infinite and the finite always remains, proximity in its highest degree cannot yield identity with
God. Full and actual participation in God is the nearest thing to

---

180 Aenig; PL 180: 399A.
181 *De Interiori domo* 39; PL 184: 547D.
182 Javelet, *Image*, 1: 129–34.
183 Bernard, Gra 9.29; SBOp 3: 186: 'Qui ipsi [Deo] esset proximior, homo
in paradiso conditus est'.
184 *Vita*, 182, 199: 'vicinius'.
185 *In Hierarchiam* 5; PL 176: 1009B.
186 Augustine, *De Trinitate* 7.6.12; PL 42: 946.

identity with God man can ever attain.[187] As Augustine pointed out, and the twelfth-century mentors of the *mulieres religiosae* after him,[188] 'In the measure we become like God, in that measure do we come closer to him. And this closer proximity is dependent on the state of virtue we attain during our lifetime'.[189] Man indeed comes closer to God, not in spatial distance, but in likeness.[190] 'He does not conform God to himself but himself to God. He asks of God nothing but himself and the means of moving toward him. He is satisfied to enjoy (*frui*) nothing but him or in him and even to use anything except as directed toward him'.[191]

The vernacular in which Hadewijch and Beatrice wrote does not lend itself as clearly as Latin in expressing nuances between vicinity and proximity. We may suppose that through their contact with their mentors they had some awareness of these nuances. Hadewijch seems to have had proximity in mind when she wrote in a letter:

When the Trinity demands from us our debt, we receive the grace to live divinely as we should. And if we fail because of our alien will or if we fall out of this unity because of our comfortable self-centeredness, we no longer grow and make progress toward the perfection to which we have been exhorted from the beginning by the [God who is] Unity and Trinity.[192]

In her first *maniere*, Beatrice stated that 'the soul desires so to lead its whole life as to work, grow, and ascend to a greater height of love and a closer knowledge of God, until it reaches that full

---

187 Bell, *The Image*, 9.
188 Javelet, *Image*, 2: 108, n. 45.
189 Augustine, *Ep*.187, 5.7: PL 33: 837–38; - Bernard, SC 83.1; SBOp 2: 298–99; – William, Exp Rm 2.4: PL 180: 583B.
190 Sullivan, *The Image*, 17–18.
191 William, Cant; PL 180: 480CD. See also Gilson, *The Mystical Theology*, 212.
192 Letter 30; VM, *Brieven*, 1: 254, ll. 68–76.

perfection for which it is made and called by God'.[193] 'Closer understanding' seems to refer to vicinity, while the striving for virtue points to proximity. In contrast to the first *maniere*, where 'an active longing' is at work, the fourth *maniere* speaks about what we would call infused love or, as Beatrice expressed it, 'a love which, without any human collaboration, embraces [the soul] so lovingly that it is totally conquered by love'. Through this 'the heart feels a great closeness to God'.[194] The way to a 'closer knowledge of God' of the first *maniere* has become 'a great closeness to God' in the fourth, and both have to do with likeness to God, but in different stages of development. Tending toward a closer proximity and nearer vicinity to God expresses the desire of the *mulieres religiosae* to move with liberating grace toward uniting grace.

UNITIVE GRACE

Image and likeness were bestowed on man together at the moment of his creation, and together they became distorted or lost when he did not follow the course set by God's primordial plan. When the *mulieres religiosae* spoke about restoring the image and regaining the likeness they were no more systematic than their mentors. They spoke about will, liberty, and love according to the topic they were treating and according to their different points of view. It is therefore nearly impossible to avoid some repetition. Since we are better informed about Hadewijch and Beatrice than about other *mulieres religiosae*, we prefer to quote their sayings, and compare them with those of Bernard, William and Richard to whom they seem close in this matter. Image and likeness are considered here not so much as gifts

---

193 R-VM, *Seven manieren*, 4, ll. 19–24. The biographer misshaped the *Seven Manieren* when trying to integrate them into the biography. He only once (248, 93) speaks of *vicinior*, to say that Beatrice, by striving toward virtue, 'seemed closer to supreme purity', an expression which does not occur in the original.

194 R-VM, *Seven manieren*, 14, ll. 16–17.

received at creation but rather as a dynamic *striving* toward the ultimate goal for which they were given: union with God.[195] In his theocentric anthropology Bernard insisted on the divine origin of both the image and likeness,[196] and he also linked the restoration of the former to the recovery of the latter.[197]

When the soul perceives this great disparity within itself [the likeness of the image and the unlikeness of sin] it is torn between hope and despair.... Drawn toward despair by so great an evil [=unlikeness] it is recalled to hope by this great good [=the persistence of the image]. Thence it is that the more it is offended by the evil within it, the more ardently it aspires to the good which it sees equally there, and desires to become what it was meant to be [not simply an image, but a likeness], that is to say simple [by absence of cupidity], upright [by absence of fear] yet fearing God [but not God's chastisements] and departing from evil.... This it can do, be it noted, if it relies on grace, not on nature, nor even on its own zeal.... Nor does it count on grace without reason, for its conversion is to the Word. This noble kinship [kinship, since the Word is the Image, and the soul is made according to this Image] is not barren... The Spirit [introduced by the Word] will deign to admit into his fellowship this soul so like him by nature; and that for a natural reason, for like seeks like.[198]

The image, being indestructible even though it may be obscured, polluted, bemired, besmirched, covered or whatever other term is used to express its maimedness, can be raised to its former status by doing, with God's grace, the opposite of what caused its downfall. Man must accept God on his, not on man's own terms.

---

195 This union with God is only briefly touched upon in the next pages, since this topic belongs to the mystical experiences of the *mulieres religiosae* which will be treated in Part Three.

196 Div 42.2; SBOp 6/1: 256.

197 SC 36.6; SBOp 2:8.

198 SC 82.7; SBOp 2: 297; The ET is taken from the Downes translation of Gilson, *The Mystical Theology*, 150.

Both the image and the likeness are involved in this process. The image has a certain priority, since at its creation it received a metaphysical share in God's freedom. As Bernard wrote, virtues have to witness,[199] to defend,[200] to serve and to adorn[201] the image on its way to restoration. William was of the same opinion: 'Resemblance to God is the whole of man's perfection.... For this we were created and live, to be like God, for we were created to his image'.[202] It is up to the will to decide which way it will go: virtue or vice, beatitude or misery, resemblance or dissemblance.

The will, the root of man's liberty, therefore plays a primary role: 'We were created, to a certain extent, as our own in freedom of will. We become God's as it were by good will. Moreover he makes the will good who made it free; and makes it free to this end'.[203] When this free will has become good will, one can talk about the common will or an agreement of wills between God and man. For the *mulieres religiosae* and their mentors, this common will did not carry the moralistic overtones it took on in later times. It was a spiritual connatural union, the only valid union between two spirits: God and man. 'Wills in agreement are a union, *viz.* a communion of wills and consensus in love'.[204] 'When my will wills what God wills, being one with God's will makes me one within myself and transforms me'.[205] Hadewijch advised one of her friends similarly: 'If you wish to become what God wills you to be, in order to have peace in the totality of your nature, then rise up above all lower things that are less than God himself'.[206] J[ean] B[aptiste] P[orion], speaking of Hadewijch, Beatrice and Mechtild of Magdeburg, claimed that a light linked with the experience of *minne* made them conceive the soul's purification as the manifestation (*dégagement*) of its true being, the one which

199 SC 80.2; SBOp 2: 277: 'testari'.
200 SC 82.5; SBOp 2: 295: 'defensari'.
201 SC 83.1; SBOp 2: 299: 'servare et decorare'.
202 Ep frat 2.16; PL 184: 348C.
203 Bernard, Gra 6.8; SBOp 3: 179.
204 SC 71.10; SBOp 2: 221: 'haec unio ipsis communio voluntatum et consensus in caritate'.
205 SC 71.5; SBOp 2: 217: 'unior cum transformor'.
206 Letter 1; VM, *Brieven*, 1: 62, ll. 187–90.

exists from all eternity in God's mind, so that 'we become what we are'.[207] Bernard had once said:

Man's nobler gifts,...his dignity, knowledge and virtue are found in the highest part of his being, in his soul. Man's dignity is his free will... his knowledge is that by which he acknowledges that his dignity is in him but not of his making. Virtue is that by which man seeks continually and eagerly for his Maker, and when he finds him, adheres to him with all his might.[208]

Hadewijch, already in agreement with Bernard about becoming oneself when the will becomes free, seems to echo what he said about knowledge as well. In one of her visions, she was told by Christ: 'I will give you understanding of my will and the art of true love, the blissful experience of your communion with me'.[209] On the same occasion he urged her to 'do my will with understanding, my most dearly beloved. You, who enjoy me most intimately in my nearness, activate your love toward me. Thus you will enjoy your delight in me'.[210] Hadewijch's agreement with the text from Bernard's *On Loving God* quoted above, covers the third part about virtue as well. Moreover she points at the same time to the common will, so important for union with God:

Before impetuous love ravishes a man out of himself and touches him so closely that he becomes one spirit with her and in her, man must offer noble service in all virtues and suffer obedience. He must remain willing with new zeal and with ready hands to perform all the work in which virtue is practiced, the will being ready to do all that honors the divine love, with no other intention than to render love her proper place in man.[211]

207 *Hadewijch. Lettres spirituelles*, 21.
208 Bernard, Dil 2.2; SBOp 3: 121.
209 Vision 1; VM, *Visioenen*, 1: 32, ll. 386–88.
210, *Ibid.* 1: 33, ll. 400–04.
211 Letter 6; VM, *Brieven*, 1: 69, ll. 366–73.

In another letter she wrote: 'Whoever wishes to dress richly and to be united with the divinity must adorn himself with all virtues, as God himself clothed and adorned himself when he lived as man'.[212] This is why Beatrice, like the other outstanding *mulieres religiosae* strove incessantly[213] with heart and will toward perfection.[214]

Common will implies renunciation of all self-will. 'By renouncing himself, i.e. his self-will, man recovers his liberty'.[215] This concept of liberty is more metaphysical than psychological. Following Augustine,[216] Bernard, and with him the Cistercians, spoke at this point of the will as freed will:[217] an open gate for the recovery of the lost likeness.[218] Image points to free liberty; likeness points to freed liberty, a liberty which has found its completion in participation in God.[219] 'Set free from sin, [man] can now begin to recover his freedom of counsel...while setting up in himself a worthy likeness to the divine image, restoring, in

---

212 Letter 30; VM, *Brieven*, 1: 254–55, ll. 68–76; 84–87.

213 *Vita*, 19, 64; 20, 10; 27, 79; 60, 12; 62, 63; 63, 77; 65, 6; 69, 68; 75, 71; 82, 48; 87, 6; 90, 71; 111, 7; 117, 34; 124, 91; 131, 31;168, 82; 170, 104; 186, 68; 196, 5; 197, 34; 212, 80.

214 *Vita*, 63, 78; 82, 48; 85, 33; 91, 6; 119, 30; 124, 85; 125, 8; 171, 41; 174, 85; 208, 11; 232, 106.

215 Bernard, Div 63; SBOp 6/1: 296: 'ut abnegando seipsum, id est proprium voluntatem, sui libertatem recuperet'.

216 Gilson, *Introduction*, 212–13, n. 2, no 3: 'Le terme *libertas* [liberty] en tant qu'il désigne l'état de celui qui est 'liberatus' [freed] signifie la confirmation de la volonté dans le bien de la grâce. Il n'y a donc pas valeur fixe, puisque cette confirmation peut atteindre des degrés variables'. In her sixth *maniere*, Beatrice spoke twice about these higher growing degrees of being freed: R-VM, *Seven manieren*, 23, ll. 2–5, and 26, ll.47–51.

217 Vanneste, *Abstracta*, 75.

218 Joseph Pieper wrote that he was 'fascinated' by the words 'to like' and 'likeness' in the English vocabulary. The Latin *amor* (love) and *amare* (to love) have something to do with the radical notion of likeness. More specifically, they are related to the Greek *hàma* ('at the same time'), the Latin *similis* and the English 'same'. See J.Pieper, *About Love*, ET by R. and C. Winston (Chicago, 1974) 15.

219 Gilson, *The Mystical Theology*, 236, n.124: 'The doctrine of the renewal of the image in perfect likeness is altogether one with the doctrine of liberty'.

fact, completely his former loveliness'.[220] 'Self-will is still will but it becomes love', William wrote, 'when with liberating grace this will is set free'.[221]

The *mulieres religiosae* saw virtue in its negative and positive aspects as a preparation for and a way to the restoration of the image and the recovery of the likeness. They realized that in their present human condition and by God's never failing grace, they could succeed. Beatrice 'seeing herself unrestrained by any sinful impediment [read self-will], and progressing further without obstacle in the way of virtue, began to place herself totally at the service of love...executing in act and in conduct only the good-pleasure of love' (196,6).

By conforming to God's will and thereby coming into a common will with God, the recovered, freed liberty moves rhythmically with God's love. In her first *maniere* Beatrice wrote that

> this is its [the soul's] request, its zeal, and its supplication made to God. Its thought is: how can it arrive at this point, and how can it attain a close conformity to Love, with all the adornments of the virtues and all the purity of the highest nobility?[222]

Beatrice's questioning indicates how much she was interested in knowing how the image can be restored and the likeness regained. The answer was already present in the way she put the question: restoration came through close conformity with God. She could have found the response too in William: 'When the will is in harmony with God's helping grace, it receives advancement and the name of virtue and is made love'.[223]

---

220 Gra 10.34; SBOp 3: 190: 90. Bernard's freedom of counsel is freedom of grace or freedom from sin, spoken of above, Chapter IV, p. 111, nn. 122–123.

221 William Ep frat 2.4; PL 184: 340D; SCh 223: 310,201: 'Liberatur vero voluntas quando efficitur caritas'. Javelet, *Psychologie*, 52, n.175 : 'Pour saint Bernard également, la raison d'image est dans la liberté. La ressemblance c'est la liberté libérée, qui a retrouvé son pouvoir'.

222 R-VM, *Seven manieren*, 4, ll. 26–31.

223 Nat am 2.4; PL 184: 383A: 'Quae [anima], cum adjuvanti concordat gratiae, virtutis accipit profectum et nomen, et amor efficitur'.

Love was as important to the *mulieres religiosae* as it was to their mentors, and they lived it on a very experiential and an emotional level: love leaning over toward its object and conforming totally to it. 'God himself is love and nothing created can satisfy man who is made to God's image and likeness, except the God who is love, who alone is above all created natures'.[224] It comes as no surprise to read that Beatrice 'with her will wholly conformed to the divine will and good-pleasure, kept as the norm of her life what she knew by the inspiration of his grace to be pleasing to him'.[225] As Hadewijch put it: '*minne* cannot rest, except in what God is'.[226] She advised a friend along the same lines: 'This is your real debt which according to the truth of your nature you owe to God...thus love God in simplicity and seek after nothing else but this single love who has chosen you for itself alone'.[227]

'God is the source and cause of the love we have for him in such a way that he is loved both by and for his love'.[228] Man can understand that his roots are in God's love and that the norm of his own love is God's love; that the main task of his life is to respond to this love. It is evident that a God whose love is infinite cannot be loved by man with an equal love. But man can and should love God with all the love he is capable of: total human love. Such a love is by no means easily attained. 'With focused eyes', advised Hadewijch, 'you must gaze undividedly and intensely at God with single affection, always seeking the service of the Beloved...for he who does so will deny himself nine hundred times rather than neglect one of the works prescribed by the worthy love of which Christ is the foundation'.[229] Hadewijch

---

224 Bernard, SC 18.6; SBOp 1: 107: 'Deus caritas est, et nihil est in rebus quod possit replere creaturam factam ad imaginem Dei, nisi caritas Deus, qui solus major est illa'.

225 *Vita*, 224, 47; 226, 93; 236, 4. See also above nn. 193–194.

226 Letter 18; VM, *Brieven*, 1: 155, l.84. Hadewijch uses here a sentence from William's Nat am 8.21; PL 184: 393A. See J. Van Mierlo, 'Hadewijch en Willem van St.Thierry, *OGE* 3 (1929) 45–59; 51.

227 Letter 18; VM, *Brieven*, 1: 154, ll.56–62.

228 Dumeige, *Yves, Epître*, 65, l. 16: 'Dat unde et facit quare ametur, ut de suo et pro suo pariter diligatur'.

229 Letter 18; VM, *Brieven*, 1: 159–60, ll. 159–64; 174–76; 198–201.

insisted on this undivided intensity: God's totality demands man's totality. As she wrote in another letter: 'Remain undivided and withhold yourself from all meddling with good and bad, high or low; let anything be and keep yourself free to be devoted to your Beloved'.[230] Or, as Beatrice wrote: the soul 'has to be made wholly free from itself until love reigns powerfully within it'.[231] In another passage, she not only repeats that love for God should be straightforward, but she also enumerates a series of vicissitudes one has to go through in order to arrive at God's love:

This is a laborious life, because the soul does not wish to be lifted up to consolation here, unless it has obtained what it so incessantly seeks. Love has pulled it and led it; Love has taught the soul to travel Love's paths, and the soul has followed them faithfully, often in great labor and with many kinds of work, in much longing and vehement desire, in many kinds of impatience and great sadness, in weal and woe and in much pain, in seeking and in asking, in lacking and in possessing, in climbing and remaining suspended, in following and striving, in need and distress, in fear and in cares, in languor and in ruin, in great faithfulness and much unfaithfulness, in joys and sorrows.[232]

To give more vigor to her striving, she 'pledged not to make void the faithfulness she had promised to the Lord, by seeking anything contrary to the divine will', and 'would not cling to any affection of her own for any temporal thing whatsoever'.[233]

These quotations provide evidence how hard it is to become Godlike to the degree to which these mystics felt called. Hadewijch and Beatrice could speak in their own words of their lives from within. The other *mulieres religiosae,* whom we know only from biographies, speak to us from without, except when some of

---

230 *Ibid.*, 1: 154, ll. 53–56.
231 R-VM, *Seven manieren*, 26, ll. 48–51.
232 *Ibid.*, 35–36, ll. 118–33.
233 *Vita*, 166, 33; 225, 62.

their own words were reported. Their biographers, usually men, were familiar with mystical terminology, but judging from the way they wrote, few had equivalent personal experiences. Nor can they be blamed for this lack. Mystics are a very small minority. Only a few individuals have mystical experiences, and then not by their own choice, though not without their faithful cooperation. But it so happened that the *mulieres religiosae* movement included a relatively high number of mystics, showing that the movement itself had a depth in which mystics could flourish without necessarily forming a 'school'. Beatrice, for instance, wrote 'that love works and strives only for the purity, the sublimity, and the supreme nobility which *minne* itself is in its very nature, possession and fruition' and 'that *minne* teaches such activity to those who cultivate her'.[234] But there is no evidence that her biography or her treatise gave rise to other mystics in her community or elsewhere.

Mystics are pointers and are made so by God, not by men or by biographers.[235] Whatever objective and/or subjective experiences mystics have had or biographers said they had, the mystics point to God, who is also the God of everyone else. The mystics' experiences of their belief go deeper than is the case with the generality of believers, though such experiences are not so much part, but rather confirmation, of that belief. When experiencing the sweet rather than the bitter, Beatrice wrote in her sixth *maniere* that then 'all things seem small, and everything which pertains to *minne*'s dignity seems easy to do or to omit, to tolerate

---

234 R-VM, *Seven manieren*, 7, ll. 59–64.

235 Ida Lewis' biographer wrote that she became a Cistercian nun 'thirsting and desiring to serve more freely and expediently under the banner of the King of kings' (*AA SS* Oct. 13: 112,13). Ida of Leuven, who had become the focus of too much attention because she bore the stigmata for awhile, joined the Cistercian nuns of Roosendaal, 'to be able, both in mind and affection, to cleave more freely—as she was now more hidden—to the good-pleasure of God almighty' (*AA SS* April 2: 181,37). Both nuns were still young and not near the end of their spiritual journey. What could their biographers do, except write down in their way what was reported about them? The quoted passages—at least in part—go back probably to these two nuns, but they leave us nevertheless 'thirsting and desiring' to have in their own words the description of their further evolution.

or to bear'.[236] Alice of Schaarbeek's biography likewise says that
for her time flew by when love was dominant.[237] One need not be
a mystic to agree with such statements. The totality—and the
demands—of belonging to a God who is infinite love was for
them more extended than for other people, and that makes the
difference. God is God, and man is man, as Hadewijch liked to
say. She believed that the depths of God can be touched in the
depths of each person. For, as she wrote, the

soul is a way free for the passage of God's liberty from his
depths, and God is a way free for the passage of the soul into
its liberty, that is, into the depths which cannot be touched
except by the soul's depths. And if God would not belong to
the soul in his wholeness, he would not truly satisfy it.[238]

Some consequences of unitive grace illustrate a few subjects
touched on earlier. Hadewijch asserted that 'the liberty that love
can give fears neither death nor life'.[239] Beatrice said in her
seventh *maniere* that the soul 'wills to love in life and death'.[240]
Here, both Hadewijch and Beatrice used anacoluthons. The former ended her sentence by saying that 'the soul wants the whole
of love and nothing else'.[241] These grammatical non-sequiturs
show at the same time how their opinions on fear had changed.
Hadewijch, using an expression of 1 Jn 4:18, stated in her Poem
36 in Stanzas that 'love is without fear'.[242] Bernard had explained
it by saying: 'When one reads "perfect love drives away fear"',
this must be understood of the punishment which is inseparable
from servile fear [which dreads punishment]; it is a figure of

---

236 R-VM, *Seven manieren*, 24, ll. 15–19.
237 *AA SS* June 2: 478,4: 'per hujus virtutem omnis hora extitit sibi brevis'.
238 Letter 18; VM, *Brieven*, 1: 155, ll. 75–79.
239 Letter 19; VM, *Brieven*, 1: 163, l. 24.
240 R-VM, *Seven manieren*, 36, ll. 133–34. What she means to say is that in
whatever situation of weal or woe she finds herself, love will always prevail.
241 Letter 19l; VM, *Brieven*, 1: 163, l. 25. Hadewijch's saying is reminiscent
of Bernard's SC 83.6; SBOp 2: 302: 'Rightly renouncing all other affections,
does she [the bride] devote herself totally to God alone, for it is in returning love
that she is able to respond to love itself'.
242 VM, *Strophische Gedichten*, 234, l. 124.

speech in which the cause is given for the effect'.[243] This is what Hadewijch might have had in mind, for in the same Poem she wrote:

> In order to content high love
> He [man] lets it appear
> That he shall read
> All judgment passed on him
> In love.[244]

Beatrice, who had been in great fear of God's judgments, learned experientially that love is stronger than fear. When she wrote her *Seven manieren*, she began by saying that 'the first *maniere* of loving is an active longing which proceeds from love. It must rule in the heart a long time before it can thoroughly expel all opposition and it should act strongly and powerfully, and progress in this'.[245] And so she did. Growing in the realization that she was created to God's image and likeness, and made to respond to God's love, she could say of her desire to love him that

> a desire of such great purity and nobility certainly arises from love and not from fear, for fear makes one work and suffer, act and desist from acting for fear of our Lord's anger and the just judgment of the just judge'.[246]

This is no longer the case once pure love has taken over.[247] A thoroughly purified soul can stand God's judgments. Even better,

---

243 Dil 14.38; SBOp 3: 152. See also Bernard's Pasc 3.3; SBOp 5: 105: 'cesset voluntas propria, et infernus non erit' : stop self-will and there will be no [more] hell.

244 VM, *Strophische Gedichten*, 231, ll. 40–44. What is *minne* itself? Hadewijch asked in her vision 11 (VM, *Visioenen*, 1: 120–21, ll. 174–83).'It is the divine Supremacy that must have priority, and this applies to me also. For the sovereign power that *minne* itself is spares no one in hate or in love; favor is not found in it. This Supremacy hold me back to free all people in any other way than in the very manner in which she elected them'. In other words, Hadewijch willed what God willed.

245 R-VM, *Seven manieren*, 1, ll. 5–9.

246 *Ibid.*, 6, ll. 52–57.

247 Gilson, *The Mystical Theology*, 146, evaluated Bernard's teaching in this matter thus: 'She [the soul] no longer thinks of it [punishment] at all. That is

its liberty, purity, dignity, noble pride (*fierheid*)—these words are often juxtaposed by Hadewijch and Beatrice—in love are so intense that with a free, unhindered and unconcerned conscience it is completely in harmony with God. Hadewijch got a glimpse of it when she was told in her tenth vision:' The city you see here adorned is your free conscience, and the lofty beauty here is your manifold virtues which you practiced so thoroughly. The adornment is your fiery ardor which overcame all distress'.[248]

In her treatise, Beatrice spoke twice of 'free conscience', each time connected with a liberty free enough to live in common will with God. In her first *maniere*, free conscience is related to being unconstrained, unhindered by former mistakes, with nothing between herself and her God:

This is the soul's greatest concern when it is established in this manner. In it the soul should work and labor until, by its diligence and fidelity, it obtains from God that henceforth without impediment from its past misdeeds it can serve *minne* with free conscience, a pure spirit and a clear intelligence.[24]

At the end of her sixth *maniere* having won, as a result of her reclaimed liberty, the ability to form her own judgment, she came to the conclusion that when Love reigns, there is 'freedom of conscience [no longer troubled by debt or guilt], sweetness of heart [experienced by a heart which has become free], animation of the senses [exclusively oriented toward love], nobility of the soul, loftiness of mind [in union with God], and the beginning of eternal life'.[250] Beatrice's 'free conscience' and her purity of spirit only made sense to her when they were seen in relation to

---

why forgetfulness of the God of power and justice and judgment can be the work of nothing else but pure love'.

248 VM, *Visioenen*, 1: 103, ll. 30–36.
249 R-VM, *Seven manieren*, 6, ll. 44–51.
250 *Ibid.*, 28, ll. 73–76.

her 'common will' with God. The same is true of Hadewijch and of the mystics of Helfta.[251]

It would be naive, not of Hadewijch or Beatrice, but of us, to think that these women hoped to return to the paradisiacal Eden of Adam. They realized that they had existed from all eternity in the mind of a loving God and were created real and living persons, marked by the nobility and dignity of such a God and above all by his liberty, the expression of his own love. The experience of their historical condition and the realization that God himself came to their help in Christ had made them aware of his desire to have his primordial plans succeed, no matter what man did to himself and to God.[252] Hence their desire to become

---

251 Robert Lerner, *The Heresy of the Free Spirit in the Later Middle Ages* (Berkeley-Los Angeles-London, 1972) 62–63. In *DSp* 5 (Paris, 1964) col.1241–68, Romana Guarnieri published an article on the 'Frères du Libre Esprit', which is a shortened version of her lenghty book, *Il movimento del libero spirito dalle origini al secolo XVI*, Archivio italiano per la storia della pietà 4 (Rome, 1964). She considers Hadewijch, Beatrice and several of our *mulieres religiosae* as members of this heterodox movement of the 'Free Spirit' which flourished at its peak some fifty years later, particularly in Germany. In the opinion of this movement, union with God left liberty to sin wide open and intact. R. Guarnieri's reference to Beatrice's saying 'that she feared neither man nor demon, nor the angelic or even the divine judgment', occurs in the poor adaptation by her biographer of her *Seven manieren*. Guarnieri's quotation takes over A. Mens' misquotation (*Oorsprong*, 106, n.19), which does not appear as cited at p.44 or p.49 of Henriquez' *Quinque prudentes virgines*, nor is the sentence so phrased in Beatrice's original text. Bernard Spaapen made the proper rectifications in 'Le mouvement des "Frères du libre esprit" et les mystiques flamands du XIIIe siècle', *RAM* 42 (1966) 423–39, and in his more amplified publication: 'Hebben onze 13de-eeuwse mystieken iets gemeen met de Broeders en Zusters van de vrije geest?', *OGE* 40 (1966) 369–91. Albert Brounts too was—mistakenly—of the opinion that Hadewijch went off the right track, as has been noted above in n.33 of Chapter V. On the ups and downs of freedom, its use and misuse in ecclesiastical circles, see Beryl Smalley, 'Ecclesiastical Attitudes to Novelty, c. 1000–1250', *Church, Society and Politics*, Derek Baker ed. (London, 1975) 113–31.

252 Gregory of Nyssa spoke frequently of the same desire for a return to the paradisiacal state which, expressed in modern terminology, means the state of a soul attaining its perfection. See Daniélou, *Platonisme*, 59 and 265, and Balás, *Man's Participation*, 88. As Javelet remarked in *Psychologie*, 101–02: 'La ressemblance c'est l'image purifiée, révélée, émergée dans une nouvelle lumière, plus conforme à l'idée divine qui preluda à sa création et qui doit se réaliser au terme de l'existence terrestre'.

completely free from all that is not God, free from their untrue selves, even from the enjoyments connected with their growth in virtue and the delight they sometimes experienced.[253] Their great desire was to respond adequately to the immensity of God's all-inclusive love with an equally all-inclusive love for God, for themselves and for their neighbor. To be able to do so, the divine image had to be restored, the likeness recovered and their will and love made 'common' with God's will and love.[254]

The effect of a union of wills between God and man, the 'common will', should not be underestimated. When 'one allows God to move to the center of one's life…to direct it',[255] the love of God and of man work together. It is the way leading straight to union with God. Bernard, although speaking from his own experience, put it impersonally:

Who is there who cleaves perfectly to God save he who, dwelling in God, is loved by God and, reciprocating that love, draws God into himself. Therefore, when God and man cleave wholly to each other—it is when they are incorporated into each other (*inviscerari*) by mutual love that they cleave to each other—I would say beyond doubt that God is in man and man in God.[256]

---

253 Hadewijch said it frequently. See particularly her letters 18, 19 and 30. Beatrice expressed it in her treatise. See, for instance, the seventh *maniere*, R-VM, *Seven Manieren*, 35, ll. 115–17: 'and thus in all these gifts [of the Creator and of creation] the soul remains unsatisfied and unpacified until it shall obtain what it so incessantly seeks'— [God].

254 Delfgaauw, *Saint Bernard*, 151: 'Ainsi que *amor notitia est* [love is knowledge], la liberté semble—par le consensus, c.à.d. par l'adhésion qu'elle réalise—comporter une connaissance immédiate et supérieure de Dieu; car c'est elle qui récrée ainsi l'unité originelle de l'être humain et son union au Créateur par l'image et la ressemblance'.

255 W. Conn, 'Morality, Religion and Kohlberg's "Stage 7" ', *IPQ* 21 (1981) 379–89; 387.

256 SC 71.10; SBOp 2: 221: 'Quis est qui perfecte adhaeret Deo, nisi qui, in Deo manens, tamquam dilectus a Deo, Deum nihilominus in se traxit vicissim diligendo. Ergo cum undique inhaerent sibi homo et Deus—inhaerent autem undique intima mutuaque dilectione inviscerati alterutrum sibi— per hoc Deum in homine et hominem in Deo esse haud dubie dixerim'.

William spoke in the same vein: 'You [God] love yourself in us, and us in yourself when we love you through you. We are made one with you insofar as we are worthy to love you'.[257] Beatrice's biography mentions that one day Christ appeared to her and that 'in the twinkling of an eye' he showed his heart to her. Not knowing what to make of such an unexpected happening, she asked him what it meant. And she received an answer in Latin:

Fedus, inquit, ineamus; pactum pangamus: ut de cetero non dividamur, sed veraciter uniamur' (Let us enter into a covenant; let us make a pact, so that in the future we may be not divided but truly united), and the Lord of all consolation pressed her soul wholly to himself in the sweetest of embraces... and so the divine Spirit modelled her soul according to his own image, and conformed it most fittingly to his own likeness.[258]

Later in her life, when she wrote her treatise, she showed the growing depth of this union of wills in a series of pointed sentences:

---

257 Contemp 11; PL 184: 375B: 'Tu te ipsum amas in nobis, et nos in te, cum te per te amamus, et in tantum tibi unimur, in quantum te amare meremur'. In his edition (SCh 61 [Paris, 1959] 99 n.2) and in the ET (CF 3: 29–30 [Spencer, MA, 1971]), Jacques Hourlier refers to John Scot Eriugena as William's source. According to Gilson [*The Mystical Theology*, 235, n.121] 'in the absence of all certain chronological data which would enable us to correlate the works of William with those of Bernard, no hypothesis on their probable filiation can be put forward.... Till proof to the contrary is forthcoming I remain convinced of their complete independence'. The answer could, perhaps, be found along the lines shown by D.N. Bell (*Citeaux* 28 [1982] 22), who writes that William's text originates not from J.Scot Eriugena, but rather from Augustine. This could be true of Bernard also.

258 *Vita*, 166, 26. What is said in this scene in the life of Beatrice is reminiscent of Bernard's SC 83.1; SBOp 2: 298: 'Every soul standing under condemnation and without hope, has the power to turn and find it can not only breathe the fresh air of the hope of pardon and mercy, but also dare to aspire to the nuptials of the Word, not fearing to enter into alliance with God... [and] venture with confidence into the presence of him by whose image it sees itself honored, and in whose likeness it knows itself made glorious.

In this [love] the heart feels a great closeness to God, a
substantial clarity, a wonderful delight, a noble liberty and a
ravishing sweetness... *Minne*'s beauty has consumed it;
Love's strength has eaten it up; Love's sweetness has
immersed it; Love's greatness has absorbed it; Love's exalt-
edness has raised it up and so united it into itself that the
soul must totally belong to *Minne* nor should it love anything else.[259]

Hadewijch and Beatrice, and two of their mentors, thus expressed
in their own words what common will with God meant, what it
included and excluded and what it leads to: union with God
evolving into a unity of spirit, *unitas spiritus.* 'In a wondrous
way', says Bernard, '[man] forgets himself, and ceasing to belong
to himself, he passes entirely into God and, adhering to him, he
becomes one with him in spirit'.[260] Or, as he states elsewhere:
'glued together with the lime of love, adhering to God, [man]
becomes one spirit'.[261] William was no less emphatic about this
unity in spirit:[262]

When man is effected to the likeness of his Maker, he is
affected to God, that is, he becomes one spirit with God,
beautiful in his Beauty, good in his Goodness; this [occurs]
in proportion to the strength of faith, the light of understanding and the measure of love; he is then in God by grace what
God is by nature.[263]

---

259 R-VM, *Seven manieren*, 14–15, ll. 16–19.
260 Dil 15.39; SBOp 3: 154: 'quasi enim quodam modo oblitus sui, et a se
penitus velut deficiens, totus perget in Deum, et deinceps adhaerens ei, unus
cum eo spiritus sit'.
261 Div 4.3; SBOp 6/1: 96. The critical edition does not finish this sentence
'with him' (cum eo), as does PL 183: 553A: 'glutine ei conglutinatur, id est
caritate...adhaerens Domino unus spiritus est cum eo'.
262 Léopold Malevez, 'La doctrine de l'image et de la connaissance mystique
chez Guilllaume de Saint-Thierry, *RSR* 22 (1932) 175–205; 199. Unity of spirit
is a 'terme très cher à l'auteur [William] et dont il a donné maintes explications
inégalement heureuses'. The expression 'unity of spirit' does not occur in all of
William's writings and he uses other words as well to express the same thing.
See Bell, *The Image*, 174, n.27.
263 Cant 1; PL 180: 505C; SCh 82: 216–18: 'Cumque afficitur ad similitudinem facientis, fit homo Deo affectus; hoc est cum Deo unus spiritus;

Man becomes what God is, but does not become God:

> For the man who has set his heart on high, unity of spirit
> with God is the perfection of the will in its progress toward
> God. Then does the will not only will what God wills; it is
> so—not only affected—but it is so perfected in affection,
> that it cannot will anything save that which God wills. To
> will what God wills, is already to be like God; not to be able
> to will anything other than what God wills, is to be already
> what God is, for whom 'to will' and 'to be' are the same
> thing.[264]

The relation between the recovery of the likeness and the
demanding, total directedness of man toward God, is much
stressed as an indispensable element of this unity of spirit. In fact,
few are willing to go to the lengths of dropping all selfishness in
order to arrive at 'commonness of will' with God.

Strictly speaking, unity of spirit involves not just likeness of
wills, but the impossibility of the slightest unlikeness. According
to William and Bernard such conformity is possible only in
heaven, not on earth where the phrase 'cannot sin' must be
understood as 'cannot persevere in sin'.[265] But during the rare
occurrences of a 'complete' ecstasy one can for a while come to
what Bernard called the fourth degree of loving God, where one
loves even oneself, not for oneself, but for the sake of God. Then

> inebriated with divine love, forgetful of self...[one] may
> utterly pass into God, and so adhere to him as to become one

---

pulcher in pulchro; bonus in bono; idque suo modo secundum virtutem fidei, et
lumen intellectus et mensuram amoris, existens in Deo per gratiam, quod ille est
per naturam'.

264 Ep frat 2.15; SCh 223: 348, 257–58: 'Unitas vero spiritus cum Deo,
homini sursum cor habenti, proficientis in Deum voluntatis est perfectio, cum
jam non solummodo vult quod Deus vult, sed sic est non tantum affectus, sed in
affectu perfectus, ut non possit velle nisi quod Deus vult. Velle autem quod vult
Deus, hoc jam Deo similem esse est; non posse velle nisi quod vult Deus, hoc et
jam esse quod Deus est, cui velle et esse idipsum est'.

265 Bell, *The Image*, 192–96.

spirit with him…. Blessed and holy should I call that man to whom it has been granted to experience such a thing in this mortal life, were it only rarely or even but once, and this, so to speak, in passing and for the space of a moment. For in a certain manner to love yourself as though you were not, and to be utterly unconscious of yourself, and to be emptied of yourself and brought almost *(pene)* to nothing, that pertains to the life in heaven and not to the life of human affection.[266]

This is what Beatrice seems to have experienced one day, when:

Snatched up in ecstasy of mind…she was clinging inseparably by the embrace of love to the supreme, divine essence. In this union she knew she had arrived at that pristine purity and liberty of her spirit, at that clarity in which she had been created from the beginning. Just as if her spirit had been totally poured into the divine spirit, she understood for a short time that she was joined to [but not absorbed into] the most high Godhead and made totally celestial.[267]

In her sixth *maniere* she described how, at such moments, the soul 'experiences a certain divine capacity [to be able to do what God as love does do], an insightful purity, a spiritual [suprasensible] sweetness, a desirable liberty [relativizing all earthly values], a savory wisdom, the drawing near to our Lord, and experiencing God's nearness to her'.[268]

---

266 Dil 10.27; SBOp 3: 142: 'ut divino debriatus amore animus, oblitus sui… totus pergat in Deum et, adhaerens Deo, unus cum eo spiritus fiat…. Beatum dixerim et sanctum, cui tale aliquid in hac mortali vita raro interdum, aut vel semel, et hoc ipsum raptim atque unius vix momenti spatio, experiri donatum est. Te enim quodammodo perdere, tamquam qui non sis, et omnino non sentire teipsum, et a temetipso exinaniri, et paene annullari, caelestis est conversationis, non humanae affectionis'.
267 *Vita*, 236, 40.
268 R-VM, *Seven manieren*, 24, ll. 20–24. Vekeman (*Lexicografisch Onderzoek*, 1: 145–51) suggested that Beatrice is inspired here by the opening paragraph of William's Cant; PL 180: 473C–474C, and by his Ep frat 2.3; SCh 223: 342–84, which could well be the case without, however, excluding Bernard's influence. For 'nearness of God', see above, Chapter V, n.123.

Such an experience, says Bernard, 'is nothing other than love, holy and chaste, full of sweetness and delight, love utterly serene and true, mutual and deep, which joins two beings, not in one flesh, but in one spirit, making them no longer two but one'.[269] Beatrice expresses this oneness in her own way. After the passage of her sixth *maniere* quoted just above she adds that the soul 'has become love, and love within rules it strongly and powerfully.[270] The soul rests, acts and refrains from acting, without and within, as love wills'.[271]

To become as Godlike as possible, was—as we might expect—also Hadewijch's greatest desire. When the soul retains no will but lives exclusively according to his [God's] will alone, and when the [selfishness of the] soul is brought to naught, and with God wills all that God wills and is engulfed in him...the soul becomes with him all that he himself is.[272]

Here we touch the core of man's being as well as the basis and height of human dignity. Man is not merely called to be, but to be in love with his God who is in love with him. While the 'distance' between the infinite and the finite has not been eliminated, this God of infinite love can and does call a being made to his image and likeness, to come and grow into an all-absorbing love-

---

269 Bernard, SC 83.6: SBOp 2: 302. For the exact meaning of 'holy' and 'chaste', see Gilson, *The Mystical Theology*, 131, nn. 192–193.

270 'Powerful' is the equivalent of Beatrice's *geweldelike*, a word which she uses six times in the sixth *maniere*. She says that *minne* reigns potently and that both God's love and Beatrice's free consent and loving response to it have complete dominion in her heart. In fact, it is the main theme of the whole sixth *maniere*. Hadewijch also uses the same word with the same meaning. For references to that expression in her *Poems in Stanzas*, and in her other writings, see Reynaert, *Beeldspraak*, 339 and 362, and Willaert, *De poëtica van Hadewijch*, 220.

271 What *Minne* (Love) wills, Beatrice wills. See R-VM, *Seven Manieren*, 25, ll. 31–34.

272 Letter 19; VM, *Brieven*: 1, 165, ll. 55–58; 60–61. See B. Spaapen, 'Hadewijch en het vijfde visioen', *OGE* 45 (1971) 131–42, which treats this passage at length. Hadewijch speaks in her seventh vision (VM, *Visioenen*, 1: 76, l. 35) of 'growing to be God with God', but here she has in view Christ as man and as God.

relation. This is expressed not only in terms of union but of an intimate embrace, a uniting oneness.[273] Reviewing the movement of liberating and uniting grace as it is described by William, one scholar phrased it well when he wrote that 'the interpersonal loving knowledge which William calls "insinuation" is that mode of knowledge which comes from mutual penetration into each other's subjectivity, in which the other is not simply other, but the other-in-me'.[274]

CONCLUSION

The movement of the *mulieres religiosae* in Belgium flourished for some ninety years. In its spiritual aspects it was nourished by the Fathers of the Church and by such twelfth-century spiritual writers as the Cistercians and the Victorines. All of them began with the conviction that without God neither man nor any other creature could exist.This God made man (*mensch*) the crown of his creation, when he made him to his image and likeness. Man was in God's mind from all eternity and was actualized at creation, and this out of love to which man was expected to respond lovingly and therefore freely. Man's historical condition indicates that the unfortunate course he took affected him so deeply that the image was obscured and the likeness lost. God's plan to have man as his partner in a love-relationship with him could not be wrecked by a creature, and so God himself saw to it that man was given the opportunity to help restore this relation, provided he cooperated freely with the help God put at his disposal. This plan implied—always with God's grace—the practice of *ascesis* and, more important, the striving toward virtuousness, in all its aspects

---

273. Here can clearly be seen what difference there is between the *mulieres religiosae* spoken of here, and the first manifestations of the 'heresy of the new spirit'—a variant of the term 'free spirit'. Some *mulieres religiosae* in Ries (in the diocese of Augsburg, in Swabia) spoke so freely about union with God, that it became interpreted as having the meaning that man could by his own nature become God. See Grundmann, *Religiöse Bewegungen*, 416–26, and Lerner, *The Heresy of the Free Spirit*, 14–19.

274 Dominic Monti, '"The Way Within": Grace in the Mystical Theology of William of Saint Thierry', *Citeaux* 26 (1975) 31–47; 44.

and facets. Biographies and writings of a few of the *mulieres religiosae* show not only that a union in love with God is possible but effectively took place. Because of Christ, the visible expression of God's love, and by the adequate reponse of the inborn human need of love to so superabundant a manifestation of love, the image became restored, the likeness regained, and union between God and man a reality.

PART TWO

THE *MULIERES RELIGIOSAE* AND CHRIST

INTRODUCTION

T HE FINAL SENTENCE OF PART ONE points to the thirteenth-century religious women's conviction that Christ is the mediator between God and man. The ultimate call of man, union with God, requires of necessity the complete, i.e. the completed process of man's healing: the restored image and the regained likeness to which man was created by God. In this process Christ stands central, or to put it more correctly, Christ and man together are central, since their tandem collaboration is pivotal.

The title '*Mulieres Religiosae* and Christ' seems more appropriate than 'The Christology of the *Mulieres Religiosae*', for these women cared more about Christ himself than about speculative Christology.

Their first source of the knowledge of Christ was manifestly Scripture, not merely the Gospels, but both Testaments, which they read as the Fathers of the Church had maintained they were intended to be read: 'in the light of the Holy Spirit'.[1] Beatrice's biographer, for example, tells us that 'divine grace had opened her mind to understand the Scriptures... dictated by the divine Spirit for man's salvation' (85,17; 85,31). Following their patristic

---

1 William expressed it in a lapidary sentence: 'It is the Spirit who authored the Scriptures and who must operate in [the spirit of] anyone who wishes to understand them. It is in the same Spirit that they must be read', Ep frat 1.10; PL 180: 327A; SCh 223: 238,121. William's dense text has thus been aptly paraphrased by P.Dreyfus in his study ' L'Actualization de l'Ecriture.2. L'action de l'Esprit', *RBibl* 86 (1979) 161–93; 165–66 and n.20.

215

and pre-scholastic mentors, the *mulieres religiosae* read and
interpreted the Old Testament in the light of the New. Christ is
the central subject of the Bible, and consequently all its texts refer
to him.[2] It is Christ whom Scripture reveals in the prophetic
provisions of the Old Testament and in the testimony of the
apostles.[3] In one of her Poems in Stanzas Hadewijch wrote:

Each prophet gave us
A beautiful promise beforehand:
That he [God's Son] was rich, elegant,
Mighty, and would bring us
The peace of *Minne*.
Moses and Solomon
Praised particularly his power;
His wisdom and his miracles:
Tobias, Isaiah, Daniel,
Job, Jeremiah, Ezekiel.[4]

Ida of Nivelles stated that 'the incarnation of God's Son took
place according to the concordant prophesies of the ancient
Fathers',[5] and Alice of Schaarbeek applied herself to the fear of
God and humility, for this was what she learned from Scripture,
especially the Psalms and Sirach.[6]

---

2 Denis Farkasfalvy, *L'Inspiration de l'Écriture Sainte dans la Théologie de
saint Bernard*, Studia Anselmiana 53 (Rome, 1964) 104: 'Les paraléllismes
entre la structure divino-humaine de la Bible et celle du Verbe incarné se
reduisent, en dernière analyse, à une dépendence de l'Ecriture à l'égard du
mystère du Christ. De fait, ces textes qui établissent un parallèle entre les
antithèses lettre-esprit et chair-Verbe, n'expriment qu'un seul aspect des rapports de l'Ecriture avec le Christ. Il y a d'autres textes qui, en plus de cette
structure commune, relèvent le fait que le Christ est l'unique objet de toute la
Bible, et que par conséquent tous ces textes doivent lui être référés'.
    3 Farkasfalvy, 105: 'C'est en lui qu'elle est chargée de révéler, tout d'abord
ses prévisions prophétiques, puis par le témoignages des apôtres qui vécurent
avec lui'.
    4 Poem 29; VM, *Strophische Gedichten*, 188, ll. 51–60. See also Reynaert,
Beeldspraak, 408–11: 'Het oude Testament'. In the critically edited text, the
punctuation is confusing.
    5 *Quinque*, 287: 'Filius incarnatus, qui ex antiquorum Patrum convenie¡te
prophetia ad notitiam nostram... prolatus est'.
    6 *AA SS* June 2: 478,3: 'Intelligens ex Scriptura, timorem Domini fore initium
sapientiae, recta ratione indagatione ipsum humilitati applicare nitebatur'.

One's understanding of Scripture depends largely on the approach one takes. The historical method of exegesis is an intellectual effort aimed at knowledge. In Cistercian spirituality, the interpretative procedure is a work of feeling, of experience and of love, which aspires to taste, to savor, to see, and to contemplate: in a word it aims at wisdom.[7] Hadewijch very often wove texts from Matthew, John and the Epistles into her writings, and the Book of Revelation inspired her visions.[8] Beatrice would often 'ruminate what she had read in Scripture' (55,26), 'gathering in the basket of her memory from everywhere in the gardens of Scripture' (103,67) what she needed. Alice of Schaarbeek likewise spent much time in prayer and meditation because Scripture told her that this was what Jesus did.[9] These few references suffice to show how the *mulieres religiosae* approached Scripture: in the usual way of that time. As Jean Leclercq has pointed out:

> In the Middle Ages, the principles of human conduct all came from Scripture such as it was transmitted and understood by a living tradition. The word of God was immediately operative; it did not go through a phase of objectification, but was assimilated immediately to a living subject who had the capacity for integrating it into his own existence, setting up thereby a vital relationship between himself and Scripture. Such a man lived his own experience inside Scripture, as it were, and in reference to it and with

---

7 Maurice Dumontier, *Saint Bernard et la Bible* (Paris, 1953) 173: 'La méthode historique en exégèse, est une oeuvre d'intelligence visant à la science. Le procédé interprétatif, en spiritualité cistercienne est oeuvre de sentiment, d'expérience et d'amour, visant à la dégustation, au goût d'abord, *gustare*, à la vue, *videre*, à la contemplation: d'un seul mot à la sagesse, *sapientia, sapere*. Henri de Lubac confirmed Dumontier's view, in *Exégèse Médiévale*, première partie, 2, Théologie 41 (Paris, 1959) 586–99, as did Jean Leclercq, 'De quelques procédés du style biblique de S.Bernard', *Citeaux* 15 (1964) 330–46.

8 Reynaert, *Beeldspraak*, 403–08.

9 *AA SS* June 2: 478,5: 'audierat in Evangelio, quod Dominus cum tribus discipulis montem ascendebat; cujus vestigia imitari cupiens ut montis Dei cacumen attingeret, studium operis nec non meditationis orationi conjungebat'.

the assurance that it transmitted a word of God endowed with a value as a practical norm for daily living.[10]

How deeply the *mulieres religiosae* took Scripture to heart has already been mentioned and does not need to be elaborated further.[11] Equally important for understanding the relation of the *mulieres religiosae* to Christ are the patristic and pre-scholastic writings on which they drew.'It is often affirmed that [medieval] monasticism maintained tradition by copying, reading or explaining the words of the Fathers, and this is correct; but it did so also through *living* by what these books contained'.[12] In the preceding pages we have seen how much the *mulieres religiosae* were influenced by their mentors, whether they came to know them by reading or hearing.[13]

They were, moreover, nourished daily by the rich food of the liturgy, itself saturated with scriptural and patristic readings. The

---

10 Jean Leclercq, 'Psycho-history and Medieval People', *CSt* 11 (1976) 269–89; 277–78.

11 To ask if the *mulieres religiosae* were fundamentalists is irrelevant. Fundamentalism is a modern phenomenon emphasizing the literal interpretation of Scripture as opposed to a non-literal interpretation. Likewise it could not have occurred to them to ask which were the *ipsissima verba Christi*, the strictly authentic sayings of the Lord. This question too is part of a modern, scientifically oriented approach to the Bible. People of the Middle Ages cannot be expected to have read the Bible as we do. At the end of the preceding quotation from J. Leclercq, the author adds the pointed remark 'that today, even when we accept its message, the Bible does not ordinarily transform our lives to the same extent or in the same way as it did formerly'.

12 Jean Leclercq, *The Love of Learning*, 135.

13 Hearing refers to readings in public. The better educated *mulieres religiosae* who could read and write had, just as anybody else, to listen to readings in public. Since such readings were destined for all, they were selected in order to have them digestible by all. Hence the sermons written by the mentors of the *mulieres religiosae* stood a greater chance of being read in public than did their treatises. Hearing refers also to spoken sermons. See Jean Longère, *La prédication médiévale* (Paris, 1983) particularly 54–68; 78–126. Of Alice of Schaarbeeek, for instance, it is said that she enjoyed listening to sermons which she considered as the choice food of divine eloquence: 'Sermo divinae eloquentiae, pabulum videlicet animae praeelectum,... audire delectabat' (*AA SS* June 2: 478,4). One day, Ida of Leuven, listening to a sermon had the impression that it

Vitae of the *mulieres religiosae* often testify that their mystical experiences, visions and raptures were related to the liturgical year. The prayers they sang or recited could not but intensify their desire to love Christ. The canon of the Mass, the Psalms and their doxologies, and the liturgical prayers kept ringing in their ears and hearts, singing there about Christ, the Trinity, God's love for man, man's praise of God and his appeal to God's mercy and hope for unending union with him.[14] 'On Sundays and feast days of the Saints, Beatrice had the custom of setting aside a certain portion of time to meditate on the theme of the solemnity' (89,50). This was not the practice of her alone, as the *Vitae* of the various *mulieres religiosae* testify. The biography of Ida Lewis, for instance, mentions the great joyfulness she experienced on Saturday and her inward tranquillity in mind and body on Sunday.[15]

The *mulieres religiosae*'s belief in regard to Christ and the incarnation was as solidly based on the teaching of their mentors as was their belief in man's creation to God's image and likeness. Both the abundance of texts about Christ from the same mentors and the plethora of sayings, practices and experiences of the *mulieres religiosae* themselves advise against substantiating them by references to their mentors, except occasionally in the footnotes. These women *lived* Christ, or at least, they did their uttermost to live him. Their spirituality was christocentric and trinitarian, the one quality leading to the other.

---

came down on the audience as rain. To her amazement, peoples' clothes were still dry when she fingered them, *AA SS* April 2: 177,24: 'Vidit in ipso sermonis exordio pluviarum imbres descendentes desuper omnem illam collecti populi multitudinem... in vestimentis auditorum appareret omnimoda siccitas'. This text says as much about Ida's appreciation of auditive instruction as it does about the value of the spoken word as the prevalent communication medium in a society where most people were illiterate.

14 Joseph A. Jungmann, *The Place of Christ in Liturgical Prayer*, ET by A. Peeler, 2nd ed. (London, 1965) 105–23.

15 *AA SS* Oct. 13: 114, 22: 'per totum sabbatum leatabunda, semper die dominica subsequenti tranquillitatem penitus, tam spiritus quam corporis, fere tota die spatio [suscepit] inauditam'. Her joyfulness and tranquillity are related to her weekly reception of the Eucharist on Sunday, as will be indicated below, in Chapter XI.

In the Middle Ages, biographers did not use quotation marks to indicate their sources, and thus it is not always easy to distinguish what the *mulieres religiosae* said from what the biographers reported they said, or had them say. Ordinarily, though, the biographers ended each chapter by adding some personal reflections or they addressed the 'dear reader' directly. In Beatrice's *Vita*, for instance, the sentence: 'the Son of God, co-eternal with the Father' (78,64) is introduced by 'O truly happy soul with the Son of God'. Similarly an 'ecce', 'see, behold or Lo!' introduces a saying that before the incarnation 'the wisdom of God was not yet veiled in flesh'[16]; thus it is clear who is speaking. In other instances it is more difficult to discern who says what. The biographer should be given the right to clothe what he intends to say in his own words, and yet it should be kept in mind that the biographers and the *mulieres religiosae* lived in the same social and religious environment and shared the same beliefs, though not the same experiences.This is particularly true when a biographer wrote soon after the death of his subject, as was the case for the five biographies published in Henriquez' *Quinque prudentes virgines* and for several others.[17] The credulity of the biographer or/and his sources can sometimes make biographies look like touched-up paintings. But this handicap notwithstanding, it can be said that the biographers present a fair picture of 'the *mulieres religiosae* and Christ'.

---

16 *Vita*, 19,112; 71,11. In fact, the biographer borrows a sentence from Bernard's Div 29.3; SBOp 6/1: 212.

17 Ida of Leuven's biographer had to depend on the notes of a certain Hugh, Ida's confidant.

CHAPTER SEVEN

THE INCARNATION

T HE HUMANITY OF THE LOGOS, God's Word, was created, like everything else, by the one God who is Trinity. Ida of Nivelles stated correctly that 'it was not the Trinity who became incarnate, but...the three persons of the Trinity cooperated in the incarnation of the Lord'.[1] If the Son, not the Trinity, nor the Father, nor the Holy Spirit, became a human being, this happened because 'Jesus Christ, the Son of man, deigned to vivify the world in accordance with the will of the Father and by the cooperation of the Holy Spirit'.[2]

The question of the incarnation can be approached by searching out what it means and how it happened. Of no less importance is the reason why. Why should a God who is said to be Absolute become incarnate in the first place? Why should a God who is pure Spirit become mingled with perishable matter, even if such a union of opposites is possible and actually took place? It is at this point that the relation between an absolute God and man takes on its deepest meaning and greatest importance, for it was by this means that the Creator envisaged union with his creature, man.

---

1 *Quinque*, 270: 'Cum Trinitas non sit incarnata, quod credere alienum est a fide catholica, sed tantum easdem personas incarnationi dominicae... cooperantes'. In fact, Ida repeats the text of Lateran IV (1215).

2 *Ibid.*, 187–88: 'Itaque filius hominis, Jesus Christus,... ex voluntate Patris, venit ad homines, cooperante Spiritu Sancto... mundum nostrum vivificare dignatus est'.

221

The Son is the Archetype of creation and especially of man. While the Father is the Supreme Archetype of his Logos, and the Logos totally directed toward the Father, it was up to man's Archetype to take care of man his image, toward whom he is already turned precisely as Archetype.[3] Man on his part, as image of the Archetype, was made to share in the directedness of the Word toward the Supreme Archetype, as we have already mentioned.[4] Man's creation originated in God's love,[5] and his re-creation through the incarnation evidenced God's love even more. For Hadewijch, the incarnation can only be explained by God's invincible love.[6] Beatrice says that 'nothing was or will be greater than this love', [that is] 'the incarnation of the only Son of the living God, and the performance of his mission',[7] while Ida of Nivelles states that 'it is out of gratuitous kindness that God Almighty took on the form of a slave'.[8]

The incarnation resulted from God's unchangeable love; it was not God correcting a mistake he had made or adjusting his plans gone wrong, but the actualization of his eternal plan. As

---

3 Javelet, *Image*, 1: 102–10: 'L'Archétype'. See also Berard, Adv 3,11; SBOp 4: 175: 'Venit siquidem universitatis Creator et Dominus, venit ad homines, venit propter homines, venit homo.... Nec sanum inglorium maiestate apparere propria in similitudine sua, quam fecerat ab initio, nec indignum Deo, a quibus in substantia sua non poterat agnosci, in imagine exhiberi, ut qui fecerat homines ad imaginem et similitudinem suam, ipse hominibus innotesceret factus homo'.

4 See above, Chapter III, nn. 175–76.

5 To Beatrice, (*Vita*, 138, 165) it was evident 'that the *loving* God had created her to his image and likeness'.

6 Reynaert, *Beeldspraak*, 43–45; 56–57.

7 *Vita*, 147, 52. This sentence is reminscent of Bernard's IV HS 4; SBOp 5: 58. Moreover, the Magnificat antiphon (composed of Eph 2:4 and Rm 8:3) sung each year at the first vespers of the feast of the circumcision, reminded the nuns of the supreme expression of God's love for men: 'Because of this excessive love with which God loved us, he sent his Son in the likeness of sinful flesh'. After Beatrice had spent a year in Rameya (1216–17) she was deeply struck by this antiphon (54,15), which became the occasion of her first mystical experience.

8 *Quinque*, 275: 'Ipsum Dominum omnipotentem sua bonitate gratuita... [accepit] formam servi'. This gratuitous kindness is nothing else than the 'wonderfully compelling immensity of his most ardent love (*ibid.*, 274): 'mira immensitate ardentissimi illius amoris coactus'.

Hadewijch wrote: 'Christ lifted us up and raised us to our [God-given] first dignity'.[9] The restoration did not happen because God mercifully closed his eyes to whatever man had done. It took place—to quote Hadewijch's whole sentence—because 'the Son of God, by his divine power and human claims' effected it. The accent here is more on the 'who' and the 'how' than on the restoration itself. The combined 'divine power and human claims' of Christ gave the primordial dignity of man an unexpected augmentation. It became apparent, when this Son came to share in man's humanity, that this dignity included, from the very beginning, man's ability to share in the Sonship of God's own Son. Theologically speaking, Christ as Son of God means that he is the Son of the Father; man too becomes a son of the Father by participation in the eternal Sonship of the Only begotten.[10] Not man, but God's Word in his humanity is the climax of God's creation.[11] Through the incarnation God offered man the ontological reality of his self-communication.

Christ is true God who became true man. God's Son is personally man and the man Jesus personally God the Son. Two natures, the divine and the human, belong to one and the same person,[12] without mixture and without separation.[13] Christ's human nature was not first created and then assumed, for that would mean uniting two previously existing elements. Christ's humanity is created by being assumed (*assumptione creatur*) as Augustine

9 Letter 6; VM, *Brieven*, 1: 68, l. 339.
10 See Amatus Van den Bosch, ' Pourquoi l'Incarnation du Fils, non d'une autre personne de la Trinité ?', *Citeaux* 9 (1958) 99–104.
11 Pierre Benoît, 'Préexistence et Incarnation', *RBibl* 77 (1970) 5–29.
12 Augustine, *Ep.* 169.2; PL 33: 745: 'Sicut in homine... anima et corpus una persona, ita in Christo Verbum et homo una persona'. This whole question has been treated by E. Schiltz, 'Aux sources de la théologie du mystère de l'incarnation. La Christologie de saint Augustin', *NRT* 12 (1936) 689–713; – Bernard, Csi 5.8.18; SBOp 3: 483: by reason of the enobling unity (*dignativa unitas*) whereby our clay was assumed by the Word of God in one single person.
13 This union is called the hypostatic union. 'Objectively the affirmation of the one divine person in Jesus Christ can with certainty only mean that the (in the modern sense) personal, human reality of Jesus Christ has entered into such a unique God-given union with God that it becomes God's real self-utterance'. See Karl Rahner, 'Jesus Christ', *SM* 3: 207. The hypostatic union is, as Bernard put it (Dil 7.22; SBOp3: 137): 'God's gift of himself: se dedit'.

expressed it.[14] In his created humanity Christ has a true, not a merely apparent or heavenly, body and also a human, sensible and spiritual soul. He was born of a mother in true human fashion,[15] and is man just as we are. It is God's Son who expressed himself in Christ. Hence Christ is not two sons, but one. Augustine put it elegantly in his *Sermo* 184.2.3 especially when the text is presented rhythmically.[16]

Natus est Christus	Christ is born
de patre et de matre	from a father and from a mother
et sine patre et sine matre	& without a father & without a mother
de patre deus	from the father: God
de matre homo	from the mother: Man
sine matre deus	without a mother: God
sine patre homo.	without a father: Man

The term 'hypostatic union' has been in use since the Council of Chalcedon (451) to express the God-Man.[17] At the time of the

---

14 *Contra sermonem Arianorum* 8.6; PL 42: 688. This seems to be more accurate than 'Christ's humanity was assumed by being created' (*creatione assumitur*), because creation does by itself not imply assumption. See Felix Malmberg, 'The Human Existence of Christ', in *A New Look at the Church. Readings in Theology*, compiled at the Canisium in Innsbruck, 2nd ed. (New York, 1963) 221–42; 237.

15 In Christian belief, God effected the conception of Christ in Mary's womb with her consent. Hadewijch expressed this in Poem 29 in Stanzas (VM, *Strophische Gedichten*, 188, ll. 41–46:

> The Father kept from all eternity
> His Son, the *minne*,
> Hidden in his bosom
> Until Mary
> In such deep humility
> Disclosed him for us in a mysterious way.

This mysterious way is God's intervention to begin by his will in Mary's womb what usually happens with the help of a male partner.

16 Christine Mohrmann, *Études sur le latin des chrétiens*, vol.1,: *Le latin des chrétiens* (Rome, 1961) 366.

17 The original Greek text and a sixth-century Latin translation have been published in the critical edition by E. Schwartz in his monumental *Acta*

mulieres religiosae this expression was only indirectly known in the West through the 'Athanasian' Creed,[18] the Latin Fathers, and a Latin translation—made at the request of the Cistercian pope Eugene III—of John Damascene's *De fide catholica*.[19] The Council of Lateran IV (1215) made its own statement about Christ's divinity and humanity:

> The only-begotten Son of God Jesus Christ, incarnate by the whole Trinity working in common, conceived of Mary ever a virgin by the cooperation of the Holy Spirit, made true man, composed of a rational soul and a human body, one person in two natures, showed the way of life more clearly. That very same [person] although immortal and impassible in his divinity, became passible and mortal in his humanity; he suffered on the wood of the cross for the salvation of mankind and died, descended into hell, rose from the dead, and ascended into heaven: but he descended in the soul and rose in the body; but ascended equally in both. He will come at the end of time to judge the living and the dead, to render each according to his works, to the rejected as well as to the elect.[20]

The *mulieres religiosae* and their biographers were familiar with this statement, though some of their expressions occasionally provoked objections.[21] As one person, Christ, the *homo*

Conciliorum Oecumenorum (Berlin-Leipzig, 1927–44) second part 1, 2, 129–30 and 3, 2, 134–89. These texts were reproduced with a lengthy commentary by Ignacio Ortiz de Urbina, 'Das Symbol von Chalkedon. Sein Text, sein Werden, seine dogmatische Bedeutung', in *Das Konzil von Chalkedon,* A. Grillmeyer and H. Bacht eds, 3rd ed., vol.1 (Würzburg, 1962) 389–418.

18 Not surprisingly several Western writers in the twelfth century lacked a precise terminology in regard to God's Son assuming a human nature. See Ludwig Otto, 'Das Konzil von Chalkedon in der Frühscholastik', *Das Konzil von Chalkedon*, vol.2 (Würzburg, 1962) 873–923.

19 See above, Chapter IV, n. 155.

20 The translation is taken from J. Neuner and J. Dupuis, *The Christian Faith,* 431.

21 The short and incomplete biography of Beatrice of Zwijveke, for instance, says that she saw 'in the spirit' the human person of Christ (*humanam Christi personam*), *OGE* 23 (1949) 243.

patens et Deus latens,[22] manifested his 'double' love for all people,[23] and the *mulieres religiosae* responded with their whole being to his all-embracing love. Because the man Jesus of Nazareth is at the same time God and the second Person of the Trinity, an immense longing for the Trinity surged up in their hearts. In the writings of Hadewijch and Beatrice and in the biographies, one can easily follow how this longing blossomed and culminated in what they called *minne*: the everlasting, unchangeable love of God, the astonishing love of Christ for them and for all of humankind, and their response to this love, a human love embracing God and their fellow men with all the implications such love involved.[24]

Christianity is not an easy religion. Besides all its ascetical and moral demands, it confronts the believer with many mysteries: the mystery of God's existence, the mystery of God as Trinity, the mystery of Christ as one person in two natures, the mystery of his real presence in the Eucharist, the mystery of his Church, not in its human institutional form, but as his 'mystical body', to say nothing about the mystery that man is himself. All this requires faith, but this faith remains unshaken when it is supported by the knowledge and experience of that other mystery which contains the answer to all mysteries: a God who is love and who desires to have man as a love partner and provides him with all the means to become such effectively. All the social, economic, cultural and other elements which put their stamp on the *mulieres religiosae*, were only human ingredients of the much deeper and far more embracing encounter between God and them.

Yielding to his Father's love for man and inclining himself toward man whose Archetype he is, the Son of God voluntarily

---

22 Christ as one person (*et erat una persona*) is disclosed in his humanity and concealed in his divinity. This is the way Garnier of Rochefort, abbot of Clairvaux (1186–93) put it in his *Sermo* 5; PL 205: 607B.

23 In her fourteenth vision, Hadewijch saw Christ's divine and human love, unbearable for human eyes; VM, *Visioenen*, 1: 161, l. 78.

24 In Chapter XV, *minne* will receive more extensive attention. Both Hadewijch and Beatrice personified *minne*, and this concept includes other elements beyond those considered at this point.

became man, showing how God acts in his relation to man.[25] Hadewijch, for instance, was astounded 'that God's Son inclined himself in three ways toward us: the first is that he gave his nature [*viz.* his divinity], the second that he delivered up his substance [i.e. his concrete humanity, his body], the third that he relaxed time [i.e.patiently waited for our answer].[26] The *mulieres religiosae* would sometimes emphasize Christ's humanity and at other times his divinity, but they never considered the one without the other.[27] In his divinity, Christ is 'the only Son of the living God' (147,46); he is, as Ida of Leuven said, 'perfect God and man born of the Virgin Mary';[28] he said to Hadewijch:'In my nature [as God]... I myself went forth from my Father to you'.[29] Because he is God, Ida of Nivelles called him 'the Lord of Majesty, born of the Virgin Mary'.[30]

The incarnation indicated also that Christ is 'the incarnated lover of men', as Ida Lewis' biographer expressed it.[31] Hadewijch spoke of the incarnation as Christ's 'fall' from sublimity as God into a bottomless abyss as man.[32] She was not at all amazed

---

25 Bernard called Christ, the incarnate Word of God, the *Verbum abbreviatum*, God's 'shortened Word': Nat 1; SBOp 4: 244. See Vl. Lossky, 'Études sur la terminologie de Saint Bernard', *Archivum Latinitatis Medii Aevi* 17 (1942) 79–96; 87–90.

26 Letter 22; VM, *Brieven*, 1: 193, ll. 133–36. R. Vanneste, *Abstracta*, 30–32, considering the fluctuating meaning of the term 'substance' in Hadewijch's time, is of the opinion that this term probably means Christ's concrete humanity. The expression 'Hi neighende den tijt' is problematic. For its suggested meaning, see VM, *Brieven*, 1: 194, n.155, and Reynaert, *Beeldspraak*, 211–12.

27 Christian spirituality today tends to pay more attention to the incarnation in its temporal and social implications, including the conquest of the cosmos. The *mulieres religiosae*, honoring the horizontal dimensions of Christ as man among men, did not do so at the expense of the vertical dimensions of the God-Man.

28 Ida of Leuven, *AA SS* April 2: 180,34: 'Perfectus Deus et homo, natus ex Maria Virgine, Dominus Jesus Christus'.

29 Vision 8; VM, *Visioenen*, 1: 85, ll. 45–47.

30 *Quinque*, 250: 'Dominus Majestatis de Virgine natus est'.

31 *AA SS* Oct.13: 117,1: *Humanator amator hominum*. Some manuscripts have only *amator hominum*. *Humanator* seems to be a misspelling of *humanatus*.

32 Poem 2 in Couplets; VM, *Mengeldichten*, 17, ll. 65–66. The bottomlesss abyss refers to Mary's womb. This 'fall' has some similarity with Bernard's saying (Csi 2.9.18; SBOp 3: 426) 'that the Author [of human nature] joined what is highest with what is lowest': *Summa imaque sociat*.

to realize that God was God and that man was man,[33] but she was utterly struck by the love of a God who through the incarnation bridged the distance between the absolute dignity of God and the misery of sinful man.[34] The incarnation does not merely point to the assumption by God's Son of *a* human body. Although without sin, he plunged himself into man's misery by taking such a body; by this act man's misery became his misery. God's incarnate Son made himself so vulnerable that he died on a cross.[35] Thus it was that Christ 'the mediator between God and man' (42,20) became our saviour (254,45) and our redeemer as the *mulieres religiosae* said.[36] Through his incarnation 'the Lord's body, born of the Virgin, became the price of our redemption' (206,9). Ida of Leuven spoke of him 'as the most zealous for all faithful souls',[37] and Beatrice, putting it more accurately, said that 'Jesus Christ is the universal Lord and friend of the human race' (137,55). Two weeks before she died on December 11, 1231, Ida of Nivelles stated that

---

33 Letter 28; VM, *Brieven*, 1: 238, ll. 231–33.

34 Misery meant for Hadewijch, as it did for Beatrice (Vekeman, *Lexicografisch Onderzoek*, 2: 130), alienation, being cut off from one's original state and destiny. See Christilla Kerstens, 'De wazige spiegel van Hadewijch. Het onuitsprekelijke Diets gemaakt in beelden', *OGE* 47 (1973) 367. 'Misery' will be more extensively treated below.

35 Kerstens, 360. Hadewijch here agrees with Bernard who, for all his reputation as a pioneer in devotion to Christ's sufferings, was more deeply touched by the assumption of mortal flesh by God's Son than by his passion and death. See A. Van den Bosch, 'Le mystère de l'incarnation chez saint Bernard', *Citeaux* 10 (1959) 250: 'L'aspect [of the incarnation] qui le touche, c'est l'abaissement, cette venue jusqu'à nous, le Christ assumant notre infirmité '. Or as Friedrich Ohly (*Hohelied-Studien*, 149) said it: 'Der Gedanke der Erlösung durch die Passion tritt für Bernhard zurück hinter dem Wunder der Liebensoffenbarung Gottes in seiner Menschwerdung'. This was not an uncommon view in the twelfth century. See Javelet, *Image*, 1: 306, referring to several authors. See also Dinzelbacher, *Vision*, 240, where he compares Anselm's *Cur Deus Homo* with Bernard's position.

36 Alice of Schaarbeek, *AA SS* June 2: 482, 32; – Ida Lewis, *AA SS* Oct.13: 114, 24; – Ida of Leuven, *AA SS* April 2: 179, 29.

37 *AA SS* April 2: 178, 27: 'omniumque fidelium animarum perfectissimus zelator'.

the Trinity thunders. This thunder is, if I am not mistaken, nothing else...than the incarnation of the Son. As the rubbing of the clouds causes thunder, so the incarnate Son... thunders his message of salvation for repentant sinners and those who observe his precepts, or for the damnation of obdurate sinners.[38]

The yearly recurring feast of Christmas spontaneously attracted the attention and affection of the *mulieres religiosae* to the incarnation. On one Christmas, Beatrice 'applied her whole heart's intention to fervent meditation and to treating carefully in her heart the holy mystery of the Lord's incarnation' (125,42). On two related occasions (216,56; 217,90) she said 'that the Lord is the Son of God, eternally born from the Father and [was] begotten temporally from his mother at the end of time'. Sick in bed one Christmas day, Ida Lewis was reflecting on God's love manifested in and through the incarnation. Her biographer reports that, as midnight mass was being celebrated, she suddenly saw in a great light, radiant as a lamp, an inexpressibly beautiful person (*persona*) carrying the child Jesus in his arms. And that person said to her: 'Behold, this is my beloved Son. I have no greater gift, but for this very day I give him to you and to the community'.[39]

From these citations, we can gather that the *mulieres religiosae* accepted Christ as God and man, or better, the one God-Man, their loving Lover and their ardently loved Beloved.[40] Their emotion-laden expressions vibrated in harmony with God's love

---

38 *Quinque* , 287: 'Tonitruum, Sanctae Trinitatis est filius incarnatus... ad notitiam nostram quasi ex nubibus concussione prolatus est'. For Hadewijch's use of thunder, 'the terrible voice of menace', see above, Chapter VI, n.72.

39 *AA SS* Oct.13: 117, 34: 'Ecce dilectus filius meus... quo carius donum nihil habens, hunc tibi et conventui die conferam hodierna'.

40 The *dilectus* and *dilector* theme occurs in Ida of Nivelles' biography (*Quinque*, 251), as it does in all the other biographies, but it can take different forms. For instance, in the biography of Ida of Leuven (*AA SS* April 2: 179,29), the expression is applied to Ida in relation to Christ of whom she is the *dilecta* and *dilectrix*.

as perceived in the incarnation of his Son: 'Our Creator and Lord took on our form and shape, [and] is a creature in our nature. Great is this honor!'[41]

---

41 Ps.- Hadewijch (late thirteenth century); VM, *Mengeldichten*, 116, ll. 13–16.

CHAPTER EIGHT

CHRIST, MAN AMONG MEN

B Y BECOMING MAN AND DWELLING as 'man among men', as Beatrice expressed it,[1] God made himself known to us by what he did for us, and by doing so made known something of what he is in himself. At the same time he manifested what man, made to his image and likeness, meant to him. Christ's incarnation was the means God used to make even more evident that he was intent on having man as a partner in love.

Christ was sent to redeem man from his sins, from his many refusals of God's love, and to save him, that is, to help him use his redeemed freedom to say 'yes' to God's offer of self-revelation and communication. In his incarnation God's Son 'emptied himself to assume the condition of a slave'.[2] Of the *kenosis*—as this self-emptying is called—his passion and death are the highest visible expressions. One day a nun of Ida Lewis' community asked her which was of the greatest value to Christ: his birth or his passion? Ida gave her a straight answer: 'If the Lord had not been born he could not have died, but because he was born it was necessary for him to suffer the torment of death'.[3]

---

1 'Inter homines homo', *Vita*, 42, 21; 128, 64.

2 Ph 2:7. The emptying refers to his glory as God of which he deprived himself voluntarily in his humanity; 'slave' is here opposed to 'Lord'. Only after his resurrection (Ac 2:36) is he proclaimed 'both Lord and Christ'.

3 *AA SS* Oct. 13: 117,32: 'Ex eo quo natus fuerat, mortis pati supplicium oportebat'. Probably without knowing it, Ida expressed in another way what

231

But to overemphasize Christ's *kenosis* in his passion and death can de-emphasize all that his incarnation included.[4] For the *mulieres religiosae*, as for their mentors, the incarnation of Christ meant his whole human existence on earth and even his glorified humanity, which, although glorified, remains humanity. Ida of Nivelles, explicitly referring to Luke 15:6, directed her affective attention to the human Christ, 'almighty God who, emptying himself and taking on the form of a slave, looked in his saving humanity after the hundredth sheep [Ida] and put it on his sacred shoulders to bring it back to the fold'.[5] Both aspects of Christ are considered when Christ—'the lover of men',[6] it should not be forgotten—is seen as the bridegroom of the Church, his mystical Body, and of the individual soul.[7] The *mulieres religiosae* saw themselves loved by Christ with his twofold love as God and as man,[8] each one in her own personal and individual way, within the framework of all they had in common as human beings and as Christians and as women sharing a cultural and temporal background.

To present Beatrice in her context, we need not explain how Christ lived as man, with his emotions and experiences, or to clarify the content of his teaching. Our interest is rather to show how the *mulieres religiosae* saw him. Their descriptions of how

---

Gregory of Nyssa had said centuries earlier. See J. Gaïth, *La conception de la liberté*, 173: 'En parlant du Christ, Grégoire ne craint pas de dire que la naissance n'est pas la cause de la mort. C'est au contraire à cause de la mort que Dieu a accepté de naître'.

4 As has been noted, for instance, by J.A. Fitzmyer, 'The Ascension of Christ and Pentecost', *TS* 45 (1984) 409–40.

5 *Quinque*, 275: 'ut ovem centesimam quae erraverat suis sacris humeris dignaretur imponere et sic ad gregem reportare'.

6 So wrote Beatrice's biographer (148,69), repeating what the nuns of Rameya called Christ in 1218 (*Quinque*, 227), when they appealed to him on Ida's behalf, who seemed then close to death.

7 Edmund Mikkers, 'De Kerk als bruid in de hoogliedcommentaar van sint Bernardus', *Sint Bernardus van Clairvaux* (Achel, 1953) 195–214; H. Riedlinger, *Die Makellosigkeit der Kirche*, 151–53.

8 What Ohly (*Hohelied-Studien*, esp. 148–51) wrote about Bernard applies also to the *mulieres religiosae* in relation to Christ's 'double love': 'Bernhard [begründet] die Christus zugewandte Liebesmystik mit der doppelten Liebe zu dem auf Erden menschlich-leidenden Jesus und der ewig herrlichen zweiten Person der Trinität, die das Wort ist, dem die Seele sich vermählt'.

they experienced him as a baby or a boy and especially how they were deeply touched by his passion and death are sufficiently eloquent. They did not stress his resurrection disproportionately, convinced as they were that the risen and glorified God-Man came to meet them in the Eucharist. That encounter empowered them to follow and to imitate him on the way back to the Father. Their most pressing desire—union with God—had become realizable through Jesus Christ.

To become man among men, God's Son experienced human birth and childhood. During the Christian centuries many cases have been recorded of males sensitive to a God who manifested his vulnerability as a baby.[9] But these men were outdone by the instinctive attraction and affection most women feel toward a baby.[10] The virginity of the *mulieres religiosae* in no way impeded such spontaneous feelings.

Christ Jesus was seen as a new born baby or as a child by Ida of Nivelles[11] and by Ida of Leuven.[12] Hadewijch saw him as a three-year old boy,[13] and Ida of Nivelles when he seemed to be twelve.[14] Apparitions of the baby or child were often related to

---

9 For bibliography, see below n. 14 and 31 of this Chapter.

10 Gradually the baby became more and more dressed up. In the visions of Caterina Ricci (1522–89) he had a complete nursery setup. See Benz, *Die Vision*, 537: 'Dieser Visionsbericht [of Caterina Ricci] zeigt, wie rasch die Vision des Kindleins zum Idyll wird—nicht nur das baby-kissing, das sich in allen Klosterchroniken des 13. und 14. Jahrhunderts findet, wird Mode—sondern auch das ganze Krippen-und Körbchenidyll.... Die Strick-Fantasie der Nonnen hat alsbald die Jäckchen und Mützchen hinzugefügt, und bei Caterina Ricci sind die Windeln bereits durch eine ganze Baby-Ausstattung ersetzt'.

11 *Quinque*, 251 and 257–59.

12 *AA SS* April 2: 166,32; 176,21; 177,22.

13 This took place in her seventh vision, when the child turned into an adult. See VM., *Visioenen*, 1: 77, ll.59—74.

14 *Quinque*, 247: 'His hair was curly and almost blond'. If Ida had been Irish or Mediterranean, the boy's hair would probably have been auburn or black. The boy 'walked around in the refectory where the nuns sat down for a meal, looking at them, but often coming back to Ida. The biographer explains the boy's preference for Ida by saying that 'she loved him with a more ardent love and a greater desire'. The biographer is adapting Ida's story to some similar stories found in Caesarius of Heisterbach's *Dialogus miraculorum*, Conrad of Ebrach's *Magnum Exordium*, or the *Liber visionum et miraculorum* compiled under prior John of Clairvaux (1171–79). See Brian P.McGuire, *AC* 39 (1983) 27–62.

the Eucharist,[15] as was the case with Ida of Nivelles,[16] Ida of Leuven,[17] and Hadewijch,[18] or took place on such feasts of the liturgical cycle as Christmas,[19] the circumcision,[20] or Epiphany.[21]. The child came to sit on the arms of Ida Lewis when she was in choir,[22] and Ida of Leuven fainted in the street when she saw him in front of her father's house.[23]

On several occasions Our Lady brought the baby to them, as happened to Ida of Nivelles,[24] Ida Lewis,[25] and Ida of Leuven.[26] These apparitions lasted only a short time, though on one occasion the child remained in Ida of Leuven's company for two days.[27] These apparitions had few psychosomatic effects, although this was to be expected in the case of Ida of Leuven.[28]

---

15 Thomas of Cantimpré made it a collective experience in Douai in 1254. See Platelle (Chapter IV, n.160) 482, and P. Browe, *Die eucharistischen Wunder des Mittelalters*, Breslauer Studien zur historischer Theologie, N.S. 4 (Breslau, 1938) 100–01. This work is henceforth cited: *Die eucharistischen Wunder*.

16 *Quinque*, 247.

17 *AA SS* April 2: 177, 22–23.

18 VM, *Visioenen* 1: 77, l. 59.

19 Ida of Nivelles (*Quinque*, 251–53); – Ida Lewis (*AA SS* Oct.13: 117, 34).

20 *Vita* 242, 39. Beatrice who had just had the regular phlebotomy (*minutio sanguinis*) responded weakly to the *puerulus* (a small boy). The biographer says that he did not know who this boy was or where he came from, but thought it to be 'some angelic vision sent by the Lord to comfort her; or else he was the Lord Jesus Christ himself, circumcised that day for us' (242, 48). The biographer does not seem to have considered that in this instance the vision could as well have been a mere phantasm.

21 Ida of Leuven, *AA SS* April 2: 166, 31–32. She had for a year greatly desired to adore him as the Magi did.

22 *AA SS* Oct.13: 118, 37. This occurrence will be more amply treated below in n. 207 of Chapter XIV.

23 *AA SS* April 2: 167, 34.

24 *Quinque*, 257–58. On this occasion Our Lady said to her: 'take him on your lap, kiss and embrace him and have a good time'.

25 *AA SS* Oct.13: 118,37. Mary carrying the child in her arms presented him to her.

26 *AA SS* April 2: 177,22–23. Ida came from a well-to-do family and was an intentional school drop-out. She dressed herself deliberately in poor clothing which irritated one of her sisters, who scolded her for that reason. Her biographer tells us that the next night the child Jesus came to this sister's bed and kicked her with his feet and fists. (*ibid.*, 167,36).

27 *Ibid.*, 176, 21: 'per totum illum diem insuper et sequentem'.

28 *Ibid.*, 167,34; 176,36.

The baby or child was evidently always very beautiful.[29] Mention is made that after such an apparition they were not able to recount what they had experienced.[30] Apparitions of the child Jesus happened seem to have been experienced more often to *mulieres religiosae* gifted with charisms, but they did not identify with Mary to the point of feeling physically pregnant or nursing the infant, as happened with some women visionaries a generation later.[31] Of much greater importance is what the man Jesus did, since his birth took place only in function of his adult life. The incarnation—meaning the whole life of our Lord—was often the topic of the *mulieres religiosae*'s meditations. Of Beatrice, still in her early teens (42,21) we read:

Whatever she heard or read concerning everything the man Jesus Christ, mediator between God and men, did or suffered for our redemption while he lived on earth as man, from the first day of his holy birth to the hour of his ascension...all this she daily remembered and pondered in humble meditation. Dwelling on each aspect individually, with groans and sighs, she gave thanks to the loving Lord for all the benefits of his mercy, and this with full affection. In her meditations she used to recount in an orderly way whatever the infant Christ bore at the time of his birth, the

---

29 To quote all the texts would inevitably lead to tedious and unnecessary repetition. The attention of the *mulieres religiosae* went chiefly to the beauty of a loving God who became a human being, to whom the familar psalm verse (45:2) was applied: 'Of all men you are the most handsome'.
30 Ida of Nivelles, *Quinque*, 247; – Ida of Leuven, *AA SS* April 2: 166,33.
31 Grundmann, *Religiöse Bewegungen*, 414–15. For more *exempla* of this baby Jesus type, see W.A. Van der Vet, *Het Biënboek van Thomas van Cantimpré en zijn Exempelen* (The Hague, 1902) 109–12; C.G. De Vooys, *Middelnederlandse Legenden*, 135–42, and especially Rosemarie Rode, *Studien zu den mittelalterlichen Kind-Jesu-Visionen* (Frankfurt/M, 1957) who considers in her unpublished dissertation particularly German *mulieres religiosae*, the nuns of Helfta, the fourteenth-century Dominican nuns (23–48), and the 'Situation der Kind-Jesu-Visionen (49–93). For pregnancy in a mystical sense, see Reynaert, *Beeldspraak*, 293–300: 'Het mystieke moederschap'.

miracles he showed in his youth, the disgrace, the spittle, the scourges, the cross and death he endured in the virile strength of his passion, and what he powerfully accomplished after his death, smashing the gates of hell and snatching his own people from the darkness. Thus she arrived in her meditation at the glory of the Lord's ascension.

There she stopped short, not because an ascension was not part of the incarnation, but because, 'thinking herself unworthy to ascend after Christ to loftier heights, she thought she had not yet deserved such a privilege of grace by a worthy exercise of virtues'.[32] When she was in her twenties (95,87), she was no longer inhibited by this objection.

She most devoutly gave thanks to our Lord Jesus Christ for the work of our redemption by which he deigned to fulfil the work of our redemption by being born of a virgin, living with man, preaching, baptizing,[33] working miracles, and finally bearing the disgrace of the cross, dying, rising again, and placing the substance of our nature at the right hand of the divine Majesty.

Hadewijch, the great lover of Christ in his divinity and humanity put it this way:

When Christ lived on earth as man, he did all his works at the right time. When the hour came, he acted: in words, in deeds, in preaching, in doctrine, in reprimands, in consoling, in miracles, in penance, in troubles, in disgrace, in calumny [all culminating] in the agony of the passion and of death. In all these things he patiently awaited his time. And when the

---

32 *Vita*, 42, 34. The quoted text seems to be a direct or indirect reminiscence of Richard's *De Trinitate*, PL 196: 890B, and borrows also some statements from the Council of Lateran IV.

33 In fact, Christ himself never baptized (see *TDNT* 1: 538), but in letting himself be baptized he expressed his solidarity with sinners.

hour came in which it befitted him to act, he did what he had to do with great effort and without flinching.With perfect fidelity he acquitted the debt of human nature to the Father's divine truth. Then mercy and truth met together, and justice and peace kissed each other.[34]

In their love for Christ as a man among men, the *mulieres religiosae* were not afraid to look more closely at his humanity. As a woman, Ida of Nivelles observed judiciously that

He is gracious and of all men the most handsome and beautiful, and he embraced and kissed her. She was greatly affected by the joyful remembrance of his holy members, *viz.* his hands, eyes, lips, torso, face, heart, etc. As a candle melts in front of a fire, so in her frequent remembrances she felt her whole body suddenly liquified to the point of failing her. It was as if a very limpid river, gushing out from a source of delight, overtook her.[35]

To feel a physical attraction to the 'most handsome and beautiful' of all men is quite natural for a woman. Some *mulieres religiosae* had no hesitation in using what to us seems to be erotic terminology. Mechtild of Magdeburg, for instance, spoke of the 'bridal bed where she would kiss and with naked arms embrace' her Beloved.[36] But we do not have to go to Germany for

---

34 Letter 6; VM, *Brieven* 1: 58, ll. 102–16.

35 *Quinque*, 223.

36 The quoted text can be found in the edition of Mechtild's *Offenbarungen* by Gall Morel (Regensburg, 1869, rpt Darmstadt, 1963) 175. Grundmann, (*Religiöse Bewegungen*, 412–13), is of the opinion that these expressions arose from overstressing the *connubium spirituale*, the 'spiritual marriage' terminology, resulting in sentences with an erotic ring. Hans Neumann, admitting that Mechtild used daring expressions, pointed out that she nevertheless stayed within the limits of acceptable descriptions of her spriritual experiences, and did not glide into depicting erotic excitement, as happened in later times. See his 'Beiträge zur Textgeschichte des "Fliessenden Lichts der Gottheit" und zur Lebensgeschichte Mechtilds von Magdeburg', in *Altdeutsche und Altniederländische Mystik*, K. Ruh ed. (Darmstadt, 1964) 175–239; 237.

expressions of this kind. Ida of Leuven's biographer made the observation

> that when a woman is embraced by a man taking her in his
> arms, she tastes inwardly and experientially the pleasant
> affections of friendship. Likewise, Ida's soul experienced
> divine embraces and felt not dissimilar contractions in some
> parts of her body. With pleasant and amorous affections, in
> mutual embraces and congratulatory wishes, she was joined
> with her Bridegroom, the Lord Jesus.[37]

Hadewijch too spoke of physical repercussions to her love for Christ's humanity. One day, after she had received Communion, she stated: 'He [Christ] came himself to me, took me entirely in his arms and pressed me to him. All my members felt his in all contentment according to my humanity and to the desire of my heart. Then I was outwardly fully satisfied'.[38] This statement, however, should be understood in the light of what she said previously in the same vision:

> I desired to have full fruition of my Beloved and to under-
> stand and to taste him to the full. I desired that his humanity
> should to the fullest extent be one in fruition with my
> humanity and that mine should then stand firm and strong

---

37 *AA SS* April 2: 172,5: 'Sicut ab homine corporalium brachiorum adminiculo quis amplectitur, et sicut in amplexibus brachiorum extrinsecis interioris affectus amicitiae jucunda quadam experientia degustatur; sic a divinis amplexibus omnem animam suam illa sensisse dicitur, haud dissimiliter in una sui corporis parte recolligi, jucundisque pariter et amorosis affectibus, ipso sponso suo Christo Domino, per mutuae complexionis et congratulationis officia, firmissime copulari'. The terminology used by the biographer is nuptial. As the text stands, there is undoubtedly an erotic element involved, which at that time did not allude to sexuality as it does in our time. It would be unfair to project our modern understanding and interpretation into texts written some seven centuries ago in a culturally very different climate.

38 Vision 7; VM, *Visioenen*, 1: 78, ll. 74–80. Paul Mommaers has fittingly commented on the physical, erotic but not sensual, aspects of Hadewijch's saying. See his 'Het VIIe en VIIIe visioen van Hadewijch. Affectie in de mystieke beleving', *OGE* 49 (1975) 105–31.

enough not to shrink when the whole of his humanity would
come down on me. I wished to content him without imperfection. In this way I would purely, exclusively and totally
practice all the virtues to his contentment. To that end I
wished that he might inwardly, in unity of spirit, content me
with his Godhead and that he should be to me all that he is,
without withholding anything from me.[39]

Hadewijch was no puritan and was unhindered by the taboos of
later times in this regard. Without any pathological traces, she
simply expressed her intense desire to be one with the total
Christ, as God and as Man, in a mystical union, as the many
commentaries on the Song of Songs available in her time formulated it.

Beatrice had a similar desire, experienced in her own personal
way, and with less stress on the 'handsome' man. One day she
had 'a vehement desire to understand and know in what way the
Lord was pleased with her soul' (192,10):

Caught up into an ecstasy of mind, she saw the sweetest
spouse of her soul, the Lord Jesus Christ, standing and
waiting at the altar with arms outstretched.... He attracted
her so strongly with the bond of that love which surpasses
all human understanding that she could scarcely await the
usual time for Communion. With open heart and enlarged
veins, as if she were mad with excessive desire, she
aspired...to receive the Lord's saving Body. Refreshed by
this health-giving Communion, Beatrice suddenly felt her
whole soul diffused through all her bodily members, so
vehemently drawn together in such a wonderful embrace
of the Godhead that even her frail body in each of its
members seemed gathered up by this mighty embrace. In
the union of this sweet embrace the Lord applied his chosen
one's heart to his own heart, and absorbed her spirit wholly

---

39 For a balanced view on Hadewijch's 'erotic' experiences, see Reynaert,
Beeldspraak, 301–20.

into himself. There Beatrice's soul, having become heavenly, so to speak, tasted the heavenly affluence of love
which eye has not seen, nor ear heard, and which has not
entered into the heart of man.[40]

Given his condition as one being composed of body and soul, a
human being experiences not only the conjunction of both, but
also their mutual effect on one another. One day, asked how the
body could share in the enjoyment of the soul transported in
spiritual delight, Ida Lewis answered:

The soul is the body's guest and joined to it by the confine
of a great love. What is there to wonder about if the body
too should feel [in its way] what its spirit feels and congratu-
lates itself greatly for such a beloved guest, particularly
when the soul is inebriated by the sweetness of measureless
divine delight?[41]

As Joseph Pieper once remarked, eroticism differs from the
libidinal gratification which the term eros too often means in our
contemporary society.[42]

---

40 *Vita*, 193, 15. Dinzelbacher states rightly that Beatrice spoke here, as did
Lutgard and Gertrud the Great, about a mystical union with the Lord, metaphorically expressed. See his 'Das Christusbild der Heiligen Lutgard von
Tongeren im Rahmen der Passionsmystik und Bildkunst des 12. und 13. Jahrhunderts', *OGE* 56 (1982) 217–277; 238.

41 *AA SS* Oct. 13: 122, 50: 'Cum anima sit hospes corporis et amoris tanti
confinio ipsi tam dulcius conjungatur; cum anima tota medullitus dulcedine
divini gaudii sine mensurae termino debrietur, quid mirum est si corpus sentiat
quod sentit spiritus et prae laetitia dilecti hospitis gratuletur?'.

42 Joseph Pieper, *About Love*, 100: 'The Christian tradition of European
thought shows a constantly recurring stress on the 'erotic' elements, even in the
love of God'. See also, *ibid.* 92: 'If every form of love really and essentially
seeks oneness and has union for its fruit, then it must be said that such union,
such merging of subjects who are nevertheless different from one another and
remain so, finds its complete realization in what is called erotic love. This,
however, gives rise to a certain misunderstanding.... On the one hand the sexual
act can take place without love or even without love in the narrower erotic sense.
On the other hand, love between man and woman, as the closest imaginable
union of persons, includes in addition to sexuality many quite other things—so
much so that a sexuality set apart and therefore "absolutized" tends rather to

The human Christ the *mulieres religiosae* sought was not primarily the handsome man, but Jesus the Lord, the God-Man. Since they never saw Jesus physically when he lived on earth, moreover, it is hardly relevant to ask whether they saw him 'really' or as a projection or the after-effect of a dream. If we read the biographies and the writings of some *mulieres religiosae* in the hope of understanding them, we cannot ignore the mystical terminology used to express their encounter with Christ as Man or as God. Kisses and embraces are intended only to stress the depth of their mutual love. By what words could they express the inexpressible, except through the terminology of human love? The human vocabulary is limited to expressing what is within its capacity. So they used amorous expressions—mostly borrowed from the Song of Songs—to voice as best they could what they had experienced. Some of them managed to communicate something of how these spiritual encounters affected them, while others, with different personalities and abilities, did not.

Alice of Schaarbeek is a case in point. When she became a leper and entered the cabin which had been built to segregate her from her community,[43] Christ appeared to her with his arms wide open. He took her in his arms and embraced her saying: 'Welcome, my very dear daughter, welcome in this tabernacle of my covenant! As long as you live in your body I will stay with you and I will act as your cellarer'.[44] Three months before she died (1250), her disease was so painfully eating away at her body that she admitted she was 'at times crucified in hell, at times in purgatory, and nevertheless it was as if she was always lying in the embraces of Jesus'.[45] And when, at the end, she disintegrated

---

block love, even erotic love, and to alienate people from one another as personal beings'.

43 For the treatment of leprosy at that time, see Saul N. Brody, *The Disease of the Soul. Leprosy in Medieval Literature* (Ithaca-London, 1974) 6–106: 'The Leper and Society'.

44 *AA SS* June 2: 479,12: 'In eodem domo apparuit ei Dominus, stans expansis brachiis in medio domus; suscepit eam in ulnas suas cum amplexu et dixit: "Bene venisti, carissima filia... diu desiderata in isto foederis mei tabernaculo; quanto degueris in hoc corpore, tecum manebo et ero tamquam tuus cellerarius" '.

45 *Ibid.*, 481, 25: 'modo crucior in inferno, modo in purgatorio.... Attamen semper quasi in amplexu Jesu jacuit quodammodo'.

physically, lost her eyes and had only her tongue left, she felt 'as if she were clothed with the divinity and wrapped all the time in divine embraces'.[46] Such kisses and embraces are expressions, not of physical emotions, but of spiritual experiences.

Ida of Nivelles too was used to kissing and embracing the Lord, but 'in the secret chamber of her heart, with ardent love and shedding of tears'.[47] Beatrice was once so taken up by her love for Christ that at his presence (at the elevation during Mass) 'she melted as though before a strong fire, and she was immediately and wholly absorbed like a little drop flowing into the ocean' (206,10). Called to the parlor soon afterwards, she was afraid of not being able to control herself and she ' quickly left and fled to her private place. There she gave herself up with freer zeal to meditation, claiming her secret for herself, and in the sweet arms and kisses of her Bridegroom she rested in the sleep of contemplation' (207, 35).

On an Easter day, the other Beatrice, from Zwijveke, had *in spiritu* an apparition of Christ in human form: 'he lifted her off her feet and pressed her tightly to his heart'.[48] 'Are you not my bride', Christ asked the oft-complaining Ida of Leuven, 'whom I cured from her former deformity and whom I, as Bridegroom, come running toward as to my bride to press her to my heart with amorous affection?'.[49] This is how these unutterable experiences were expressed in human terminology. These are not stories about physically living men and women in love, but about the encounter of the *mulieres religiosae* and their God who had dwelt as man among men.

---

46 *Ibid.*, 482, 31: 'Ex eo tempore quo lumine privabatur oculorum, erat anima ejus quasi amicta Deitate et in divinis amplexibus semper comprehensa'.

47 *Quinque*, 223: 'Quem [Christum] ipsa frequenter intra secretum cordis sui cubiculum consueverat osculari et amplexari cum ardenti caritate et lachrymarum abundantia'.

48 L. Reypens, 'Nog een dertiendeeuwse mystieke Cisterciënsernon', *OGE* 23 (1949) 245, ll. 70–72.

49 *AA SS* April 2: 179,31: 'Nonne es tu, carissima sponsa mea... quam fugato pristinae deformitatis omnique foeditatis obstaculo... quam ut occurrentem sibi delectabiliter amplexetur, et [tamquam sponsus] ad pectus suum affectu stringat et applicet amoroso?'.

In the preceding passages we heard Christ speak of his heart. This marks another aspect of his love.[50] Some instances where the love of Christ's heart or the love for Christ's heart are spoken of could be called 'soft' or allusive indications. In these cases the *mulieres religiosae* spoke about leaning on Christ's heart as some inferred that John the Evangelist had done at the passover meal, to listen to the heartbeat of Christ's love or to drink from his heart.[51] More frequent are direct statements about the heart of Christ, the man. Some speak of an 'exchange of hearts'.[52] Peter Dinzelbacher has shown that the exchange of hearts is a favorite metaphor to express the 'residing presence of the Beloved in the heart of the partner', as in Lutgard's case.[53]

The heart is the symbol of Christ's love as man and can be looked at from different angles, all focusing on the mutual love between the God-Man and man. Kisses and embraces are but the expressions of a much more deeply situated stimulator: the heart.[54] For the *mulieres religiosae* the 'devotion' to the heart had not yet taken the ever growing dimensions of later times.[55]

50 For an overview of this subject, see Auguste Hamon, 'Coeur (Sacré)', *DSp* 2: 1023–49, a short version of his five volumes *Histoire de la dévotion au Sacré-Coeur* (Paris, 1921–40).

51 For Hadewijch, see J. Reynaert, *Beeldspraak*, 420–22 and bibliography. For Ida of Leuven, *AA SS* April 2: 173, 11; see Carl Richstätter, *Die Herz-Jesu-Verehrung des deutschen Mittelalters* (Paderborn, 1919) vol.2: 233–37, and Cl. Jean-Nesmy, 'La dévotion au Sacré-Coeur est elle une dévotion particulière? Jalons pour une recherche méthodique des thèmes et de leur portée', *Dr.Reypens -Album*, A. Ampe, ed. (Antwerp,1964) 241–56; 248–49, for several people.

52 Numerous instances are cited by Cl. Jean-Nesmy (see preceding note, 249). The Flemish Lutgard, 'eine echt deutsche Heilige' as Richstätter (see preceding note, vol 1: 158) called her, is said to have experienced an 'exchange of hearts' described by Amand Bussels, 'Het hart van Sinte Lutgart', *Coll* 8 (1946) 257–83. Alfred Deboutte is his 'Sainte Lutgarde et sa spiritualité' *Coll* 44 (1982) 73–85; 82 is more reserved and not of the same opinion.

53 Dinzelbacher, 236–38 of his study mentioned above in n.40.

54 See the illustrations published by Peter J. van Schaick in his study 'Le coeur et la tête. Une pédagogie par l'image populaire', *RAM* 50 (1974) 457–78.

55 See Gabriele Winter, 'Die Herz-Jesu-Mystik bei Mechtild von Magdeburg, Mechtild von Hackeborn und Gertrud von Helfta', *Jahrbuch für salesianische Studien* 17 (1984) 72–82; 80: 'Im Verlauf des Mittelalters vollzieht sich eine Verlagerung der Herz-Jesu-Verehrung von der Theologie...zur Mystik und Volksfrömmigkeit'.

Beatrice, one among many examples, spoke of the heart of Jesus in a way that points to the hearth of burning love rather than to radiant flames of the heart.[56] Another example is given by Alice of Schaarbeek. When already a leper, preparing herself to receive the Eucharist, she 'could not allow any transitory thing, anything mundane to penetrate the inner chamber of her heart'. When it was time to receive communion, 'she sensed that her heart was opened by the Lord as if it were a door and her heart filled with sweet-smelling aromas. And immediately the Lord entered the garden of his bride's heart with inestimable delightfulness and with inexpressible spiritual jubilation'.[57]

A vignette taken from Ida of Nivelles' biography illustrates what was meant by heart and how central and important the man Jesus was for these women during their journey on earth.

> One day the aforesaid [Beatrice] was praying to the Lord for her beloved Ida, and when, as is customary with all the saints, she began praising the Lord from the depths of her heart for all the good things he so often worked in his spouse Ida, the Lord replied to her, saying: 'Why do you praise me for these things which I do from the depths of my heart in my beloved? Is a man to be praised when he loves his heart and his soul, as he does by nature in such a way that he cannot not love it? Is not Ida my heart and my soul?' Hearing this, Beatrice felt wonderfully comforted, and not hesitating because of his reply she continued the prayer she had begun, saying: 'I ask you, Lord, in your loving kindness guard forever this love you have deigned to show your beloved, and which she ardently returns to you'. Then the Lord said to her: 'Why do you press me with your prayers to guard my heart? Can a man and his heart be separated

---

56 See the text cited in n. 258 of Chapter VI.

57 *AA SS* June 2: 479,13: 'Sensit cor suum more ostii a Domino sibi aperiri and quasi aromatibus odoratissimis in circuitu resarciri, et statim Dominus inaestimabili jucunditate inenarabili spiritus jubilatione, hortum cordis sponsae suae dignatus est introire'. Ida of Leuven had a similar experience—without aromas: *AA SS* April 2: 163,18.

separated from each other?' When Beatrice heard this, she was forced to interrupt her prayer, being overcome by such great sweetness (*suavitas*). Thus with a happy silence she admired the wonderful sanctity of the venerable Ida to the glory of her spouse, our Lord Jesus Christ.[58]

Talk about heart and love and its expressions should not draw us away from the comprehensiveness of Christ's humanity. The *mulieres religiosae* had not yet arrived at their goal: permanent union with God. But they were on their way to it, thanks to Christ, God's Son, who became man to save them from the possible inhumanity of their own humanity. As Ida of Leuven said: 'He is the kindest maker and redeemer of humankind,[59] 'the lover of men', as Ida Lewis expressed it.[60] He is 'full of all consolation and grace' (147,47), 'kind and compassionate, always ready to console those in sorrow'.[61] 'The lover of men and spouse of the souls, the reward of labor, the healer of the sick and the consolation of the distressed'.[62] He is 'Bridegroom, Redeemer and Lord'.[63]

So all-encompassing for them was Christ that at times they called him 'Father', meaning that his concern and compassion made him seen like a father. This title was not new,[64] but it meant a great deal to them. For Alice of Schaarbeek Christ was 'the father of compassion',[65] for Ida Lewis 'the kind, patient and

---

58 *Quinque*, 263. Reprinted, after collation with two manuscripts from the Royal Library in Brussels, by L. Reypens, *Vita*, 219–20.

59 *AA SS* April 2: 179, 29: 'benignissimus humani generis Opifex et Redemptor'.

60 *AA SS* Oct. 13: 107, 1: 'amator hominum'.

61 *AA SS* April 2: 179, 30: 'pius et miserator Dominus ac moestorum consolator'.

62 As Beatrice's biographer put it: *Vita*, 148, 29.

63 *AA SS* April 2: 187, 19: 'Ipse quidem sponsus ejus, ipse redemptor et Dominus.

64 Adalbert de Vogüé, 'La paternité du Christ dans la règle de saint Benoît', *VS* fasc. 105 (1964) 55–67; ET: 'The Fatherhood of Christ', *MnS* 5 (1968) 45–57.

65 *AA SS* June 2: 480, 20: 'Pater misericordiarum'.

merciful father'.[66] On one occasion Ida of Leuven called him 'my father',[67] just as Beatrice 'perceived him, and not without wonderfully sweet gratitude, as a father wanting to enrich his favorite daughter with the fullness of many graces' (74,35). That these women felt less need than did men to apply the metaphor 'mother' to Christ is worth noting.[68] Beatrice used the metaphor only once and then partially. She meant virtually what she meant by Christ as father. She was deeply touched 'by the abundance of graces which she had received in her life from the Lord's generosity... how sweetly he had nourished her with the milk of consolation and with motherly affection all her days' (208,8). When Alice of Schaarbeek felt 'tired, depressed or empty, she would in the awareness of her littleness run to Christ's breast and wounds to suck as from a mother's breast the liquid of restoration from her distress'.[69]

Not too much emphasis should be given to the 'motherhood' of Jesus. Though the society the *mulieres religiosae* lived in could not exactly be called patriarchal, it was nonetheless a society run by men.[70] In speaking about Christ as master (74,23), shepherd (74,31), abbot (112,124), or bridegroom (74,39) or referring to his maternal affection (208,8), Beatrice—and any of the *mulieres religiosae* for that matter—were using imagery to express Christ's concern and care for them and all people. When Hadewijch, however, referred to motherhood, she had in mind princi-

66 *AA SS* Oct. 13: 123, 55: 'benignus et patiens Pater misericordiae Jhesus Christus'.

67 *AA SS* April 2: 172, 7: 'Pater meus'.

68 Christ's divinity and humanity are the two breasts of Christ as mother. See Caroline Walker Bynum, *Jesus as Mother. Studies in the Spirituality of the High Middle Ages* (Los Angeles-Berkeley-London, 1982) 129–35, and B. Fischer, 'Jesus, unsere Mutter', *GL* 59 (1985) 147–56. See also Gertrud J. Lewis, 'Christus als Frau. Eine Vision Elisabeths von Schönau', *Jahrbuch für Internationale Germanistik* 15 (1983) 70–80.

69 *AA SS* June 2: 479, 10. For more similar cases, see Peter Dinzelbacher, 'Das Christusbild der H. Lutgard' *OGE* 56 (1982) 251–52, and C. Walker Bynum, see preceding note.

70 See S. Shahar, *Die Frau im Mittelalter*, ET by C. Galai (London-New York, 1983), has a chapter on the treatment of nuns by ecclesiastical and secular authorities (22–64). In an otherwise well documented study the author seems at times overly biased against 'the males'.

pally Mary or the *imitatio Mariae*.[71] In her eleventh vision, she herself is called 'bride and mother', a phrase which has been interpreted in various ways.[72]

At first sight all these references look like a compilation of statements without systematic coherence. This is true insofar as the *mulieres religiosae* had no intention of presenting us with a methodical approach to Christ. Their primary concern was to live Christ and therefore to discern how he lived when he was on earth. But his death did not put an end to his humanity. His resurrection and ascension were the glorious exaltation of this same humanity. As we will point out in Chapter XI on the Eucharist, Christ, God and Man, no longer physically man among men on earth, had still a way to be present to them and in them, to be met in his divinity and glorified humanity in the Eucharist. It did not escape the *mulieres religiosae* that, after his resurrection, the Lord went back to his Father. The ascension meant a great deal to them: not only because Jesus, the man, was glorified 'sitting at God's right hand', to use a biblical expression, but because they knew that the goal of their existence pointed toward their own ascension, *viz.* their endless union with God. It has been recently shown how important were the resurrection and ascension of the glorified Lord for some Cistercians.[73] One can perceive what Christ meant to Alice of Schaarbeek when on one ascension day she sighed in her solitude: 'Today, Jesus, a part of

---

71 Reynaert, *Beeldspraak*, 293–300 and bibliographical footnotes.

72 Paul Mommaers, *Hadewijch. Visioenen* (Nijmegen-Bruges, 1979) 98–99, sees it in the sense of *imitatio Mariae*, and Herman Vekeman, *Het visioenenboek van Hadewijch* (Nijmegen-Bruges, 1980) 231, is of the opinion that motherhood refers here to her leadership, a sense it had for several twelfth-century Cistercians. See also C. Walker Bynum, 'Maternal Imagery in Twelfth-Century Cistercian Writings', *Noble Piety and Reformed Monasticism*, CS 65, R. Elder ed. (Kalamazoo, MI, 1981) 68–80.

73 Bernard McGinn, 'Resurrection and Ascension in the Christology of the Early Cistercians', *Citeaux* 30 (1979) 5–22, taking into consideration Bernard, Hugh of Pontigny, Guerric of Igny, Aelred and Isaac of Stella. Garnier of Rochefort and Helinand of Froimont are mentioned in n.20 on p.20. Javelet, *Image*, 1: 312 adds the importance of ascension and glorification for William and Thomas the Cistercian.

my heart, went back to the Father, and my other part left me too with him. And so he left me behind without me'.[74]

In all this Christ as man among men has been seen mostly from the point of view of the *mulieres religiosae*.[75] There still remains the question of Christ's understanding of himself, of his own divinity. This question is still debated among contemporary authors.[76] Among the *mulieres religiosae* there is perhaps no one who has spoken, or rather was spoken to, about this subject more clearly than was Hadewijch. In her first vision the Lord said to her:

I have one thing against you which makes me indignant at this point and which I wish to show you. You are young in days, and you want me to acknowledge the aching pain in your body, the fidelity of your handiwork, your assiduous always overflowing will toward charity, the desire of your heart, the languishing of your senses and the love of your soul. All this I do recognize. But acknowledge on your part that I lived as mere man, and that my body suffered great pain and that my hands worked diligently. My will over-flowed always anew with charity over the whole world both for strangers and for friends. My senses languished, my heart desired and my soul loved. And during my whole time [on earth] I waited all the time till the hour would come when my Father would take me up to him.

---

74 *AA SS* June 2: 480, 19: 'Hodie pars cordis mei Jesus ad Patrem rediit, et altera pars me deseruit, simulque cum eo abiit, et sic me sine me relinquit'.

75 He is 'the saviour of the world, who holds in his hand heaven and earth and all powers' (Ida of Nivelles, *Quinque*, 250); he is 'the author of peace' (*ibid.*, 250); 'the king of kings' (173,65) and 'the king of glory' (*Quinque*, 267).

76 A few references can suffice: K. Rahner, 'Dogmatic Reflections on the Knowledge and Self-Consciousness of Christ', *Theological Investigations 5*, ET by K.H. Kruger (London-Baltimore, 1966) 193–215; E. Schillebeeckx, 'Het Bewustzijnsleven van Christus', *TT* 1 (1961) 227–51; *Who is Jesus?* by several contributors in *Concilium 37* (ET: New York, 1966). For the view by theo-logians in Hadewijch's time, see C. Ernst, 'De kennis van Jesus naar mid-deleeuwse interpretatie' *TT* 10 (1970) 151–78.

You have at times said to me that it was easy for me to live because I possessed the seven gifts. This is true: not only did I have them, but I myself was the gift which is called the seven gifts of the Spirit. And you have said about me that my Father was with me. That is true. Never were we separated. But I make known to you a hidden truth concerning me, perceptible however for one who knows how to understand it: never did I, at any given time, call upon my [divine] power to give myself relief when I was in need. And never did I claim the gift of my Spirit. I won them at the price of painful practice of virtues, and because of my Father, for he and I were wholly one, even before the day of my exaltation [*lit.* the day of my full-growness]. Never did I relieve my grief or my pains with the help of my [divine] perfection.[77]

Having shown Hadewijch that she had no reason ever to complain about being abandoned by God, Christ exhorted her to keep striving toward God by practicing the virtues and by God's help, and to accept the experience of her human limitations. He then continued:

When I lived as man, I took upon me all the misery which belongs to man's humanity, except sin alone. I never cheered myself up by my own inner power, but only with the consolation that I was certain of my Father.

You know also that I lived a long time on earth before I became well known to people and before I worked wonders. And when I performed them and became better known, few friends remained to me in this world. At my death almost all men alive abandoned me.[78]

---

77 VM, *Visioenen*, 1: 28–29, ll. 307–41. For a theological approach to Christ's human experiences as man, and his 'beatific vision', see Raymond Maloney, 'The Mind of Christ in Transcendental Theology: Rahner, Lonergan and Crowe', *HJ* 25 (1984) 288–300.

78 VM, *Visioenen*, 1: 31, ll. 359–69.

If Christ told Hadewijch that as man he never used the powers he had in his divinity, he seems to have done this not only to show how he lived as man, but also to hold in view what his followers would have to go through if they really wanted to become like him. On their degree of likeness would depend the depth of their union with God forever. In his love for humankind, God marked us by creating us to his image and likeness. By re-creating us he marked us with the likeness of his Son, a man among men.

CHAPTER NINE

CHRIST, THE MAN FOR OTHERS

THE 'HARSH AND ROUGH THINGS THE LORD Jesus Christ suffered in our mortal flesh' (44,65) culminated in his passion and death. This final offering affected the *mulieres religiosae* greatly. The man who died on the cross was not merely a man. He was 'the Lord of Majesty who deigned to die for us', as Ida of Nivelles said.[1] He did it, not because some human authorities, who were only instrumental, had decided that he had to die. He went to his passion and death voluntarily, as Bartholomew, Beatrice's father said (12,86). If there was compulsion, it came, not from men, but from his own love: 'compelled by the astonishing immensity of his most ardent love, the Lord of Majesty deigned to deliver himself into the hands of pernicious men and to undergo the torture of his crucifixion', as Ida of Nivelles expressed it.[2]

Hadewijch had the same conviction: 'He delivered up to death his substance, that is to say his holy body, which fell into the

---

1 Ida of Nivelles, *Quinque*, 216: 'pro nobis mori dignatus est Dominus Majestatis'.

2 *Quinque*, 275: 'ardentissimi amoris illius cujus mira immensitate coactus, Dominus Majestatis dignatus est se manibus tradere nocentium et crucis subire tormentum'. The last part of this sentence is taken from the collect on Maundy Thursday in the Cistercian breviary. The *mulieres religiosae* did not blame 'the Jews' for Jesus' passion and death. They attributed it correctly to his love for mankind.

hands of his enemies for the love of his friends'.[3] She stressed 'that Christ indicated thereby the strength of his love. His love, *minne*, wields an almighty scepter over all that God brought into existence. She brought him even to death'.[4] Christ's passion and death'are the signs of his love' (147,51). 'In view of man's salvation, the Lord of mercies suffered the disgraces of the passion in his body with a quiet affection of mind' (209,25), but, as Hadewijch remembered, in the loneliness of his abandonment on the cross 'he was certain of his Father'.[5]

Surrendering himself to his tortures, Christ surrendered in fact to his Father's will to bring about man's salvation. Beatrice 'devoutly understood that the old writ of damnation had been destroyed and the salvation of all mankind repaired through this work of redemption'.[6] Or, as Ida of Nivelles said: 'His passion and death meant man's vivification'.[7] On a Good Friday, Alice of Schaarbeek longed to see the scene on Calvary, and Christ appeared to her showing the marks of his passion, saying: 'Look attentively and consider how many and what great disgraces I sustained for your redemption and that of the human race'.[8] It is worth noticing that the last sentence expresses the redemption of the human race in general, without omitting the personal I-Thou relation of one or another of the *mulieres religiosae* to Christ.

---

3 Letter 22, VM, *Brieven*, 1: 193, ll. 143–45.

4 Poem 13 in Stanzas, VM, *Strophische Gedichten*, 82, ll. 58–61. It is evident that Hadewijch speaks here about 'God brought to death', in a way totally different from the 'God is dead' theologians of the late nineteen-sixties.

5 See above, Chapter VIII, n.78.

6 *Vita*, 95, 95, where she quotes Col 2:14.

7 *Quinque*, 287–88: 'per mortem et passionem nostrum mundum vivificare dignatus est'.

8 *AA SS* June 2: 482, 30: 'Intuere ergo diligenter et considera, quanta et qualia pro te et humani generis redemptione, sustinui opprobrium'. Appearances of this kind happened to Lutgard (S. Roisin, *L'Hagiographie*, 171), and are mentioned in Ida of Nivelles' biography (*Quinque*, 223), and not infrequently in *Legendaria*, such as Caesarius of Heisterbach's *Dialogus miraculorum* or Conrad of Eberbach's *Exordium Magnum*. Soon this desire to see Christ hanging on the cross developed into a visual presence at the scene on Calvary, as happens in the case of Mechtild of Magdeburg and others. See Dinzelbacher, *Vision*, 118.

In the thirteenth century, Christ was seen more as the suffering than as the triumphant Saviour,[9] but not yet in the grisly detail depicted a century later.[10] Their culture (from which our modern technology and multinational business corporations were absent), the evolution of their theological thinking and devotional practices, their way of life, their personalities, all influenced their approach to Christ. Ida Lewis, for instance, was so wholly taken by Christ's presence in the Eucharist that her biography has no explicit reference to Christ's passion.[11]

In one of her letters Hadewijch wrote:

He himself [Christ] cast all away when he was sent by his Father, and when he finished the work *minne* had commanded him to do, he said in the gospel: 'Father, the hour has come'. After that he said to his Father: 'I have finished the work you gave me to do'. Consider therefore how he lived.[12]

Ida of Nivelles dialogued with Christ about the bitterness of his passion and cross. Attributing the cause of his passion to her own sins, she could not look at a crucifix without feeling great pain, nor could she stand hearing others speak of his passion.[13] In contrast, Alice of Schaarbeek is said to have carried the memory

---

9 This can be clearly seen in the iconography of the time. Among the extensive bibliography, see Emile Mâle, *Religious Art in France. The Twelfth Century*, Bollingen series 90, 1; *idem., The Thirteenth Century*, Bollingen series 90, 2, ET by Marthiel Mathews (Princeton 1978 and 1985). See also the *Lexikon der christlichen Ikonographie*, Engelbert Kirschbaum et al., eds, 8 vols (Rome, 1968–74).

10 M. J. Picard, 'Croix (Chemin de)' *DSp* 2: 2575–2606, where (2579) the author, alleging the influence of the Ps-Bonaventurean treatise *Meditationes Vitae Christi* says that Angela of Foligno (d.1309), to refer here to this one example, describes Christ's passion as if she had been an eyewitness. The devotion to the twelve or fourteen stations of 'the way of the cross' appeared more than a century later.

11 Antoon Steenwegen, 'De Gelukz. Ida de Lewis', *OGE* 57 (1983) 243.

12 Letter 16, VM, *Brieven*, 1: 133, ll. 35–41. The biblical references are Jn 17:1 and 17:4.

13 *Quinque*, 173: 'Non poterat sine magna acerbitate crucis imaginem intueri, nec audire alios loquentes de passione Christi'.

of the Lord's passion as a bride carries a little bundle of myrrh between her breasts.[14] Ida of Leuven 'directed the keenness of both her meditation and affection toward the remembrance of the Lord's passion'.[15] Beatrice of Zwijveke 'kept in mind daily, with thorough consideration the remembrance of Christ's passion; wherever she was she smelled the odor of violets'.[16] Bartholomew, Beatrice's father, 'had the memory of our Lord's passion in his heart and on his lips' (12,83), while Beatrice herself

distrusting the defect of forgetfulness, found an appropriate method of expelling it continuously from the limitations of her memory. Day and night she wore on her breast a wooden cross, about a palm in length, tightly tied with a knotted string. On it were written the titles of the Lord's passion, the horror of the last judgment, the severity of the judge and other things she wanted always to keep in mind. Besides this, she also carried tied to her arm another image of the Lord's cross, painted on a piece of parchment. A third one she painted on a piece of wood set before her when she was writing, so that wherever she went, or whatever exterior work she did, all forgetfulness would be banished. By means of the image of the cross she would keep impressed on her heart and memory whatever she feared losing.... Through this constant remembering of the Lord's passion, she seemed always more vigilant in progressing in virtue.[17]

---

14 *AA SS* June 2: 479, 8: 'passionem Domini, quam more sponsae ut fasciculum myrrhae inter ubera deportabat'.

15 *AA SS* April 2: 162, 13: 'Totam in memoria Dominicae passionis summam intentionis suae considerationisque locaverat, ad quam, tamquam ad praecipuum et singulare praesidium, in omni necessitate articulo, meditationis simul et affectionis aciem dirigebat'.

16 Reypens, *OGE* 23 (1949) 243, ll. 6–10: 'contingit [ut] odorem quasi violarum ubicumque fuerat sentiret'.

17 *Vita*, 70, 85. The several titles written on the cross she wore on her breast concur with the iconography of the cross at that time. Her *Vita* mentions on several occasions her custom of keeping the Lord's passion in her consciousness, for instance 71, 14; 72, 28 (for about five unbroken years); 109, 50; 209, 25.

Cistercian nuns were *choro addictae*, to use a modern and official expression, meaning that they were, not 'addicted', but obligated to participate in the choral offices. The liturgy provided a rhythm to their daily living. Beyond this, Beatrice herself was methodical in her personal life, as can be observed in her habit of looking for ways to improve her spiritual life.[18] This is seen, for example, in the way she began each day:

when at night the usual signal for rising for the matins office sounded in her ears, she would immediately sit up and fortify herself with the sign of the life-giving cross. With humble prayer she would beg the Lord that all her thoughts, words and deeds the coming day would be directed to the praise and honor of the holy and undivided Trinity. After this she recited the Lord's Prayer three times in succession. Then she would promptly jump from her bed with a fervent spirit, and would prepare herself for the divine office with the correct composure.[19]

Her *Vita* mentions 'that at all the choir offices by night and day she held in her mind in devout meditation that part of the Lord's passion which he had suffered at that hour' (43,57; cf. 95,93). In this practice she was in conformity with an ancient, if intermittent, tradition,[20] but she felt free to change it some time later: 'From the hour of terce until sext she kept her mind's eye upon the whole sequence of the Lord's passion' (128,57) and from sext till the hour of none, she followed in her meditation 'the model which Jesus as a man among men showed by teaching and example to his followers'.[21] Beatrice of Zwijveke too seems to

---

18 Some of her personal practices reported in the two first books of her *Vita* have sometimes been seen as shortened treatises by her. See R-VM, *Seven manieren*, 76*–81* and Simone Roisin, *L'Hagiographie*, 65; this opinion was correctly no longer shared by Reypens when he published the *Vita*, 58*.

19 *Vita*, 125, 14.

20 M.J. Picard, 'Croix', *DSp* 2: 2579–80.

21 *Vita* 128, 63. Edmund Rich, archbishop of Canterbury (d.1240), in his treatise *Speculum Ecclesiae* recommended meditating before the hour of the Divine Office on that aspect of Christ's passion to which it was customarily

have observed this practice,[22] which is not otherwise mentioned in the biographies of the *Quinque prudentes virgines*.

Praying in common or in private, the *mulieres religiosae* had a whole range of expressions at their disposal to describe what Christ did for them and how they felt about it. The heart has less difficulties in expressing itself than does the mind. One day Ida of Leuven went to a church and was totally inebriated by the sweetness of love; 'she knelt in front of the tabernacle where the pyx was kept for emergencies. She gave vent to the feelings of her heart and said: "Hail... Jesus, who for our redemption sought out the pillory of the cross and by your precious blood redeemed us from the bonds of everlasting death'.[23] In Ida we have an example of a woman who had refused to become educated (which here meant going through the school curriculum and learning Latin), but whose prayer, flowing from her heart, corresponded to the liturgical prayers of the Church.[24]

Whether the *mulieres religiosae* looked at Christ as the suffering man or as the glorified God, the marks (stigmata) of his passion spoke with an unmistakenly clear voice about his love for his Father and for man himself. Beatrice 'dwelling like a simple dove in the clefts of the rock, made her nest in the hollows of the

---

attached. See M. Philomena, 'St. Edmund of Abingdon's Meditations before the Canonical Hours', *Ephemerides Liturgicae* 78 (1964) 33–57, where the whole evolution of this practice is briefly traced. Beatrice adapted this tradition to her own needs. The older practice, connecting the praying of the hours with the sequence of Christ's passion was still used in the fourteenth-century. See Jacques Laurent, 'Un opuscule ascétique inédit attribué à saint Bernard', *Saint Bernard et son temps*, Vol.2 (Dijon, 1929) 111–14. The 'opuscule' is in a manuscript of the fourteenth-century, and has as its title *mediationes secundum septem horas diei*.

22 Reypens, *OGE* 23 (1949) 243, l. 8. The text is not too clear at this point: 'memoriam beate passionis ihesu cristi cogitando cotidie in se collegit et quid singulis horis pro nobis pertulit sollicita consideratione signavit'.

23 *AA SS* April 2: 172,6: 'Ave... Jesu, qui pro nostra redemptione crucis patibulo expetisti, nosque a perpetuae mortis nexibus tuo pretioso sanguine redemisti'.

24 Wilmart, giving several examples of private prayers similar to the one of Ida, says at the end of his study: 'Pour les prières de dévotion', *Auteurs spirituels*, 13–25, that 'la piété et la liturgie, la libre dévotion et le culte officiel sont fait pour s'entendre. L'expérience des siècles établit qu'il n'y a aucune raison de sacrifier l'une à l'autre, l'une et l'autre correspondant à des besoins profonds et légitimes'.

wounds of Jesus Christ' (42,18). At another time she was said to have seen in them 'at what price he [man] was redeemed and restored by such an exchange' (147,53). Indeed, Christ retained imprinted in his glorified body the marks of his passion as visible signs of his love. In a rapture Beatrice saw 'the all-powerful and eternal Father emitting from himself a great river from which many brooks and brooklets branched forth hither and yon; they offered a drink of water springing up to eternal life to those who willed to approach them' (215,48). She understood the symbolic meaning of this vision (216,56) thus:

the river itself was the Son of God, the Lord Jesus Christ, eternally born from the Father, and begotten in time from his mother for human redemption and salvation. The brooks were the signs of our redemption, that is the marks of the Lord's passion which he deigned to bear in his body on the wood of the cross for us sinners.

Stigmata were sometimes seen imaginatively, as in the case of Beatrice of Zwijveke. When meditating on Christ's humanity she saw the wounds of his hands, feet, and side.[25] The stigmata were seen in a vision when Christ appeared one Good Friday to Alice of Schaarbeek, his hands bleeding, his feet nailed, his side pierced.[26] These scenes could well have been inspired by, or were at least contemporary with, the 'rhythmic prayer to each member of the suffering Christ hanging on the cross', a well-structured poem expressing deep feelings in regard to Christ's wounds and heart, written by Arnulph, abbot of Villers (1240–48).[27]

---

25 Reypens, *OGE* 23 (1949) 244, ll. 58–59: 'de cristi humanitate cogitare cepit, et vulnera manuum et pedum laterisque inspexit'. The iconography at that time already showed each foot pierced separately.

26 *AA SS* June 2: 482,30: 'Cruentatis manibus, clavatis pedibus, perfossoque latere'.

27 D. Adolf Stracke, 'Arnulf van Leuven, O.Cist versus Gelukz. Hermann Jozef, O.Praem.', *OGE* 24 (1950) 27–90. Comparing the extant manuscripts (the text is also in PL 189: 1319) of this 'Rythmica oratio ad unumquodlibet membrorum Christi patientis et a cruce pendentis', Dr. Stracke attributes this poem to Arnulph.

At times, most frequently during Mass, which is the memorial of the passion, Christ was seen to display the marks of his passion to the Father as an intercessory gesture for man's needs. At the consecration 'Christ offered his body on the altar of the cross as an appeasing sacrifice to God the Father' (127,50). Beatrice of Zwijveke saw the same offering several times, also at Mass.[28] The same vision also occurred at times unconnected with the Eucharist, as happened in Lutgard's case.[29]

Ida of Leuven, 'the imitator and companion of Christ's passion', as her biographer called her, still living as a *mulier religiosa* before she joined the nuns of Roosendaal, received the stigmata.[30] She tried medication and surgical treatment (whatever that meant in her time), and when this did not remove the stigmata, she prayed and was granted that they become invisible, though for the rest of her life she occasionally felt pain from them.[31] At seven centuries distance there is little chance of determining whether Ida's stigmata were real, imagined or counterfeit. It speaks in her favor that she was eager to have them made invisible to escape the attention she would attract. In itself this does not certify that the stigmata or their disappearance were not due to intense auto-suggestion. Ida manifested other paranormal phenomena, such as bodily elongation.[32] The ecclesiastical

---

28 Reypens, *OGE* 23 (1949), 246, ll. 26–30: 'Vidit celum apertum et ihesum se offerentem Patri in altari et Pater wulnera manuum et lateris ostendenten'. The text suggests that the Father points at Christ's stigmata.

29 Dinzelbacher, 'Das Christusbild', *OGE* 56 (1982) 267, with references to the iconographical representations of the fourteenth century where, at the last judgment, Christ the Man of Sorrows and Our Lady with bared breasts intercede conjointly for man, the sinner. See also Dieter Koepplin, 'Interzession', in *Lexikon der christlichen Ikonographie* vol.2 (Rome, 1970) 346–52.

30 *AA SS* April 2: 162,14: 'haec Christi passionis aemulatrix et socia'. She had the five stigmata and the wounds caused by the crown of thorns.

31 *Ibid.*, 162, 14–16.

32 *Ibid.*, 166,31; 167,34; 184,10; 186,17. Once she had an elongation in reverse. She shrank to the size of a two or three year old child, *ibid.*, 171,2. Ida's disproportionate swellings, lasting a short time, are attributed by her biographer to her burning love for Christ or God. The vehemence of her love cannot be questioned, but her psychic balance can. Medical observations have shown that certain individuals, when they become deeply and emotionally disturbed, are unable for a short span of time to ensure the normal physiological water-

authorities, usually skeptical, if not antipathetic, in such cases, allowed nevertheless Cistercians and Benedictines to celebrate Ida's feast day and office in 1719, and extended them in 1854 to the diocese of Beauvais as well.[33] The *oratio* or prayer of this office mentions explicitly that she had the stigmata.[34] Curiously enough Ida escaped the attention of Herbert Thurston, a 'devil's advocate' in paranormal phenomena.[35]

Inspired perhaps by 1 Peter 1:18, which states that the ransom of man's redemption was paid by the precious blood of Christ, the spotless lamb, some *mulieres religiosae* had the mystical experience of their being cleansed by Christ's blood. To a modern mind this image may seem distasteful, but it was not to people used, as they were, to the symbolic meaning. When Beatrice had been prioress in Nazareth for several years it happened that

> when she had approached the Sacrament of the Lord's body and had received from the priest's hand at the altar the price of our redemption as the nourishing support of man's journey, she rested with delight in the passion of Christ the Lord. It seemed to her that all the blood which flowed from his wounds was poured into her soul, and that all the drops of that precious liquid were so sprinkled on it that it was

metabolism at the intra- and intercellular level. As a result the water remains in the body, weight increases accordingly, and an outsider has the impression of an abnormal, bodily elongation.

33 W. Van Caster, 'Notice historique sur Waelhem et de l' ancienne abbaye de Roosendaal', *Bulletin du Cercle Archéologique de Malines* 2 (1891) 249–270. The text of this office was printed in folio, 'Typis Caspari Brimbaum' in Cologne, 1721.

34 'Domine Jesu, qui beatae Idae virginis corpori tuorum vulnerum stigmata igneo amoris stylo impressisti'.

35 Herbert Thurston, *The Physical Phenomena of Mysticism*, mentions (40–43) Elisabeth of Spaalbeek or of Herkenrode (d.1304) and Lukardis (d.1319), another Cistercian nun in Oberweimar. Thurston asserts (122–23) that 'while in the course of the last seven centuries there have been an immense number of female mystics about whose complete stigmatization no doubt is possible, there are only two men being marked with all the five wounds' (St. Francis and Padre Pio of Foggio). The author states also that Francis' case created what he calls a 'crucifixion complex' among pious imitators, 'so much so that in a few exceptionally sensitive individuals the idea conceived in the mind was realized in the flesh'.

wholly washed by these drops and most perfectly cleansed from all the dust of sin. In that spiritual washing she was wonderfully and superhumanly kindled and set on fire by love. As though her whole spirit had been invaded by the fervor of love, she burned with the marvelous fire of delight beyond what human strength can stand, and she was enraptured.[36]

Experiences of this kind were not uncommon, though often expressed in different words or with variations. Hadewijch, for instance, mentions in her 'List of the perfect' that Sarah, a Jewess who became a Christian, had a rapture 'and was bathed in the blood of Christ'.[37] The blood-theme metaphorically indicated redemption by, and union with, Christ, a goal very dear to these mystics. What Christ's blood effected was explained by Christ to Ida of Leuven: 'Was it not by my precious blood that, doing away with your pristine deformity, I restored the former comeliness of your wonderful beauty and admirable elegance?'.[38] Ida had an experience somewhat similar to that of Beatrice:

When the priest was on the point of drinking of the cup [during Mass], the venerable woman, deprived of her human senses, was lifted up in contemplation..... She saw how the chalice, which the priest had still in his hand, was totally poured out upon her attentively gazing soul, and at this moment...she felt as if she was completely reddened by Christ's precious blood.

---

36 *Vita*, 238, 4. Several themes we met in the first part of this study are bundled together here. Sin has become 'dust of sin', the 'spiritual washing' set her so much on fire that she was enraptured, an effect she would try to express in her treatise *Seven manieren*, but attributed there to *minne*.

37 VM, *Visioenen*, 1; 186, ll. 153–54. The context of this passage shows that this figure of speech includes both a cleansing and a consuming by the fire of *minne*.

38 *AA SS* April 2: 179, 31: 'non ergo es tu illa quam...meo sanguine pretioso decorem in te mirae pulchritudinis et eminentis elegantiae, fugato pristinae deformitatis...reparavi?': a reference to her being created to God's image and likeness.

Greatly terrified by this outpouring, Ida came back to herself
but could not see with her physical eyes what she had witnessed
in her mind. At this point, her biographer declares that the
meaning did not escape her, though in his next sentence he seems
to say what it meant to him rather than to Ida:' The Lord himself
showed in this fact, as we can conjecture from Scripture [proba-
bly Revelation 7:14–15], that she [Ida] was added to the number
of those who have whitened their garments in the blood of the
mystical lamb, [and who] stand in front of God's throne and serve
him very devoutly day and night.[39]

The theme of the lamb also appears with variations, depending
on the biblical passages in view: the epistles of Paul or Peter and
especially the Book of Revelation. To Lutgard, for instance, it
seemed as if Christ under the form of a lamb had so positioned
himself on her breast that one leg rested on her right shoulder, the
other on her left, and the lamb placed its mouth on her mouth: a
metaphorical indication of the sacrificed and glorified Christ,
expressing his love for Lutgard and the union between them.[40] In
her eleventh vision, Hadewijch speaks in an unclear way of a
comparable experience of a lamb, to which Peter Dinzelbacher
attributes a typological meaning.[41]

The whole account of Christ's passion, his wounds on the cross
and his death in loneliness inevitably stirred the *mulieres religiosae*'s compassion in the double meaning of having compassion on and of suffering with (*com-passio*). Lutgard thought of
Christ, the Man of Sorrows, as her 'bloody Bridegroom'.[42] Beatrice on her part

> found copious matter for compassion and devotion as often
> as she raised her eyes to consider the Lord hanging on the

39 *Ibid.*, 179, 29.

40 Dinzelbacher, 'Das Christusbild der H.Lutgard', *OGE* 56 (1982) 262. The
author adds (263–64) further examples of this theme as found in the biographies
of mystics who lived a generation after Lutgard.

41 Dinzelbacher, *ibid.*, 262. J. Van Mierlo, *Visioenen*, 1: 110, n.15, thought
that the text could perhaps have something to do with the lamb theme expressed
in iconography (as shown by Dinzelbacher), though VM refers it to the union of
the divine and the human in Christ.

42 Dinzelbacher, *ibid.*, 269.

cross. She saw him, who was beautiful above the sons of men, pierced through, bloody and hanging on the cross, and she meditated on his stripes and wounds. Then, like wax melting before the fire, her whole soul, melting with the fire of compassion, flowed totally into the chalice of Christ's wounds.[43]

Recalling (as she often did) the disgraces Christ suffered for our redemption, Beatrice 'aroused herself to reciprocal compassion' (128,61). Some texts indicate clearly the holy women's compassion, their intention to suffer with the suffering Christ. This was the case of Ida of Leuven, though we are not in a position to check the psychic elements involved here. When her biographer began to talk about her stigmata he said explicitly that she received them from the Lord 'to suffer with him'.[44] To suffer and to die with Christ should, however, not be underestimated, for it claimed the whole humanity of the *mulieres religiosae*, who were—as will be seen below—more than willing to be so claimed. Christ's passion seen as an expiatory sacrifice invited and incited them to make the same offering. In her first vision Hadewijch saw a tree of wisdom with three branches:

The first branch was the fear that each person must die by the same death whereby our Beloved died: with wisdom to be perfect in each and every virtue in order to die of that death every hour, and to carry that cross and to die on it each day: to die [in expiation] for all who go astray and die [in sin].[45]

Shortly before she became a leper, Alice of Schaarbeek saw in a dream a golden cross lowered by a cord from heaven until she could clearly gaze at it. This indicated, comments the biographer, that she would present herself to God as a martyr when the

---

43 *Vita*, 109,38.
44 *AA SS* April 2: 163,13: 'ad sibi compatiendum'.
45 VM, *Visioenen* 1: 18, ll. 130–37.

passion of our Lord had been consummated in the martyrdom of her affliction in heart and body.[46] To speak here of her 'affliction in heart and body' is quite justified. Yet, in all cases the 'affliction of the heart' is basic. Hadewijch, keeping in mind, as she usually did, the immeasurable distance between God and man, realized that a 'complete' imitation of Christ was out of the question. The suffering of a mere man cannot be compared with the sufferings of a God-Man.

> Those who follow...Christ as he delivered up his substance [i.e. his humanity] to death, live as in hell. This comes from God's redoubtable exhortation. What they experience is quite fearful: their spirit understands the grandeur of Christ's abasement, but their reason cannot understand it. Therefore they condemn themselves all the time. Whatever they say, do, or perform, seems to them to be of no account. Their spirit does not believe that it can attain that grandeur. This leaves their heart without hope. Nevertheless this way leads them very deep into God.[47]

The notion of sacrifice is not always presented as it is by Hadewijch, as a challenge wherein one suffers because one cannot possibly reach the dimensions of Christ's sufferings, since he is God as well as man. Man can only do so much, as Hadewijch herself admitted, and here she is echoed by other *mulieres religiosae*. When Ida Lewis was not at work, she devoted all her time to prayer and offered herself to her Beloved as a pleasing sacrifice.[48] This too 'was the whole occupation of Beatrice's mind and the whole intent of her heart: to be attentive... and always to offer him[Christ] a clean, pleasing and acceptable sacrifice' (197,33). It was not the first or the last time that she did so (184,33; 241,35). When she was thirty-two, 'mindful that the Lord suffered the disgrace of his passion in his body', she was convinced

---

46 *AA SS* June 2: 479, 8: ' cujus crucis visio et transmissio non indebite passionem Domini... nobis demonstrat'.

47 Letter 22; VM, *Brieven*, 1: 194–95. ll. 169–80.

48 *AA SS* Oct.13: 113,19: 'se dilecto placentem hostiam offerebat'.

that she in turn would have to suffer disgrace and contumely for him (209,25). Uneasy with the signs of respect, if not veneration that she received, she intended to feign madness to arrive at her goal.[49] But 'before she presumed to move toward the accomplishment of her heart's proposal, she was eager to get counsel from some wise man...lest poorly on her guard she would repent after the deed' (211,51). This man was out of town at that time and she had to wait three months before he was able to visit her. He told her then that

> this way of abjection by which you would follow in your redeemer's footsteps, is not a diabolical suggestion as you suspect; love alone taught your mind to conceive it. But if you acquiesce to my advice, you will in no way try to put into effect this fiction of pretending you are insane or a fool. The chief reason is that you might perhaps incur in this way no small loss in your progress, and so by following too stubbornly a less useful way of piety, you would be forced to omit what was more useful, not so much to your own as to your neighbor's harm and loss. When she heard this...she did not delay withdrawing her foot quickly from the forbidden path. Hastily she rejected from the bottom of her heart the desire she had conceived in her mind, but the integrity of her will from which such a proposal had flowed, remained always vigorous and firm in following the divine good-pleasure.[50]

For all the *mulieres religiosae*, the immensity of Christ's love towered above their insufficiency and incapacity, and his love

---

49 To feign insanity was not uncommon, and did happen occasionally in the West and even more in the East. See 'Fous pour le Christ', *DSp* 5: 751–61: 'En Orient' (Thomas Spidlík) and 'En Occident' (François Vandenbroucke) *ibid.*, 761–70. See also the recent publication by John Saward, *Histoire des saints fous pour le Christ* (Paris, 1983). Hadewijch deemed it opportune to advise a *mulier religiosa* under her guidance to strive for humility, but not up to the point of showing signs of foolishness: Letter 23 VM, *Brieven*, 1: 206, l. 17.

50 *Vita*, 212, 74.

itself gave them a beneficial boost against all the psychological drawbacks they experienced in their human condition. Remembering Christ's ardent love, they were urged to concentrate on his love for them as it was shown in his passion and death, and in this they found great joy. When Ida of Nivelles thought that her human behavior had caused Christ's sufferings, she felt depressed. But pondering the love with which he had undergone his passion, 'she was then filled with such an overwhelming sweetness that her heart, anointed with the oil of salutary gladness, changed her former grief into a vehement joy'. When she meditated on the successive stages of Christ's passion, 'the power of love was interiorly so strong that her heart suddenly could not stand it: it melted and she broke down physically'.[51]

Ida of Leuven too meditated in succession on what Christ had suffered in each member of his body and found there an antidote for any self-centeredness she experienced. She broke free (*libera*) of all selfish pull and, remembering the Lord's passion, was able 'to ascend to the summit of delight with all her affection and intention'.[52] Beatrice, with her profound compassion for the suffering Christ, expressed how: 'with a special remembrance she rested with delight in the Lord's passion. There she sought with daily insistence the food for her spirit, there she delighted to find quickly without visual image and without delay, whatever was useful for her salvation and protection'.[53]

Her compassion led her to com-passion, suffering with him. Both her compassion and com-passion were inspired by the awesome love of a God who for her and the whole human race became the God-Man. It even brought her, as we have seen, to the point of thinking that feigning madness would make her more Christlike, for—as her biography says—it was by the enormity of

---

51 *Quinque*, 274–76: 'tanta interius repleatur dulcedine, ut corde ejus oleo laetitiae salutaris inuncto, dolorem pristinum vehementi gaudio mutavit... sicut fluit cera a facie ignis, sic subito vim amoris interius sentiens, et tota liquescens corpore deficiebat'.

52 *AA SS* April 2: 160, 9: 'ut... ad vere delectationis culmen ascenderet, quam in memoria Dominicae passionis, totis affectionum conatibus ac intentionis viribus exquirebat'.

53 *Vita*, 109,45.

his love that she was 'immediately rekindled by the fire of devotion' (154,55).

In a high-minded text which stresses love, free consent to love in return, and a straight path toward union with Christ, Hadewijch wrote:

He [Christ as God's Son] bowed himself toward time [through his incarnation], that is, he awaits with great patience for our improvement in virtuous living, if we are willing to do so. We see his mouth proffered to us to kiss anyone who wishes it. His arms are outstretched, ready to embrace anyone who runs toward him. Yes, briefly put: God has inclined himself toward us, in time, in all we can have and wish to have and to know, as much and as heartily as we wish.[54]

As Alice of Schaarbeek drew close to death, she grew physically deformed and totally deprived of the use of her bodily members; she had to be put to bed as if she were a decaying corpse, consumed as she was by the rottenness of her leprosy. And yet 'as a bride receives from her bridegroom a long-desired little present', she accepted these usually unwelcome sufferings, infirmities and deformities with joyful delight. Her hands were of little help, for her great infirmity had long since crumpled them like the bark of a shrinking tree. Enraptured, she used to sing: 'my hands are roundish, full of hyacinths'.[55]

In various ways and words, these *mulieres religiosae*—and especially Hadewijch and Beatrice—said much the same thing that Bernard wrote of his relation to Christ, the Man for others:[56]

---

54 Letter 22, VM, *Brieven*, 1: 194, ll. 155–64.

55 *AA SS* June 2: 482, 31: 'unde tripudiando cantare solebat: manus meae tornatiles, plenae hyacinthis'; a reference to Sg 5:14 and described by Richard, *Explicatio in Canticum*; PL 196: 513C. It is at this point that Alice is said to be 'clothed with the Divinity', see above nn. 43–44 of Chapter VIII.

56 SC 43.4 as presented in rhythmic form by C. Mohrmann, *Études sur le latin des Chrétiens*, 2: 366.

Haec mihi in ore frequenter

  sicut vos scitis
  haec in corde semper
  sicut Deus scit

Haec stilo meo admodum
familiare
  sicut apparet
  haec mea subtilior
  interior philosophia

Scire Jesum et hunc
crucificum.

These sentiments are often
on my lips
  as you well know,
  are always in my heart
  as God knows.

They are a familiar theme
to my pen
  as is evident.
  This is my refined,
  interior philosophy

To know Jesus and him
crucified.

CHAPTER TEN

FOLLOWING CHRIST

T O KNOW JESUS AND HIM CRUCIFIED is not merely to know what he did. Through Christ's incarnation, passion, and death, God himself cries out the immensity of his love for the humanity he created and re-created, and the requirement that the response to his love be a free and total human love for him. The model of this response to love's call was provided by Christ. In becoming man, the Son of God humbled himself, performed all that the Father sent him to do, and in obedience died an infamous death on a cross. Thus he set upon his human life the seal of his total and unconditional love for his Father and for man. Through his resurrection and ascension into glory, his humanity took its place at the Father's right hand, manifesting how from all eternity God planned the union between the divine and the human.

All this opened new horizons for the meaning and purpose of human life: union with God, through Christ. Our creation to God's image and likeness, our re-creation by Christ's incarnation set us on the way to consummation. Hadewijch recapitulated this whole process in her thirtieth letter:

Through the wisdom of the Son and the goodness of the Holy Spirit summoning the omnipotence of the Father, man was created. But because man did not respond to the summons of Unity, he fell. Through the summons of the Trinity, God's Son was born, and to satisfy his debt to the Unity he

died; through the summons of the Trinity he rose again
among men, and to satisfy the debt to the Unity he ascended
to his Father. And so it is with us also. When the Trinity
demands of us our debt [to strive toward and arrive at union
with God], grace is given us to live worthily according to
the noble Trinity as is fitting. But if we thwart this because
of alien [self-] will, we fall in what pleases us. Then we no
longer grow and make no progress in that perfection which
was demanded of us from the beginning by [God who is] the
Unity and the Trinity. But if rational man's noble reason
would recognize its just debt and follow Love's leading into
her land, that is, follow Love according to her due, then he
would be capable of attaining this supreme Good and be rich
with divine riches.[1]

The journey begins with self-knowledge; by it man becomes
aware of his personal relationship with his Creator.[2] Consequently, by accepting God's self-revelation he can come to the
realization that this relationship is much deeper than it seems to
be at first sight. When man turns from self-knowledge to self-
acceptance, he advances from being humbled to being humble,[3]
and this humility will help him to accept himself and to love God.

For Christ the relationship between humility and love is the
other way around. Lovingly drawn toward his image he became
man in order to help mankind recover its lost likeness: not merely
as a repairman to save man from his mistakes, but as an exemplar
to teach him how to exert himself toward union with God, his
God-given goal. As Hadewijch wrote: 'He who wishes to be
clothed and become rich and one with the Godhead must adorn

---

1 VM, *Brieven*, 1: 254, ll. 55–83. Love's land is union with God in heaven,
man's homeland.

2 See above, Chapter III, pp. 65-66.

3 This process can be closely followed in Beatrice's *Vita*. For instance, the
first half of her biography speaks more often about humiliation (25,46; 90,67;
105,8) than about humility, which is more frequently mentioned in the second
half (110,57; 115,70; 116,10; 126,35; 187,77; 199,69). Hadewijch went through
a similar process. See B. Spaapen, 'Hadewijch en het vijfde visioen', *OGE* 44
(1970) 21–23.

himself with all the virtues that God clothed and adorned himself
with when he lived as man. One must begin this by the same
humility with which he also began it'.[4]
By doing what he did, Christ gave man the opportunity to
practice humility no longer by necessity alone but out of love.[5]
'Taking Christ as the cornerstone for structuring her life' as
was said of Ida of Leuven,[6] Beatrice, 'the Lord's devout and
eager follower, ordered her life the best she could to follow in the
way of humility and patience the Lord Jesus Christ who said in
the Gospel: learn from me that I am meek and humble of heart'
(128,65). Similarly, Ida of Nivelles, 'learned from the Master
Jesus Christ to be humble of heart before God and man'.[7] Ida
Lewis' biographer called her 'the daughter of humility',[8] and
Beatrice cherished humility as 'her treasure' (61,39).

Ida Lewis' biography mentions that 'the more she descended
into humility in regard to herself and the more humble she was in
all her dealings with her neighbors, the more she ascended to a
more sublime level of virtuous living and contemplation'.[9] The
topos 'descending/ascending' is also found in Beatrice's biography.[10] Hadewijch too used it when she wrote that 'saints and

---

4 Letter 30, VM, *Brieven*, 1: 255, ll. 84–89. Humility was not seen by
Hadewijch only as a way of accepting her human condition, but also as a
deepening within herself which let her become more open to God's presence
within her.
5 It is striking how close the *mulieres religiosae* were at this point to Bernard.
See R. De Ganck, 'Nederigheid uit waarheidsdwang en uit liefdedrang bij
Bernardus', *Sint Bernardus van Clairvaux* (Achel, 1953) 165–94. It is in relation
to this humility out of love that Bernard called God: *humilium gloria*, the glory
of the humble. See Csi 5, 25; SBOp 3: 487, and J.Ch. Didier, 'L'Ascension
mystique et l'union mystique par l'humanité du Christ selon saint Bernard', *SVS*
22 (1930) [140]–[155].
6 *AA SS* April 2: 160,9: 'ipsum angularem lapidem in structurae suae fundamento composuit'.
7 *Quinque*, 202: 'humilitatem coram Deo et hominibus... inspiravit magister
humilitatis Christus'.
8 *AA SS* Oct. 13: 123,56: 'humilitatis filia'.
9 *Ibid.*, 113, 19: 'Quantoque vitae meritis contemplativo spiritu ascendebat
sublimior, tanto sibi et proximis humilior omnibus descendebat'.
10 See above, Chapter VI, pp. 192-211, Unitive Grace. To the *mulieres
religiosae* can be applied what has been said of Hadewijch: humility did not
threaten but fostered reciprocity in the relation with the Beloved. See M. J. Van
Baest, *De fierheid als kernmoment ...van Hadewijch*, 156.

others still journeying on earth, have in perfect virtues followed him [Christ] up the mountain of an outstanding life from the deep valley of humility, and have climbed this high mountain with strong faith and great confidence in the contemplation of his cordial love'.[11]

It did not escape the *mulieres religiosae*'s attention that God's Son became man in obedience to his Father and combined thereby humility and obedience, both flowing from love. To follow Christ meant therefore to follow him lovingly, humbly and obediently. Before there can be any question of becoming united with God, 'man must', as Hadewijch wrote, 'offer *minne* noble service and the life in exile: noble service in all works of virtue, and a life of exile in all obedience'.[12] In one of her methods to gain control of herself, Beatrice established in her heart a spiritual monastery, of which 'humility and obedience were the warders' (114,70). 'They surrounded and guarded this convent of virtues on every side that none of them might transgress the regular boundaries of this cloister by their own presumption' (114,72). Ida of Nivelles' biographer said of her that 'obedience always accompanied and flanked humility. Without fail she took great care of them from the moment she entered the monastery till the end of her life. For obedience intermingles with all other virtues and thus preserves them'.[13]

Sincere, faithful and consistent orientation of one's being and life toward God demands following Christ everywhere and at all times. Hadewijch advised thusly:

Just as Christ's humanity surrendered itself on earth to the will of the Majesty [of the Father], you must here surrender yourself with love to both in unity. Serve humbly under their sole power, stand always before them as one prepared to follow their whole will, and let them bring about in you

---

11 Letter 15; VM, *Brieven*, 1: 125–26, ll. 36–44.
12 Letter 6; *ibid.*, 1: 69, ll. 365–68.
13 *Quinque*, 283: 'obedientia enim ceteras virtutes inserit, insertasque custodit'.

whatever they will.... This is the way in which God's Son took the lead. Of this he gave us knowledge and understanding when he lived as man. The whole time he dwelt on earth, from the beginning to the end, he did and with discernment accomplished the will of his Father in all things and at all times, with all he was and with all the service he could perform in words and works, in weal and woe, in grandeur and abasement, in miracles, in scorn, in pain, in exertion, in anguish and in the agony of bitter death.[14]

Of those *mulieres religiosae* about whom we are better informed, it could be said that they too 'did and accomplished' or at least tried hard to do and to accomplish, 'with discernment the will of the Father in all things and at all times, with all they were and with all the service they could perform'. To quote Hadewijch once more:

You must ask about the way. He himself said: 'I am the way'. Oh, since he is the way, consider what ways he went. How he worked and how he burned interiorly with charity and exteriorly in works of virtue for strangers and for friends. And hear how he commanded men how greatly they should love their God: with all their heart, with all their soul, with all their strength. And that they nevermore forget this, sleeping and waking. Now consider how he himself did this, though he was himself God: how he gave all, and how he lived totally for the sake of his Father's veritable love and out of charity for man. He worked with vigilant charity, and he gave to love his whole heart and his whole soul and all his strength. This is the way that Jesus teaches, and that he himself is, and that he himself went. Therein lies eternal life and the fruition of the truth of his Father's glory.[15]

---

14 Letter 6; VM, *Brieven*, 1: 58–59, ll. 117–27; 67–68, ll. 324–35.
15 Letter 15; *ibid.*, 1: 125, ll. 16–35.

It could be pointed out that the *mulieres religiosae* did not so much speak about 'the imitation of Christ',[16] as about 'following Christ' or living 'in conformity with him'. Beatrice's biography mentions for instance, that she 'followed without any deviation the footsteps of her Redeemer leading the way to life. And this she clung to until the very end of her life'.[17] She considered Christ 'as her guide and leader, walking beside her on the slippery path of this life, and wherever she turned or went, she used to follow eagerly and without stumbling the Lord who went before her'.[18] The biographer of Ida of Leuven says that 'leaning on her Beloved, she walked after him with unobstructed steps in the way of patience. For this was the way the Lord himself, going before her, has showed his followers'.[19]

The biographies and the writings of the *mulieres religiosae* indicate plainly why and how they strove with their whole being and by all possible means to make their way back to God by following Christ. We find here a clue to the dilemma of the 'distance' between God the Absolute and man the contingent. As Beatrice wrote: God is 'incomprehensibility, fathomlessness, and inaccessible sublimity. The deep abyss of the Divinity is wholly present in all things and remains incomprehensible above all things'.[20]

----

16 The imitation they had in view was the stretching of the image toward its archetypal form as a throrough search for unity through conformity with the Exemplar. Robert Javelet rightly observed: 'L'imitation n'est pas un mime extérieur. L'imitation est la tension de l'image à sa Forme archétype, tension de son être qui cherche son unité en vertu d'une *participation* fondamentale. L'imitation est l'aspect ontologique qui, sous son aspect noétique, se définit par pérégrination vers la *contemplation*. Une spiritualité médiévale ne doit jamais se confondre avec un moralisme ni avec une imitation de Jésus Christ purement phénoménale, à fleur de conscience, en fonction de sa vie anecdotique'. See his 'Sens et Réalité ultime selon Hugues de Saint-Victor', *Ultimate Reality and Meaning* 3 (1980) 84–113; 106.

17 *Vita*, 41, 76.

18 *Vita*, 41, 26 See also 71, 8; 123, 76; 128, 68; 136, 132; 141, 9, etc.

19 *AA SS* April 2: 162, 15: 'per viam patientiae, quam suis sequacibus ipse Dominus praecedendo monstraverat, innixa super dilectum suum, post illum inoffensis gradibus ambulavit'.

20 R-VM, *Seven manieren*, 29, ll. 9–12.

When compared to God, man's finiteness can only be expressed by opposites. In one of her letters, Hadewijch advised others to do what she herself practiced: 'look at your littleness and his greatness, your lowliness and his sublimity, your blindness and his clear sight, penetrating all things'.[21] Ida Lewis said that 'as this little rose does not belong to me, so the gift God presents me with does not belong to me'.[22] Hadewijch expressed it poignantly in the twenty fifth of her Poems in Stanzas:

When the loved soul is so joined to the Beloved
That it cannot be parted from its dear Beloved
And the soul with love so fully enjoys its Beloved
That it lives for the Beloved on the Beloved's word.
When reason then assaults it
By showing the incongruity thereof
Because reason considers the lovers unequal,
Then the loving soul is ever most wounded, when it
Self loved, experiences the Beloved already as Beloved.[23]

The way this dilemma is approached is of great importance. When, with the right disposition, one compares oneself with God, one stands in pure humility. According to Hadewijch 'this [pure] humility professes with wise fear God's greatness and her own littleness... and does not know what she should extol herself in'.[24] Norbert De Paepe made the correct observation that the opposition between man and God was experienced by Hadewijch on the ontological, rather than on the moral level.[25] This emphasis on humility did not prevent both Hadewijch and Beatrice from speaking of their noble pride (*fierheid*).[26] Against the

---

21 Letter 27; VM, *Brieven*, 1: 221, ll. 14–16. C.Kerstens collected the many passages where Hadewijch speaks about following Christ's ways: 'De wazige spiegel van Hadewijch', *OGE* 47 (1973) 347–85; 376–82.

22 *AA SS* Oct. 13: 118, 38: 'sicut haec rosula non pertinet ad me, sic ad me non pertinet donum quod mihi dominus propinavit'.

23 VM, *Strophische Gedichten*, 163, ll. 61–70.

24 Vision one; VM, *Visioenen*, 1: 13, ll. 52–59.

25 De Paepe, *Hadewijch. Strofische Gedichten*, 162.

26 See above, Chapter VI, pp. 149-50.

humbling limitations of their human situation, they proudly affirmed their creation to the image and likeness of a loving Creator, pointing to the ultimate goal: union with God.

God himself provided man with the lever by which, if he was willing, he could be lifted up to everlasting union with him, as God had planned from all eternity. By suffering the miseries of the historical human situation, Christ 'christianized' the miseries of this condition. This belief was the main reason why the *mulieres religiosae* strove with great hope toward a timeless union with God. This belief provided a God-given stimulus to avoid vices and sins, to practice virtues, to conform themselves to God's will in everything. All this they did out of love, and it all led to some equality with him.

Total equality with God in being is absolutely out of the question in christian belief, and equally so is total equality in love, as has been pointed out already.[27] Nevertheless God gave man ways and means to come to some measure of equality with him. Through the totality of his Son's incarnation, he proved that he loves man with total love. When man responds to God's total love with the totality of the love of which he is capable, then there is between them an equality of totality, however unequal these totalities might be. The inequality derives from the difference between the Absolute and the contingent, of the Creator and the creature, of God and man. The equality lies in the realm of the totality in love of both partners in this love-relationship.[28]

De Paepe has asserted that for Hadewijch 'the following of Christ is to be seen not primarily as a striving toward virtue. To live like Christ means first to be removed (*verwijdering*) from the

---

27 *Ibid.*, Chapter VI, pp. 198-99.

28 Bernard also pointed this fact out in his SC 83.6; SBOp 2: 302; CF 40:186; 'The stream of love does not flow equally from her [the soul] who loves and him who is love, the soul and the Word, the bride and the Bridegroom, the Creator and the creature, any more than a thirsty man can be compared to a fountain. Will the desire of her heart, her burning love... fail in their purpose because she has not the strength to keep pace with a giant, or rival honey in sweetness, the lamb in gentleness, or the lily in whiteness, because she cannot equal the brightness of the sun and the love of him who is love? No! Although the creature loves less, being a lesser being, yet if it gives love with its whole heart nothing is lacking, for it has given all'.

Father, but remaining in association (*verbondenheid*) with him.
The separation is the cause of the desolation (*troosteloosheid*) of
the terrestrial situation; the association, however, is the motive for
patience, steadfastness in affliction and opposition, fidelity, exertion to''satisfy'' God in everything and to acquire this fruitive
oneness with him'.[29] That the following of Christ should not be
seen *primarily* as the striving toward virtue is right on the mark.
But the roots of 'the desolation of the terrestrial situation' are
found in man, since he caused the separation,[30] which causes the
desolation.

The incarnation of God's Son changed the whole outlook of
man's condition of separation from God. Man has to reach the
depths of painful excruciation as Christ has done. He demanded,
or rather commanded, that Hadewijch do likewise.[31] In her first
vision Hadewijch was told by Christ:

> I wish you for my sake to be prepared for every kind of
> affliction.... I give you a new command: if you wish to be
> like me in my humanity as you are eager to be wholly united
> with me in my divinity, then you shall be poor, miserable
> and despised among men.[32]

29 De Paepe, *Hadewijch. Strofische Gedichten*, 169–70. My translation.
Hadewijch's text (VM, *Visioenen*, 1: 30, ll. 350–54) reads: 'Since you are a
human being (*mensche*), live as such in misery. It is my will that you live so
perfectly toward me in all virtues on earth, that you do not fail me in any point'.

30 See above, n.1 of this chapter and the implicit references to the fall as
mentioned by De Paepe, *Hadewijch. Strofische Gedichten*, 163, n.113, and by
Reynaert, *Beeldspraak*, 215 and 442.

31 See Chapter VI, n.154, which refers to the text about the 'new command'
and its meaning. Hadewijch was an outstanding *mulier religiosa*, exceptionally
gifted as a person and as a spiritual leader, who seems to have known it. Peter
Dinzelbacher called the strong self-consciousness encountered in her visions,
'ihre ungewöhnliche hohe Selbsteinschätzung' (self-appreciation). See his
'Hadewijchs mystische Erfahrungen', *OGE* 54 (1980) 267–79; 277. Higher
giftedness calls for more responsibility. Her undeniable 'Selbsteinschätzung'
indicates as well that Hadewijch's strong personality was psychologically quite
in touch with her deep self.

32 VM, *Visioenen*, 1: 26–27, ll. 288–93. Hadewijch warned a friend of hers:
'you have much to do if you are to live the divinity and humanity of Christ and
come to full growth as befits your dignity in which you are loved and claimed':
Letter 18; VM, *Brieven*, 1: 151–52, ll. 7–10.

This text is very important in understanding not only Hadewijch, but the other outstanding *mulieres religiosae* as well. At creation, man received a dignity he did not request and did not live up to. In accordance with God's unchangeable plans from all eternity, man's primordial dignity was not only repaired and restored, but immensely enhanced by the incarnation of God's Son, seen in its totality. Man's alienation, restoration and the consummation of his God-given finality now bear Christ's stamp. In his Son, God came to share man's humanity and made man capable of sharing his divinity in and through Christ.

The *mulieres religiosae* took this to mean that anything they had to go through as human beings took on special and specific meaning when it was permeated with a deep-seated desire to follow Christ all the way. This made their lives a movement toward God, as Christ had shown them and entreated them. Hadewijch summarized this whole process in her sixth Letter:

We must be continually aware that noble service and suffering in exile are proper to man's condition as they were to Jesus Christ when he lived as man. We do not find it written anywhere that Christ ever, in his entire life, had recourse to his Father or his omnipotent nature [as God] to obtain fruition and repose. He never gave himself any satisfaction, but continually undertook new labors from the beginning of his life to the end. He said this himself to a certain person,[33] whom he charged to live according to his example and to whom he himself said that this is the true, genuine *Minne*: where love is, there also are great labors and burdensome pains. Love, nevertheless, finds all pains sweet: *qui amat non laborat*, that is, he who loves does not labor.[34]

---

33 Hadewijch herself. See the text referred to in n.77 of Chapter VIII.
34 Letter 6; VM, *Brieven*, 1: 57–58, ll. 86–101. The 'qui amat non laborat' could have been inspired by Bernard's SC 85.3.8; SBOp 2: 312: 'ubi amor, labor non est, sed sapor': where there is love, there is no toil but added savor. Hadewijch could have found it also in Richard's fourth degree of violent Love. See G. Dumeige, *Les quatres degrés*, 173, [45].

Beatrice, in full agreement with Hadewijch her contemporary,[35] wrote:

It [the soul] knows and feels that love does not consist in labor and sorrow for those in whom it reigns. But all those who desire to attain *Minne*, must seek it with fear, and exercise it with longing, and this they cannot do if they spare themselves in great labors and many pains, in bearing trouble and in suffering contempt. And they must reckon all little things great until they arrive at the point where Love reigns within them and works its mighty works of love, making everything little, every labor easy, softening every pain and remitting every debt.[36]

The two last quotations encapsulate the spirituality of the *mulieres religiosae*. Although Hadewijch stated it more frequently and skillfully, Beatrice's biography, her treatise and the biographical accounts of the other four women under consideration here, show sufficiently how they all practiced love 'in noble service and suffering in exile'. A study of the other *mulieres religiosae* we know about show that they all did the same. 'Suffering in exile' refers to their own lives; 'noble service' to their relations with their fellowmen.

Beatrice 'established two cells in her heart...aspiring with a marvelous fervor and devotion to win the favor and grace of the Beloved' (101,1). In the lower cell she stored the six 'general miseries of the human condition', from birth to death, including the chores required by physical needs and care of health. Reflecting attentively on these necessities, she used them as 'antidotes of

35 De Paepe, *Hadewijch. Strofische Gedichten*, 159, n.101, stands by his impression that Hadewijch was not born before 1200 and thinks that she wrote her visions between 1239 and 1246. Reynaert accepts the possibility that she was still alive in the second half of the thirteenth century. See his 'Over Hadewijch naar aanleiding van drie recente publikaties', *OGE* 54 (1980) 280–92; especially 284, and VM, *Visioenen*, 2: 121, who admits 1260 at the latest. Hadewijch was certainly a *mulier religiosa*, but not necessarily a beguine in the strict sense.

36 R-VM, *Seven manieren* 27, ll. 64, 67–72.

human humiliation', efficacious in expelling the disease of inconstancy (102,22). In the upper cell 'she gathered whatever goods [she could], either natural or gratuitous', and 'pondered those spiritual gifts of fidelity and grace by which she was daily anticipated, and all those general deeds which the loving Lord did for the reparation of human salvation' (103,58). She then enumerated all the aspects of the incarnation in its totality, from birth to death, resurrection and ascension (103,63).

To become perfectly conformed to Christ, the God-Man, and 'fully grown', *volwassen*, as she called it, Hadewijch was told in her fourth vision that she had to practice virtues as Christ had made known to her in different ways: to live in misery and insecurity; to experience despair because all her efforts would seem to fall short of arriving at full conformity with him. Most painful of all, her lack of being *volwassen* would deprive her of him 'whom she must love above all', with the result that she would fall into even greater despair and be thrown in total darkness. But this very fall would bring her to that perfection of love whereby she would be pleasing to God, surrendering herself completely to him in total conformity.[37]

Biographers do not usually describe at length the 'miseries' or 'the sufferings in exile' of the *mulieres religiosae* they write about. Yet we read that a year before she was to die, Alice of Schaarbeek was told by the Lord in an apparition that the bodily and spiritual sufferings she had endured as a leper in the previous years notwithstanding, 'she could expect to suffer still more in her body and to be oppressed by more abundant tribulations in her heart'.[38] Ida Lewis' biographer stated that she suffered greatly 'because she was detained in the valley of misery'.[39] Ida of Leuven labored daily to make progress in the exercise of good works. She was not downcast by the many adversities she had to endure. Remembering the Lord's passion, she patiently accepted it all, and frequently sang God's praises in a clear and beautiful

---

37 VM, *Visioenen*, 1: 53–55, ll. 90–129.
38 *AA SS* June 2: 480,22: 'Multo amplius corporis debilitates multoque graviores cordis tribulationes'.
39 *AA SS* Oct. 13: 108,3: 'in valle miseriae detineri'.

beautiful voice all by herself.[40] But when the enthusiasm of her youth was over, she asked the Lord 'how long he would allow her to be oppressed and afflicted in the valley of misery,... separated from his presence'.[41]

When Beatrice was in her early teens, she too 'rejoiced greatly to follow Christ, her head, through many tribulations, being weighed down by continuous sickness and lack of necessities' (36,13), but when she was about thirty, her biographer could write a whole chapter on 'the grave inconvenience she suffered from weariness of the present life' (156,1), seen in contrast with 'the unfading riches of the heavenly fatherland' (157,46).

Hadewijch's many sayings about human misery have been collected by Christilla Kerstens.[42] The texts indicate the various ways in which Hadewijch looked at misery, *ellende*, and how she used different expressions, images, and combinations of images to describe the whole range of 'misery'.

For both Hadewijch and Beatrice the noun misery, *ellende*, had kept its original etymological meaning of being alienated, exiled in a foreign land, far away from their true home, which was none other than God himself.[43] By no means does 'misery' express an attitude hostile to the world or to life. It is simply related to their insatiable desire for God, and to their immense longing for union with him in an intimate loving fruition. As Beatrice put it:

> The soul always wills to follow Love, to honor Love and to enjoy Love, which cannot happen to it in this exile. Therefore the soul wills to proceed to the fatherland where it has built its home, and directed its whole desire, and where it rests in love; for it well knows that every impediment will

---

40 *AA SS* April 2: 160,10: 'Per bonorum operum exercitia quotidiano labore... in Dei laudem...in concentuum exquisito modulamine'.

41 *Ibid.*, 180, 35: 'Quamdiu me sustinebis in hac valle miseriae comprimi et affligi, praesentisque corporis et fragilis domicilio relegata a tua me praesentia separari?'

42 C. Kerstens (above n.21), 367–75.

43 For Hadewijch: Kerstens, *OGE* 47 (1973) 367; for Beatrice: Vekeman, *Lexicografisch Onderzoek*, 2: 139.

be removed from it, and it will be received with love by the Beloved.[44]

Moreover the respect the *mulieres religiosae* had for creation, for their earth and all its beauty which they greatly enjoyed, the zesty relish they took in their own existence and in the nobility and dignity of every person do not suggest that those women were discontented, weary *mulieres taediosae*.[45] Aware of what they were, where they were and where they belonged, they expressed their yearning to be there and not here, using such metaphors as exile, prison, desert, pilgrimage and others,[46] as a few examples will show.

On one occasion Ida of Nivelles asked: 'How long do I have to remain in this exile?',[47] while Beatrice spoke of 'the long-drawn-out exile of this world: this harmful protraction which overwhelms human affection with worldly fluctuations, and does not permit everlasting freedom'.[48] In her treatise, the miseries of the exile are more emphatically stressed in the paradoxical effects they had on her emotions:

Earth is a great exile, a strong prison and a great annoyance for the soul. It despises the world, earth wearies it and what belongs to earth cannot calm the soul or satisfy it. The soul's great sadness is to have to be so far away and to seem so alien. It cannot forget its exile; its desire [to be with God] cannot be calmed; what the soul longs for, vexes it miserably and thus afflicts and torments it beyond measure and without respite. For this reason the soul greatly longs and

44 R-VM, *Seven manieren*, 37, ll. 143–51.

45 Siegfried Wenzel, *The Sin of Sloth: Acedia in Medieval Thought and Literature* (Chapel Hill, NC, 1960) 3–12; Reinhard Kuhn, *The Demon of Noontide. Ennui in Western Literature* (Princeton, NJ, 1976) 39–64. See also Stanley W. Jackson, 'Acedia the sin and its relationship to sorrow and melancholia in Medieval times', *Bulletin of the History of Medicine* 55 (1981) 172–85, with a helpful bibliography.

46 Francesco Lazzari, *Mistica e ideologia tra XI e XIII secolo* (Milan, 1972).

47 *Quinque*, 226: 'quamdiu morabor in hoc exilio?'.

48 *Vita*, 102, 38. She often spoke of her burdensome exile: 102, 42; 125, 5; 157, 46; 160, 92; 162, 27; 164, 68; 204, 81.

strongly desires to be freed from this exile and loosed from the body.[49]

Hadewijch advised in her twenty-fourth Letter: 'Be humble in your outward behavior...and be free from within, continually longing for him with a miserable, exiled heart'.[50] So also in her fifteenth Letter: 'Pass through this exile so uprightly and so purely and so ardently, that you may find God, your love, at the end'.[51] She said it more cogently in her sixth Letter: 'To live here in noble service in all the works of virtue and a life of exile in all obedience....This is to be crucified with Christ, to die with him, and to rise with him'.[52]

Earth as exile is also described as a prison. While Ida Lewis' biography spoke of her body as a prison,[53] and Ida of Leuven asked the Lord how long he would 'detain her in the prison of her body',[54] Beatrice applied the term to her life on earth: 'she grieved at being assigned to this world as if she were held in a dark prison', but the next sentence explains why this was so: 'thinking the world indeed nothing but a squalid prison, the more she saw herself constantly and heavily burdened with its miseries and hardships, the more frequently she sighed for the freedom of the heavenly fatherland' (156,18).

In her *Poems in Stanzas* Hadewijch spoke of the miseries experienced in wandering in the wilderness of the desert.[55] 'Wandering in the desert' evokes in the mind of those familiar with the Old Testament the idea of a pilgrimage through the desert to the promised land. The figurative language used in the Bible has a built-in capacity for being re-expressed in different ways. For the

49 R-VM, *Seven manieren*, 32–33, ll. 61–75.
50 VM, *Brieven*, 1: 211, ll. 76–80.
51 *Ibid.*, 1: 129, ll. 119–21.
52 *Ibid.*, 1: 69, ll. 366–68; 374–76.
53 *AA SS* Oct. 13: 123, 57: 'carnis carcer'.
54 *AA SS* April 2: 180, 35: 'Quamdiu me patieris in hoc carnis ergastulo detineri?'.
55 VM, *Strophische Gedichten*, 140, ll. 28. Benedicta Ward's 'The Desert Myth. Reflections on the Desert Ideal in Early Cistercian Monasticism', *One Yet Two*, CS 29, M. B. Pennington, ed. (Kalamazoo, MI, 1976) 183–99, does not precisely cover this aspect, but has some passages expressing the same ideas.

mulieres religiosae and their mentors, the promised land is manifestly the kingdom of God's love.

Hadewijch wrote in her fifteenth Letter of 'our pilgrimage to God, in which we shall seek the kingdom of God and his justice in perfect works of love'.[56] Beatrice connected pilgrimage with following God's will, as her biography shows: 'Since the time for rest had not yet come, and the rainy, harsh winter of this pilgrimage still hung over her, she did not delay in the meantime to apply the whole intention of her heart to follow the divine goodpleasure'.[57] Exactly a year before her death, Alice of Schaarbeek received the promise that the next year on the same day she would 'happily migrate from exile to the fatherland'.[58] Theirs was a one-way migration; the peregrination ended once and for all when they crossed the finish line.

One cannot expect from a biographer a description of how the *mulier religiosa* he wrote about felt after she had a vision or an ecstasy. Such experiences were unsuspected if they were not expressed by the recipient. Hadewijch and Beatrice are the two in whose writings we can detect the psychological effects of such experiences. In most instances they savored what they had perceived. Sometimes, however, they became painfully aware that they were back in the ordinariness of human life.[59] To stay within the context of this study, we limit ourselves to a few references to Hadewijch and Beatrice.

At the end of her fifth vision Hadewijch wrote: 'And I am back into my grief with many a woe';[60] after her sixth vision she said:'and I was woefully brought back to myself'.[61] Or she was told: 'Go back into your body'.[62] At the end of her eighth vision,

---

56 VM, *Brieven*, 1: 125, ll. 13–15.
57 *Vita*, 199, 60. Beatrice is here in company with the early Cistercians. See Jean Leclercq, 'Monachisme et pérégrination du IXe au XIIe siècle', *StM* 3 (1961) 33–52; 47–49.
58 *AA SS* June 2: 480,2: 'de exilio ad patriam feliciter migratura'.
59 Benz, *Die Vision*, 119.
60 VM, *Visioenen*, 1: 62, ll. 71–72. Her third vision (1: 44, ll. 21–22) says simply: 'that she came back to herself'.
61 *Ibid.*, 1: 70, ll. 103–04.
62 Vision 8; VM, *ibid.*, 1: 91, ll. 123. The original text has *materie*, which according to Vanneste [*Abstracta*, 32] means the bodily existence on earth.

she wrote :'Then I came back to myself as someone in new severe heart pain'.[63] Her tenth vision expresses it still more strongly: 'and I came back, piteously lamenting my exile, as I have done all this winter'.[64] At the end of her eleventh vision she wrote: 'afterwards I returned to myself, where I found myself poor and miserable'.[65]

Occasionally, Beatrice would say how hard it was to return to herself. At the end of her first ecstasy 'she saw that she had been recalled from heavenly delights to the miseries of the human condition, and finding herself on earth...began to sigh and sob violently, bathing her face with tears' (56,55). After a revelation, 'coming back to herself, she fell again into the abyss of violent fear, and as if going from paradise to hell, she knew by revelation of the Holy Spirit that she could not dwell any longer in this sweet fruition of heavenly joy in which she had not yet deserved to remain eternally, but would have to be brought back to her fleshy dwelling place'.[66]

Not all *mulieres religiosae* were as high-spirited as those we meet in biographies and writings. Nor did these exceptional women have illusions about themselves. Because more focused than most people, they perceived more sharply that man's miseries not only came from without and from within, but emerge more refined and dangerous when they come from within. Hadewijch could be considered as their representative when she made the following statement in her sixth Letter:

> We all indeed wish to live God with God [Christ's divinity] but God knows there are few of us who want to live as man (*mensche*) with his humanity, or want to carry his cross with him, or want to hang on the cross with him and pay humanity's debt to the full.... We do not live with Christ and we do

63 VM, *Visioenen*, 1: 91, 127–28.

64 *Ibid.*, 1: 105, ll. 74–76.

65 *Ibid.*, 1: 114, ll. 72–73.

66 *Vita*, 174, 81. After a vision of the Trinity, Abundus of Villers is said to have returned to the vale of tears [*Citeaux* 10 (1959) 17]. The Latin text has 'ad vallem plorationis', an expression found in Augustine's *Ennarrationes in Psalmos*, PL 37: 1606.

not carry our cross with God's Son, but we carry it with Simon [of Cyrene] who received pay for carrying the Lord's cross.... So it is with our struggles and sufferings: for we demand God as a reward for our good works, and we wish to feel him present in this life, and we suppose that we rightly deserve it. We take it to be right that he, in return, should do what we want him to do. We hold in great esteem what we do or suffer, and we never resign ourselves to be left without recompense or without knowing and feeling that it pleases God. We very quickly accept from him pay in hand, *viz.* satisfaction and repose. We also accept pay a second time in our self-complacency...and a third time, when we are satisfied that we have pleased others, and we accept honor and praise and credit from them. All this is to carry that cross with Simon [of Cyrene] who carried it for a short time, but did not die on it.[67]

In the same letter she wrote that 'we show plainly that we do not live with Christ as he lived, neither do we forsake all as he did, nor are we forsaken by all as Christ was'.[68] Living within the confines of her community, Beatrice took 'vigilant care in spiritual exercises', yet felt 'that time was always lacking for what she had undertaken, while negligent and slack religious, who delight in ease rather than in effort, used to have time to spare' (87,7). 'It cost me much grief of heart to see many robust, healthy nuns sometimes passing their time in idleness' (87,10), neglecting to follow Christ totally.

---

67 VM, *Brieven* 1: 64, ll. 230–35; 65–66, ll. 275–92. Simon's receiving pay for carrying the cross is not mentioned in Scripture. Hadewijch could have been expressing her own insight as Benz [*Die Vision*, 448–49], referring to other instances, mentions. Hadewijch could have read or heard the second reference to Simon, who carried the cross but did not die on it, in the *Moralia* of Gregory the Great (PL 75: 846) or else in the tenth meditation of the Carthusian Guigo II (d.about 1188). See Edmund Colledge and James Walsh, *Guigo II le Chartreux... Douze méditations*, SCh 163 (Paris 1970) 186, ll. 114–16; ET: *Guigo II: Ladder of Monks and Twelve Meditations*, CS 48 (Kalamazoo, MI, 1981) 122–23. For other references to Simon carrying the cross but not dying on it, see Reynaert, *Beeldspraak*, 418, n.30.

68 VM, *Brieven*, 1: 65, ll. 256–60.

Ida of Nivelles' biographer made the observation that while the enraptured Ida was lying motionless on the floor, some nuns more advanced in the spiritual life glorified God, while the small-minded were scandalized, 'each interpreting it differently'.[69] Similar remarks are found in nearly all the biographies of ecstatic *mulieres religiosae*. Beatrice's biographer, for instance, mentions criticism a few times.[70] When Beatrice was 'chided, despised, blamed or insulted',[71]... 'she fled to the safe bosom of patience and quickly embraced with the arms of a wonderful gratitude every adverse happening' (117,28). 'Annoyances and mockery...could not recall her from her intention to approach Christ through this path of insults' (157,40).

Ida of Nivelles 'considered that the wickedness of evil does not kill but instructs. She did not dread all the darts of persecution, nor was she frightened by the poisonous detractions of stinging tongues'.[72] Alice of Schaarbeek, suffering from leprosy, was not subjected to detractions, yet 'desired to be despised'.[73] Before Ida of Leuven became a nun she was often praised and often ridiculed. At one time, thought insane, she was for a short while tied up by her relatives and released only when her santiy became apparent. Meanwhile 'from within, her heart was so fortified with invincible freedom, that she praised God, rejoicing in this insulting treatment'.[74] At another time she was suspected of having been made pregnant by a Dominican; when she was informed of this suspicion, it caused her great distress.[75] Hadewijch experi-

---

69 *Quinque*, 282: 'aliter et aliter interpretantes'.

70 As in *Vita*, 158, 37, where criticism is said to be frequent. In 220, 47 a distinction is made between the nuns who understood Beatrice's condition, and the nuns who did not.

71 *Vita*, 117, 26. The biographer, by choosing the verbs he did, could be excused from peppering somewhat the real situation.

72 *Quinque*, 284: 'Considerans quia malorum pravitas non occidit sed erudit'.

73 *AA SS* June 2: 481,28: 'contemptui singulorum optaret se haberi'.

74 *AA SS* April 2: 163,19: ' interiori cordis invincibili libertate munita, in Dei laudibus exultabat'.

75 The biographer dwells at length on this topic: *ibid.*, 175,17–176,20. The suspicion was deduced from the fact that the Dominican visited the bedridden Ida in her room with its shutters closed. To shutter the windows to keep the distracting light out was not uncommon among ecstatics. See Benz, *Die Vision*,

enced hostility, as Christ said she would.[76] Her writings indicate that she was indeed threatened and rejected by some of her peers—as can be seen, for instance, in her fifth and twenty ninth letters.

In their desire to follow Christ totally, the *mulieres religiosae* were careful not to fall prey to vainglory.[77] Without developing an inferiority complex, they stressed submissiveness,[78] and considered themselves less worthy than others,[79] just as they were careful not to make hasty judgments about others. Of Ida of Nivelles it is explicitly said that when she knew that people were entangled in sin, she did not judge them at once, but with great affection felt compassion for them, hoping to hear later that they had changed for the better.[80] Hadewijch was forbidden by the Lord to take revenge and was told why she should not:

I [Christ] forbid you for ever, even for the twinkling of an eye, to dare to take offence, to strike back or to take revenge for any reason. If you dare to do that in any way whatever, you will be the one who wills to attack my right and who mars my sovereign power of judgment.[81]

Beatrice 'bore the load of insults laid on her shoulders with a joyful heart, without rancor or murmuring as if she had received a

---

228. To shutter the windows was 'eine Abschirmung gegen alle Störungen von aussen, die die Seele an ihren Begegnungen mit Gott hindern könnten', as for instance, 'das Abdunkeln der Fenster'.

76 Spaapen, 'Hadewijch en het vijfde visioen', *OGE* 44 (1970) 381–94.

77 See Chapter VI, n.140.

78 As Hadewijch did in one of her letters: 'In perfect humility be submissive in everything and never glory in anything'.Letter 27; VM, *Brieven*, 1: 221, ll. 12–13.

79 Ida of Nivelles, *Quinque*, 282; – Beatrice, *Vita*, 99, 4;

80 *Quinque*, 278: 'Si quando vero sciebat aliquos peccatis irretitis, non statim judicabat eos, sed ex nimio cordis affectu compatiebatur illis, sperans in posterum audire de eis meliora'.

81 Vision one; VM, *Visioenen*, 1: 26–27, ll. 283–88. This text is reminiscent of Rm 12:19, and an example of what Dinzelbacher calls *Lehrvision*, a teaching vision: what a seer has learned elsewhere is expressed in a vision (*Vision*, 85). For detailed study of biblical motives in Hadewijch's figurative language, see Reynaert, *Beeldspraak*, 414–23.

special gift from God's loving kindness' (117,32). Alice of Schaarbeek did not repay a wrong done to her,[82] while Ida of Nivelles was of the opinion 'that it is better to flee a hurt by keeping quiet than to prevail by arguing'.[83] The same Ida did not dread suffering persecution or detraction for Christ's sake.[84] When she did not experience them, she complained about the lack. Her biographer adds 'that she frequently and vehemently desired adversities, but had few imitators'.[85] Ida Lewis felt uneasy when she did not experience her usual vexations and feared that for one reason or another she had deserved to be forsaken by the Lord.[86] Alice of Schaarbeek refused to be healed even if she could have been,[87] and Beatrice asked for sufferings.[88] Whatever secondary motives the biographers might have had in mind, their primary intention was to show that those women did what Hadewijch advised in her sixth Letter:

The affliction of our sweet God which he suffered when he lived as man, deserves that for his sake one gladly bears all affliction and all sorts of derision. Yes, even to desire them. The eternal nature of his sweet love deserves very much that each man should perform with perfect will the virtues in which God, his Beloved, is honored.[89]

Following Christ utterly sometimes seemed to demand that the *mulieres religiosae* inscribe a square circle. To be called by the

---

82 *AA SS* June 2: 478, 4: 'Injuria sibi illata vices non reddebat'.

83 *Quinque*, 284: 'Melior est injuriam tacendo fugere, quam loquendo superare'.

84 *Ibid.*: 'Non formidavit pro Christo pati universa persecutionum jacula, nec ad venenosa mordacium linguarum detractiones expavit'.

85 *Ibid.*: 'Quare, Domine, tam diuturno somno dormis et me ancillam tuam vexationis tribulationes carere permittis? Desiderabat haec beata et frequenter et vehementer adversitates, sed paucos habebat aemulatores'.

86 *AA SS* Oct. 13: 112,16: 'Quotiens hostis perfidus aliquanti temporis spatio cessabat a verberibus et a vexationibus assuetis, timebat mirabiliter ne per offensionculam qualemcumque meruisset a Domino derelinqui'.

87 As has been mentioned in Chapter VI, n.106.

88 *Vita*, 184, 26; 189,100. The reason for this request has been given in the text referred to in n.112 of Chapter VI.

89 VM, *Brieven*, 1: 61, ll. 164–71.

God-Man to follow him to the very end, and to be determined to
do so, is indeed very demanding, as Beatrice noted: 'All who
desire to attain Love must seek it with fear and follow it faithfully
and exercise it with longing, and this they cannot do if they spare
themselves in great labor and many pains, in bearing trouble and
in suffering contempt'.[90]

Gripped by Christ's love for them and their love for him, the
mulieres religiosae were constantly tossed around, tasting now
the sweet, and now the bitter. Taken by their great desire to
follow the God-Man out of love and totally, painfully aware of
not being able to satisfy his love fully, their hearts were enlarged
into a greater capacity to become more Christlike.[91] As Hadewijch wrote: 'At times Love so enlightens me that I know what is
wanting in me: that I do not content my Beloved according to his
dignity. At other times the sweet nature of Love blinds me so
much by tasting and feeling her, that this is enough for me'.[92]

Christ reminded Beatrice that 'the vehement attraction by
which I have provoked you to follow me with a certain indefatigable vehemence and violence of spirit', made 'you walk with
continuous steps of virtue through things both sweet and bitter,
harsh and smooth' (171,42). Her biographer noted that

> by a certain marvelous vicissitude both the smooth and the
> rough, the sweet and the bitter flowed from the same spring
> of love. The sweet, because the abundance of heavenly
> delights was often poured forth copiously for her drinking;
> the bitter, because she could not make the worthy return of
> love due to her Bridegroom, according to her heart's insatia-
> ble desire.[93]

---

90 R-VM, *Seven manieren*, 27, ll. 62–67.
91 The scope of the biographies of the other *mulieres religiosae* does not
include this kind of autobiographical information. This fact does not mean that
the other women did not experience what Hadewijch and Beatrice did, but only
that they did not write down their own experiences or speak about them.
92 Eleventh letter; VM, *Brieven*, 1: 96, ll. 40–45.
93 *Vita*, 204,74.

Reflecting on her experiences at a later stage in her life, Beatrice wrote that the third *maniere* of loving

has many sorrows connected with it, namely when it [the soul] desires to satisfy and yield to Love in all service and all obedience and all loving submission. Sometimes, this desire so greatly agitates the soul that it strives vigorously to undertake everything, to follow after every virtue, to suffer and endure everything, to fulfil all its works in love, withholding nothing and without measure. In this state the soul is very ready for every service, and is eager and unafraid in labor and sorrow; yet it remains unsatisfied and unappeased in all its works.[94]

Hadewijch shared Beatrice's desire 'to satisfy and yield to Love in all obedience and all loving submission'. In her seventh vision she wrote:

Above all gifts I ever longed for, I chose this gift: that I should give satisfaction in all great sufferings. For that is the most perfect satisfaction: to grow up to be God with God. This means suffering, pain and misery and living in great new grief of soul; letting everything come and go without grief, experiencing in all this no other taste but sweet love, embraces and kisses....In this sense I desired God's gift of himself to me, to give him satisfaction.[95]

Beatrice herself wrote that 'the soul desires to lead its whole life so as to work, grow and ascend to a greater height of love and a closer knowledge of God, until it reaches that perfection for which it is fully made and called by God'.[96]

To 'grow up to be God with God', one must, go through adversity and find consolation in the darkness which comes in its wake. As Hadewijch stated in her twenty-eighth Letter: 'God

---

94 R-VM, *Seven manieren*, 9–10, ll. 3–16.
95 VM, *Visioenen*, 1: 75–76, ll. 32–37.
96 R-VM, *Seven manieren*, 4, ll. 19–24.

Letter: 'God gave the noblest of men insight through all adversity and through all adversity withdrew this insight. And when he withdrew this insight, he gave him the sharpest insight of all. I found my consolation with God in all adversity'.[97] This insight is what made Hadewijch speak of 'sweet misery'.[98]

Near the end of the chapter in Beatrice's *Vita*, before he speaks about the foundation of Nazareth, the biographer says that for some time she was totally deprived of her [self-] will (222,1), and that 'from then on, the more vexed she was in body or mind by any corporeal or spiritual trouble, the more sweetly she was refreshed by this supreme Good [God's will] and thus would stand all hard and harsh things, not only patiently but also very willingly... bearing everything with equanimity.[99]

Experiencing their own incapacity to measure up to Christ in the totality of his *kenosis*, the *mulieres religiosae* found in Christ's love the stimulus to trust in him who provoked them to follow him to the very end. 'From this exercise in humility and patience, Beatrice gathered so much confidence in the Lord that, even if she knew beforehand that the whole human race, except one person was going to be condemned by the Lord, trusting in his goodness she would have striven with all her might and main that this prerogative of grace should be reserved for her' (136, 131). It is also said of her (142,32): 'Having firm hope and confidence in him, she had so based all her strength in him that she was sure that neither death nor life nor anything afterward could ever separate her spirit from his love'.

In her last Letter Hadewijch also makes a distinction between relying on Christ alone and relying on him through one's own works:

---

97 VM, *Brieven*, 1: 238, ll. 236–41.
98 Ninth Poem in Stanzas; VM, *Strophische Gedichten*, 55, l. 21. William said also in his *Golden Epistle* (CF 12: 98, 272) that 'it is sweet for man to be abased together with the supreme Majesty, to become poor with the Son of God, to be conformed to divine Wisdom, to make his own the mind which is in Jesus Christ our Lord'.
99 *Vita*, 227,101.

We come close to God by satisfying him in love and trusting in him above everything else. We come most close to him by confidence. He himself said to a person [most probably Hadewijch] that true prayer is nothing else than lofty confidence in him, to trust him completely in all that he is [as God-Man]. He himself said: 'People who do not know me and my goodness as I am, serve me with fasting and vigils and with sundry labors, and with these labors they rely on me. But nothing has so much power over me as the perfect trust of lofty fidelity.[100]

Christ had done the same himself when he took upon himself the miseries of the human condition. He performed the task he was sent to do. He went confidently into the darkness and the agony of his death on a cross, certain that this was the way his Father wanted him to express God's love for man.[101] From his cross he signaled to the *mulieres religiosae* the kind of following to which he called them, and the degree of conformity to which he lovingly invited them. And they went and went, following him to the very end of a blossoming Christ-likeness. In her fourteenth Letter Hadewijch expressed this when she wrote to a correspondent:

May God [here Christ] be your help and consolation of your whole being. May he teach you the veritable virtue by which we render Love the most honor and justice. God must teach you the well-pleasing oneness which he offered to his Father, when as man he lived undividedly and totally for him. And may he teach you the holy oneness he taught and prescribed for his holy friends, who for the sake of his love renounce all alien consolation. May he make known to you in truth and in deed that delightful sweet union, the experience of which he still gives to his dear friends who conform above all things to his holy sweet love.[102]

---

100 Letter 31; VM, *Brieven*, 1: 262–63, ll. 2–14.
101 As he told Hadewijch. See the text referred to in n.78 of Chapter VIII.
102 VM, *Brieven*, 1: 119–20, ll. 5–18.

Surveying how Beatrice tried to follow Christ, the biographer could state that 'in everything she was quiet and patient, conforming herself in all ways to the divine good-pleasure, in things both sweet and bitter, adverse and prosperous' (205,86). 'Thus bearing everything with equanimity and confiding in the great goodness of her God, Beatrice with the help of God's grace, perfected for the rest of her life the work which the heavenly Father had given her to do, being firmer in faith, more constant in hope, and more fervent in love'.[103].

Since the society the *mulieres religiosae* lived in was feudal, they did not speak of 'civil liberties' or 'human rights' as we do in today's real or alleged democracies. As Christians they believed that all human beings have 'divine rights and obligations'. Beatrice referred to both when she 'saw man made to the image of God, framed according to his likeness, and she recognized with certitude and by reasonable judgment that she was bound by the precept of charity to love him' (108,32). Love for neighbor is rooted in God's relation to him and his relation to God. Moreover, by becoming man among men, God's Son proved and manifested that the meaning of man's life is not limited to the man himself or to a one-way relation to God. To be complete in his own totality man has to care for all his vertical and horizontal relationships, the former not based on the latter, but the latter flowing from the former. Christ has shown how love for neighbor is practiced. To follow Christ implies following him in his relationships with men whose neighbor he became when he became incarnate—that is, when he made his vertical relation as God horizontal as well. Hadewijch spelled this out in her third letter:

Here [on earth] we should to a large extent understand and perform the customs of heaven, if the shackles of love drew us far enough away from this world's customary way of acting, and if we had enough assiduity toward God and brotherly love for men in all things of which they are in need. To Love's greatest need and Love's most urgent task I

---

103 *Vita*, 227,106.

attend first. So does brotherly love that lives in the charity of Jesus Christ. It supports fraternal love in whatever way it may be: in joy or sadness, in severity or mildness, with services and counsels, in consoling or in warning. In order that God may have nothing to reproach you, keep your vigor always in readiness for his sake. This is how we touch him in the side where he cannot defend himself, for we do so with his own work and with the will of his Father, who commanded him to do this and which he fulfilled. And that is the message of the Holy Spirit.[104]

Hadewijch herself practiced what she advised others to do, as can be seen in her twenty-ninth Letter: 'I have lived with people, with all the works I could perform in their service. They found me prepared with ready virtue for all their needs'.[105] The *mulieres religiosae* could not look at their neighbors without seeing them in a larger context: as human beings made to God's image and likeness, with a dignity and nobility in need of and on the way to salvation.[106] When speaking of Beatrice's love for neighbor, her biographer wrote that: 'in a marvelous way, her heart quickly seemed to enlarge and to extend over the whole breadth of the world. Her heart spread out like a vast net, catching within it the whole human race (218,119). Or, as he said at another place (263,8):

---

104 VM, *Brieven*, 1: 33–34, ll. 19–38. Some ideas expressed in this text are close to Bernard's saying: 'If he [God's Son] had not first had that mercy which knows nothing of misery, he would not have come to that of which misery is the mother. If he had not had that, he would not have attracted us to himself; and if he had not attracted us, he would not have extracted us from the morass of misery and from the miry bog': Hum 3.12; SBOp 3: 26: 'Si illa, quae miseriam nescit, misericordia non praecessisset, ad hanc, cujus miseria mater est, non accessisset. Si non accessisset, non attraxisset; si non attraxisset, non extraxisset. Unde autem extraxit, nisi de lacu miseriae et de luto faecis?'. The last part of this sentence is a biblical citation of Ps 39:3.

105 VM, *Brieven*, 1: 244, ll. 61–64.

106 Beatrice's biography several times says that she put her talents to the use of people in need: 123, 68; 199, 71; 210, 47; 212, 82; 217, 107; 221, 63. This was also the stand taken by Bernard, William and Richard. See Javelet, *Image*, 1: 420–26.

It was fitting that she pour forth that nectar-like taste of charity, sharing it for her neighbors' use, because like a chosen bride she had been brought into the wine cellar where the heavenly king had set charity in order within her. It was becoming that she, as a lavish dispenser of the heavenly talent, should pay out for the profit of others the gift of charity which she has received. The duty of well-ordered charity is to serve with attention and devotion the neighbors' salvation. Just as love unceasingly embraces God, the creator of all, with outstretched arms, so it should incline to the needs of creatures, loving good and bad alike.

Ministering to his [Christ's] Lordship, Beatrice 'revered him with a necessary kindness so to speak, as a pupil her teacher or as a servant her mistress; and like a good housewife she obeyed him faithfully in every expression of his will' (264,32).

For this reason she was weak with the weak, and she burned with fire daily with those who were scandalized. For this reason also she necessarily took upon herself whatever servitude the other person was suffering, not being able to withhold her mercy and compassion in any needy situation. The more closely she clung to the Creator of all things through the affection of love, the more faithfully she gave to his creatures a loving service that was not so much voluntary as necessary.[107]

The other *mulieres religiosae* had the same affective concern for their neighbors' needs as did Hadewijch and Beatrice, even if their biographies do not describe it at length. Ida of Nivelles' biography amply indicates that 'with her whole heart she desired the salvation of her fellowmen. Through her efforts, effusive prayers, tears, counsel and example she called many back to the way of salvation'.[108] As her biographer points out, 'she would occasionally leave God for God's sake, lovingly to serve her

---

107 *Vita*, 264,32.
108 *Quinque*, 273: 'Quorum [proximorum] salutem toto corde desiderans, et ad hoc frequenter laborans, orationes orationibus et lachrymas lachrymis addens, plurimos eorum consilio et exemplo suo ad viam salutis revocavit'.

neighbors'.[109] A priest who had his doubts about the same Ida's reputation, came to see her but remained skeptical. To make his point, the biographer used a vignette much appreciated at that time. One day, as this priest was celebrating Mass, he saw Ida's face and heard a voice saying: 'My son, I show you Ida's outward face but instantly you will see her interior one, that you may see that Ida is my beloved, welling up as a fountain from the earth, so that whoever comes to that fountain can draw from it abundantly and without difficulty'. It was then revealed to this priest 'with what compassion Ida assumed to herself the misfortunes of all those who came to her to be relieved by appropriate alleviations'.[110]

Alice of Schaarbeek, 'pressed by the vehemence of her charity, was very anxious for the salvation of the human race, and did what she could to save her neighbors who were in distress or mentally disturbed or sexually tempted'.[111] 'With great ardor she bore her physical and spiritual sufferings in the hope that the human race would come to the enjoyment of its Redeemer'.[112]

---

109 *Quinque*, 280: 'Deum propter Deum dimittere, ut proximis per caritatem deserviret'. Hadewijch said similarly 'that one is sometimes so wounded by charity for others that he must renounce the fruition and blessedness of God for the sake of sinners who live in sin, preferring to be deprived of his Beloved until assurance is given him that these sinners are not despairing of God's grace'. (Letter 2; VM, *Brieven*, 1: 29–30, ll. 124–31). This too is part of following Christ, as Richard pointed out in the fourth and highest degree of love (Dumeige, *Les quatre degrés*, 173–74). Henri Bergson supports this for all 'great mystics'. See his *The Two Sources of Morality and Religion*, ET by R. Audra and C. Brereton (Garden City, NY, 1935) 231–36. See also Javelet, *Psychologie*. 170–71.

110 *Quinque*, 264: 'Vidit infra missae canonem faciem venerabilis Idae, audivitque vocem Domini dicentem sibi: "Ecce fili, quemadmodum ostendo tibi faciem Idae exteriorem, sic ostendam tibi statim ejus interiorem, ut cognoscas Idam dilectam meam esse quasi fontem de terra iugiter emanantem, ad quem quicumque venerit et exhauriat, hauriat abundanter et sine difficultate"'... itaque divinitus revelatum est ei quanta compassione Ida omnes omnium calamitates in se traheret, et omnes necessitates aliorum qui ad se confluebant congruis consolationibus relevaret'.

111 *AA SS* June 2: 480,21: 'In se patiebatur caritatis violentia, [et] pro humani generis salute gestabat solicitudinem pro vivis non paucis contribulatis, mente quoque conturbatis atque a carnalibus tentationibus per eam saluti traditis'.

112 *Ibid.*, 482,30: '... quali modo humani generis, ut suo Redemptore posset frui'.

Ida Lewis was 'submissive to all, agreeable in her words and compassionate with the grieving',[113] while Ida of Leuven 'offered daily the libation of her prayers for the liberation [from sin] of a dear friend and for the salvation of all the faithful'.[114] Conscious of who they were, the *mulieres religiosae* felt a deep solidarity with their neighbors in need, as two occurrences in Ida Lewis' biography show. One day, a nun of her community came to her asking for help, for she was constantly troubled by a certain vice. Ida advised her to go to communion and tell the Lord that Ida had sent her. Afterwards this nun said to Ida that, at her request, the Lord had effectively subdued the overpowering sway of the troublesome vice.[115] On another occasion, a nun approached her to explain the distress she was in. Ida replied to her: 'If I ever did any good, I give it all to you, and you give to me all the wrongs you have done and leave them entirely to me. But with this agreement: henceforth you must be watchful to follow the path of virtue with renewed spirit and right living, and apply yourself to keep doing so faithfully'.[116]

At the time of the *mulieres religiosae* there were not yet any public or private organizations to succor the needy in a systematic way. Communities of monks were better equipped than communities of women to help many individuals and small groups,[117] and some were well known for their dedication to social welfare on the local level.[118] Women, whether beguines or nuns, were

---

113 *AA SS* Oct. 13: 118,38: 'humilis omnibus, dulcis operibus, dolentibus compatiens, tota virtute spiritus imminebat'.

114 *AA SS* April 2: 178,26: 'de liberatione sui familiaris aliorumque salute fidelium pro omnibus orationum libamina quotidie transmisit ad Dominum'.

115 *AA SS* Oct.13: 116,28: 'percepit quod Dominus voluit veraciter vitium per merita dilectae virginis terminari'.

116 *Ibid.*, 118,39: 'Si bona aliqua umquam feci, ego vobis omnino confero universa, vestraque mala omnia mihi detis, et ea mihi penitus dimittis, tali videlicet pactione, quod vos de caetero virtutis semitam et novitatem spiritus vitaeque rectitudinem sequamini sollicite, sicque spiritu fideli de caetero permanere studeatis'.

117 Lekai, *The Cistercians. Ideals and Reality*, 378–99.

118 Among them Villers, for instance. See E. de Moreau, *L'Abbaye de Villers*, 261–66: 'L'organisation de la bienfaisance'. This lasted till the end of the thirteenth century, when the heavy taxes imposed by governing princes, including the duke of Brabant, bled them to the point of forcing them to disband temporarily, as indicated by several *Statuta* of the General Chapter.

much less able than men to alleviate the poverty of their neighbors.[119] They compensated for their inability to provide economic assistance by giving moral and spiritual support within the
restrictions imposed by the ecclesiastical, secular and social conditions of their time. They were manifestly not the therapists with
which the twentieth century is familiar, but they shared freely the
personal gifts they themselves had received freely, and had freely
cooperated with and developed.

Men no less than women used to go to the outstanding *mulieres
religiosae* for help and advice. 'Men and women, religious and
lay, come often to see Ida of Nivelles and to talk with her'.[120] The
same is said of Beatrice: 'Persons of different ages, conditions
and professions were to be seen daily coming with their needs to
her' (265,40). Lutgard too had many visitors of both sexes who
came to her for help with their spiritual needs.[121] Her leprosy
notwithstanding, Alice of Schaarbeek knew what was going on
socially and offered the loss of her eyes for two royal causes.[122]
These *mulieres religiosae*, being known as ecstatics, undoubtedly
attracted the merely curious, but these were not in the majority.[123]
The *mulieres religiosae*, for their part, regarded it as their duty to
their neighbors not primarily to alleviate them temporarily but to
advance them to the eternal bliss to which each person is called.
In her passion for God's love and her compassion for sinners,
Hadewijch said antithetically in her eleventh vision:

> I would have wished that he [God] give his love to others
> and withdraw it from me. I would gladly have purchased
> love for them [sinners] by obtaining that he should love

---

119 Except for a few, most communities of women had limited, slowly
growing, assets.

120 *Quinque*, 207–08: 'Religiosi et non religiosi viri et mulieres venientes as
ipsam'. The *Liber specialis gratiae* 5,10 of Mechtild of Hackeborn (ed. by the
monks of Solesmes [Paris-Poitiers, 1877] 347) mentions that the supervising
prelate ordered her not to divulge her revelations for fear that making them
public would attract people and disturb the community.

121 *AA SS* June 4: 205,4 and 7.

122 *AA SS* June 2: 481, 23 and 27: William of Holland, elected emperor of the
Holy Roman Empire, and Louis IX of France.

123 Ida Lewis' biography, for instance, states explicitly that ecstatics inevitably attracted peoples' attention and curiosity. See *AASS* Oct.13: 108, CD.

them and hate me.[124] And at times too, because he did not do this, I would willingly have turned away from him in love and would have loved them in spite of his wrath. For the unfortunates could not realize how sweet and hearty is the love which resides in his [God's] holy nature.[125]

'Due to God's love as is fitting' was Hadewijch's favorite expression when she spoke of man's responsive love for God. This and the salvation of man, collectively and individually, were the two major stimuli of the *mulieres religiosae* to love their neighbors. A few examples help make this clearer.

Before Ida Lewis joined the nuns of Rameya, she one day went with her sister to a place where people were behaving licentiously.When she realized where she was heading, 'pierced with the sword of love and unable to stand the disgrace done to her Beloved, she followed his example and had great compassion with the folly of straying sinners'. She took leave of her sister and went straight back home.[126]

Expected to die in June 1249, Alice of Schaarbeek had a nocturnal vision of the Lord, who told her that she would die exactly one year later on 11 June 1250. He told her she would have 'to suffer much more in body and heart during that year than she had suffered during her whole life'. He also explained why: 'by her patience and prayers she would purify sinners from their sins'.[127] Alice was aware that one of her tasks was to suffer

---

124 Lutgard made a similar request. See *AA SS* June 4: 269. For more examples of this kind, see Bernard Spaapen, 'Hadewijch en het vijfde visioen', *OGE* 44 (1970) 38, n.54.

125 VM, *Visioenen*, 1: 120, ll. 170–74. In her sixth Letter (VM, *Brieven*, 1: 56, ll. 73–75), Hadewijch wrote that the most effective way to help sinners is to love God more intensely: 'What is more profitable to sinners: the love we give to God. The stronger love is, the more it frees sinners from their sins'. Like Beatrice, Hadewijch is here in agreement with Richard, William and Bernard, see n. 106 above.

126 *AA SS* Oct. 13: 110,11: 'Dilecti sui dedecus non modice graviter sustinens, ardentique mente compatiens errantium stultitiae proximorum, caritatis transfixa gladio, vulnerata non mediocriter amoris jaculis, compassione laqueo suffocata... domum quam citius est regressa'.

127 *AA SS* June 2: 480,22: 'Innotuit ei Dominus quod respectu temporis totius vitae prioris, multo ampliores corporis debilitates multoque graviores cordis

vicariously for sinners.[128] Some months later her blood sister was deeply grieved at Alice's excruciating pain; to her Alice replied that her sufferings were needed to ease sinners out of the snares in which they were entangled and from the temptations by which they were continually seduced.[129] One day, Ida of Leuven in a rapture thought she had died and was joyfully standing in front of her Saviour who told her to go back quickly to her body, re-clothing herself with 'the tunic of her flesh' to save a friend of hers and others from the danger of committing grave sins.[130]

Some of the *mulieres religiosae* also had charismata, which must be distinguished from those of our contemporary charis-matic prayer-groups.[131] To indicate that the charisms of these women were not self-induced, the biographer of Ida of Nivelles pointed out that God the Holy Spirit is the distributor of heavenly charisms.[132] Ida of Leuven's biographer speaks of Christ as 'the generous giver of all graces and the distributor of charisms'.[133]

---

tribulationes, omniumque membrorum passiones, per illius anni circulum deberet sustinere et quod per ipsius patientiam similiter et orationes... in corpore adhuc degentium animae, ac in statu periculoso existentium vita, a sordibus emundari'.

128 *AA SS* June 2: 481,26. The text is quoted in the next note. Similar vicarious sufferings are related in the biography of Beatrice (267,86). Lutgard, Alice and some others seem to have 'specialized' in vicarious sufferings not unrelated to their physical illnesses.

129 *AA SS* June 481, 26: 'Non me putes pro peccatis meis hujusmodi exponi tormentis, sed pro defunctis in locis poenalibus diu cruciandis, et pro pec-catoribus mundi a laqueis venantium jam miserabiliter irretitis et sine fine seducendis, nisi per poenam qua me vides sic consumi, defuncti mereantur liberari, et vivi, a laqueis similiter relaxari'.

130 *AA SS* April 2: 178, 26. Similar stories with variants about assumably deceased people resuming their dead body, appear before and after Ida's life-time. See, for instance, Benz, *Die Vision*, 267–70; the *Exordium Magnum* (ed. Br.Griesser), 360; C.G. De Vooys' *Middelnederlandse Legenden*, 270, and similar *legendaria* mentioned above in Chapter VIII, nn. 14 and 31.

131 The references given by Roisin, *L'Hagiographie*, 165–92 show this difference sufficiently.

132 *Quinque*, 257 and 268.

133 *AA SS* April 2: 172,7 and 189,28.

The charism we call ESP (extrasensory perception) was one of them. Hadewijch may have had it,[134] and Ida of Nivelles was particularly gifted in this regard. She had extrasensory perceptual knowledge that a priest was sexually attracted to a young woman. In her desire to help him, she suffered sickness for six months until this priest was able to integrate his sexual attraction.[135] She knew that another priest, as well as a layman and a woman, had committed fornication.[136] In another case she had extrasensory knowledge that a man known to her had committed incest with his daughter. She called him to the parlor, asking him about his spiritual life. The man made a confession of his sins, but omitted the incest. When Ida began to weep, the startled man asked her why she was crying, and she confronted him with the incest. The man also began to weep and did an (unspecified) penance in her presence.[137] Each time she knew by ESP of carnal deviations, she was so overcome by compassion that she herself did not feel any sexual stimulation.[138]

Though this Ida 'desired ardently to die to be inseparably united with God', she nevertheless declared herself ready to remain, God willing, 'a long time in the miseries of this life, for no other reason than to help the desolate and sinners by counsel and assistance'.[139] Her friend Beatrice was told that her life 'was

---

134 In her Letter 29 (VM, *Brieven*, 1: 244–45, ll. 61–84) Hadewijch makes an allusion to them. Van Mierlo (*Brieven*, 1: 244, note) and M.J. Van Baest (*De Fierheid als kernmoment...van Hadewijch*, 31) are of the opinion that she could be referring to miracles. Bernard Spaapen (*OGE* 43 [1973] 383–84) understands it as ESP. Herman Vekeman ('Haderwijch. Een interpretatie...', *TNTL* 90 [1975] 346–47) offers another interpretation: to be overbusy in activities is not compatible with the demands of the primacy of God's infinite love.

135 *Quinque*, 214.

136 *Ibid.*, 215 and 230–31.

137 *Ibid.*, 228–30. In several of the extra-sensory perceptions of grave sins, she vomited blood, as has been noted above, Chapter VI, n.119.

138 *Quinque*, 279: 'in auditioni carnalium illecebrarum et horrendorum facinorum numquam, sicut ipsa testabatur, vel primum saltem motum se sensisse meminerit. Nec mirum, statim enim cum aliquis ei loquebatur de peccatis vel flagitiis suis, valido caritatis igne interius eam accedente, tota ejus anima liquescebat ad compassionem; et hoc erat ei salubre remedium quo non permittebatur vel modicum saltem sentire carnis tintillationem'.

139 *Ibid.*: 'Dicebat se libentissime velle, si Domino Deo placeret in hac vita calamitatibus plena diu morari, non ob aliud sane nisi ut desolatis et peccatoribus consilium et auxilium posset impertiri'.

not going to end as yet. Instead it would still be prolonged for some time in order that she might be exercised in the services of love and charity' (239,30). Hadewijch mentions in her thirteenth vision that despite her burning desire to enjoy union with God in heaven, she preferred to remain a while longer on earth to help the members of her group to grow into the fullness of love for God which she herself so painfully had learned.[140] Closely connected with ESP is the charism of clairvoyance, which can take different forms.[141] Hadewijch 'could see in what state of grace, or absence of it, people were'.[142] Beatrice 'knew without disclosure the whole origin and process of sinners' interior state' (267,78). Ida of Nivelles could 'plainly see peoples' state and thoughts'.[143] 'It was divinely given to her to know the state of people, good and bad'.[144] Ida Lewis also 'often knew through many signs, manners, and words, when, how long, and in what way God visited a person's spirit',[145] and Ida of Leuven had clairvoyance occasionally, 'with the insight, not of bodily but of interior eyes'.[146]

If they deemed it helpful, they would use their clairvoyance to tell respected people to their face what hidden defects blocked their way toward God. One day, Ida of Nivelles, travelling with an abbess, stayed overnight with beguines. To one of them, who was highly thought of by the others, Ida spoke of her three major defects and their consequences.[147] Ida Lewis told a nun of her

---

140 VM, *Visioenen*, 1: 152–53, ll. 243–46.

141 Benz, *Die Vision*, 186–90: 'Die Unterscheidung der Geister kann aber auch in einer psychologisch verfeinerten Form auftreten'.

142 Second vision; VM, *Visioenen*, 1: 38, ll. 7–10. When she wrote down this vision she seemed no longer to possess this clairvoyance. See H. Vekeman, *Het visioenenboek van Hadewijch*, 216.

143 *Quinque*, 243: 'perspicue [videbat] status et cogitationes hominum'.

144 *Ibid.*, 270: 'ita ut statum tam de bonis quam de malis ei daretur divinitus cognoscere'.

145 *AA SS* Oct. 13: 120,44: 'Cognovit etiam, et hoc saepius, signis, modis et verbis plurimis, quando, quamdiu, qualiter Deus spiritum personae visitabat'.

146 *AA SS* April 2: 169,43: 'non corporalibus sed internorum oculorum acie' [pervidebat].

147 *Quinque*, 241–42. When the beguine thought that Ida could only have known it through an indiscretion of an abbot to whom she had gone to confession, she was told what she was thinking by the telepathic Ida and thus received

community about a hidden vice, to which the nun retorted harshly: 'Did you see visions?'[148] The concern of the *mulieres religiosae* for their neighbors' needs did not stop when they died. Beatrice (28,97), her father (19,11), and Ida of Nivelles all prayed for the deceased. Ida, moreover, was sick for six weeks to alleviate the pains of a man held in purgatory.[149] Lutgard is too well known for her sufferings on behalf of the dead to escape mention here.[150] It took Alice of Schaarbeek a long time of practicing special penances before one certain soul in purgatory was liberated, though usually it took less time.[151]

Apparitions of souls in purgatory are mentioned in the biographies of Lutgard,[152] Ida of Nivelles,[153] and Alice of Schaarbeek.[154] Nor were Alice's sufferings offered only on behalf of individuals. To the physical pains caused by her leprosy she incessantly added prayers and groans to obtain the liberation of all the souls in purgatory.[155] No figures are claimed to illustrate the effectiveness of Alice's efforts, and we may compare this with the fantastic figures of the mass-liberation of a century later. A Dominican nun, Adelheid Langmann (d.1375), is supposed to have liberated 30,000, 60,000 and 100,000 souls on three different days, while another Dominican nun, Christine Ebner (1277–1356) holds a record for liberating one million souls all at once.[156] Simone Roisin made the justified remark that the

---

the affirmation that Ida knew her defects by God's revelation. For the combination of these two charisms, see Benz, *Die Vision*, 198.

148 *AA SS* Oct. 13: 116,29. Ida told her that she knew about this through God, and that the nun would not escape God's anger if she did not mend her ways.

149 *Quinque*, 213.

150 *AA SS* June 4: 179, 4 and 7. See also Jacques Le Golff, *La naissance du purgatoire* (Paris, 1981) 434, and Adriaan H. Bredero, 'Le Moyen Age et le purgatoire', *RHE* 78 (1983) 429–52.

151 *AA SS* June 2: 481, 26 and 29.

152 *AA SS* June 4: 199,12; 205,51: the Cistercian abbot Simon of Foigny and pope Alexander III among them.

153 *Quinque*, 213.

154 *AA SS* June 2: 480,20; 482,29.

155 *Ibid.*, 480, 21: 'Deum precibus incessanter et gemitibus oravit ut poenam purgatoriam defunctis omnibus relaxaret'.

156 Dinzelbacher, 'Das Christusbild', *OGE* 56 (1982) 265.

mulieres religiosae here under consideration appear quite modest in this regard because their hope of salvation was greater than their fear of perdition.[157] Ida of Nivelles' biography mentions how she tried unsuccessfully to get an unwilling woman out of purgatory.[158]

In passing, mention could be made of television.[159] Centuries before technological television, Ida of Nivelles experienced the effect, though in a quite different way. The day her friend Beatrice received the 'consecration of virgins', the enraptured Ida, at Rameya, followed the ceremony taking place in Maagdendaal and saw how the consecrated nuns were affected. When asked by a nun of her own community where she had been, she told her what she had seen. When shortly afterwards a laybrother from Maagdendaal (probably Beatrice's father, who had a daughter in Rameya) came to visit Ida's community, the inquisitive nun asked him about what happened in Maagdendaal and received a report confirming Ida's television.[160] Ida experienced other televisions of this sort.[161]

Prophetic visions are related to television,[162] and some *mulieres religiosae* used them in the service of their own and others' spiritual progress. In her first vision Hadewijch was told by the Lord: 'With understanding you shall wisely carry out my will to all those who need to know, through you, my will which is still

---

157 Roisin, *L'Hagiographie*, 199: 'Les anecdotes de ce genre, toutefois, sont peu nombreuses dans nos *Vitae* du XIIIe siècle. On sent que celles ci sont écrites dans et pour un autre milieu où l'espoir du ciel fait plus impression que la crainte de l'enfer'. It would be misleading if one were to limit Roisin's correct conclusion to the diocese of Liège. Dinzelbacher (*Vision*, 118–19) made the observation that from the seventh till the beginning of the thirteenth century, fear of hell and damnation played an important role in the 'great' visions, while (except in Italy) in the thirteenth century, reaching for the felicity of heaven became dominant.

158 *Quinque*, 221–24. Dinzelbacher has commented extensively on this case in his 'Ida von Nijvels Brückenvision', *OGE* 52 (1978) 179–94.

159 For this kind of television, see Benz, *Die Vision*, 208–21.

160 *Quinque*, 268 and 272.

161 *Ibid.*, 268–69. More ecstatic televisions by Ida are mentioned in *Quinque*, 259, 261, 264 and 266–67.

162 Dinzelbacher, *Vision*, 48: 'auch des prophetische Schauen kann so bezeichnet werden', as television.

unknown to them'.[163] Ida of Nivelles could see what had happened in the past and what would happen in the future.[164] At one time, she was informed about what wrongs would be done to her and by whom.[165] A short while before Alice of Schaarbeek was stricken with leprosy she received a premonition that she would be afflicted in heart and body but that, having once consummated her martyrdom, she would be able to present herself as a martyr before God.[166] More premonitions, previsions and prophetic visions granted to Cistercian monks and nuns could be mentioned,[167] but the above-mentioned cases illustrate sufficiently the charisms of the *mulieres religiosae* and their use in 'noble service'—as Hadewijch called it—all were part of their following Christ.

---

163 VM, *Visioenen*, 1: 32–33, ll. 391–94. In her second and short vision (VM, *Visioenen*, 1: 38, ll. 2–10) Hadewijch 'saw the will in which they [people] were either in the truth or in falsehood'.

164 *Quinque*, 280: 'vidit praeterita et futura'.

165 *Ibid.*, 284–85: 'aliquando Dominus volens praemuniri eam, in spiritu revelavit ei, quando vel a quibus personis injurias illatas et modum earum sustinere deberet'. Ida told this revelation to her close friends, asking them to be tolerant.

166 *AA SS* June 2: 479,8: 'et quod cordis corporisque afflictione martyrio in se consummato, martyrem se Deo praesentaret'.

167 See, for instance, Roisin, *L'Hagiographie*, 190–92.

CHAPTER ELEVEN

CHRIST IN THE EUCHARIST

T HE LIFE AND MISSION OF JESUS ended in failure with his crucifixion and death. So it seemed from the human point of view. Yet his life, crucifixion and death were a precondition for the realization of God's much vaster plan. That plan called for God's Son to become man and to suffer and to die as a sacrificial lamb for the salvation of all. The Saviour and the saved belong together. By the same token his 'failure' could never be the end. His resurrection and ascension and glorification are also part of what God had in mind when the Son became man. As Archetype of the man who was created to God's image and likeness, Christ in his life, death, resurrection and glorification has an archetypal meaning for man himself. Man's suffering and death—which are inescapable—have significance and value beyond all expectation. The restoration of his God-likeness has not only become attainable, but this whole process now stands under the banner of the glorified Christ, who left the world a memorial to perpetuate his passion, death and glorification throughout the ages. The accounts of what took place at the Last Supper indicate that this memorial is what we call today the Eucharist.

The Eucharist is not a mere symbolic reference to what happened historically on Holy Thursday and Good Friday. The same bloody sacrifice, which took place once, is now offered on the

307

altar in an unbloody, ritual way.[1] Christ's explicit command 'take and eat: this is my body, given for you', points to his true and real presence in the Eucharist.[2] By partaking in the Eucharist, man cooperates with Christ toward the finalization of God's plan of creation and re-creation. In both cases God's position is as immutable as God himself. The weak link lies in man, for a Christian can still become and act as unchristlike and inhuman as any other human being.

The bibliography about the Eucharist is immense, accessible and need not be referred to here. The same could be said about the diverse ways of understanding and interpreting the Eucharist during the later centuries, particularly at the Reformation. The *mulieres religiosae* under consideration here did not witness the proliferation of devotional practices of later times, nor did they know about the exploitation of christian belief by the greed and politics of ecclesiastical and secular authorities in the fifteenth century, which in the end provoked, at least initially, the Reformation.

The Eucharist, 'the ocean of God's love' as Beatrice called it (206,12), was for the *mulieres religiosae* the highest expression of God's desire to have man as a partner in a love-relationship. God had revealed his desire when he was known as Yahweh; he demonstrated it when his incarnate Son ended up in the clutches of death, to rise again and to enter into his glory. He cries it aloud in the Eucharist, when the same God gives himself as food in the com-union, preliminary to everlasting union. The Eucharist is

---

1 Joseph Ratzinger, 'Is the Eucharist a Sacrifice?, *Concilium* 24 (New York, 1967) 66–77.

2 Thomas D.Stanks, 'The Eucharist: Christ's self-communication in a Revelatory Event', *TS* 28 (1967) 27–50; 45: 'Any call from one person to another, and *a fortiori* the call of the bodily-risen Christ who is invisible, must of necessity be embodied in a word or gesture. Christ communicates with us in a fashion conformable to that of a body-person. But the form his communication takes at the Last Supper as encapsulating his whole life is that of self-giving. Christ gives himself under the form of bread and wine.... For the Hebrew mind symbolism does not exclude realism. The sign performs what it signifies. Therefore Christ would have to be present, because the word and gesture signify Christ giving himself'.

'the aqueduct of love' as Ida of Nivelles put it:[3] inviting and demanding a commensurate love on man's part, even if human love is immeasurably less than God's unlimited love, as Hade-wijch pointed out.[4]

The *mulieres religiosae* believed what the Fourth Council of Lateran (1215) taught them:

> Jesus Christ is both priest and sacrifice, whose body and blood are truly contained in the sacrament of the altar under the species of bread and wine; the bread having by the power of God been transubstantiated into the body and the wine into the blood, whereby we receive of his what he received of ours so that the mystery of unity may be perfected.[5]

To say that the *mulieres religiosae* believed this teaching firmly is to put it not only too mildly but also inappropriately. In fact, they had a passion for it, as the following pages will show. Occasionally they would even express precisely what had never yet been stated or at least never so clearly.

All accounts of the institution of the Eucharist indicate that at the consecration the body of the Lord Jesus Christ becomes present in the Eucharist. The transubstantiation itself, however, is effected by God as Trinity. One day, when Ida of Nivelles attended mass and the words of the consecration were pronounced,

> she saw the three persons marvelously and ineffably gathering together on the altar: not under the form of bread, since the Trinity did not become incarnate, but only that the same three persons who cooperated in the incarnation of the Son did so also in the life-giving sacrament of Christ's body. Several days later it happened that wherever she was, Ida knew that the Trinity was present in the way she had seen

---

3 *Quinque*, 250: 'aquaeductus amoris'.
4 See above, Chapter IX, n. 47.
5 The translation is taken from J. Neuner and J. Dupuis, *The Christian Faith*, 203.

earlier. But she could find no words to express this inscrutable mystery. The only way to explain it was to compare it
with the impression made by a seal: as if stamped by a seal,
her soul kept the image of that seal. With the lime of the
most ardent love she was so deeply impressed by the seal of
the Trinity that her spirit became one spirit with God.[6]

In this text, as in so many others, the accent is on personal union
with God.

The *mulieres religiosae* expressed in different ways the different aspects of the Eucharist. At times, they put the stress on 'this
most noble of all sacraments', as did Ida of Leuven's biographer.[7]
Or, like Beatrice, they would speak of 'the sacrament of the
Lord's body' (79,5; 192,6; 238,4), 'the salutary and life-giving
sacrament' (65,13; 67,29; 152,19), or of 'the health-giving sacrament of his body and blood which he left to the human race, both
as a reminder of himself and as a support and travelling provisions in this wandering exile' (95,99). At other times they spoke
of 'the mystery of our redemption' (24,21), 'the price of our
redemption' (206,9;238,5), or 'the revered price of our redemption',[8] 'the salvific mystery of our Redeemer' (67,12).

The Eucharist, this 'treasure of the divine Majesty' according
to Ida of Nivelles,[9] 'the wholesome food' (202,49), 'this heavenly
food' (154,55), was 'the nourishment from the Lord' for Alice of
Schaarbeek;[10] 'the tower of refuge and the castle of protection'
for Ida Lewis, using a metaphor appropriate to the feudal society
she lived in,[11] 'a supreme remedy, special refuge and protection
throughout the laborious struggle of life'. (*Vita* 151, 4). When
Beatrice went to communion she felt 'remade by this salubrious

---

6 *Quinque*, 270–71. The first part, *viz.* the statement that the Trinity effected
the incarnation of the Son, could have come from Bernard's Div 57; SBOp 6/1:
288.
7 *AA SS* April 2: 179,30: 'Sacramentum illud omni sacramento nobilius'.
8 *Ibid.*, 172,6: 'Illud venerandum nostrae redemptionis pretium'.
9 *Quinque*, 274: 'divinae majestatis thesaurum'.
10 *AA SS* June: 480,5: 'dominica refectio'.
11 *AA SS* Oct.13: 112,16: 'frequenter postulans Eucharistiam, Christum sibi
turrim refugii, castellumque'.

sharing in the Eucharist, and immediately began to experience its power by the expulsion of her former torpor and ignorance... and to recognize already in herself then and thereafter the benefits of her Lover and Beloved' (66,33). It made her 'not only stronger but also more spirited in her resistance against the hostile attacks of the vices (151,120). Moreover, 'the spiritual affection and special loving devotion she felt for it [the Eucharist], forbade her abstinence from it' (155,59).

The Lord was Ida Lewis' physician.[12] Ida of Leuven said that 'the Lord's body is medicinal',[13] and Beatrice found in the Eucharist 'medicinal support' (152,24) and 'medicinal nourishment' (160,92). These expressions convey not only physical invigoration.they meant also that the *mulieres religiosae* found in the Eucharist spiritual help and remedies for the integration of all hardships, trials, temptations, feelings of emptiness and similar experiences they had to go through in the course of purification.[14] Above all, the Eucharist is 'the food of eternal life' (67,31), 'the food of immortality'.[15]

---

12 *Ibid.*, 114,14: 'medicus'. The idea of Christ as physician or as medicine, expressing his healing presence was not exceptional in the *mulieres religiosae* movement. The State Library of Berlin has a manuscript probably written at the end of the thirteenth century, perhaps in Lille, now in France, but then still part of Flanders, which speaks of Christ as medicine. See Alfons Hilka, 'Altfranzösische Mystik und Beginentum', *Zeitschrift für romanische Philologie* 47 (1927) 121–70; 121–22. Augustine spoke already of Christ as physician, see J. Courtès, 'Saint Augustin et la médecine', *AM* 1: 43–51; 48–49: 'Le Christ médecin'. Rudolf Arbesmann lists the passages in Augustine's writings where he speaks of Christ as the humble healer and physician: 'Christ the *Medicus humilis* in St. Augustine', *AM* 2; 623–29. See also Gervais Dumeige, *DSp* 10 (1978) 891–901: Médecin (le Christ) and M. Honecker, 'Christus medicus', in *Der kranke Mensch im Mittelalter und Renaissance*, von Wunderli, ed., Studia humariora 5 (Düsseldorf, 1986) 27–43.

13 *AA SS* April 2: 171,5: 'medicinale Dominici Corporis Sacramentum'.

14 Beatrice's biographer comments (81,37) that according to the state of spiritual growth one is in, the Eucharist has different effects, giving 'sweetness to the sucklings and nourishment to the robust'.

15 Ida of Leuven, *AA SS* April 2: 174,12: 'Cibus immortalitatis'. Ignatius of Antioch, martyred in Rome between 97 and 111 A.D. wrote to the Ephesians about the Eucharist as 'the medicine of immortality, the antidote which results, not in dying but in living forever in Jesus Christ'. See Robert Grant, *The Apostolic Fathers* 4 (Camden, New York-Toronto, 1966) 53.

If the *mulieres religiosae* combined a heightened sensitivity and swift pliability to all the demands emanating from the Eucharist and themselves, this trait is due to their conviction that in the Eucharist they came in contact not with something, but with Someone in an encounter or co-inherence that surpasses phenomenological models.[16]

The one encountered so intimately in the Eucharist is no other than the living Christ, the God-Man. When Alice of Schaarbeek attended mass 'she longed for the divine presence and allowed nothing else to occupy her mind and heart'.[17] Ida of Leuven asserted that when she was present at mass, praying and giving thanks, 'her heart enlarged in the presence of the salutary Host'.[18] According to Beatrice, 'this sacrament is nothing else than the true body of Christ, born of the Virgin' (160,86), and when she went to communion, she received 'the life-giving body of the Lord' (67,13;126,40; 151,6), his 'life-giving body and blood' (65,8).

A nun of Ida Lewis' community, intrigued by Ida's extraordinary relation to the Eucharist, asked her what went on in her when she went to communion. She received as answer: 'when I go to communion I feel without doubt (*certius*) that the true humanity as well as the perfect divinity dwell in my mind, transmitting and imparting themselves delightfully to my spirit'.[19] She received then 'the body of Jesus Christ',[20] 'the body of her Redeemer or of her Saviour',[21] 'the body of her Beloved'.[22] One day, when Ida of

---

16 William A. Luijpen, *Existential Phenomenology*, 3rd ed., Duquesne Studies. Philosophical Series 12 (Pittsburg PA-Leuven, 1963), 'Phenomenology of Intersubjectivity', 176–231.

17 *AA SS* June 2: 479,13: 'Tota semper die, ante perceptionem sanctae Eucharistiae, tam magno aestuabat intrinsecus desiderio,... tam vigili thalamum Sponso suo praeparabat intentione, quod nulli rei transitoriae nullique rei mundanae ad penetralia cordis ipsius patuit ingressus'.

18 *AA SS* April 2: 163,19: 'Cor suum in oratione et gratiarum actionibus [dilatavit] in praesentia salutaris Hostiae'.

19 *AA SS* Oct.13: 122,50: 'sentio certius quod et vera humanitas et perfecta divinitas mentem meam inhabitant, seque meo spiritui dulcius conferant et transfundant'.

20 *Ibid.*, 114,24; 117,31; 121,46: 'Corpus Christi'.

21 *Ibid.*, 116,30; 120,40: 'Corpus Redemptoris'.

22 *Ibid.*, 123, 57: 'Corpus dilecti'.

Leuven went to communion she interiorly heard a voice saying: 'This is my Son, my Beloved'.[23] The point is that she and the other *mulieres religiosae* believed unshakably that in the Eucharist they received Christ in his totality, as God and as Man.

Such a total gift on Christ's part demanded a correspondingly total gift of man to God, as has been explained above to some extent.[24] For Beatrice to receive the Lord in the Eucharist meant also to receive grace 'to increase in virtue' (126,43); for the 'deifying sacrament', as she liked to call the Eucharist (66,32; 80, 29; 151,13; 239, 25), could not deify man more than man is freely willing to cooperate in the process.[25] The Eucharist is not merely a reception by a man of the eucharistic Christ, but implies a quite positive effort of man to respond by his own self-gift to Christ's self-gift. 'Christ has given himself to be eaten and to be drunk, as much and as heartily as one wishes it'.[26] When speaking of the Eucharist, Hadewijch stressed both eating and being eaten. One eats the Eucharist to be eaten by Christ, which is another way of saying that sharing in this meal unifies the partners.

> As one eats his flesh and drinks his blood,
> The heart of each devours the other's heart
> One soul thrusts itself impetuously into the other
> As he, who is love, showed us:
> This surpasses all human understanding.[27]

At the time of the *mulieres religiosae*, the celebration of the Eucharist 'which Christ left to his Church throughout the ages as

---

23 *AA SS* April 2: 184, 9. Hearing a voice is an hagiographical topos.

24 See above, Chapter VI, pp. 192-211: Unitive Grace. Any desire or need of man to love God has been built by God himself into the depths of man's being. There is no indication that any of the *mulieres religiosae* we are informed about thought otherwise. However strong a desire man might have to be united with God it can only be a freely willed human response, elicited by God's prior desire to have man united with him in a love-relation.

25 For a theological explanation of this necessary cooperation, see Thomas D. Stanks, 'The Eucharist', *TS* 28 (1967) 27–50.

26 Hadewijch, Letter 22, VM, *Brieven*, 1: 193, ll. 145–47.

27 Poem 16 in Couplets; VM, *Mengeldichten*, 79, ll. 30–34.

a pledge of his love' (126,43), retained its character as a communitarian meal.[28] Listening together to the scriptural readings and worshipping as a community during mass was still the normal way of celebrating the Eucharist.[29] The custom of going privately to communion was not yet common, except for the sick and the dying.[30] This communitarian aspect of the eucharistic celebration was often stressed in the official documents of the Cistercian Order,[31] and in the biographies of Cistercian *mulieres religiosae*.[32]

In the thirteenth century, Cistercian nuns went to communion every Sunday, as did the monks,[33] a relatively high frequency.[34]

---

28 Victor Warnach, 'Symbol and Reality in the Eucharist', *Concilium* 40 (New York, 1969) 82–106; 96–97: 'The mass is not *just* a sacrificial action, it is also a sacrifical meal... constituting a table fellowship among those present, uniting them first with Christ, then through him with one another in the one spiritual body of the Church'.

29 It would be superfluous to describe here the evolution of the celebration of the Eucharist. Scholarly publications are easily available, as of instance, J. A. Jungmann's often reprinted *Missarum Solemnia*, 2 vols. (Vienna 1949), ET by F.A. Brenner and C.K. Riepe, *The Mass of the Roman Rite*, 'a new and [too] abridged edition in one volume' (New York, 1959); *L'Eglise en Priére. Introduction á la Liturgie*, A.G. Martimort ed. (Paris, 1961).

30 P. Browe, 'Wann fing man an die Kommunion ausserhalb der Messe auszuteilen?', *Theologie und Glaube* 23 (1931) 755.

31 Bruno Griesser, 'Die "Ecclesiastica Officia Cisterciensis Ordinis" des Cod. 1711 von Trient' (written between 1130–34), *AC* 12 (1956) 229, n.66: 'In die nativitatis, cene, pasce, pentecostes debent fratres pacem sumere et communicare omni occasione postposita... omnibus vero dominicis diebus qui potuerit'.

32 Alice of Schaarbeek: *AA SS* June 2: 480,12; – Ida of Nivelles: *Quinque*, 209; – Ida Lewis: *AA SS* Oct.13: 115,25; – Ida of Leuven: *AASS* April 2: 182,40.

33 See Griesser, above n.31, and the biographies of the nuns. This weekly communion was one of the reasons why Ida of Nivelles joined a Cistercian community: *Quinque*, 207.

34 Canon 21 of the Fourth Lateran Council (1215) made communion mandatory for all Christians in the West once a year at Easter. For a developed treatment of the frequency of communion in the Middle Ages, see P. Browe, *Die häufige Kommunion im Mittelalter* (Münster/W., 1938). It should be noted that in the thirteenth century local bishops and religious Orders had much freedom to determine their own regulations. The strict centralization of the Roman curia started at the Council of Trent in the sixteenth century, and was only able to impose itself more forcefully only at the end of the Napoleonic wars, when it stepped in and filled the authority gap brought about by the French Revolution which tore apart the fabric of the 'Ancien Régime' in the West.

Ida Lewis identified the reception of the Eucharist so deeply with Sunday that she yearned to die on a Sunday (*dies dominica*), and did, three years later.[35] Novices were allowed to go to communion only three times a year.[36] Ida of Nivelles found this hard. One day she went to the chaplain, asking him to give her communion secretly. He did so when he celebrated mass the next day, while the community was meeting in the chapter room. Ida pretended to suffer from spiritual sloth and said to him that before joining the community she had been told in Nivelles that the Eucharist was very helpful in overcoming this disturbance.[37] Ida of Leuven too felt quite frustrated when she was a novice in Roosendaal. Her biographer mentions that one day she slipped unnoticed into the ranks of the professed nuns and went with them to communion.[38]

The expression 'communion' means what it says: com-union, the union of two as one if and as far as the communicant is open for it. Hadewijch expressed this when she wrote:

He, who gave us himself to be eaten
Thereby made known to us
That true and most intimate love
Is through eating, tasting, and seeing from within.
He eats us while we think we eat him
And, indeed, we do eat him.
But because he remains so unconsumed
And so untouched and so undesired
Each of us remains uneaten
And so far separate from each other.[39]

---

35 *AA SS* Oct.13: 120,40: 'Cumque diem dominicam ad diem sui obitus exoptasset,... desiderium complevit pius Dominus. Ipsam enim [the following] anno tertio, quadam die dominica, de corporis ergastulo liberavit'.

36 This is explicitly mentioned in the biography of Ida of Leuven, *AA SS* April 2: 182,1. One wonders what happened to that papal permission her biographer says (*ibid.*, 180,33) she received when still living in Leuven, allowing her daily communion.

37 *Quinque*, 208–09.

38 *AA SS* April 2: 182,2. The biographer makes it appear as if she had become invisible on that occasion.

39 Poem 16 in Couplets; VM, *Mengeldichten*, 79, ll. 35–44.

Love is a uniting bond which cannot be made uniform, for true love accepts, respects and fosters the intransferable individual uniqueness of the other. In his relations with human beings God respects all they have in common and all that distinguishes them from each other. The impetuous Ida of Leuven, intellectually and culturally so different from the talented Hadewijch, exclaimed one day when she went to communion: 'Let us go and devour God',[40] and her whole biography shows that 'devouring God' meant to her what it meant to Hadewijch.[41] This 'devouring' was a sharing in God's love in time as the beginning of a timeless union with God. As Beatrice's biographer put it:

> By receiving the sacrament of the Lord's body and blood [she] thereby approached—if not yet with the abundance of eternal enjoyment, at least by frequent sharing and communion—the heavenly things to which she always aspired, for this sacrament is nothing else than the body of Christ.[42]

---

40 *AA SS* April 2: 164,22: 'eamus, inquit, et devoremus Deum'. The presentation of the Eucharist as a mutual eating and being eaten is not altogether new. Pierre Courcelle pointed out ('Tradition neo-platonicienne et traditions chrétiennes de la région de dissemblance', *AHDL*, 32 [1958] 12, n.1) that Richard, following Augustine, expressed it in so many words in his *Declarationes nonnullarum difficultatum Scripture* which he wrote for Bernard (PL 196: 262C). Bernard himself (Courcelle, 10, n.3) and Aelred (ibid,.32, n.57) say it also, but less explicitly than Richard. Their reference to the Eucharist is made in connection with the return of the prodigal son (symbolizing man) from the 'land of unlikeness' to 'the land of resemblance'. See also, J. B. Auberger, *L'Unanimité Cistercienne*, 302–05: the restoration of man's original likeness to God in which he was created, is made possible by Christ. In his SC 71.5 (SBOp 2: 217), however, Bernard speaks explicitly about a mutual eating and being eaten.

41 This meaning of 'devouring' is supported by K. Rahner, 'Developing Eucharistic Devotion', in his *The Christian Commitment*, ET by C. Hastings (New York, 1963) 171–294; 189, where he writes that 'theologically the sentence "take and eat, this is my body", is the first and basic proposition of eucharistic theology, and not the sentence "Christ is here present". The food Christ offers is not a thing but himself'. Rahner restates what Maximus the Confessor (d. 662) had expressed earlier: 'The Eucharist, the meal of the Lord, has been constituted to be consumed, not to be contemplated'. See Alain Riou, *Le monde et l'Église selon Maxime le Confesseur*, Théologie historique 22 (Paris, 1973) 113.

It can be safely assumed that Hadewijch, Ida, and Beatrice expressed what the great majority of the *mulieres religiosae* desired when they went to communion. The surviving biographies and writings of the most outstanding among them leave little doubt about the dispositions of the 'silent majority', as they testify equally to a 'silent minority' of mediocre,[43] and sometimes less than mediocre, *mulieres religiosae*[44] inevitably present in any movement.[45]

It is worth noticing that the verbs used in this regard by the *mulieres religiosae* were not limited to eating and devouring. Union with God was their God-given destination. Using other verbs of their vocabulary, the *mulieres religiosae* were, in their way, 'hungry and thirsty' to be united with God, as he himself was, in his way, 'hungry and thirsty' for that same union. Their own existence, the incarnation of God's Son, and the Eucharist brought them closer to attaining that goal.[46]

---

thoroughly biblical'. Christ is present *in order* to be eaten. In her treatise Beatrice speaks of *minne*, Love, wherein she wrote that 'Love's beauty has consumed it [the soul], *minne*'s strength has eaten it up', R-VM, *Seven manieren*, 15, ll. 27–28.

43 About 1262, Thomas of Villers chided his sister Alice, a Cistercian nun in Vrouwenpark, some ten miles north of Leuven for her mediocrity: 'Vos semper pusillanimis et tristis estis, quia sicut dicitis dulcedinem internam non habetis'. Another of her brothers, also a monk in Villers, was the opposite. Though he did not have any extraordinary experiences or visions, he was always joyous and concerned about others. See Edmund Mikkers. 'Deux lettres indites de Thomas, chantre de Villers', *Coll* 10 (1948) 161–73.

44 For instance in the biographies of Ida of Nivelles, *Quinque*, 234 and 242; and of Ida Lewis, *AA SS* Oct. 13 : 116,29.

45 Occasionally biographers would weave into their accounts stories taken from or inspired by *Legendaria*, as when Ida Lewis saw the Lord expressing satisfaction or dissatisfaction when people went to communion (*AA SS* Oct.13: 118,36). It is said that one day she saw an angel taking the consecrated host out of the mouth of someone who had dishonorably received communion (*ibid.*, 118,36). Similar or nearly similar stories can be found in the *Magnum exordium* (ed. Griesser [Rome, 1961]). The purpose of such stories was to inculcate the need of the right dispositions required of the communicant and the celebrant. One day, when Ida of Leuven did not feel her usual delight at mass, she learned afterwards that the priest who had celebrated mass was suspended (*AA SS* April 2: 178,28). For a detailed study of this kind of stories in different settings, see Browe, *Die eucharistischen Wunder des Mittelalters*, 31–44.

46 In her zeal to restore women's equality with men, Caroline Walker Bynum at times in her otherwise well documented study gives a twisted interpretation of

In the thirteenth century, the two high points of the eucharistic celebration were the consecration and the reception of the Eucharist. To stress the consecration, the clergy began to elevate the consecrated bread at the beginning of the thirteenth century,[47] and the Cistercians introduced this custom in 1210.[48] Two factors contributed to the introduction of the elevation: the first was a twelfth-century theological dispute over whether Christ was already present after the consecration of the bread or only after the consecration of the bread and the wine.[49] Consistent with the

---

some phenomena occurring to *mulieres religiosae*. She corrects some conclusions of 'feminists', but she herself projects twentieth-century preoccupations to phenomena occurring in the thirteenth century. Though her paper 'Women Mystics and Eucharistic Devotion in the Thirteenth Century', *Women's Studies* 11 (1984) 179–214, has many correct quotations and references, the 'facts' are too often 'explained' without seeing them in their mystical context and meaning. On p.192, for instance, the question is asked: Why did ecstasy and *humanitas Christi* matter so much to women? Part of the answer seems to be that the women's ecstasy served 'as an alternative to the authority of priestly office'. On the next page the author says that 'the eucharist and the paramystical phenomena that often accompanied it, were substitutes for priesthood in two complementary ways. Firstly, eucharistic ecstasy was a means by which women either claimed "clerical" power for themselves, or by-passed the power of males, or critizied male abuse of priestly authority. Secondly, ecstasy was a means of endowing women's non-clerical status—their status as lay recipients—with special spiritual significance'. Women certainly have reason to complain about the way they were and still are treated, not treated, or mistreated by men, and to request equality between the sexes. The *mulieres religiosae* spoken of in this book, however, would never side with Bynum's interpretations of their behavior. We could contrast this study with Brenda Bolton's saying that 'the *Vitae* of the beguines make it plain that the role of the priesthood was in no danger from feminine zeal.' See Bolton's paper, 'Some Thirteenth-century Women in the Low Countries', *Nederlands Archief voor Kerkgeschiedenis* 61 (1981) 7–29; 7.

47 V.L. Kennedy, 'The Moment of the Consecration and the Elevation of the Host', *MS* 6 (1944) 121–50.

48 *Statuta*, 1210,5: at the elevation of the host, all were to prostrate on their knuckles till after the elevation of the consecrated wine.

49 This question has been treated by Ludwig Höld, 'Der Transsubstantionsbegriff in der scholastischen Theologie des 12. Jahrhunderts', *RTAM* 31 (1964) 230–59, and by J.J. Megivern, *Concomitance and Communion. A Study in Eucharistic Doctrine and Practice*, Studia Friburgensia, N.S. 33 (Freiburg, 1963). The different opinions lingered for quite some time. In the 'distinctio nona' of his *Dialogus miraculorum* (ed. Strange) 2: 185, Caesarius says that Peter Cantor, the famous theologian in Paris (d.1197) did not believe in the transubstantiation before the consecration of both the bread and wine. In a

command of Christ, 'do this in memory of me', the bread and the
wine were consecrated in separate formulas, sacramentally
expressing what happened at the Last Supper and the next day on
the cross. In the Eucharist, at the consecration, the Christ who
becomes present is the risen and glorified Lord whose body and
blood cannot be separated: he is present at the consecration of the
bread. This was clear to Alice of Schaarbeek, who was not
allowed to drink from the chalice because of her leprosy. Her
biographer does not explain it theologically, but instead of speaking of the total presence of the risen and glorified Lord by
concomitance as it is technically called, he has—in accord with
the hagiography of his time—recourse to a voice from heaven
which said:

> My very dear daughter, do not be disturbed and stop com-
> plaining that something of me has been withdrawn from
> you. It quite conforms to true faith, that whoever tastes my
> body should similarly and undoubtedly rejoice for having
> been re-created by my blood. Where a part of me is present,
> my whole self is present. A part should not even be called a
> part, but should be considered as the whole of me.[50]

The elevation was further fostered by the growing desire of the
faithful to see the consecrated host,[51] which led to the introduc-

---

fragment of a later addition to the unfinished *Libri VIII Miraculorum* published
by A.Kaufmann, (*Caesarius von Heisterbach. Ein Beitrag zur Culturgeschichte
des zwölften und dreizehnten Jahrhunderts* [Cologne, 1862] 162–96; 173–74),
Caesarius says that Stephen Langton, archbishop of Canterbury (1207–28) told
his abbot Henry that the transubstantiation took place at the consecration of the
bread. Stephen Langton spent five years (1207–12) in exile in the abbey of
Pontigny, and abbot Henry could have met him there when he went to the
General Chapter.

50 *AA SS* June 2: 480,15: 'Firmae congruit fidei, ut quicumque de corpore
meo gustaverit, similiter et de sanguine gaudeat se indubitabiliter recreari: quia
ubi pars, ibi totum; nec pars potest dici, sed totum debet reputari'.

51 Edouard Dumoutet, *Le désir de voir l'hostie et les origines de la dévotion
au Saint-Sacrement* (Paris, 1926). Gazing at the host was one way of compensat-
ing for the rareness of receiving communion.

tion of the feast of Corpus Christi in 1251,[52] and later to a flood of eucharistic devotions.[53] The consecration received a third emphasis when, about 1200, the custom was introduced of ringing the bells of the church tower at that moment.[54] The Cistercians adopted it in 1214.[55]

Ida of Leuven's biography speaks of a celebrating priest who took his time before elevating the consecrated host. But Ida who felt the presence of the Lord at the right moment went down on her knees, regardless of the moment the bell was rung, and she convinced the priest afterwards to correct his procrastination.[56] According to Ida Lewis' biographer, 'as the mother of John the Baptist felt the presence of the Lord when Mary visited her, so Ida felt the coming of the Lord on the altar'. The chaplain tested the veracity of her perception and secretly ordered the bell to be tolled earlier or later, but Ida could not be deceived by this trick.[57] Whether in church or sick in bed in the infirmary, Ida of Nivelles likewise sensed when the Lord became present on the altar.[58]

---

52 M.C. Hontoir, 'La dévotion au Saint-Sacrement chez les premiers Cisterciens', *Studia Eucharistica* (Antwerp, 1964) 133–55; 152–55. The introduction of the feast of Corpus Christi was especially due to the efforts of Juliana of Cornillon (d.1258) with the support of the monks of Villers and several communities of Cistercian nuns. Together with the older study of J.B. Bertholet, *Histoire de l'Institution de la Fête-Dieu avec la vie des bienheureses Julienne et Eve* (Liège, 1846), see E. Denis, *Sainte Julienne de Cornillon* (Liège, 1927), and especially the articles by C. Lambert on this subject, republished together in *RBen* 79 (1969) 215–315. For a good overview in English, see McDonnell, *The beguines*, 299–319. [An English translation of the life of *Juliana of Mont-Corneillon*, translated by Barbara Newman, is now available (Toronto: Peregrina Press, 1988)—ed]

53 Emile Bertaud, 'Efflorescence du culte eucharistique', *DSp*: 4, 1622–38.

54 N.M. Denis-Boulet, *L'Église en prière* (see above n.29), 402, n.1.

55 *Statuta*, 1214, 16: at the consecration during the community mass the bell in the belfry was to be tolled once, and all, even those who were not present in the church, were to kneel down for a while.

56 *AA SS* April 2: 173,9.

57 *AA SS* Oct. 13: 117,35. Browe, *Eucharistichen Wunder*, 36–40 has some more cases of this kind.

58 *Quinque*, 275: 'Quotiescumque missa celebrabatur, si contingebat eam esse in choro, sive in lecto prae infirmitate jacere, dominum descendentem in altare sentiebat'.

Both Ida Lewis[59] and Ida of Leuven[60] knew when a consecration took place in a nearby church.

Bell or no bell, at the elevation Beatrice 'began to feel his presence within her with immense fervor and devotion. At his presence she melted as though before a strong fire, and she was wholly absorbed like a little drop flowing down into the ocean of love' (206,8). She fainted and laying 'head and body prostrate on the floor, she noticed nothing around her until the mass was over'. At another time, 'at the elevation of the deifying sacrament Beatrice saw a ray of an incomprehensible clarity flashing like lightning from the Lord's sacred body' (239,24). Ida of Leuven had a similar experience when, as a child, she went with her mother to mass.[61] Beatrice's biography mentions also that on one occasion 'she received a command by divine revelation that at the moment of the elevation she should... hold herself in the presence of the divine Majesty, as an advocate for those for whom Christ offered his body on the altar as an appeasing sacrifice to God the Father' (127,47).

The reception of the Eucharist, the eating and being eaten implied therein, so affected the outstanding *mulieres religiosae* about whom we are well informed that it was often accompanied by physical phenomena revealing the intensity of their desire and their love,[62] and at the same time the diverse ways in which it burst out. Hadewijch wrote in her first vision:

---

59 *AA SS* Oct. 13: 117,35: 'Virgo praedulcissima sentiebat adventum Domini descendentis praesentialiter in altare'.

60 *AA SS* April 2: 172,8: When visiting a recluse, Ida suddenly cried out:'the Supreme Pontiff is present' (Summum adesse Pontificem). The recluse opened the wooden panel allowing her to look at the altar where indeed she saw a celebrating priest at the moment of the consecration. The biographer states that this awareness occurred often: 'nec hoc semel aut raro, sed saepe repetitis vicibus'. A similar story is told in the biography of Juliana of Cornillon (*AA SS* April 1: 450,22.

61 *Ibid.*, 158,2. Her biographer called it a *mistica visio*, a vision symbolizing or signifying the Lord's presence.

62 What has been said above, Chapter VI, pp. 168–211, about liberating and unitive grace should be kept im mind for a better understanding of what the Eucharist meant to the *mulieres religiosae*.

It was on a Sunday, the octave of Pentecost,[63] when the Lord was brought to me privately at my bedside. I felt such an attraction of my spirit inwardly that I could not control myself outwardly enough to go among people; it would have been impossible for me to go among them. The desire I had interiorly was to be one with God in fruition.[64]

When Ida Lewis was in the infirmary one day, she greatly desired to receive the Eucharist without delay (*festinanter*). When the priest brought her the Eucharist, she was so affected by the vehemence of her burning desire that she seemed near to death and turned black in the face. It was as if she underwent an ecstasy (*quasi extasim experiens*) and was unable to receive the Eucharist, whereupon the priest took the sacrament back to the church.[65] On another occasion the same Ida

was so taken by her fervor and desire that she could [again] no longer wait for the Eucharist. The vehemence of her madness was so overwhelming that her love, delight, the influx of sweetness or the lavishing of grace were not enough for her heart set on fire. She willed to receive the Lord and God immediately. [66]

Alice of Schaarbeek

longed so strongly to receive communion that by the excessive effervescence of her desire, her veins seemed to suffer violence to the breaking point. The Lord inebriated the heart of his beloved, that no longer aware of what went on, she

---

63 Which in the fourteenth century became Trinity Sunday in the general calendar of the Church.

64 VM, *Visioenen*, 1: 9, ll. 1–9.

65 *AA SS* Oct.13: 115, 25.

66 *Ibid.*, 123, 54: 'erat tanti fervoris spiritus tantique desiderii ut non posset ullatenus prae vehementia furoris animi sui sustinere quod ipsa corpus Domini non haberet'. Hadewijch and Beatrice called this 'furor' *orewoet*, as will be seen below.

seemed to lose control of herself and went into a spiritual dance (*tripudium*).[67]

Alice was not the only one whose veins threatened to burst when she was preparing herself to receive communion. It happened often (*saepius*) that when Ida of Leuven went to mass she began bleeding so profusely from her mouth and nose that a puddle was formed on the pavement.[68]

Of Beatrice we read (193,18) that she was 'so strongly attracted by the bond of that love [of Christ] which surpasses all human understanding that she could scarcely wait for the usual time of communion, but with open heart and oozing veins, as if she were mad (*ac si demens*) from excessive desire, she aspired in a certain wonderful gesture to receive the Lord's saving body'. Some years earlier

she used to aspire so continually for communion with that life-giving body, that when the time for communion came, her mind was not only filled with inner spiritual sweetness,[69] but the delight breaking out in all the members of her

---

67 *AA SS* June 2: 479,11: 'Tanto aliquando affectu in Missarum celebratione ad divinam suspirabat praesentiam, quod ex nimia desiderii scintillatione, totius venae corporis pati violentiam et dirumpi videbantur... tanta mentis exultatione inebriarat cor Dilectae [Alice], quod prae nimio animi tripudio, quid sentiret quidve secum ageretur penitus ignoraret'.

68 *AA SS* April 2: 163,19: 'Ex nimia gratitudine devotionisque supereffluenti dulcedine...ex ore simul et naribus tanta sanguinis abundantia confestim erumpendo coepit effluere quod ipsum quoque pavimentum ecclesiae visus sit in multa copia...irrigasse'.

69 *Vita*, 79,10: 'spirituali dulcedine'. The writings and biographies of *mulieres religiosae* speak often of sweetness, preceded by such adjective as 'spiritual'. This sweetness is a metaphor indicating a spiritual delight and is used by Scripture, the liturgy, the Fathers of the Church and the *mulieres religiosae*'s mentors. Other expressions are *suavitas, dulcis, jucundus, benigitas, laetitia, deliciae*, all referring to God's sweetness (*dulcedo Dei*). Psalm 33:9, God's *dulcedo*, is a recurrent theme in the writings of Cistercians and Victorines (among the latter especially Richard). See Dumontier, *Saint Bernard et la Bible*, 185, q.v. *Gustate*. This psalm verse translated from the Ugaritic (Mitchel Dahood, *Psalms 1–50*. The Anchor Bible 16 [Garden City NY] 1966, 204) runs as follows: 'Taste and drink deeply, for Yahweh is sweet'. Ida of Nivelles' sixth contemplation was about God, not only because of his creation and his gifts

body, like an inebriating nectar, made her move excitedly in a kind of spiritual dance.... She showed her heart's desire by the melting of her heart, the abundance of her tears or her unusual unrestrained laughter. By such tokens she showed her interior feelings however much she willed to resist.[70]

The visions some *mulieres religiosae* occasionally had at the consecration or when receiving the Eucharist could, [71] at times, put them in embarrassing situations. One Christmas—a day when three masses were celebrated—Ida of Nivelles, being sick, took her place in the stalls reserved for the infirm.

During the midnight mass, when the priest elevated the host, she saw that he held in his hand a very beautiful, newly born child and she was seized with fear and trembling. She had never desired to see him in human form, thinking that her faith would prove deficient in her belief in the mystery of this wonderful sacrament... but the Lord assured her and told her to put all scruples aside. When the second mass was celebrated she again took a seat in the place reserved for the infirm. At the consecration she again saw the child in the priest's hands. She stood up with the others to proceed to the reception of the Eucharist, but hesitated and went with

---

bestowed on man, but also because he is in himself ineffably good and he let her experience his *suavitas* (*Quinque*, 276). Sweetness and its equivalents have nothing to do with sweets tasted by the mouth. All the quotations from the *mulieres religiosae* in this context refer to their experience of 'tasting' God's sweetness. For a good summary on this subject, see Jean Chatillon. 'Dulcedo. Dulcedo Dei', *DSp* 4: 1777–95. See also Friedrich Ohly, 'Geistige Süsse bei Otfried', *Typologia literarum. Festschrift für Max Mehrly* (Zurich, 1969) 85–124, reprinted in *Schriften zur Mittelalterlichen Bedeutungsforschung* (Darmstadt, 1977) 93–127, and the study covering several centuries by Henri de Lubac, *Exégèse médiévale* 1/2 (Paris, 1959) 599–620, or R. Kereszty, 'Die Weisheit in der mystischen Erfahrung beim hl. Bernhard von Clairvaux', *Citeaux* 14 (1963) 6–24; 105–34; 185–201.

70 *Vita*, 79,8.

71 Hadewijch, for instance, not infrequently had ecstasies and visions related to the Eucharist. See Reynaert, *Beeldspraak*, 117.

lagging feet back to her place, not being able 'to eat the infant'.

She asked her Lover and Beloved to temper these wonderful visions so she might receive communion without impediment. Remaining in the church till the third mass she saw Christ again, this time somewhat older, coming to her from the altar to embrace and to kiss her: 'If I show you my humanity', he said, 'this is not because I doubt your faith, but to show you the zeal of my love for you'.[72] Afraid to scandalize her sisters by abstaining again from communion on this solemn feast, she asked to be able to receive Christ's body without difficulty. The vision disappeared and she was able to receive 'peacefully the author of peace'. This experience touched her so deeply that she remained 'inebriated' till the feast of Candlemas [2 February].

The biographies give no hint of any initiation into or imitation of such psychosomatic phenomena,[73] nor is there any indication that they took collective proportions, except perhaps in Rameya, as we shall see below. Some biographers' accounts assume that these phenomena were signs of the sanctity of the *mulier religiosa* they were writing about, but by themselves these effects do not indicate a higher degree of holiness. They are incidental, outwardly disturbing happenings related to the fieriness of the nuns' desire to be united with Christ, which was sometimes so

---

72 *Quinque*, 251–53. Siegfried Ringler made the pertinent remark that visions of the child in the consecrated host are too easily discarded as products of stirred up (*erregter*) imagination of women or as theologically unacceptable nonsense. In fact, it is a literary topos with a specific meaning: at the consecration, the second person of the Trinity is personallly present. See S. Ringler's 'Die Rezeption mittelalterlicher Frauenmystik als wissenschaftliches Problem, dargestellt am Werk der Christine Ebner', P. Dinzelbacher and D.R. Bauer eds, *Frauenmystik im Mittelalter* (Ostfildern, 1985) 178–200; 183–84.

73 C. Walker Bynum's *Jesus as Mother* (see above, Chapter VIII, n.68), 180, n.1, says that 'thirteenth-century women mystics, especially in the Low Countries, were more likely than their male counterparts to cluster together in a few well-known houses, to belong to spiritual networks, and to become subjects of admiring biographies that propagated a spirituality based on mysticism'. The examples given in the footnotes do not justify this deduction, which seems too sweeping. The monks of Aulne, Ter Duinen, and especially Villers were more 'clustering' than any community of nuns or groups of beguines.

strong that their sensory perceptions were obscured or at least out of focus. In other words, these women were so swept away by the overwhelming love of Christ and their own consuming longing for him that they fainted. Moreover this process has variations, depending on the women's physical strength, health, and the level of their psychic growth, as an in-depth study of other biographies would show.

Since the *mulieres religiosae* considered in these pages were nearly all Cistercian nuns, a word about the prescribed ritual for the reception of the Eucharist will help clarify the disturbances caused by the psychosomatic phenomena. Though they went to communion as a community,[74] the nuns not only realized that in the Eucharist they received Christ, their Lord and God in person, as is explicitly stated by Ida Lewis,[75] but they were also conscious of a deep interpenetration occurring between the Lord and each of them personally.

When the celebrating priest and his assistants had taken or received communion under both species, the celebrant went to the right, *viz.* the epistle side, of the altar to distribute the consecrated bread.[76] The deacon and the sub-deacon went to the left,

---

74 This does not exclude some *mulieres religiosae* not having a clear perception of the communitarian aspect of the Eucharistic meal. A case in point is Ida of Leuven. One day, in Roosendaal, the Lord told her at mass that he would totally come into her heart when she went to communion, and would do the same with the other nuns. The unschooled (*ignara*) Ida wondered how Christ could enter totally in the others and at the same time into her. The Lord told her that 'in opposition to what happens in the physical order, he would not be split in parts but could totally infuse himself into the hearts of all those who desire him piously. What is impossible to nature is not to God' (*AA SS* April 2: 182, 40). This small vignette shows that Ida, who had refused a school education, was not only ignorant but also naive and credulous, and the same could, unfortunately, be said of her biographer. Contemporary *Legendaria* indicate even more how ignorance was a fertile soil for naivité and credulosity.

75 *AA SS* Oct.13: 123,54: ' Ipsum Dominum et Deum [percepit] praesentialiter'.

76 The 'eating' of the Lord's body was realistic in the sense that the 'hosts' were not little white wafers to be swallowed, but bread to be eaten. Ida of Leuven's biography (*AA SS* April 2: 182,2) mentions that she 'dentium officio masticavit', with her teeth she chewed the consecrated bread. The use of unleavened wafers began, to the scandal of the Greek branch of Christianity, in the ninth century in the Western Church 'to facilitate the reverent handling of

or gospel side, with the chalice and the gilded silver pipe (*fistula*) through which the consecrated wine had to be sucked. The nuns first stood in line, according to seniority, at the entrance to their choir, and when the first nun had received the kiss of peace from the sub-deacon, she gave it to the next sister and so it went down the line. There were no grills or altar rails at that time, and the nuns went up in single file to the right side of the altar. There they received the consecrated bread, walked around behind the altar—which was free-standing—and on the gospel-side received the consecrated wine. As they made their way back to choir, each took a sip of unconsecrated wine from a cup which the sacristan, who stood waiting at the choir's entrance, provided as an ablution after communion.[77]

One day, when Ida of Nivelles went to communion, 'her soul became inebriated by such a sweetness of delight that she had to make a great effort to return to the choir'.[78] She was not always able to return to the choir, for she would be, 'as usual', rapt in ecstasy.[79] 'Realizing what a treasure of the divine Majesty she had received, she immediately fell on the floor and lay there a long time', disrupting the regular order. Blamed by her friends for being a cause of scandal to some of her sisters, she claimed that 'she had no power to act otherwise. If she were to fall straight into hell, she could in no way have avoided it'.[80]

---

the sacramental species', See Frank C. Senn, 'The Lord's Supper, not the Passover Seder', *Worship* 60 (1986) 362–68; 364.

77 For a brief overview of this ceremony, see Fulgence Schneider, *L'Ancienne Messe Cistercienne* (Tilburg, 1929) 201–09.

78 *Quinque*, 246: 'Tanta suavitatis dulcedine amima ejus inebriata est, quod grandis fuit ei labor chorum intrare'. Her biographer sometimes used figurative language to express her inebriating union with Christ: 'She passed from the refectory of the salvific Eucharist to the spiritual dormitory and, alienated from her bodily senses, "went to sleep", most happily resting in the arms of her Bridegroom', *ibid.*, 274.

79 *Quinque*, 267. *CCH*, 224 published a sentence left out by C. Henriquez, which says that when Ida had drunk from the cup she became so greatly inebriated that she lost control over her body.

80 *Quinque*, 274–75.

Ida Lewis, a nun of the same community of Rameya, one day received communion under both species,[81] and two nuns could barely bring her back to the choir. It happened frequently that she was too absorbed to return to choir in accord with the prescribed rite. Because other nuns acted this way also, the community decided that those who could not return in an orderly way should no longer go to the altar to receive communion.[82] With great grief, the nuns involved gave priority to obedience. The biographer comments on this decision by referring to a philosopher who had said: 'Who is going to impose a law to lovers? Love is unto itself a greater law'. The decision of the community seems to have been in effect for a year, and during that time Ida made 'spiritual communions'. 'You know, Lord', she said, 'that I do not dare to come to you [in the Eucharist], but you are free to come to me'. Each Sunday he visited her 'sweetly and divinely', giving her the taste and sweetness she had enjoyed when she went to communion.[83] Some time later, she went up to the altar and when she had received the Eucharist she became unable to stand on her feet. Falling flat on her back, she lay there for quite some time. When they tried to lift her up, she was so stiff that her body could not be bent and she was later transported to her bed.[84]

---

81 *AA SS* Oct. 13: 113,19. Remi De Buck, who published her biography, said (*ibid.*, 114, n.9) that there is no evidence that she ever drank the consecrated wine. The text, however, mentions that she went up to the altar to receive the Eucharist and was 'nourished (*impinguata*) by the marrow of wheat and inebriated by the wine'. De Buck may have interpreted this sentence as a figure of speech, which it is, but does not necessarily exclude what is signified. Cistercian nuns would in any case have followed the Order's custom.

82 *AA SS* Oct.13: 113,19: 'perpenditque sententia generalis inter ipsas, ut quaecumque non redirent ordinate de altari, nullatenus accedere praesumerent ad altare'.

83 *Ibid.*, 113,20. K. Rahner, (*The Christian Commitment*, 195–98) supports the 'spiritual communion' in the way Ida did.

84 *Ibid.*, 117,31. Ida was thirteen when she joined the community some years before 1225. See A. Steenwegen, 'De gelukz. Ida de Lewis', *OGE* 57 (1983), 221. She went at least once to communion under both species. This custom diminished in the thirteenth century. M.J. Van Baest, *De Fierheid als kernmoment...van Hadewijch*, 50, n.27) refers to Alexander of Hales (d.1245) who said it was customary for laypeople to receive communion under one species. The Cistercians decided in 1261 (*Statuta*, 1261,9) that because of 'pericula gravia', monks, laybrothers and nuns would henceforth have to abstain from partaking of

Asked if she did not feel pain in her head because she had fallen backwards, she replied that she felt it later, not at the moment it happened.[85] Like the other two Idas, Ida of Leuven too was so overcome when she went to communion that she fainted and afterwards had to go to bed 'burning with the fire of love, weakened in body but very sound in mind'.[86] Before and after she joined the community of Roosendaal, overwhelmed with 'a special copious sweetness', she was unable to move and fell frequently on her back. Some people, whom the biographer does not specify, became envious and believed or made themselves believe that she did it out of vainglory or to attract attention, a suspicion which is not supported by her biography. Ida asked in her prayers and was granted not to faint any more.[87] She was already in Roosendaal when one day, having received communion, her heartbeat raced and,

---

the consecrated wine. It is unlikely that the 'sententia generalis' of the nuns of Rameya, quoted above in n.82, refers to the General Chapter of 1261. Before that year, the expression 'to receive the body of the Lord' did not mean receiving the consecrated bread only. Ida of Leuven's biographer, who wrote after 1261 had to mention communion under both species when he reported that in her great desire to drink from the cup, she started bleeding in mouth and nose and was unable to drink. See *AA SS* April 2: 164,21: 'tam fortissimo desiderio mox ex eo [calice] bibere concupivit... in tantum ei fraena laxaverit, ut impetuoso suo conamine, confestim ex ejus ore simul et naribus, immensos cruoris rivos excuteret...ob nimiam sanguinis effusisonem,...ad perceptionem Hostiae salutaris... efficere non praevaluit'.

85 *AA SS* Oct. 13: 120,44: 'Respondit dulcius, quod ad horam illam non doluit, nec sensit penitus casum illum, sed aliquanto tempore post elapso, laesionem in capite sensit gravitatem'.

86 *AA SS* April 2: 175,16: 'Amoris dumtaxat incendio conflagrata, caritatisque delicioso vulnere sauciata, corpore quidem languida, sed mente sanissima, feliciter inter dilecti sui brachia conquievit'. Without questioning Ida of Leuven's soundness of mind, the expression 'mente sanissima', used here and in the text quoted below in n.88, could as well have been taken from Beatrice's biography, where the same wording appears (191,45). Ida's biographer made frequent use of Beatrice's biography.

87 *Ibid.*, 180,32: 'ut sacratissimae Communionis hora, qua veneranda libamina foret annuente Domino post futuro tempore perceptura, virium siquidem corporalium non deficerent, sed potius ascrescerent adjumenta, devotissimis precibus omnipotentis Dei magnificentiam exoravit. Qui clementer illius precibus annuens, in hora Communionis, ex tunc in antea, vitae vires corporales ei attribuit'.

panting, she had to sit down behind the altar 'exhausted in body but sound in mind', unable to proceed or incapacitated to drink from the ablution cup.[88]

Beatrice often experienced ecstasies and, not surprisingly, had them also when she went to communion. Then 'she forthwith lost the use of her exterior senses so that she could neither walk nor do any work with her hands'.[89] The biographer mentions (81,35) that after several years (between 1225 and 1231): 'in a second stage, as often as she approached this life-giving sacrament, she experienced the divine strength in herself and quickly recovered from all sickness, if she had any, by receiving the spiritual food and by being visited by divine grace'. In 1232 she seems to have gone back to the 'first stage'.

> Going to communion and tasting the Eucharist, her bodily senses failed and she fell to the floor since her feet could not support her, or keep her standing or let her advance further. Therefore the nun who was her usual nurse in sickness, went to her and held her up in her arms lest she fall. She guided her through the choir, but when she had gone half way, she could no longer hold Beatrice up since she was bereft of all her bodily senses, and so [the nurse] left Beatrice prostrate full length on the floor until she returned to herself. When Beatrice did return to herself, the nun led her to the infirmary and put her to bed, where she rested with the Lord all day long in tranquil peace of conscience, in exultant jubilation, drunk with inestimable sweetness of mind.[90]

Some time later she seems to have been back in the 'second stage', for 'Beatrice received from the Eucharist much strength of

---

88 *Ibid.*, 184,10: 'nequaquam ad Vini libationem ex calice percipiendam, ut moris est communicantibus, appropinquare valuit: sed post altare cum ingenti labore se transferens, ibidem infirmata quidem corpore, sed mente sanissima decubuit'.

89 *Vita*, 80,20. The biographer made the remark that her joy was combined with thankfulness: 'she used to melt with enormous gratitude as often as she approached this sacrament to communicate'.

90 *Vita*, 194,34.

heart and body to support more evenly the weight of heavenly delights. Formerly she had failed under this wholesome food, totally wearied in body by it. But afterwards refreshed by it, she used to arise stronger to carry the weight of divine visitation, which is beyond every bodily sense, but also more lively and brisk'.[91]

Ida Lewis, 'her heart set on fire, and longing with such a vehement madness to receive the God-Man could not wait to receive communion',

> but when she had received him who includes everything (*habens habentem omnia*), she wanted nothing more and nothing else.Her body was then perfectly subjected to her spirit and her spirit enjoyed the greatest peace. The unspeakable delights which reigned in her heart prevented her from sleeping for several nights.[92]

However exceptional these faintings and ecstasies might be, they do not look like self-induced syncopes. They began and ended, not at the command of the *mulieres religiosae* themselves but by the powerful invasion and retreat of the divine. At times the women requested that these effects cease. The psychosomatic happening itself was visible and open to criticism, but the accent should be placed not on the *soma* or body but on the *psyché* which could not always stand the weight of the spiritual delights. These lovers were so eager to eat Christ in the Eucharist and to be eaten by him that it became more than their bodies and their hearts could take.

It was perhaps in relation to these psychosomatic effects that a nun in Ida Lewis' community talked with her often about the Eucharist. One day she asked Ida how long the sacred species remained, once the words of the consecration were pronounced. From Ida's answer one can see that the question referred, in fact, to the presence of the Lord, once the consecrated bread was eaten,

---

91 *Ibid.*, 204,42.
92 *AA SS* Oct. 13: 123,54. Earlier (*ibid.*, 115,24) the biographer remarked that God did not mean to put an end to her enjoyment, but wanted to teach her where to draw the line: 'voluit Deus non metam imponere gaudiis, sed mensuram'.

for she replied simply: 'When I receive God [in the Eucharist], after a short while I feel his coming over into my soul; but he is not carried away by the time-bound food into the parts of the body'—meaning here the digestive tract.[93]

On several occasions the desire of some *mulieres religiosae* to receive communion gave rise to stories about receiving the Eucharist from Christ himself,[94] or from a suddenly appearing hand,[95] or from a dove,[96] or from an angel,[97] or in some other strange way.[98] One finds similar stories in the *Legendaria* in circulation; the biographers kept the central idea of the Eucharist as an exceptional gift, but inserted it into the biographies in their own version of *mirabilia*. This hagiographical pattern served both

---

93 *Ibid.*, 122,49: 'Quando Deum recipio, brevis spatio temporis ipsum animam sentio subeuntem ad partes corporis per cibi limites corporalis'. This text is open for an alternative translation: 'when I go to communion, for a short while I feel God penetrating my soul after the manner of bodily food [penetrating] to the [digestive] parts of the body. De Buck, who published the biography in the *AA SS* (Paris, 1883) has 'nec translatum ad mentem corporis' and refers in the margin to the 'ad partes', whereas Henriquez in his *Quinque*, (xv–xvi) says that he used the same manuscripts and another which has since disappeared. His text indicates, as usual, only one reading: 'ad partes corporis' ('the digestive tract'). According to K. Rahner 'it can be difficult for ascetics and mystics to confine themselves only to the theses of systematic theology which have been defined by the magisterium or are otherwise beyond doubt. See his *Theological Investigations* 4, 'On the duration of the Presence of Christ after Communion', 312–20; 313. Ida put in a short sentence what Rahner explained in nine pages.

94 Mens, *Oorspong*, 232, n.37 mentions several instances. In her first vision Hadewijch saw Christ giving her communion in heaven (VM, *Visioenen* 1: 79, ll. 60–74). Paul Mommaers treated this visionary communion in *OGE* 49 (1975) 105–31; 116–17. Herbert Thurston, *The Physical Phenomena of Mysticism*, speaks in this regard of *telekinesis* (141–61), or 'the alleged transference of the Host through the air by some unexplained agency from the altar or the hand of the officiating priest to the lips of the expectant communicant'. While he does not reject *a priori* the possibility of such transference, he admits for certain that 'fraud and hysterical delusion have often availed themselves of similar manifestations to establish a very ill-deserved reputation'.

95 Ida of Nivelles, *Quinque*, 220–21: 'Apparuit ei manus quaedam, quae sanctam Eucharistiam tradidit ei'.

96 Ida of Nivelles, *ibid.*, – Ida of Leuven, *AA SS* April 2: 173,12.

97 Ida of Leuven, *AA SS* April 2: 163,20. A variant shows up in A. Kaufmann's *Caesarius von Heisterbach*, 177, where the same happening is told of a certain Ida, said to be living in Brussels.

98 Browe, *Die eucharistischen Wunder des Mittelalters*, 21–31.

to edify the readers and to stimulate awe for the Eucharist and a greater appreciation for the eucharistic-oriented heroines. Though such stories have no significance as far as the Eucharist itself is concerned, they show at least what the imagination of some writers of those and later times would do to stress the real and exceptional eucharistic devotion of the *mulieres religiosae* and similar people.[99]

Another consequence of the bodily impact of the Eucharist on the *mulieres religiosae* was their reluctance or inability to take ordinary food afterwards. There are mild cases as when Beatrice, often enraptured and physically weakened, would 'like the mad and insane, apply her sense and her mind to take some food only under external coercion or rebuke' (159,80). On the feast, Alice of Schaarbeek was deeply moved by the ascension of the Lord,[100] and [after communion] declined to eat before evening because her heart was full of great jubilation.[101]

There were also more pronounced instances of repugnance and incapacity to take food after communion. Ida Lewis said that when she had received the Eucharist she 'wanted nothing more and nothing else',[102] and this has to be taken literally: she did not and could not take ordinary food. One time she lost all appetite from Wednesday in Holy Week till Low Sunday, i.e. for twelve days.[103] On another occasion, the nurse concerned about her physical condition put a piece of meat into her mouth when she seemed to come out of a rapture, but 'inebriated with delightful nectar, she went to sleep again', and the morsel remained between her teeth.[104] At times, she was simply incapable of

---

99 Possibly some *mulieres religiosae* had such 'experiences' because they knew such stories through reading or hearing.

100 See above, Chapter VIII, n.74.

101 *AA SS* June 2: 480,19: 'Prae nimia cordis adhuc jubilo terrenis refici renuit, sed usque ad coenam jejunavit'.

102 *AA SS* Oct.13: 123,54: 'Sed cum ipsum susceperat, habens habentem omnia, nihil umquam ulterius requirebat'.

103 *Ibid.*, 117,35: 'A quarta vero feria ante Pascha, tota illa hebdomada et etiam subsequenti...tantis refecta gaudiis laetabatur, quod amittebat penitus ciborum corporalium appetitum'.

104 *Ibid.*, 118,36: 'bucellan carnium in ore retinens, obdormivit iterum jocundo nectare debrieta'.

eating.[105] When chided about it, she replied: 'how can you believe that a mouthful of bread could enter my body when I am so full with God's sweetness that not even a hair could go through?'[106] Another time at the insistence of the nurse she took a little food, but could not sleep the following night. On one Ascension day she was so filled with joy and delight that she could not eat at all. The next day she tried five times and could absorb only a tiny bit.[107] Ida of Leuven had the same troubles in eating. At some time, 'wounded by the dart of love' she could not take any food for thirteen days.[108] When she had received communion, ordinary food simply disgusted her,[109] or she could only take a little bit in the evening.[110] Other anecdotes are mentioned in her biography.[111]

---

105 *Ibid.*, 121,45; 121,46: 'Manducare minime potuit'. In medical terms this is called *anorexia (mentalis)*: people, who become emotionally so taken that through an irresistible impulse they cannot eat or refuse to eat.

106 *Ibid.*, 121,49: 'Quomodo creditis panis bucellam in corpus proprium introire, in quod capillus minimus prae multitudine Dei dulcedinis nullatenus subingredi praevaluit?'

107 *Ibid.*, 122,51: 'Tentans quinquies si posset aliquatenus aliquid cibi sumere, sed nec pro toto nisibus se vincere praevaluit, nisi parum'.

108 *AA SS* April 2: 167,35: ' vulnerata amoris spiculo... continuo tredecim dierum spatio...solo per id temporis amoris nutrita ferculo, caput a lectulo non levavit'.

109 *Ibid.*, 183,3: 'ipsum [cibum] cum taedio simul et maxima cordis angustia degustavit'.

110 *Ibid.*, 185,12: 'Jejuna permansit usque post solis occubitum... et tunc quidem, alieno quam suo potius acquiescens desiderio, cibi sumpsit permodicum'. Similar stories are told in the *Dialogus miraculorum* of Caesarius of Heisterbach and in other collections. Several are spoken of by Browe, *Die eucharistischen Wunder*, 44–55. Thurston, speaking of 'The Mystic as Hunger-Striker' (*The Physical Phenomena*, 341–62) in the thirteenth and later centuries, indicates cases in which the revulsion toward food, as in Ida Lewis and Ida of Leuven, seems to be only token when compared with that of women of later times. Thurston writes that 'in these states of mystical union, the normal function of sentient and nutritive processes of the body often seems to be profoundly altered, or at any rate partially inhibited', adding (343–44) the remark that 'similar symptons are common in hysterical disorders'. In his *Holy Anorexia* (Chicago-London, 1985) Rudolph M. Bell studies anorexia as it occurred in Italy, especially in Umbria and Tuscany, from the thirteenth till the twentieth centuries. The cases presented confirm the remarks made by Thurston.

111 The biographer at times wove some 'fioretti' into the biography: when still a *muliere religiosa* in Leuven, Ida went one day to church and called the

The psychosomatic phenomena and other circumstances related to the Eucharist should not distract us from the basic and essential element: the encounter with Christ himself. Or, to put it another way, these phenomena were only side effects, outward reflections of what went on inside the heart of these women. The expression 'encounter' can mean a merely passing meeting with somebody, but in no way renders the full intimacy, depth, and union that occurred between Christ and the *mulieres religiosae*. Theirs was a relation between a divine Bridegroom and a human bride, wherein both were seeking a personal, loving interconnection. They looked at Christ as their Bridegroom who came in the Eucharist as the God-Man with his divine and human love for his brides. A routinely performed eucharistic ritual was unthinkable to them. Alice of Schaarbeek spent the whole day before her Sunday's communion 'preparing with watchful intention the bedroom of her heart for the reception of her Bridegroom'.[112] Their relation with Christ in the Eucharist was as intense as it was intimate. Using verse 2:9 of the Song of Songs, Hadewijch wrote in her sixteenth Poem in Couplets:

> He who is secured by this bond [of love]
> Can eat his fill
> If he wishes to know and to taste
> Thoroughly beyond his dreams.
> The bond of love makes known what is meant by:
> 'I to my Beloved and my Beloved to me'.[113]

Conscious that their Bridegroom was Christ, the God-Man, some *mulieres religiosae* wished to receive him ceremoniously. When Lutgard went up to the altar, she is said to have been

---

chirping bids of both sexes to church where they followed the service quietly and intently, till Ida gave them permission after the gospel to fly away (*AA SS* April 23: 166,30). When she happened to see a girl folding corporals, she started to feel hot inside herself (*ibid.*, 170,45). At another occasion Ida saw her soul as if it were a great temple in which Christ proceeded to the altar, surrounded by a phalanx of beautifully dressed assistants and chanters (*ibid.*, n. 180,34).
112 *AA SS* June 2: 479,13. The text has been quoted in n.17 of this Chapter.
113 VM, *Mengeldichten*, 79, ll. 45–50.

accompanied by two angels as bridesmaids, and on another occasion by Mary and John the Baptist.[114] Ida of Leuven 'rejoicing greatly in the presence of her Bridegroom', went up to the altar and said to him 'If my bridegroom were a fuller or a peasant or a mechanic he would not let me go to the betrothal banquet without a retinue. How can you, to whom I am engaged as a bride, bear to let me come to you without a decent and graceful company?'. Her request did not fall on deaf ears, for according to the biographer, Mary and John the Evangelist appeared to escort her to the altar.[115]

When Ida of Nivelles had to pass in front of the altar where the pyx with the Eucharist was kept for emergencies,[116] she started to shake and her entrails began to tremble.[117] Likewise, when Ida Lewis had to cross over to the priest's choir, the succor (*consolatio*) she felt radiating from the ciborium was so strong that—in accordance with her emotions—her face looked rosy or pale.[118] Ida of Leuven, still a *mulier religiosa* in Leuven went one day to church and greeted Christ in the Eucharist with 'Hail, kind, gentle and sweet Jesus'. He saluted her in return by knocking on the pyx so hard that a strong sound reverberated from it.[119] At another time she went to a church, and when she found herself alone there, she became bold enough to lower the suspended pyx on to

---

114 *AA SS* June 4: 203,39.

115 *AA SS* April 2: 148,8: ' O Domine, si sponsum aliquem aut fullonem haberem aut rusticum, aut cujuscumque mechanici operis architectum, non sine ducatu familiariter obsequente sponsale tenderem ad convivium, quanto magis et me...tuo tamen sponsalitio subarrhatam, absque venusto comitatu non decet incedere.... et ecce Regina virginum ad dextram illius apparuit, ad laevam vero ille discipulus, cui Christus in cruce Matrem virginem virgini commendavit'.

116 In Ida's time the pyx, usually made in the form of a dove, was suspended above the altar. See Archdale King, 'Eucharistic Reservation in Cistercian Churches', *Coll* 20 (1950) 114–27; 243–49.

117 *Quinque*, 275: 'tremebat et concutiebantur interius omnia viscera ejus'.

118 *AA SS* Oct.13: 117,32: 'Quotiens virgo nobilis seu lente seu celeriter juxta chorum sacerdotum transmeabat, consolatio spiritus ipsi sic de ciborio mittebatur ut facies ejus exterior, quandoque rosea, quandoque pallida, motum sequens intrinsecus, videretur'.

119 *AA SS* April 2: 172,6: 'Ave, inquiens, benigne, pie et dulcis Jesu... quo dicto, ictus quidam validus ipsum pyxidem ab interiori suae parte vehementius impulit, sonum faciens validum et excussum ...vice resalutationis'.

the altar, press it to her heart and kiss it. In her impulsiveness she tried to open it but was unable to do so.[120]

The psychosomatic effects of, and the sometimes unusual behavior around, the Eucharist do not show any indication of being induced or simulated to attract attention by an ostentatious self-display. In the preceding pages we heard Hadewijch speak of her aloneness or of being abandoned. Alice of Schaarbeek, as soon as she became a leper, received what was available at that time: not preventive or curative medical prescriptions, but sequestration. It is frequently said of the others that they sought solitary places to relish their experiences or to ruminate about God's love.[121] The three Idas did.[122] When Beatrice returned from her stay in Rameya, her sisters complained because her desire for solitude deprived them of her comforting presence.[123] To cool off emotionally or undisturbedly to digest her experiences she often went to her 'secret place' (201,13; 207,28 and 35; 220,29) and was not always displeased when she had to stay in the infirmary where a greater tranquillity prevailed (190,129). When Ida of Nivelles felt she was dying she asked to be left alone, except for her abbess and nurse,[124] while Ida Lewis asked the nurse to cover her face with a veil after she had received for the last time on earth—while dying—'the body of her Beloved'.[125]

Well aware that they were created to God's image and likeness, they realized that, thanks to Christ, they were able to have the

---

120 *Ibid.*, 178,27. Chapter 20 of the Fourth Lateran Council (1215) had ordered the pyx to be kept under lock and key. Since Ida's attempt did not take place in Roosendaal, and the Cistercians adopted the Lateran rule in 1238 (*Statuta*, 1238,1), this date helps to determine whether she joined this community before 1238.

121 It has been pointed out that for them relationships with people were often felt to be annoying. See Dinzelbacher, *Vision*, 152: 'die charismatische Begnadeten [empfunden] an dem Umgang mit dem Menschen oftmals Überdruss'.

122 Ida of Nivelles, *Quinque*, 288–89; – Ida Lewis, *AA SS* Oct.13: 114,23; 116,31; 120,43; 121,48; 123,57; – Ida of Leuven, *AA SS* April 2: 181,36; 182,15; 185,15.

123 *Vita*, 60,20: 'amica solitudinis'.

124 *Quinque*, 289.

125 *AA SS* Oct.13: 123,57: 'cum dilecti corpus recepero, velare faciem nostro velamine memor sitis'.

damaged divine image restored and the likeness recovered. The gateway to restoration was opened by Christ and by means of the Eucharist the *mulieres religiosae* passed through it on their way to never-ending union with the One, Trinitarian God. It is remarkable that all six of the *mulieres religiosae* considered in these pages expressed their burning desire for just that: oneness with the Trinitarian God, an aspect which will be more closely considered in Chapter Seventeen.

It has already been mentioned that Alice of Schaarbeek, a decaying leper, felt 'clothed with the Godhead... all the time wrapped in divine embraces'.[126] After one of Beatrice's ecstasies when she had received communion, her delight was to seek the Supreme Good, and the whole intention of her mind was to cling constantly but humbly to the essence of the Supreme Trinity, both praising and loving it, giving thanks for benefits received and contemplating God's marvels with a purified mind.[127]

At the beginning of her third vision Hadewijch wrote that

One Easter Sunday I went to God [in the Eucharist] and he embraced me in my interior senses and took me away in spirit. He brought me before the countenance of the Holy Spirit who in one essence possesses the Father and the Son; and from the total being of that countenance I received all understanding.[128]

When we turn to the three Idas we hear the same tidings. On the feast of the apostles Philip and James [11 May], Ida of Nivelles went into an ecstasy during mass. When she returned to herself, she was asked where she had been and she replied that she had been plainly enraptured in the Trinity. In this ecstasy

---

126 See above, note 45 of Chapter VIII.

127 *Vita*, 195,49.

128 VM, *Visioenen*, 1: 42, ll. 1–7. In the text which follows, Hadewijch was taught what God is: Love in action, made evident in creation and in man's recreation through Jesus Christ. By following God in *what* he is, as manifested in the man Jesus, she would be able to come in union with the *who* of God: transcendent Love, reposing in himself in fruition.

she had tasted and perceived the Trinity more than ever before. As best she could, she tried to explain that it was unveiled to her 'how the essence of the Father is in the Son, and the Son's essence in the Father's, and the essence of both of them in the Holy Spirit. The one God as Trinity had sweetly talked with her as with his beloved and she herself had sweetly and in a friendly manner conversed with the Trinity.[129]

The last six months of her life 'she ineffably contemplated as in a mirror herself in the Trinity and the Trinity in herself'.[130] During a vision on one Christmas, Ida Lewis had seen 'some mysteries of the Trinity and how the Father was joined to the person of the Son'.[131] One day, she was given a friendly reminder that she had not drunk from the cup of ablution after communion, and she answered: 'How can you think that I could drink from the cup presented by the sacristan, when the Trinity rejoices in me and the Godhead delights in me and my own spirit becomes one spirit with the Beloved?'.[132] One day, Ida of Leuven went up to the altar thinking about 'the holy and undivided Trinity', and in an intellectual vision she was told that she was on the point of receiving 'the Beloved Son of the Father'.[133]

---

129 *Quinque*, 271: 'Exponens quemadmodum poterat sibi revelatam fuisse essentiam Patris in Filio et Filii in Patre, et Spiritus Sanctus in utroque. Et adjiciens dixit: beatam Trinitatem tamquam dilectum cum dilecta dulciter secum allocutam fuisse, seque beatae Trinitati dulciter etiam et amicabiliter fuisse conversatam'.

130 *Ibid.*, 286: 'Sacratissimam Trinitatem quasi per speculum intuebatur. Et miro modo semper se in beata Trinitate et beatam Trinitatem in se ineffabiliter contemplabatur'.

131 *AA SS* Oct.13: 117,34: 'Viditque virgo nobilis in lumine divino undique confuso quaedam mysteria Trinitatis, Patremque Filio praesentialiter cohaerentem'.

132 *Ibid.*, 121,48: 'Sic respondit: "cum laetatur in me Trinitas et Deitas in mente jubilat, et spiritus meus unus effcitur cum dilecto, cum ista sentiam, soror dulcissima, quomodo creditis quod possem calicem a custode suscipere seu gustare?"'.

133 *AA SS* April 2: 184,9: 'Priusque ad altare precederet.... Sancta siquidem et individua Trinitas, desuper influente illius in anima exili quodam susurrio, se venturam esse praedixit, et sine morae quovis interstitio mox quod promiserat

No one should be surprised that this *mulieres religiosae* movement attracted attention. When James of Vitry wrote the biography of Mary of Oignies (d.1213) he dedicated it to Foulques of Toulouse. Foulques, a former troubadour turned Cistercian, had become bishop in 1205. He came to Belgium to recruit support for his fight against the Albigensians in his diocese and to see for himself the *mulieres religiosae* he admired.[134] Less known is the desire of Francis of Assisi to come to Belgium to be among the *mulieres religiosae* whose devotion to the Eucharist the had heard so much about.[135] When the Franciscans decided in 1217 to split into provinces, Francis wanted to be part of the *Gallia Belgica*-province, which included a great part of Belgium, already known to him as the country where cloth-industry flourished, that is in Flanders and Brabant. His protector, Cardinal Ugolino, thought he was more needed in Italy and did not let him have his wish.[136]

King Louis IX of France was well disposed toward the beguines and a supporter of the Cistercians and the mendicant Orders.[137] He also knew of the *mulieres religiosae* in the Low Countries, as they knew of him. Alice of Schaarbeek lost her left eye, the only one left, before her death in 1250. She offered this deprivation for the success and welfare of the king, at that time crusading in Palestine.[138] In 1267 Louis IX wrote to the Dominicans of Liège asking that the *mulieres religiosae*, 'so numerous in

---

implevit. Sic ergo dilatata simul et ampliata, processit ad altare Dominicum, percepitque Corporis illius et Sanguinis Sacramentum'. It is on this occasion that she heard a voice saying: 'This is my Beloved Son'.

134 Anselme Dimier, 'Folquet ou Foulques de Marseille', *DHGE* 7, 777–80; R. Lejeune, 'L'Evêque de Toulouse, Foulques de Marseille', *Mélanges F. Rousseau* (Brussels, 1958) 433–48; Brenda Bolton, 'Fulk of Toulouse. The Escape That Failed', *Church, Society and Politics*, Derek Baker ed. (London, 1975) 83–93.

135 Grundmann, *Religiöse Bewegungen*, 172, n.6. Both James of Vitry and Francis were in Perugia when Innocent III died there on July 16th, 1216.

136 For a detailed treatment, see Mens, *Oorsprong*, 245–51 and bibliography.

137 Anselme Dimier, *Saint Louis et Citeaux* (Paris, 1954).

138 *AA SS* June 2: 481,27.

that country', should keep him and the royal family in their prayers.[139]

Before concluding this Chapter, we need to point out another characteristic of the *mulieres religiosae* in the Low Countries.[140] However intense was their desire for union with Christ, the God-Man, and through him with the Trinity, they did not allow their subjective emotions to lead them away from orthodoxy in this matter. Their faithfulness to God matched God's faithfulness to them so well that orthopraxis coincided perfectly with orthodoxy, the latter continuously nourishing and fostering the former. They proved to be true religious women, *mulieres religiosae*, an expression in which each word has its own importance. They really never had enough of God as God himself never had enough of them.

CONCLUSION

In Part Two of Beatrice's 'context', an effort has been made to indicate what the incarnation of God's Son meant to the *mulieres religiosae*. They were deeply impressed by Christ coming as man to men and living among them and for them. Spurred by his love and realizing that his life on earth called them to love him in return 'as his due'—as they often expressed it—they tried through thick and thin to follow the way he went as man. They knew that by following in his footsteps they would be able to become not only intimately united with Christ the man, but also drawn into him, the God-Man.

Christ showed them what love does. They became ready to do whatever love can do. Their first concern was the primacy of God, who in the all-inclusiveness of his love embraces all his creatures, particularly man made to his image and likeness. Christ had shown them how dear man is to God. The *mulieres religiosae*

---

139 A. Mens, *Oorsprong*, 27

140 A comparison between different movements of *mulieres religiosae* in Belgium and Germany can be found in Grundmann, *Religiöse Bewegungen*. For a comparison between the Belgian and German movements and those of Italy, see Mens, *Oorsprong*. This interesting topic falls outside the scope of our study.

concluded from his example how they had to love their neighbors, if they ever were to prove that they loved their God.

Christ gave them the strength to work at this most difficult task: to let themselves be loved by God and to give him reciprocal love with their whole being. In the Eucharist, Christ gave himself to be eaten, and to the degree that they would really 'eat him' with all the love they were capable of, they would 'be eaten by him'. In this union of love they experienced a foretaste of the unassailable and enduring love of God as Trinity and Unity.

A complete Bibliography will appear at the end of the next volume (Cistercian Studies 122)

CISTERCIAN PUBLICATIONS INC.
Kalamazoo, Michigan

TITLES LISTING

CISTERCIAN TEXTS

THE WORKS OF BERNARD OF CLAIRVAUX

Apologia to Abbot William
Five Books on Consideration: Advice to a
 Pope
Grace and Free Choice
Homilies in Praise of the Blessed Virgin
 Mary
The Life and Death of Saint Malachy the
 Irishman
Parables
Sermons on the Song of Songs I-IV
Steps of Humility and Pride

THE WORKS OF WILLIAM OF SAINT THIERRY

The Enigma of Faith
Exposition on the Epistle to the Romans
The Golden Epistle
The Mirror of Faith
The Nature and Dignity of Love

THE WORKS OF AELRED OF RIEVAULX

Dialogue on the Soul
The Mirror of Charity
Spiritual Friendship
Treatises I: On Jesus at the Age of Twelve,
 Rule for a Recluse, The Pastoral Prayer

THE WORKS OF JOHN OF FORD

Sermons on the Final Verses of the Song of
Songs I-VII

THE WORKS OF GILBERT OF HOYLAND

Sermons on the Songs of Songs I, II, III
Treatises, Sermons and Epistles

OTHER EARLY CISTERCIAN WRITERS

The Letters of Adam of Perseigne I
Baldwin of Ford: Spiritual Tractates
Guerric of Igny: Liturgical Sermons I-II
Idung of Prüfening: Cistercians and Cluniacs:
 The Case for Cîteaux
Isaac of Stella: Sermons on the Christian Year
Serlo of Wilton & Serlo of Savigny
Stephen of Lexington: Letters from Ireland
Stephen of Sawley: Treatises

MONASTIC TEXTS

EASTERN CHRISTIAN TRADITION

Besa: The Life of Shenoute
Cyril of Scythopolis: Lives of the Monks of
 Palestine
Dorotheos of Gaza: Discourses
Evagrius Ponticus: Praktikos and Chapters
 on Prayer
The Harlots of the Desert
Iosif Volotsky: Monastic Rule
The Lives of the Desert Fathers
Menas of Nikiou: Isaac of Alexandra & St
 Macrobius
Pachomian Koinonia I-III
The Sayings of the Desert Fathers
Spiritual Direction in the Early Christian East
 (I. Hausherr)
The Syriac Fathers on Prayer and the Spiritual
 Life

WESTERN CHRISTIAN TRADITION

Anselm of Canterbury: Letters I-[II]
Bede: Commentary on the even Catholic
 Epistles
Bede: Commentary on Acts
Bede: Gospel Homilies
Gregory the Great: Forty Gospel Homilies
Guigo II the Carthusian: Ladder of Monks
 and Twelve Meditations
Peter of Celle: Selected Works
The Letters of Armand-Jean de Rance I-II
The Rule of the Master

CHRISTIAN SPIRITUALITY

Abba: Guides to Wholeness and Holiness
East and West
Athirst for God: Spiritual Desire in Bernard
 of Clairvaux's Sermons on the Song of Songs
 (M. Casey)
Cistercian Way (A. Louf)
Fathers Talking (A. Squire)
Friendship and Community (B. McGuire)
From Cloister to Classroom
Herald of Unity: The Life of Maria Gabrielle
 Sagheddu (M. Driscoll)
Life of St Mary Magdalene... (D. Mycoff)
Rancé and the Trappist Legacy (A.J.
 Krailsheimer)
Roots of the Modern Christian Tradition
Russian Mystics (S. Bolshakoff)
Spirituality of Western Christendom
Spirituality of the Christian East
 (T. Spidlék)

MONASTIC STUDIES

Community and Abbot in the Rule of St
Benedict I-II (Adalbert De Vogüé)
Consider Your Call: A Theology of the
Monastic Life (Daniel Rees et al.)
The Finances of the Cistercian Order in the
Fourteenth Century (Peter King)